# WEST'S LAW SCHOOL
# ADVISORY BOARD

# CRIMINAL PROCEDURE

## CONSTITUTIONAL LIMITATIONS

# IN A NUTSHELL

Seventh Edition

By

## JEROLD H. ISRAEL
Ed Rood Eminent Scholar in Trial Advocacy
and Procedure, University of Florida,
Fredric G. Levin College of Law
Alene and Allan F. Smith Professor of Law Emeritus,
University of Michigan

## WAYNE R. LaFAVE
David C. Baum Professor Emeritus of Law and
Center for Advanced Study Professor Emeritus,
University of Illinois

Mat #40452841

*Nutshell Series, In a Nutshell*, the Nutshell Logo and West Group are trademarks registered in the U.S. Patent and Trademark Office.

COPYRIGHT © 1971, 1975, 1980, 1988, 1993 WEST PUBLISHING CO.
© West, a Thomson business, 2001
© 2006 Thomson/West
   610 Opperman Drive
   P.O. Box 64526
   St. Paul, MN 55164–0526
   1–800–328–9352

Printed in the United States of America

**ISBN–13:** 978–0–314–16775–0
**ISBN–10:** 0–314–16775–7

*TEXT IS PRINTED ON 10% POST
CONSUMER RECYCLED PAPER*

# PREFACE

This brief text is intended primarily for use by law students taking courses in the field of criminal procedure. In preparing these materials, we have attempted to set forth as succinctly and clearly as possible an analysis of the constitutional standards of major current significance. In doing so, however, we have not wavered from our firm conviction—which we believe is manifested in our casebook on *Modern Criminal Procedure* (with Professors Yale Kamisar, Nancy King and Orin Kerr)—that there is no substitute for in-depth study of the basic sources: the leading cases in the field, and the critical and extended analysis of the cases to be found in the legal literature. Rather, we have undertaken this work on the assumption that the diligent student might also profit from a less cluttered look at some of the principal problems in the field. On the basis of our own experience with students and that reported to us by other teachers of criminal procedure, we believe this assumption is valid—that at some point it is useful for the student to examine only the forest and not the trees.

This is not a text on criminal procedure, but rather about constitutional criminal procedure. As anyone who has followed the work of the Supreme Court in recent years well knows, we have, in many aspects of criminal procedure, about reached the point—to borrow Judge Henry Friendly's phrase—where we may view "the Bill of Rights as a code of criminal procedure." Whatever one may think of this significant development, it is apparent that most of the difficult problem areas in the field of criminal procedure are now constitutional in dimension. In concentrating upon the "constitutionalized" parts of the criminal justice process, we have avoided the task—almost impossible for a book of this size— of describing the various non-constitutional standards applied to the criminal justice process in the 50 states and our federal system. Those standards are treated in much larger works, such as *Modern Criminal Procedure* and our hornbook, *Criminal Procedure*.

Criminal procedure curriculums vary considerably from one school to another. Some schools offer a single course, focusing on constitutional regulation, and covering most of the major steps in the process. Our coverage matches the full range of such a course, and may well exceed it in certain chapters. Other schools divide the subject matter into two courses. The first concentrates on criminal investigations (and possibly also considers aspects of the right to counsel unrelated to investigations). Such courses also tend to focus on the constitutional regulation of the process. Our coverage here also provides a very good match; chapter 1 describes the general doctrinal foundation of constitutional criminal procedure, chapters 2–6 treat in greater depth the constitutional regulation of police investigations, chapter 8 adds material on self-incrimination issues presented in grand jury investigations, and chapter 7 considers various aspects of the right to counsel.

The second course in the usual two-course package (commonly nicknamed the "Bail to Jail" course) typically concentrates on the post-investigative portion of the process, and places greater emphasis on non-constitutional regulation. While our coverage is not as good a match for that course, it still should be of considerable help. Chapters 1, 7, 8, and 9 treat almost all of the elements of constitutional regulation considered in such a course (albeit, in a somewhat summary fashion as to chapter 9).

By including more than is needed for some courses, we have managed (we hope) to provide coverage of use to students taking any of the different criminal procedure courses. Of course, even where a particular course does not deal with the subject matter considered in one of our chapters, there is no prohibition against reading that chapter and thereby acquiring a more complete backdrop for analyzing the role of the federal constitution (as interpreted by the Supreme Court) in the regulation of the criminal justice process.

For the sake of brevity and ease in reading this text, we have departed from the traditional citation style for cases. Where it would not be ambiguous, we have used abbreviations for the name of the governmental unit in the case name (e.g., U.S., N.Y.), and have placed all citations in the table of cases itself. There, we have cited only the official reporter for Supreme Court decisions, unless that citation was not available. A previous discussion of the same case (or, occasionally a subsequent discussion is noted by a section and subsection reference within a parentheses. Reference to subsections within the same section refer to the subsection letter—e.g. ((d) infra). Traditional introductory signals ("see," "see e.g.," and "accord") have been omitted where the case supports the text either through direct ruling, dicta, or the decision's general treatment of a particular case.

To make our sentence structure as short and direct as possible, we generally have not used the phrases "he or she" or "his and her." Consistent with traditional rules of construction in statutes and legal texts, masculine or feminine pronouns should be read to refer to both female and male actors unless the context clearly indicates otherwise.

This text includes cases decided by the United States Supreme Court through July, 2006, the conclusion of the October 2005 Term.

J.H.I.
W.R.L.

July, 2006

# OUTLINE

*OUTLINE*

# OUTLINE

# OUTLINE

## OUTLINE

## OUTLINE

*OUTLINE*

# TABLE OF CASES

**References are to Pages**

# TABLE OF CASES

# TABLE OF CASES

# TABLE OF CASES

# TABLE OF CASES

\*

# CRIMINAL PROCEDURE

## CONSTITUTIONAL LIMITATIONS

# IN A NUTSHELL

Seventh Edition

*

# CHAPTER 1

# THE CONSTITUTIONALIZATION OF CRIMINAL PROCEDURE

## § 1.1  INTRODUCTION

### (a)  The "criminal justice revolution"

During the latter half of Chief Justice Warren's tenure (i.e., over most of the 1960s), the Supreme Court instituted a reshaping of the constitutional regulation of criminal procedure so extensive that it came to be known as the "criminal procedure revolution." In subsequent decades, the Supreme Court retreated from some aspects of that criminal procedure revolution, but accepted most of its foundational elements and in many areas used that foundation to extend constitutional regulations to areas that had been largely untouched by the Warren Court. The end result was the establishment through Supreme Court rulings of a substantial body of constitutional standards governing the structure and administration of both state and federal criminal justice systems.

This nutshell provides an overview of the current constitutional regulation of the criminal justice process, along with a more detailed analysis of specific constitutional standards governing selected aspects of the process. Chapter 1 discusses the doctrinal foundations of the constitutional regulation of the process. Chapters 2–6 then describe the constitutional regulation of police investigations. The analysis here brings together the various different constitutional guarantees that bear upon different police investigative procedures. In Chapters 7 and 8, we consider the constitutional right to the assistance of counsel and the constitutional prohibition against compelled self-incrimination as they bear upon procedures other than police investigations. We have given these constitutional rights individual treatment because of their pervasive significance, as they impact all stages of the process. In chapter 9, we add a brief survey of several additional constitutional restrictions that are applicable to the non-investigative portions of the process.

It would take far more space than we have available to restate even in the briefest fashion all of the Supreme Court rulings that have shaped the constitutional standards currently applicable even as to the investigative stage alone. Prior to the 1960s, space limitations would not have been a problem. Indeed, those constitutional rulings applicable to the state criminal justice systems—which produce the vast bulk of criminal investigations and criminal prosecutions in this country—could readily have been surveyed in less than a quarter of these pages. Since that time, however, no field of constitutional adjudication has consistently occupied a more substantial portion of the Supreme Court's efforts than the regulation of criminal procedure. Almost every Supreme Court term has been marked by at least a few decisions producing significant new developments in constitutional criminal procedure, and by a larger group of rulings that have finetuned previously announced standards. The end result is a substantial body of precedent, creating as to some subjects (e.g., police searches) a body of constitutional regulation so extensive that it rivals a complex statutory code in its comprehensiveness and intricacy. Our discussion focuses on the most basic of those constitutional standards, mentioning the "exceptions" to those standards (and the "exceptions to the exceptions") only where they have a significant practical impact.

### (b) The criminal procedure provisions of the Constitution

To understand how constitutional limitations come to play such a significant role in the regulation of the criminal justice process, one must start by examining the provisions in the Constitution that deal with criminal procedure. The Constitution as originally adopted had only a few provisions relating to the administration of the criminal <sup>1</sup> (the most significant of these provisions bei<sup>r</sup> Article III requirements that the "tr<sup>i</sup> Crimes, except in Cases of Impeachm<sup>r</sup> by Jury," in the "the State where shall have been committed"). B<sub>1</sub> of obtaining state ratification <sub>f</sub> ment to add amendments g<sup>r</sup> rights of individuals (and there. the federal government's lack of au.

these rights), it became obvious that the criminal justice process would receive considerable attention in those amendments. The various state constitutions in their "Bills of Rights" had given great emphasis to the rights of individuals subjected to the criminal justice process, recognizing the potential, as reflected in English and colonial history, for the government's misuse of that process to persecute political and religious dissidents. Those state constitutions did not seek to set forth all of the basic protections of suspects and defendants that were recognized at common law, but concentrated on certain celebrated guarantees that had been established in response to notorious misuses of the criminal process by the English Crown (some of these guarantees having been established in the distant past and others being of more recent vintage, reflecting the colonial experience). The federal constitution's "Bill of Rights" (the first ten amendments, adopted in 1791) adhered to this model. Even though the Bill of Rights deals only selectively with the criminal justice process, of its twenty-seven guarantees of rights of individuals (i.e., excluding the structural safeguards of the Ninth and Tenth Amendments), fifteen deal specifically with the criminal justice process.

The Fourth Amendment guarantees the right of e people to be secure against unreasonable rches and seizures and prohibits the issuance of ants unless certain conditions are met. The Amendment requires prosecution by grand dictment for all infamous crimes (excepting certain military prosecutions) and prohibits placing a person "twice in jeopardy" or compelling him in "a criminal case" to be a "witness against himself." The Sixth Amendment lists several rights that apply "in all criminal prosecutions"—the rights to a speedy trial, to a public trial, to an impartial jury of the state and district in which the crime was committed, to notice of the "nature and cause of the accusation," to confrontation of opposing witnesses, to compulsory process for obtaining favorable witnesses, and to the assistance of counsel. The Eighth Amendment adds prohibitions against requiring excessive bail, imposing excessive fines, and inflicting cruel and unusual punishment In addition to these fifteen, the Fifth Amendment's due process clause clearly includes the criminal justice process in its general prohibition against the "deprivat[ion] of life, liberty or property" (which includes imposing capital sentencing, incarceration, and criminal fines) without "due process of law."

Taken together, the various Bill of Rights provisions offer an obvious potential for extensive constitutional regulation of the criminal justice process. Constitutional provisions, however, are not self-defining. Their ultimate impact depends, in large part, upon how they are interpreted by the judiciary in the course of adjudicating individual cases. Thus, it was not until the Supreme Court came to adopt certain critical interpretations of the Constitution's criminal procedure guarantees that the potential for substantial constitutionalization of the criminal justice process was realized.

## (c) Constitutionalization by judicial interpretation

Two important doctrinal developments were prerequisites to establishing, through Supreme Court rulings, extensive constitutional regulation of the nation's criminal justice procedures. First, the relevant guarantees in the Bill of Rights had to be made applicable in large part to state proceedings. Although federal criminal jurisdiction has been expanding over the years, almost 99% of all criminal prosecutions still are brought in the state systems. For the Constitution to have a major impact upon criminal justice administration, its criminal procedure provisions had to be held applicable to state as well as federal proceedings. That application eventually was achieved through the Supreme Court's reading of the Fourteenth Amendment's due process clause. Although the Fourteenth Amendment was adopted in 1868, it was not until the Warren Court adopted the "selective incorporation" doctrine in the 1960s, almost 100 years later, that the due process was held to make the critical Bill of Rights guarantees applicable to the states. That development is discussed in § 1.2.

The second major doctrinal prerequisite for the extensive constitutionalization of criminal procedure was adoption of expansive interpretations of individual guarantees. Even though applied to the states, the Bill of Rights guarantees, if interpreted narrowly, would have only a limited impact upon the criminal justice process. A narrow construction of each of the guarantees would produce a constitutional regulatory scheme that governs only a small portion of the total process and imposes there limitations fairly restricted in scope and unlikely to have a significant impact upon traditional state and federal criminal justice practices. Consider, for example, the Fifth Amendment clause stating that "no person * * * shall be compelled in any criminal case to be a witness against himself." Read narrowly, that provision might be said simply to prohibit the state from compelling the defendant to testify in his criminal trial as to any incriminating aspects of his involvement in the offense charged. Such an interpretation would establish constitutionally an important structural element of an accusatorial process, but its significance would be limited to the trial, and even there, it would only restate a prohibition firmly established in the law of all fifty states. On the other hand, an expensive interpretation of the self-incrimination privilege could render the privilege applicable to a wide range of practices occurring throughout the process, and impose limitations that extend far beyond those found in the law of most (and sometimes even all) states. The Supreme Court has, in fact, done exactly that, as discussed in Chapter 8.

Whether particular rulings are appropriately described as expansive interpretations depends, of course, on one's starting point. Very rarely can it be argued that the Court has given a particular clause its broadest conceivable interpretation, one that would take the most expansive general policy suggested by the clause and apply it without regard to limitations suggested by language and history, or alternative (and narrower) understandings of the clause's underlying policy. Some would argue that any rulings that fall short of such breadth are "restrictive" rather than "expansive". Our focus, however, is not on whether the Court's interpretation of a particular guarantee is as broad as it conceivably could be, but on how the Court approaches interpreting the guarantee. From this perspective, expansive interpretations are those that start from a presumption of liberal construction. They do not treat the guarantee as a technical, statute-like provision, but as a basic protection reflecting an important policy that must be safeguarded against circumvention and carried forward to meet changed conditions, especially growth in governmental authority. By that standard, the Court's interpretation of most, if not all, of the criminal procedure guarantees can be characterized as expansive.

The adoption of expansive interpretations of the Constitution's criminal procedure guarantees is not a new phenomenon. Indeed, it is debatable whether any Supreme Court ruling has ever adopted a broader view of the Fourth Amendment than did *Boyd v. U.S.* (1886) (§§ 6.3(b), 8.3(a)). Until the 1960s, however, Supreme Court opinions adopting strikingly expansive interpretations of criminal procedure guarantees were fairly infrequent. That was changed by the Warren Court, as its 1960s rulings marked the heyday of expansionist interpretations.

The Court's 1960s rulings substantially extended the reach of several of the Constitution's criminal procedure guarantees, particularly in their application to police investigative practices. Over the subsequent decades, Court rulings have been less pronounced in their extension of constitutional regulation. Indeed, in some instances the Court has withdrawn from earlier Warren Court rulings, and in others it has refused to extend these rulings (in contrast to what the Warren Court majority presumably would have done). Yet, each decade also has been marked by rulings that significantly extended the degree of constitutional regulation of the criminal justice process. Some of those rulings basically accepted and logically extended the core concepts of Warren Court interpretations to new situations (as the Warren Court presumably would have done); others, however, branched out to produce new expansive interpretations in areas barely touched upon by the Warren Court (in some instances, finding unconstitutional procedures that the Warren Court deemed constitutionally acceptable). Thus, while the extension of constitutional regulation arguably has stopped as to certain aspects of the criminal justice process, as to others, it has merely slowed down, and as to still others, it appears to be proceeding at a pace rivaling the Warren Court era.

## § 1.2   APPLICATION OF THE BILL OF RIGHTS GUARANTEES TO THE STATES

### (a) Introduction

The first 10 Amendments were enacted as limitations solely upon the federal government. *Barron v. Baltimore* (1833). The adoption of the Fourteenth Amendment in 1868, however, significantly extended federal constitutional controls over the actions of state governments. That Amendment provides, inter alia, that "no State" may "deprive any person of life, liberty, and property, without due process of law." From the outset, the Supreme Court found troublesome the determination of the exact relationship of the limitations that Fourteenth Amendment imposed upon the states and the limitations that the Bill of Rights imposed upon the federal government. Over the years, three separate views of that relationship have attracted the attention of the Court. The three were debated in opinions spread over a period of almost a hundred years, with the sharpest exchanges often between concurring and dissenting opinions.

### (b) The fundamental rights interpretation

The relationship between the Fourteenth Amendment and the Bill of Rights was first considered by the Supreme Court in the criminal procedure context in *Hurtado v. Cal.* (1884). The Court there adopted the "fundamental rights interpretation" of the Fourteenth Amendment's due process clause, an interpretation that prevailed until the early 1960s and that still governs that content of what is commonly described as "free-standing due process" (see 1.2(f)). The fundamental rights interpretation holds that there is no necessary relationship between the content of the Fourteenth Amendment and the guarantees of the Bill of Rights. The due process clause is viewed as incorporating, whether or not included in the Bill of Rights, those rights "so rooted in the traditions and conscience of our people as to be ranked as fundamental." *Snyder v. Massachusetts* (1934). As applied to criminal procedure, those fundamental rights basically require that the state adhere to "that fundamental fairness essential to the very concept of justice." *Lisenba v. Cal.* (1941). While the recognition of a procedural right in one of the specific guarantees of the Bill of Rights is a likely indicator that the right is an essential component of fundamental fairness, that recognition is not conclusive. Similarly, the absence of a specific Bill of Rights guarantee prohibiting a particular practice does not necessarily mean that the practice complies with fundamental fairness.

In support of the fundamental rights interpretation, it frequently was argued that not all Bill of Rights guarantees necessarily reflect in all their aspects that process needed to achieve basic fairness. Some Bill of Rights guarantees were seen as reflecting only the "restricted views of Eighteenth Century England regarding the best method for the ascertainment of facts." *Adamson v. Cal.* (1947) (Frankfurter, J., con.). Still other guarantees were viewed as encompassing a fundamental right in their general conception, but not in every aspect of the guarantee as it had been interpreted by federal courts. For example, the Fifth Amendment's double jeopardy clause had been held to prohibit the federal government from retrying a previously acquitted defendant both where the government's only justification for seeking a retrial was its interest in gaining a second chance to prove guilt and where it alleged that the original verdict of acquittal had been tainted by a trial error that worked to the prosecution's disadvantage. The Supreme Court held, however, that a retrial did not bar fundamental fairness in the latter situation, as the government was only seeking one fair opportunity to present its case. At the same time, it suggested that the retrial in the former situation would deprive the defendant of fundamental fairness. Moreover, even as to the retrial where the acquittal had been flawed by trial error, it pointed to special circumstances that contributed to its conclusion that fundamental fairness was not violated (e.g., this was not a case where the state had made repeated attempts to convict the defendant). *Palko v. Conn.* (1937).

### (c) The total incorporation interpretation

Though it won majority support for roughly eighty years, the fundamental rights interpretation was criticized over most of that period by various dissenting justices. They contended that the fundamental rights interpretation promoted a largely ad hoc, personal application of the Fourteenth Amendment. They argued that its imprecise standards (e.g., "fundamental fairness") granted a largely "unconfined power" to the judiciary that was contrary to the basic premise of a written constitution. *Duncan v. La.* (1968) (Black, J., con.). In response to these contentions, the justices in the majority frequently stated that a fundamental rights analysis was not basically subjective, but rested upon the pervasive consensus of society, which could be determined independently of a justice's personal views.

The dissenting justices who criticized the fundamental rights interpretation generally argued for a much broader reading of the Fourteenth Amendment as "incorporating" the entire Bill of Rights and making all of its guarantees applicable to the states. Justice Black, the primary proponent of this view, found support for this incorporationist position in his reading of the Fourteenth Amendment as a whole; he took into consideration the Amendment's prohibition against state abridgement of the "privileges and immunities of citizens of the United States" (notwithstanding precedent limiting that clause to the protection of elements of federal citizenship), as well as its due process clause. Justice Black further argued that the due process clause, standing apart from its incorporation of the Bill of Rights, should not be interpreted as requiring recognition of such additional rights as the Court might characterize as "fundamental," but simply as requiring even-handed adherence to the process otherwise provided by local law (i.e., the process that was "due"). Other adherents to the total incorporation position rejected this limited interpretation of the due process clause, and their position therefore was described as "total incorporation plus".

Responding to the total incorporation position, opinions supporting the traditional fundamental fairness approach argued that, had the drafters of the Fourteenth Amendment intended to make the Bill of Rights guarantees applicable to the states, they would have said so directly, and would have had no need to include a due process clause in the Fourteenth Amendment (as one was already in the Fifth Amendment). They also rejected Justice Black's contention that "total incorporation" would avoid much of the subjectivity inherent in the fundamental rights approach. The focus of judicial inquiry, they argued, would simply be shifted from the flexible concept of "fundamental rights" to the equally flexible terms of the specific Amendments, such as "probable cause," "unreasonable search," and "speedy and public trial." Although the total incorporation position never gained majority support, some of the criticism it proponents directed at the fundamental rights interpretation did appear to influence the Warren Court's subsequent adoption of the selective incorporation doctrine.

### (d) The shift to selective incorporation

In 1961, Mr. Justice Brennan, in a dissenting opinion, advanced what is commonly described as the "selective incorporation" view of the Fourteenth Amendment. *Cohen v. Hurley* (1961) (Brennan, J., dis.). This view combines aspects of both the "fundamental rights" and "total incorporation" interpretations of the Fourteenth Amendment. Selective incorporation accepts the basic premise of the fundamental rights interpretation that the Fourteenth Amendment encompasses rights, substantive or procedural, that are so basic as to be ranked as "fundamental." It recognizes too that not all rights specified in the Bill of Rights are necessarily fundamental. It rejects the fundamental rights interpretation, however, insofar as that doctrine looks only to the character of the particular element of a specified right denied in the particular case, and evaluates that element with reference to the "totality of circumstances" of that case. Evaluating the fundamental nature of a right in terms of the "factual circumstances surrounding each individual case" is viewed as "extremely subjective and excessively discretionary." Limiting a decision to only one aspect of the specified right also is rejected as presenting the same difficulty. Accordingly, in determining whether a specified right is fundamental, the selective incorporation doctrine requires that the Court look at the total right guaranteed by the particular Bill of Rights provision, not merely at a single aspect of that right nor at the application of that aspect in the circumstances of the particular case. If it is decided that a particular guarantee is fundamental, that right will be incorporated into the Fourteenth Amendment "whole and intact." The specified right will then be enforced against the states in every case according to the same standards applied to the federal government. With respect to those guarantees within the Bill of Rights held to be fundamental, there is, as Justice Douglas put it, "coextensive coverage" under the Fourteenth Amendment and the Bill of Rights. *Johnson v. La.* (1972).

The selective incorporation doctrine gained majority support during the 1960s. The debate as to its adoption was presented largely in concurring and dissenting opinions, as the majority opinions typically applied the doctrine without any extensive discussion as to why the focus should be on the whole of an enumerated right. Justices opposing selective incorporation argued that it was no more than an artificial compromise between traditional fundamental fairness and the total incorporation doctrines. *Duncan v. La.* (1968) (Harlan, J., dis.). Supporters of the doctrine stressed that selective incorporation reduced the potential for subjectivity and "avoid[ed] the impression of personal, ad hoc adjudication" by discarding an analysis that focused on the totality of the circumstances of the individual case. Selective incorporation was also praised as promoting certainty in the law, and thereby facilitating state court enforcement of due process standards; once a specified right was held to be fundamental, the state courts were directed to the specific language of the Bill of Rights guarantee and the various past decisions interpreting that guarantee in the context of federal prosecutions. This stood in contrast to the case-by-case rulings under fundamental fairness, which left the state courts at sea as to whether other circumstances and other elements of a particular right would produce a different result as to what was fundamental. Although selective incorporation would also expand federal constitutional regulation of the state criminal justice systems, that was viewed as consistent with the interests of federalism because the regulation was limited to rights which were fundamental and therefore too important to allow the states to disregard in the interests of local experimentation. *Pointer v. Tex.* (1965) (Goldberg, J., con.).

The adoption of the selective incorporation position during the 1960s was accompanied by a movement towards a broader view of the nature of a "fundamental procedural right." A right was to be judged by reference to its operation within the "common law system of [criminal procedure] * * * that has been developing * * * in this country, rather than its theoretical justification as a necessary element of a 'fair and equitable procedure.'" *Duncan v. La.* (1968). The fact that another system of justice could operate without a particular right (as the civil system operated without jury trials) did not work against finding the right to be fundamental in our system. Also, greater emphasis was placed upon the very presence of a right within the Bill of Rights as strong evidence of its fundamental nature.

Applying this approach, the Supreme Court during the 1960s held fundamental (and therefore ap-

plicable to the states under the same standards
applied to federal government) the following Bill of
Rights guarantees of the Fourth, Fifth, Sixth, and
Eighth Amendments: the freedom from unreasonable searches and seizures and the right to have
excluded from criminal trials any evidence obtained
in violation thereof, *Mapp v. Ohio* (1961), and *Ker v.
Cal.* (1963); the privilege against self-incrimination,
*Malloy v. Hogan* (1964); the guarantee against double jeopardy, *Benton v. Md.* (1969); the right to the
assistance of counsel, *Gideon v. Wainwright* (1963);
the right to a speedy trial, *Klopfer v. N.C.* (1967);
the right to jury trial, *Duncan v. La.* (1968); the
right to confront opposing witnesses, *Pointer v. Tex.*
(1965); the right to compulsory process for obtaining witnesses, *Washington v. Tex.* (1967); and the
prohibition against cruel and unusual punishment,
*Robinson v. Cal.* (1962). Moreover, in light of these
rulings, two earlier cases were characterized as incorporating within the Fourteenth Amendment the
Sixth Amendment rights to a public trial and to
notice of the nature and cause of the accusation.
See *In re Oliver* (1948); *Cole v. Ark.* (1948). Prosecution by grand jury indictment, on the other hand,
was found not to be fundamental, and therefore not
required of the states: in this regard, the original
fundamental fairness ruling of *Hurtado v. Cal.*
(1884) continued to be followed as valid precedent
See *Gerstein v. Pugh* (1975).

Somewhat surprisingly, the Court has not been
required to decide whether three other specified
rights relating to the criminal justice process are

fundamental and therefore to be applied to the states. Those rights are the Eighth Amendment prohibition of excessive bail, the Eighth Amendment prohibition of excessive fines, and the Sixth Amendment's "vicinage" requirement (i.e., the requirement that trial jury be "of the state and district wherein the crime shall have been committed, which district shall have been previously ascertained by law"). Lower courts generally have assumed that the two Eighth Amendment prohibitions are fundamental, but are divided as to the Sixth Amendment's vicinage requirement. Some view that requirement as a unique product of the geographical scope of the federal judicial system, expressing no enduring principle of a type that would justify its application to the states. Others contend that an essential element of the right to jury, already held to be fundamental, is that the jury be selected from a previously defined geographic district in which the commission of the crime occurred.

### (e) Incorporation of federal-context precedent

In holding that the Fourteenth Amendment selectively incorporated the Sixth Amendment's jury trial right, the majority in *Duncan v. La.* (1968) acknowledged the state's contention that incorporation could disrupt long established state practices by requiring adherence to past interpretations of the Sixth Amendment that were developed solely in terms of federal court practice. Justice Fortas, in a separate opinion, argued that the proper response to the state's concern was to distinguish between these past Sixth Amendment rulings that had defined the basic elements of the jury trial requirement and those that had adopted "a system of administration" for applying that right in the federal context (e.g., requiring a 12 person jury). The latter decisions, Justice Fortas argued need not be selectively incorporated, as the selective incorporation concept did not require the Court to impose upon the states the totality of the Sixth Amendment guarantee, including "all its bag and baggage, however securely or insecurely affixed they may be by law or precedent."

The Court had no need to decide in *Duncan* whether absolute parallelism (despairingly characterized by Justice Harlan as "jot for jot" and "case by case" incorporation) would be mandated in the application of the Sixth Amendment guarantee to federal and state systems. However, the *Duncan* majority clearly indicated that it was not receptive to the type of distinction that Justice Fortas suggested. It suggested that, if past decisions dealing with "administrative" aspects of the jury trial guarantee should appear to be inappropriate as applied to the states, the proper approach was to "reconsider" the constitutional grounding of those decisions, and possibly conclude that the standards announced there were not required, as a matter of constitutional law, for either the federal or state systems.

Subsequently, in *Williams v. Fla.* (1970) and *Apodaca v. Or.* (1972), the Court majority rejected the "bag and baggage" exception that had been advanced by Justice Fortas and chose the "reconsideration route" suggested by the *Duncan* majority. *Williams* reconsidered earlier rulings that appeared to require constitutionally the twelve-person jury that traditionally had been used in federal courts, concluded that the twelve-person size was not critical to the jury function guaranteed by the Sixth Amendment, and held that a state's use of six-person juries in non-capital cases did not violate the incorporated Sixth Amendment. In *Apodoca*, eight justices agreed that the constitutionally of non-unanimous jury verdicts should be resolved in the same way for both state and federal prosecutions. But on reconsideration of earlier precedent mandating unanimous verdicts in federal trials, the eight divided equally on whether the Sixth Amendment required unanimity, with four justices concluding that the state's acceptance of 10–2 verdicts was constitutionally acceptable. The deciding vote was cast by Justice Powell, who accepted Justice Fortas' earlier suggestion as to non-incorporation of constitutional rulings dealing with matters of "administration," and concluded that the 10–2 verdict was acceptable under the Sixth Amendment as applied to the states, but would not be acceptable in the application of the Sixth Amendment to a federal prosecution.

Justice Powell, in dissent, argued for a similar exception from incorporation in *Crist v. Bretz* (1975), where the state argued against application of precedent, developed in the context of federal prosecutions, which established the starting point for the attachment of jeopardy under the double jeopardy clause. The majority, once again, insisted on a parallel application in federal and state prosecutions, and on reconsideration of the earlier precedents, concluded that they had correctly identified the point at which jeopardy attached (those earlier cases had not adopted "some arbitrarily chosen rule of convenience" based on traditional federal practice, as the state argued, but a standard based upon the primary function of the double jeopardy prohibition).

*Crist* apparently put an end to the possible consideration of a "bag and baggage" exception. The Court in later years considered various constitutional claims that Justices Fortas and Powell might have characterized as relating to "matters of administration," but no member of the Court suggested that the particular requirement might have a different constitutional status as to state and federal proceedings. The distinctive treatment on the jury-unanimity issue presented in *Apodoca* is today simple an oddity, resting on the vote of a single justice who advanced an approach to incorporation that settled law now clearly rejects.

While the Supreme Court has rejected the possibility of reading a selectively incorporated guarantee as requiring more in the federal criminal justice system than in the states, the Court retains the authority to impose additional requirements in the federal system through the exercise what it has characterized as its "supervisory authority over the administration of justice in the federal courts" *U.S. v. Hasting* (1983). That authority has most prominently been used to fashion judicial remedies for actions of federal officials that violate statutory duties, see e.g., *McNabb v. U.S.* (§ 4.1(b)), but it also is available to protect the integrity of federal judicial proceedings. Thus, in several cases, after concluding that certain procedures or prohibitions were not constitutionally mandated (and therefore not required of the state), the Court relied on its supervisory power to impose that requirement on federal courts. See e.g., *Rosales–Lopez v. U.S.* (1981) (requiring voir dire questioning beyond what is constitutionally mandated).

The Court has noted, however, that federal appellate courts, which also possess this supervisory authority, may not use it simply because they view the current interpretation of constitutional requirements as not sufficiently rigorous to meet desirable procedural goals. See *U.S. v. Payner* (1980) (lower court could not rely on its supervisory power to effectively bypass standing requirement (§ 6.8) for raising Fourth Amendment objections); *U.S. v. Hasting* (1983) (lower court could not rely on supervisory power to reverse a conviction based on a constitutional violation without regard to the harmless error doctrine (§ 9.10) ordinarily applied to such violations). Also, unlike Constitutional rulings, Congress may override rulings based on the Court's supervisory authority. See § 4.1(b).

## (f) "Free-standing" due process

Early fundamental fairness cases recognized that due process could impose fairness requirements that were not to be found in the specific guarantees of the Bill of Rights. Indeed, prior to the adoption of selective incorporation, several of the most significant Supreme Court rulings invalidating state procedures rested on this concept. Thus, although an unbiased judge is not mentioned in the specifics of the Bill of Rights (the Sixth Amendment refers only to an "impartial jury"), *Tumey v. Ohio* (1927) held lack of judicial bias to be an essential element of fundamental fairness (and therefore overturned a state conviction where the trial judge had a pecuniary interest in having the case result in a conviction rather than an acquittal).

Once the Court selectively incorporated almost all of the specific guarantees dealing with criminal procedure, the independent content of due process came to be known as "free-standing due process" (i.e., standing apart from the incorporated guarantees). Notwithstanding the extensive range of the incorporated guarantees, free-standing due process plays an important role in the constitutional regulation of state criminal procedures. Indeed, constitutional requirements grounded in free-standing-due process extend across all stages of the criminal justice process, including police investigations (see § 5.4), pretrial procedures (see §§ 9.2(b),9.4), adjudication by guilty plea (see § 9.5), adjudication by trial (see § 9.8(f)), sentencing (see § 9.9(a)), and appeals (see § 9.9(b)). Many of these free-standing due process standards extend concepts found in the specific guarantees to procedural settings not covered by those guarantees. See e.g., § 7.2(a) (due process extension of right to counsel). Others impose fairness requirements that have no ready counterpart in the specific guarantees. See e.g., § 9.4(d) (due process requirements relating to defense access to evidence).

Notwithstanding the variety and scope of freestanding due process rulings, the Court has noted that, "beyond the specific guarantees enumerated in the Bill of Rights, the Due Process Clause has limited operation" and will be construed "very narrowly." *Dowling v. U.S.* (1990). Since the "Bill of Rights speaks in explicit terms to many aspects of criminal procedure," the expansion of constitutional regulation "under the open-ended rubric of the Due Process Clause" is said to "invite undue interference with both considered legislative judgments and the careful balance that the constitution strikes between liberty and order." *Medina v. Cal.* (1992). Thus, while a balancing approach has been applied to determine what procedures are mandated under due process in the field of administrative law, see *Mathews v. Eldridge* (1976), the Court has held that such an approach is inappropriate for the field of criminal procedure, where the "narrower inquiry" of the traditional fundamental fairness standard is applied. *Medina v. Cal.* (1992). So too, while constitutional violations under the specific guarantees are usually established without a showing of likely prejudice (although those violations may then be subject to a harmless error analysis, see § 9.10), rulings based on free-standing due process typically require a showing of a likely prejudicial impact upon the outcome of the proceeding to establish a constitutional violation. See *U.S. v. Gonzales-Lopez* (discussed in § 7.5(b)). Another narrowing feature found in some free-standing due process rulings is a reliance upon a "totality of the circumstances" analysis, see e.g., § 5.4, although other free-standing due process standards are as broadly stated as the standards imposed under specific guarantees, see e.g., § 7.3(h).

## § 1.3  GUIDEPOSTS FOR CONSTITUTIONAL INTERPRETATION

A variety of interpretive guideposts have influenced Supreme Court rulings applying constitutional guarantees to the criminal justice process. Some of those guideposts–such as the language of the guarantee and the history underlying the guarantee–are staples of all constitutional interpretation. Our focus here is in guideposts that, at least since the advent of selective incorporation, have been advanced as having a special relevance to the criminal justice process. The justices over the years have been divided as to the appropriateness of these guideposts. Also, those justices accepting a particular guidepost very often have differed as to how much weight should be given to that guidepost when it contradicts other relevant considerations. Thus, although all of these guideposts appear to

have played an important role in shaping the
Court's criminal procedure decisions, at one time or
another, their influence has varied (and presumably
will continue to vary) with changes in the composition of the Court.

## (a) Viewing criminal process guarantees as "civil liberty" guarantees

At least since the end of World War I, the Supreme Court has viewed the safeguarding of civil
liberties as a primary function of constitutional
judicial review. This focus has produced a willingness to extend the reach of guarantees protecting
individual liberties, responding particularly to the
restrictions accompanying the growth of modern-
day governmental authority. Thus, provisions such
as the First Amendment guarantee of free speech
have received far more expansive interpretations
than provisions dealing with property rights, such
as the prohibition against state impairment of the
obligation of contracts. For at least the past several
decades, the Court has viewed the criminal procedural guarantees of the Constitution as among
those provisions that safeguard basic civil liberties.
Thus, in one of the Warren Court's most significant
expansionist rulings, the Court noted that "the
quality of a nation's civilization can be largely
measured by the methods it uses in the enforcement of the criminal law." *Miranda v. Ariz.* (1966)
(§ 4.4). A fair criminal justice process is viewed, in
somewhat the same fashion as the right of free

speech, as a "bulwark" against "governmental op-
pression."

Closely connected to the protection of civil liberties has been a recognition of the need for especially
close judicial scrutiny where the burdens of governmental regulation fall upon "discrete and insular
minorities" who cannot count on the protection of
the political process. *U.S. v. Carolene Products Co.*
(1938). Safeguarding the rights of the accused has
been viewed, at least by some justices, as a critical
aspect of protecting the rights of minorities. Justice
Frankfurter, for example, described accused persons
as themselves constituting a highly unpopular minority (noting that "those accused of crime * * *
have few friends"), and argued that the judiciary
therefore has a special obligation to provide "alert
and strenuous resistance" to infringements of criminal procedural safeguards. *Harris v. U.S.* (1947)
(dis.). Commentators have suggested that the fact
that accused persons so frequently are members of
disadvantaged groups also has contributed to the
Court's heightened concern that the criminal justice
process be fairly administered. It is certainly true
that the Court has taken significant steps to eliminate many of the barriers that kept indigent defendants from fully exercising their procedural rights
(see e.g., §§ 4.4(b), 7.2). So too, the Court has noted
on several occasions that, to preserve the integrity
of the criminal justice process, constitutional standards must preclude any suggestion of racial discrimination in its administration. See *Rose v. Mitchell* (§ 9.2(b)); *Batson v. Ky.* (§ 9.6(b)).

Viewing guarantees from a "civil liberties" perspective typically leads to giving less deference to legislative judgments in interpreting those guarantees, and references to the deference due legislative determinations are found less frequently in criminal justice rulings than in many other areas. Yet, in certain contexts, the Court's criminal justice opinions have stressed the need to give deference to the balance struck by legislative bodies in weighing individual liberty concerns against the needs of public safety. See e.g., *Medina v. Cal.* (§ 1.2(f)). So too while acknowledging that broad prosecutorial discretion can readily be used to discriminate against various racial or ethnic groups, the Court often has stressed its reluctance to subject such decisionmaking to anything more than an extremely limited form of judicial review. Though the opinions in such cases do not directly reject the concept of treating the criminal procedure guarantees as "preferred rights," they readily can be read as giving far less weight to that viewpoint than many of the opinions adopting expansive interpretation of those guarantees.

## (b)  Giving priority to reliability guarantees

Over the years, various justices have maintained that a higher priority should be given to those procedural guarantees that serve primarily to ensure factfinding reliability, with a special emphasis on avoiding the erroneous conviction of the innocent. Such justices tend to be much more willing to give a broad reading to those guarantees that seek to achieve factfinding accuracy, as opposed to guarantees that serve other interests (e.g., the protection of privacy under the Fourth Amendment or the recognition of individual dignity in the Fifth Amendment's self-incrimination clause). Of course, certain constitutional guarantees serve both to promote accuracy and to protect other interests as well. In such cases, justices arguing that factfinding reliability should receive higher priority may be willing to extend the scope of the guarantee only insofar as it achieves the reliability objective. Thus, they would refuse to apply the self-incrimination privilege to bar most police interrogation, but would extend the policies of the privilege to exclude from evidence potentially unreliable confessions obtained through interrogation so abusive as to encourage false admissions of guilt. Similarly, the double jeopardy protection against reprosecution following an acquittal would be given a more expansive interpretation than the double jeopardy protection against multiple punishment for the commission of a single offense.

Other justices have flatly rejected treating more favorably those guarantees that seek to ensure factfinding accuracy. They argue that all constitutional guarantees should be treated alike and extensive relief should be available for any constitutional violation. They acknowledge that some remedies afforded for violations of guarantees protecting other interests (such as the exclusion of evidence obtained through a Fourth Amendment violation) often operate to protect the "guilty," but they note that those remedies also serve the interests of society as a whole. They also contend that attempts to separate the different interests protected by a single guarantee produce uneven interpretations of the guarantee that only serve to undermine the Court's authority. Expansive protection of all guarantees is essential, in their view, to ensure respect for the place of the Constitution in regulating the criminal justice process.

The significance of the position that favors truthfinding guarantees has varied with the composition of the Court and the nature of the issue being considered. That position may well have had considerable influence in the initial development of the "fundamental fairness" standard of due process. In the post-incorporationist era, its greatest influence arguably has been in determining the appropriate scope of remedial measures, with the broader remedies available for guarantees central to factfinding accuracy. Such influence is seen, for example, in *Teague v. Lane* (1989), where the Court created a fact-finding reliability exception to the general rule limiting the retroactive application of new constitutional rulings on habeas review (see § 1.4(c)). Similarly, in restricting the reach of the exclusionary rule, which bars use of evidence obtained in violation of the Fourth Amendment, the Court frequently has stressed that this remedy impairs truthfinding by excluding reliable evidence. See § 6.5(c)–(g); § 6.7(a). On the other hand, majority opinions defining the substantive content of guarantees that impede accurate factfinding have very rarely expressed concern as to that impact, and certainly have not expressed the view that such guarantees should therefore be narrowly construed.

## (c) The significance of historical acceptance

What weight should be given to the fact that a practice, now challenged as unconstitutional, was well accepted and thought to create no constitutional difficulties at the time of the adoption of the Bill of Rights, or at the time of the adoption of the Fourteenth Amendment? The Court has made clear that the sanction of settled historical usage is not a shield against constitutional attack. See *Williams v. Ill.* (1970) ("neither the antiquity of a practice nor the fact of steadfast legislative and judicial adherence to it through the centuries insulates it from constitutional attack"). On the other hand, it also has repeatedly treated the sanction of history as a strong indicator of constitutionality. The critical division among the justice's has centered on what circumstance justify finding a practice unconstitutional notwithstanding that sanction.

Is historical acceptance readily discounted where the practice in question is contrary to what the Court now views as the overriding function of the constitutional provision at issue? In some cases, that view has prevailed, particularly as to "open-ended" constitutional standards (e.g., the "reasonableness" requirement of the Fourth Amendment). See e.g., *Payton v. N.Y.* (1980) (§ 2.7(a)) (such a guarantee should not be read as having "frozen into constitutional law * * * those practices that existed at the time of the [guarantee's] adoption"). Yet, in other instances, sometimes involving the same type of guarantee, the Court majority has rejected such an analysis. See e.g., *U.S. v. Watson* (1976) (upholding police authority to make arrests in public without warrants, notwithstanding ample opportunity to obtain a warrant prior to the arrest). The Court majority here reasoned that the historical acceptance of a practice seemingly inconsistent with the function of a guarantee indicates that the purpose of the guarantee was more limited than what a logical extension of that function might suggest. The assumed "logic" of the guarantee "must defer to history and experience," *U.S. v. Watson* (1976) (Powell, J., con.), as the Court must recognize that, in determining the intended purpose of many guarantees, "a page of history is worth a volume of logic," *Ullmann v. U.S.* (1956) (Frankfurter, J., con.).

The Court has fairly uniformly accepted the position that changed circumstances can deprive historical acceptance of much of its weight. In light of "sweeping change in the legal and technological context, reliance on the common-law rule * * * [becomes] a mistaken literalism that ignores the purposes of a historical inquiry." *Tenn. v. Garner* (1985) (police use of deadly force against fleeing felons, though allowed at common law, must be assessed today in light of the greatly expanded grouping of crimes classified as felonies, the greatly restricted authorization of death penalty sentences for felonies, and the greatly increased capacity, via handguns, for police officers to use deadly force in situations posing no threat to their personal safety). But the justices often have divided us to whether a particular change is relevant and whether an admittedly relevant change truly alters the character of the challenged practice. Changed circumstances are commonplace when today's criminal justice system is compared to the process that existed at the time of the adoption of the Constitution, and justices who are general skeptical of an historical inquiry can quite readily find a change that they would characterize as rendering irrelevant the historical acceptance of the particular practice.

Notwithstanding some variations, the same underlying considerations arise where a challenged practice, or one very much like it, was held unacceptable at common law. Here, the issues that have divided the Court are: (1) whether the current practice is truly analogous to that prohibited at common law, (2) whether the common law prohibition was based on the peculiarities of the common law or upon basic constitutional principles; and (3) whether changed circumstances place the practice in a new light, and thereby undercut the significance of the earlier interpretation of the guarantee as barring the particular practice. See e.g., *Apprendi v. N.J.* (2000) (§ 9.9(a)).

### (d) The desirability of a per se analysis

In many settings the Supreme Court has viewed the constitutional question at issue as naturally calling for what might be described as a "categorical" or "definitional" standard—i.e., a standard that looks to a single characteristic or event and does not adjust to the uniqueness of each case. Such standards are imposed, for example, in determining when jeopardy attaches and what constitutes the minimum acceptable size for a jury. In other settings, the Court has viewed the constitutional question at issue as calling for a standard requiring a fact sensitive judgment geared to a variety of circumstances that differ with each case. Such standards are applied, for example, in determining whether the police had the probable cause needed to obtain a search warrant or whether a defense lawyer's performance was so deficient as to deny defendant the effective assistance of counsel. In still other settings, the Court has concluded that, while the question at issue generally calls for a case-by-case balancing of a variety of circumstances, administrative concerns justify imposing a "per se" or "bright-line" test which finds a particular action to be constitutional or unconstitutional based on a single event or characteristic.

The per se standard is similar in formulation to the usual categorical standard, but its grounding is different. The Court is not saying that the function of the applicable constitutional guarantee necessarily requires such a bright-line. Indeed, the Court is acknowledging that its per se standard is either overinclusive or underinclusive as compared to the application of that function to all relevant circumstances on a case-by-case basis. Nonetheless, practical considerations relevant to administration of the Court's ruling have convinced the Court of the need to adopt a shorthand generalization in the form of a per se rule even though the function of the guarantee might point to the ad hoc application of a totality-of-the-circumstances analysis. Illustrative are *N.Y. v. Belton* (1981) (allowing police to search the entire passenger compartment of an automobile, contemporaneously with the arrest of the occupant, without seeking to determine whether, in the particular physical setting that entire area is within the "immediate control" of the arrestee), and *Turner v. Murray* (1986) ("because risk of racial prejudice infecting a capital sentencing proceeding is especially serious in light of the complete finality of the death penalty," a capital defendant accused of an interracial crime is entitled automatically to voir dire questioning on racial issues "inextricably bound up with the conduct of the trial"). Though per se rules are often associated with the adoption of expansive interpretations of procedural safeguards, that is not necessarily the case. Thus, as illustrated by *N.Y. v. Belton*, to provide police with a clear guideline and a standardized procedure, a per se approach may result in the acceptance of a search more extensive than what would be justified if the exigency supporting the search (the arrestee's capacity to destroy evidence or seize a hidden weapon) were applied to the specific circumstances of the particular case.

While the Court has utilized per se standards in various settings, it also has rejected adoption of such standards in other settings viewed as similar by at least some members of the Court. See e.g., *U.S. v. Dunn* (1987) (refusing to adopt a "bright-line rule" that the Fourth Amendment protected area of a dwelling's "curtilage" would "extend no farther than the nearest fence surrounding a fenced house," and instead allowing for consideration of indicia of privacy that could on occasion encompass structures lying outside the fenced area); *Ristaino v. Ross* (1976) (rejecting as to non-capital cases an automatic entitlement to voir dire questioning on racial bias where the crime is interracial, as determining the presence of a "constitutionally significant likelihood" of juror bias absent voir dire questioning requires an evaluation of "all of the circumstances" presented by the case).

As might be surmised from such disagreements, the Court has not been able to develop a bright-line rule as to when administrative concerns will or will not justify adoption of a administratively based per se standard. Factors of obvious relevance include: (1) the extent to which such a standard will be overinclusive or under inclusive as compared to a case-by-case analysis; (2) whether the constitutional regulation deals with decisions made by "front line" players (e.g., police officers) who have limited time and expertise and therefore would have difficulty applying the "subtle nuances" and "hairline distinctions" of a standard geared to a variety of circumstances; (3) whether the failure to provide a clear direction to officials bound by the standard invites abuse by those officials in the form of fabricated testimony as to relevant circumstances; and

(4) the significant adjudicatory burdens that would be placed upon trial courts, and the special problems those courts would face, if required to assess certain types of factors (e.g., the motive of the official involved).

Although all of the above factors have been cited by the Court in majority opinions, the justices have disagreed as to the weight to be given to particular factors. Indeed, some justices have viewed only the first factor as critical, and would adopt per se rules only when the bright line rule provides close to a perfect fit to the result that would follow from a case-by-case analysis. Also, even where the justices agree that a particular factor (e.g., the effectiveness of case-by-case adjudication) is relevant, they may well view differently the practical impact of that factor. See e.g., *Smith v. Phillips* (1982) (disagreement as to trial court's capacity to determine through juror questioning whether the juror was biased as a result of a particular interaction with the prosecutor).

### (e) The desirability of prophylactic requirements

The Supreme Court has described only a handful of its criminal procedure rulings as imposing "prophylactic" requirements, yet that characterization has been the source of considerable controversy, extending beyond the significance of the rulings so characterized. Undoubtedly, the most prominent of the opinions characterized as prophylactic is *Miranda v. Ariz.* (§ 4.4), where the Court required

that the police give various warnings to an interrogated suspect in order to ensure that he was not
compelled by the interrogation to incriminate himself. Other prophylactic rulings include *N.C. v.
Pearce* (§ 9.9(b)) (requiring a judge who imposes a
higher sentence on retrial to set forth the reasons
for the higher sentence and to rely on justifications
that will ensure that the higher sentence is not
vindictive), and *Anders v. Cal.* (§ 7.3(h)) (prescribing procedures that must be followed by appointed
appellate counsel in withdrawing from a case in
order to ensure that such withdrawals are limited
to "wholly frivolous" appeals).

The Court has emphasized two characteristics in
explaining why a particular decision imposed a
"prophylactic rule." First, the rule is prophylactic
in the sense that it seeks to safeguard against a
constitutional violation, typically by imposing procedural requirements designed to provide a protective
shield for the underlying constitutional right. Secondly, the prophylactic rule is grounded not on the
conclusion that its violation invariably produces a
denial of the underlying constitutional right, but on
the Court's exercise of its authority to craft remedies and procedures that facilitate its adjudication
responsibilities. Two important consequences, the
Court has noted, follow from the second prong
grounding: (1) since prophylactic rules may be violated without necessarily denying the underlying
constitutional right, violations of prophylactic rules
may be given remedial consequences narrower in
range than the consequences which would follow

from direct violations the underlying right (see e.g., §§ 6.6(g), 6.7(b), 8.1(e)): and (2) the legislature may eliminate the need for the prophylactic protection added by the Court's ruling by replacing its prophylactic requirements with alternative safeguards that are equally effective.

Some justices have challenged the Court's authority to impose prophylactic safeguards. Here, they argue, by prescribing additional procedures solely as a prophylaxis, the Court engages in "pure legislation." *N.C. v. Pearce,* supra (Black, J., dis.). However, *Dickerson v. U.S.* (2000) (§ 4.5(d)), flatly rejected the contention that the *Miranda* ruling lacked a constitutional grounding, and described that ruling as similar in function to a traditional per se standard (the *Miranda* requirements simply responded to the "unacceptably great" risk of "overlooking involuntary confessions" when admissibility was tested only by the ad hoc "coerced confessions" standard).

The *Dickerson* opinion failed, however, to explain why *Miranda* and certain other rulings had been separately characterized as "prophylactic," thereby suggesting that the Court majority was divided on that question. *Chavez v. Martinez* (2003) later revealed that division. There, the eight justices commenting on the special character of the *Miranda* ruling offered quite different characterizations. Four justices utilized the traditional "prophylactic" characterization, and placed in that category, along with *Miranda*, several earlier rulings dealing with self-incrimination (see § 8.3(b)); two justices described the same group of rulings as establishing "law * * * outside the Fifth Amendment's core, with each case expressing a judgment that the core guarantee, or the judicial capacity to protect it, would be placed at some risk in the absence of such complementary protection"; two justices placed *Miranda* alone in such a special category, describing it as a constitutional measure adopted to "reduce the risk of a coerced confession and to implement the self incrimination clause." Though *Chavez* indicated that the Court majority continues to accept the constitutional legitimacy of the distinctive grounding (and distinctive remedial treatment) of the rulings that have been characterized as "prophylactic," it did not suggest any strong inclination to make use of that grounding in future rulings. Indeed, more than a decade has passed since the Court last discussed the possible adoption of a constitutional ruling that at least some justices might characterize as "prophylactic."

### (f) Administrative burdens

The more expansive a constitutional requirement, the more likely that it will impose a substantial burden upon the administration of the criminal justice process. That burden can take various forms, including increased expenses for an already underfunded system, additional hearings for already congested court dockets, and perhaps even insurmountable obstacles to the solution of some crimes. The extent to which such "practical costs" should be considered by the Court has been a matter of continuing debate among the justices. The clash of viewpoints on this score is most often found in the fashioning of standards (particularly per se standards) under the more open-ended procedural guarantees (e.g., the due process clause), and in the application of the more concrete guarantees to new settings. Thus, the Court has noted that where the text or history of a particular provision produces a "constitutional command that * * * is unequivocal," the practical costs incurred in applying that command become irrelevant. *Payton v. N.Y.* (1980). The command itself strikes a balance between the rights of the accused and society's need for effective enforcement of the criminal law, and the Court is bound to accept that balance.

Where the application of a guarantee is acknowledged to be less than clear, justices generally have taken positions that fall within a wide-ranging continuum as to the appropriate concern for practical costs. At one end of the continuum are justices who believe that administrative burdens should never be considered in reaching a result, or should be considered only where there is considerable doubt that the proposed standard would be more effective in protecting constitutional rights than a less burdensome standard. At the other end are justices who believe that, where the burden imposed would be great, the Court should extend the guarantee only if the particular extension is absolutely essential to fulfilling

the function of the guarantee. In between are justices who give practical costs varying weight depending upon a variety of circumstances. They will
look to such factors as whether the burden will be
substantial and clear (asking, for example, whether
other jurisdictions have accommodated such a burden under state law standards similar to the proposed constitutional standard), whether the burden
relates to an important state interest (thus, perhaps
giving less weight to a mere increase in the state's
financial costs than to an increase in the inconvenience to witnesses), and whether the burden can be
offset by other measures (e.g., police use of more
advanced technology).

Very often differences in perspective are reflected
not only as to the weighing of the administrative
burden but also in the justices' evaluation of the
likely scope of the burden. Thus, in *Miranda,*
though looking at the same data, the majority concluded that its decision would "not in any way
preclude police from carrying out their traditional
investigatory role" and thus "should not constitute
an undue interference with a proper system of law
enforcement," while one dissenter (Harlan, J.)
found that the Court was taking "a real risk with
society's welfare" and another (White, J.) concluded
that the Court's ruling would "measurably weak-
en" the enforcement of the criminal law and result
in an inability to prosecute successfully a "good
many criminal defendants."

## § 1.4 RETROACTIVE APPLICATION OF NEW CONSTITUTIONAL STANDARDS

### (a) Cases on direct review

The Warren Court's dramatic extension of the constitutional regulation of criminal procedure led that Court to reconsider the retroactive application of rulings imposing new constitutional limitations. Under traditional analysis, each new ruling, even if it overturned a previous ruling, announced the "correct" constitutional rule to which all past defendants (as well as all future defendants) were entitled. Thus the new rule could be raised by: (1) defendants yet to be tried; (2) defendants already convicted, but still eligible to challenge their convictions on appeal; and (3) defendants whose convictions were "final" (i.e., the opportunity for direct appellate review was exhausted), but because the defendants were still subject to custodial restraint (e.g., imprisoned), they could challenge their convictions collaterally through federal habeas corpus. Thus, where the Court announced that a particular police investigative practice, formerly thought to be acceptable, violated the constitution and required the exclusion of evidence obtained through that practice, that ruling provided the grounding for (1) excluding such evidence in a future prosecution even though the police had engaged in the now unconstitutional practice before it had been declared unconstitutional, and (2) overturning on direct appeal or on habeas corpus convictions that had been based on such evidence. In the case of habeas challenges, this extended to convictions obtained many years earlier, a factor that commonly rendered impracticable a retrial that did not use the unconstitutionally obtained evidence.

In *Linkletter v. Walker* (1965), the Supreme Court rejected the traditional position on retroactivity as resting on an outmoded Blackstonian view of the judicial process, which failed to recognize that earlier precedent was an "existing fact until overruled." *Linkletter* concluded that the retroactivity of new constitutional standards should be evaluated ruling by ruling, taking into consideration both the hardship that retroactive application imposed upon criminal justice administration and the values served by the new ruling. The "criteria guiding the resolution of the question [of retroactivity]," the Court later noted "implicate (a) the purpose to be served by the new standards, (b) the extent of the reliance by law enforcement authorities on the old standards, and (c) the effect on the administration of justice of a retroactive application of the new standards." *Stovall v. Denno* (1967). Relying on this analysis, the Court held that (1) some new rulings did not apply to future prosecutions (or past convictions) where the operative event held unconstitutional (e.g., a search) had occurred prior to the date of the new rulings; (2) other new rulings had full retroactive application in all trials, appeals, and habeas challenges pursued after the date of the new ruling.

Starting with *U.S. v. Johnson* (1982), a series of cases overturned *Linkletter* insofar as it permitted new rulings not to be extended to future prosecutions or to past prosecutions that had resulted in convictions not yet final. The *Johnson* line of cases concluded that the *Linkletter* analysis produced a result that undermined the integrity of judicial review, and violated "the principle of treating similarly situated defendants the same." As the dissenters to that analysis had noted, giving the benefit of the new rule to the defendant whose case constituted the vehicle for announcing the rule and denying it to others whose cases were at the same stage could result in "different standards for the protection of constitutional rights * * * [being] applied to two defendants simultaneously tried in the same courthouse for similar offenses."

The *Johnson* line of cases held that new rulings, even if they reflected a "clear break" from past precedents, were to be retroactivity applied (1) to all subsequent prosecutions, and (2) all prosecutions that had not yet reached the point of a conviction that was finalized by the exhaustion of the possibility of appellate review. Where a conviction has been appealed, that point of finality is marked by the denial of certiorari by the Supreme Court or the time for filing for certiorari having elapsed.

### (b)  Habeas corpus and retroactivity

After *Johnson*, there remained the possibility of applying the *Linkletter* analysis on habeas corpus, but *Teague v. Lane* (1989) held that here *Linkletter* had not gone far enough in restricting retroactivity. *Linkletter's* error there had been in failing to focus on the function of habeas review, as opposed to the general issue of retroactivity. Since federal habeas review served basically a deterrent function (ensuring that state courts recognized "established constitutional principles"), the critical issue should be whether the state decision upholding the conviction at the time it became final conscientiously applied Supreme Court precedent as to the then-existing constitutional standards.

Apart from two exceptions, *Teague* directs a federal habeas court not to apply to a prisoner's petition: (1) a ruling of the Supreme Court that came after the prisoner's conviction became final and that announced a "new rule"; or (2) the habeas court's own reading of a pre-existing Supreme Court precedent where that reading announces a "new rule" as to that precedent. In describing the "new rule" limitation, *Teague* stated that a "a case announces a new rule if the result was not *dictated* by precedent existing at the time the defendant's conviction became final." Later cases added that a result was not so dictated simply because the habeas court believes the result follows from the general rationale of the prior precedent. Thus, where two interpretations of prior precedent were "susceptible to debate among reasonable minds," the habeas court could not override the state court's adoption of the narrower of the two by itself applying retroactively the broader interpretation. *Butler v. McKellar* (1990). See also *Williams v. Taylor* (2000) (reading as consistent with *Teague* subsequently adopted federal habeas legislation, which bars relief unless the "adjudication of the [defendant's constitutional] claim by the State Court * * * resulted in a decision that was contrary to, or involved an unreasonable application of, clearly established Federal law as determined by the Supreme Court of the United States * * * ").

*Teague* recognized two exceptional situations in which the habeas court may overturn a final conviction based on a new rule. The first is a new ruling that "place[s] certain kinds of primary, private individual conduct beyond the power of the criminal-law making authority." Thus, if the new rule established that the criminal offense itself was unconstitutional, that rule could be applied even though the state court's earlier conclusion to the contrary may have been consistent with Supreme Court precedent at the time. Such jurisdictional defects have long been cognizable on habeas review, and respect for a state court's good faith application of existing precedent does not carry so far as to allow continued custody for conduct that could not constitutionally be punished.

The second exception similarly is designed "to assure that no man has been incarcerated under a procedure which creates an impermissibly large risk that the innocent will be convicted." It allows for application of a new rule that implicates fundamental fairness by mandating a procedure "central to an accurate determination of innocence or guilt."

The *Teague* Court noted that it "seemed unlikely that many such components of basic due process have yet to emerge," but should that occur, they would be applied even though not established by precedent at the time the conviction became final. Later cases emphasized that this exception applied only to a truly "watershed ruling" that altered "bedrock procedural elements essential to a fair trial" and not simply refinements of earlier established limitations designed to ensure factfinding accuracy. *Sawyer v. Smith* (1990).

# CHAPTER 2

# ARREST, SEARCH
# AND SEIZURE

## § 2.1  INTRODUCTION

### (a)  The Fourth Amendment

The Fourth Amendment to the U.S. Constitution reads: "The right of the people to be secure in their persons, houses, papers, and effects, against unreasonable searches and seizures, shall not be violated, and no Warrants shall issue, but upon probable cause, supported by Oath or affirmation, and particularly describing the place to be searched, and the persons or things to be seized." The Amendment is applicable to the states through the due process clause of the Fourteenth Amendment (see § 6.3(a)), but on both the federal and state levels governs only conduct by agents of the government (police, other government employees, and private persons acting at the direction or request of government officials). *Burdeau v. McDowell* (1921).

The same standards of reasonableness and probable cause govern both federal and state activities. *Ker v. Cal.* (1963); *Aguilar v. Tex.* (1964). A plurality of the Court concluded in *U.S. v. Verdugo–Urquidez* (1990) that the word "people" in the Amendment covers only members of our "national

50

community'' and not nonresident aliens, so that the Amendment is inapplicable to the search of such a person's Mexican residence. (Perhaps the three dissenters, together with the two concurring Justices who instead stressed the inapplicability of the Amendment's warrant clause to foreign searches, would have produced a different result had the objection been not lack of a warrant but absence of probable cause.)

Subject to the *Leon* or "good faith" exception (see § 6.4), direct and derivative evidence (see § 6.6) obtained in violation of the Fourth Amendment by police or by some but not all other government officials (see § 2.11(f)) is subject to exclusion in state, *Mapp v. Ohio* (1961), as well as federal, *Weeks v. U.S.* (1914), criminal cases (regarding other proceedings, see § 6.5), if the defendant has standing to object (see § 6.8).

### (b) Seizure of the person

Because of the exclusionary sanction, the Fourth Amendment is more commonly thought of as a limitation on the power of police to search for and seize evidence, instrumentalities, and fruits of crime. However, an illegal arrest or other unreasonable seizure of the person is itself a violation of the Fourth and Fourteenth Amendments, *Terry v. Ohio* (1968); *Henry v. U.S.* (1959), although it is no defense to a state or federal criminal prosecution that the defendant was illegally arrested or forcibly brought within the jurisdiction of the court, *Frisbie v. Collins* (1952), except perhaps when the circumstances are particularly shocking. (Even abduction of the defendant in lieu of resort to an extradition treaty is no bar to prosecution when the treaty does not provide otherwise. *U.S. v. Alvarez–Machain* (1992).)

Whether an arrest or other seizure of the person conforms to the requirements of the Constitution is nonetheless frequently a matter of practical importance. The police are authorized to conduct a limited search without warrant incident to a lawful arrest (see §§ 2.6(b), 2.7(c), 2.8(a)), and thus the admissibility of physical evidence acquired in this way depends upon the validity of the arrest. The same is true of certain other evidentiary "fruits" obtained subsequent to and as a consequence of the arrest (see § 6.6(e)).

### (c) The major issues

Several Fourth Amendment issues of current significance are surveyed in this Chapter. Consideration is first given to the areas and interests protected by the Amendment (see § 2.2), for they determine what constitutes a "search" and thus what activities are subject to the requirements of the Amendment. The most pervasive requirement of the Amendment is that of "probable cause," needed for lawful arrests and searches both with and without warrant, and special attention is therefore given to the meaning and significance of this quantum-of-evidence standard (see § 2.3). Other constitutional requirements for obtaining physical evidence by search warrant (see §§ 2.4,

2.5), without a warrant (see §§ 2.6, 2.7, 2.8), and with consent (see § 2.12) are separately considered. Finally, to illustrate the flexibility of the Fourth Amendment limitations, this Chapter also covers some unique practices for which separate rules have been developed because of the limited intrusion or special need attending their use: brief detentions for purposes of investigation (see § 2.9); grand jury subpoenas (see § 2.10); and inspections and regulatory searches (see § 2.11).

## § 2.2  PROTECTED AREAS AND INTERESTS

### (a)  Property interests vs. privacy interests

What is a search under the Fourth Amendment? The traditional approach was to speak of intrusion into certain "constitutionally protected areas," in that the Fourth Amendment protects the "right of the people to be secure in their persons, houses, papers, and effects, against unreasonable searches and seizures." This property approach was rejected in *Katz v. U.S.* (1967), in favor of a privacy approach. In concluding that a nontrespassory eavesdropping into a public telephone booth constituted a search, the Court declined to characterize the booth as a "constitutionally protected area": "For the Fourth Amendment protects people, not places. What a person knowingly exposes to the public, even in his own home or office, is not a subject of Fourth Amendment protection * * *. But what he seeks to preserve as private, even in an area accessible to the public, may be constitutionally protected."

The majority opinion in *Katz* does not elaborate upon the privacy approach, except for the helpful observation that defendant's activities were protected because the government intrusion "violated the privacy upon which he justifiably relied." Justice Harlan's oft-quoted concurrence suggested a "twofold requirement: first, that a person have exhibited an actual (subjective) expectation of privacy; and, second, that the expectation be one that society is prepared to recognize as 'reasonable.' " (But later, dissenting in *U.S. v. White* (1971), he cautioned against undue emphasis upon actual expectations, which "are in large part reflections" of what the law permits.) He also noted, quite correctly, that in asking what protection the Fourth Amendment affords people (i.e., where an expectation of privacy is reasonable), it is generally necessary to answer with reference to a place, so that many of the earlier property-based decisions are not disturbed by *Katz*.

The Fourth Amendment proscription on unreasonable "searches and seizures" extends not only to cases involving both a search and a related seizure, but also to those in which either a search *or* a seizure has occurred alone. *Soldal v. Cook County* (1992). While the "searches" part of the Amendment has to do mainly with the privacy interest, as in *Katz*, the "seizures" part concerns the interests in possession of property and liberty of person. See *U.S. v. Place* (1983) (detention of traveler's luggage

90 minutes an unreasonable deprivation of defendant's "possessory interest in his luggage" and his "liberty interest in proceeding with his itinerary").

### (b) Plain view, smell and hearing

It is not a search under *Katz* for an officer, lawfully present at a certain location, to detect something by one of his natural senses (e.g., to hear "by the naked ear" conversation in adjoining motel room). But, while "plain touch" has been analogized to plain view for some purposes, ordinarily the touching will itself constitute search activity for which a justification must be shown. *Minn. v. Dickerson* (1993). Because physically invasive inspection is more intrusive than a purely visual inspection, the squeezing of a bus passenger's luggage in the overhead rack, resulting in discovery of a brick-shaped object within, constitutes a search, as a bus passenger justifiably expects other passengers or bus employees to "move" or "handle" his bag but not to "feel the bag in an exploratory manner." *Bond v. U.S.* (2000).

It is ordinarily no search when common means of enhancing the senses, such as a flashlight or binoculars, are used. *U.S. v. Dunn* (1987); *U.S. v. Lee* (1927). But the use of such devices in particular circumstances may be so highly intrusive as to justify the conclusion that a search has occurred, as where a highpowered telescope is used to determine from a distance of a quarter mile the contents of papers being read in a high-rise apartment. In holding aerial photography of the outdoor areas of an industrial complex was no search although objects as small as half-inch pipes were detected, the Court in *Dow Chem. Co. v. U.S.* (1986) intimated the result might be different if (1) the place of surveillance had been "an area immediately adjacent to a private home, where privacy expectations are most heightened," (2) "any identifiable human faces or secret documents [were] captured in such a fashion," or (3) the surveillance involved "highly sophisticated surveillance not generally available to the public."

Also, it is a search to utilize other sophisticated means, such as an x-ray machine or magnetometer. But use of a drug dog to detect narcotics in a suitcase is no search because, unlike any other investigative procedure, it "discloses only the presence or absence of * * * a contraband item" and "does not expose noncontraband items that otherwise would remain hidden from public view." *U.S. v. Place* (1983), applied to a dog sniff of a lawfully stopped car in *Ill. v. Caballes* (2005). By similar reasoning, it was held in *U.S. v. Jacobsen* (1984) that field testing of a white powder uncovered by a private search was no search, as it would only reveal whether the powder was an illegal substance.

Sometimes even police action in opening a package will be treated like a plain view situation on the ground that the opening did not intrude upon any reasonable expectation of privacy. This is so as to containers whose "contents can be inferred from their outward appearance," such as a gun case, *Ark.*

*v. Sanders* (1979), as to reopening of a package promptly after controlled delivery following an earlier lawful government inspection of the package's contents, *Ill. v. Andreas* (1983); or reopening a package after the private person who summoned police had opened the package to the same extent but then closed it, *U.S. v. Jacobsen* (1984).

While the characterization of an observation as a nonsearch plain view situation settles the lawfulness of the observation itself, it does not inevitably follow that a warrantless seizure of the observed object would be lawful. As explained in *Ill. v. Andreas* (1983), the plain view doctrine "authorizes seizure of illegal or evidentiary items visible to a police officer" only if the officer's "access to the object" itself has a "Fourth Amendment justification." Thus, if an officer standing on the public way is able to look through the window of a private residence and see contraband, he must except in exigent circumstances obtain a warrant before entering those premises to seize the contraband.

### (c)  Residential premises

Even entry and examination of residential premises is not a search if those premises have been abandoned. *Abel v. U.S.* (1960). Consistent with *Katz,* the proper test for abandonment in this context is not whether all formal property rights have been relinquished, but whether the complaining party retains a reasonable expectation of privacy in the place allegedly abandoned. Except for a hotel or motel guest, such an expectation may exist even after the rental period has expired if the tenant has not yet departed. As for premises not abandoned, it is a search for an officer to make an uninvited entry into even the hallway of a single-family dwelling, but the result is otherwise if the entry is into the common hallway of an apartment building. In the latter instance, some courts reach a contrary result if the building is sufficiently secured so that even common areas are not accessible to the general public.

Looking in or listening at a residence or other structure within the curtilage is no search if the officer uses his natural senses and is positioned on nearby public property, on the adjacent property of a neighbor, or on part of the curtilage of the premises being observed which is the normal means of access to and egress from the house. As for reliance upon sense-enhancing devices, the Court in *Kyllo v. U.S.* (2001) held that the use there of a thermal imager, which without sending rays or beams into premises determines the amount of heat emanating therefrom by measuring differences in surface temperatures of targeted objects, constituted a search. Stating a more particularized version of the *Katz* test for this genre of cases, the Court declared "that obtaining by sense-enhancing technology any information regarding the interior of the home that could not otherwise have been obtained without physical 'intrusion into a constitutionally protected area' constitutes a search where (as here) the technology in question is not in general public use."

As for entry of the curtilage (an area to be ascertained on a case-by-case basis "with particular reference to four factors: the proximity of the area claimed to be curtilage to the home, whether the area is included within an enclosure surrounding the home, the nature of the uses to which the area is put, and other steps taken by the resident to protect the area from observation by people passing by," *U.S. v. Dunn* (1987)), the question is whether the conduct intrudes upon a justified expectation of privacy. Relevant to that determination are the place of entry (was it along a normal route of access?) and the degree of scrutiny.

Mere looking into these lands from adjacent property will seldom constitute a search, though some courts deem this a search under *Katz* if the viewing can be accomplished only by most extraordinary efforts unlikely to be utilized by any curious passer-by. In *Cal. v. Ciraolo* (1986), the Court held viewing from a plane in public navigable airspace was no search because "any member of the public flying in this airspace who glanced down would have seen everything that these officers observed." *Ciraolo* was followed in *Fla. v. Riley* (1989), involving a helicopter hovering at 400 ft., but the Court cautioned flights could be so rare at some lower level, albeit within navigable air space, as to constitute a search.

**(d)  Other premises and places**

Before *Katz,* the protections of the Fourth Amendment were "not extended to the open fields,"

*Hester v. U.S.* (1924), typically viewed as all lands not falling within the curtilage. *Hester* was reaffirmed in *Oliver v. U.S.* (1984), where the Court reasoned that such places were not covered by the Fourth Amendment's "persons, houses, papers, and effects" language, and that a case-by-case assessment of the privacy expectation in such areas (e.g., that in *Oliver* the land was fenced, locked and posted with "No Trespassing" signs) would make it too "difficult for the policeman to discern the scope of his authority." In *U.S. v. Dunn* (1987) the Court assumed that a justified expectation of privacy could exist as to a barn outside the curtilage, so that entry of it would be a search, but held it was no search merely to look into the barn from an open field vantage point.

Though the Fourth Amendment mentions only "houses," offices, stores and other commercial premises are also protected. *See v. City of Seattle* (1967). Whether a particular investigative practice directed at such a place is a search often involves considerations similar to those discussed above as to residences, though it is no search for an officer to enter where and when there is an implied invitation for customers to come in. *Md. v. Macon* (1985). Even if certain business premises are generally open to the public, surveillance into private areas therein, such as fitting rooms and rest rooms, constitutes a search. The outdoor area of business premises, such as the fenced grounds of an industrial plant, can "be seen as falling somewhere between 'open fields' and curtilage," so that it is no search to use sophisticated aerial photography at such a place, even though physical entry probably would be deemed a search. *Dow Chem. Co. v. U.S.* (1986).

## (e) Vehicles

It is no search for the police, from a lawful vantage point, to examine the exterior of a vehicle, *Cardwell v. Lewis* (1974), or to see the contents by looking through the windows, *N.Y. v. Class* (1986). Entry of the car is a search under *Katz, N.Y. v. Class* (1986), unless of course the vehicle had been abandoned in such a way that the user no longer had a reasonable expectation that the automobile would be free from governmental intrusion.

## (f) Personal characteristics

In *U.S. v. Dionisio* (1973), the Court held that requiring a person to give voice exemplars is no search because "the physical characteristics of a person's voice, its tone and manner, as opposed to the content of a specific conversation, are constantly exposed to the public," so that "no person can have a reasonable expectation that others will not know the sound of his voice." By the same reasoning the Court ruled in the companion case of *U.S. v. Mara* (1973) that it is no search to require a person to give handwriting exemplars. The Court has also referred to fingerprinting as nothing more than obtaining "physical characteristics * * * constantly exposed to the public." *Cupp v. Murphy* (1973). But seizing evidence from within the body by taking a blood or urine sample quite clearly is a search. *Schmerber v. Cal.* (1966).

## (g) Effects

It has long been accepted that the protections of the Fourth Amendment do not extend to effects which have been abandoned. *Hester v. U.S.* (1924) (containers thrown into field); *Abel v. U.S.* (1960) (items left in waste basket upon hotel checkout). After *Katz,* the question is not whether the object has been abandoned in the property sense, but rather whether the defendant has, in discarding the property, relinquished his reasonable expectation of privacy as to it. (See e.g., *Smith v. Ohio* (1990), holding there was no abandonment of a grocery bag defendant placed on the hood of a car at police order and then attempted to protect from police inspection.) One has no expectation of privacy as to "trash left for collection in an area accessible to the public" (e.g., in plastic bags placed at the curb), as garbage so placed is "readily accessible" to the public; moreover, the garbage was so placed "for the express purpose of conveying it to a third party, the trash collector," who could search it or allow others to do so. *Cal. v. Greenwood* (1988). Because only the latter reason would apply, it is unclear what result should obtain where the collector at police request takes the garbage from well within the curtilage and then turns it over to the police.

In *Warden v. Hayden* (1967), the Court discarded the so-called "mere evidence" rule, whereunder objects of evidential value only could not be seized pursuant to a warrant, *Gouled v. U.S.* (1921), or incident to arrest, *U.S. v. Lefkowitz* (1932). This rejection of the distinction between "mere evidence" and instrumentalities, fruits of crime, and contraband was based upon the conclusions that (1) nothing in the language of the Fourth Amendment supports the distinction; (2) privacy is disturbed no more by a search for evidentiary material than other property; (3) the Fourth Amendment protects privacy rather than property, so that the defendant's or the government's property interest in the items seized is not relevant; and (4) the distinction had spawned numerous exceptions and great confusion.

The Court in *Hayden* was careful to emphasize that "the items of clothing involved in this case are not 'testimonial' or 'communicative' in nature, and their introduction therefore did not compel respondent to become a witness against himself in violation of the Fifth Amendment." This led some courts to conclude that the result would be otherwise if private papers were seized, but that position was rejected in *Andresen v. Md.* (1976). The Court there held that though the Fifth Amendment privilege against self-incrimination protects a person from having to produce testimonial documents in response to a subpoena, the privilege against self-incrimination affords no protection against a search warrant, as when a warrant is utilized the person in possession has not been compelled to make the record or to authenticate it by production.

The fact that "mere evidence" is being sought, or that it is being sought from a "third party," does not limit the manner of seizure. In *Zurcher v. Stanford Daily* (1978), the respondent, a college newspaper, argued that, because it had not been a participant in the crime being investigated, the prosecutor had violated the Fourth and First Amendments by seeking evidence allegedly in its possession (photographs) through a warrant-authorized search of its offices rather than through a subpoena duces tecum. Rejecting this claim, the Court noted that nothing in the Fourth Amendment suggests third parties are entitled to greater protection against searches than suspects; indeed, a contrary rule would be unworkable in that search warrants are often obtained when the identity of all those involved in the crime under investigation is not known. The First Amendment also did not require use of a subpoena duces tecum instead of a warrant, but only that the Fourth Amendment requirements be applied with "particular exactitude."

## (h) Surveillance of relationships and movements

The courts have upheld a number of surveillance practices on the questionable ground that no justified expectation of privacy was infringed because what was discovered had been revealed in a limited way to a limited group for a limited purpose. In *Smith v. Md.* (1979), for example, police use of a pen register to record the numbers called on a phone was held to be no search, as the defendant had conveyed such information to the telephone company equipment when dialing. By an equally narrow view of the *Katz* expectation of privacy test, it has been held that use of a mail cover, recording information on the outside of incoming mail, is no search. The Court similarly has said that a bank depositor "takes the risk, in revealing his affairs to [his bank]," that the information will be conveyed by the bank to police, and thus has no Fourth Amendment protection against such transfer. *U.S. v. Miller* (1976).

As for use of an electronic tracking device or "beeper" to keep track of an object's movements, the mere installation of a "beeper" in an object and its transfer to a suspect is no search because it "conveyed no information," and is no seizure because no one's possessory interest "was interfered with in a meaningful way." *U.S. v. Karo* (1984). Monitoring a beeper to keep track of one's public movements, even if visual surveillance would not have been practicable, is no search, as one "travelling in an automobile on public thoroughfares has no reasonable expectation of privacy in his movements from one place to another." *U.S. v. Knotts* (1983). But "monitoring of a beeper falls within the ambit of the Fourth Amendment when it reveals information that could not have been obtained through visual surveillance," such as that a certain object remains inside private premises. *U.S. v. Karo* (1984).

## § 2.3 "PROBABLE CAUSE" AND RELATED PROBLEMS

### (a) When and why "probable cause" in issue

The Fourth Amendment provides that "no Warrants shall issue, but upon probable cause," and thus it is apparent that a valid arrest warrant or search warrant may only be issued upon an affidavit or complaint which sets forth facts establishing probable cause. Those arrests and searches which may be made without a warrant must not be "unreasonable" under the Fourth Amendment, and because the requirements in such cases "surely cannot be less stringent" than when a warrant is obtained, *Wong Sun v. U.S.* (1963), probable cause is also required in such circumstances. *Draper v. U.S.* (1959).

When the police act without a warrant, they initially make the probable cause decision themselves, although it will be subject to after-the-fact review by a judicial officer upon a motion to suppress evidence found because of the arrest or search. When the police act with a warrant, the probable cause decision is made by a magistrate in the first instance, but his decision may likewise be challenged in an adversary setting upon a motion to suppress. However, because of the *Leon* "good faith" rule (see § 6.4), a finding of no probable cause in a with-warrant case will not often result in suppression. But *Leon* is inapplicable when the affidavit was "so lacking in indicia of probable cause as to render official belief in its existence entirely unreasonable." *Leon* indicates that as far as the executing officer is concerned, the question is "whether a reasonably well-trained officer would have known that the search was illegal despite the magistrate's authorization." But *Leon* also requires good faith on the part of the officer applying for the warrant, and as to him the fact the magistrate acted favorably on the warrant request is irrelevant. *Malley v. Briggs* (1986).

Although there are many circumstances in which arrests and searches may be made without a warrant (see §§ 2.6, 2.7, 2.8), the Supreme Court has expressed a strong preference for arrest warrants, *Beck v. Ohio* (1964), and search warrants, *U.S. v. Ventresca* (1965), on the ground that interposing an orderly procedure whereby a neutral and detached magistrate makes the decision is better than allowing those engaged in the competitive enterprise of ferreting out crime to make hurried decisions which would be reviewable by a magistrate only after the fact and by hindsight judgment. This preference has even resulted in a subtle difference between the probable cause required when there is no warrant and that required when there is; "in a doubtful or marginal case a search under a warrant may be sustainable where without one it would fall." *U.S. v. Ventresca* (1965).

Although there is reason to question whether before-the-fact review when warrants are sought is always as cautious as presumed by the Supreme Court, the warrant process at least has the advantage of providing a before-the-fact record of the facts upon which probable cause is based. If the police have acted without a warrant, the probable cause determination must be made primarily upon the basis of the officer's testimony on the motion to suppress, and thus there is some risk that the facts brought out at that time may not be limited to those upon which the officer acted. But when the police have acted with a warrant, the factual justification is under the prevailing practice set out in a complaint or affidavit, and at the motion to suppress hearing the issue is whether those pre-recorded facts show probable cause. Thus, a defective complaint or affidavit may not be saved by police testimony that they actually had additional facts, *Whiteley v. Warden* (1971), although where not barred by statute it is possible to receive testimony that additional facts were orally presented to the magistrate under oath at the time of the warrant application.

Even an affidavit sufficient on its face may be challenged upon a later motion to suppress. If the defendant makes a substantial preliminary showing that a false statement was included therein by an affiant who either knew the statement was false or acted with reckless disregard for the truth, and it appears that the allegedly false statement was material (i.e., necessary to the earlier probable cause finding), the Fourth Amendment requires that a hearing be held at defendant's request. If the defendant then proves the allegation of perjury or reckless disregard by a preponderance of the evidence, the affidavit must then be judged with the false material excised. *Franks v. Del.* (1978). This is an express exception to the "good faith" rule of *U.S. v. Leon* (1984). The Court in *Franks* did not require invalidation because of a material false statement negligently made, as a few courts had previously done, or because of an immaterial but deliberately false statement, as many courts had previously done.

Probable cause for arrest does not necessarily constitute probable cause for a search warrant, nor does probable cause for a search warrant necessarily provide grounds for arrest; each requires the same quantum of evidence, but as to somewhat different facts and circumstances. For a search warrant, two conclusions must be supported by substantial evidence: (1) that the items sought are connected with criminal activity; and (2) that the items will be found in the place to be searched. By comparison, for arrest there must be probable cause (1) that an offense has been committed; and (2) that the person to be arrested committed it. Thus, a showing of the probable guilt of the person whose premises are to be searched is no substitute for a showing that items connected with the crime are likely to be found there, and an affidavit for a search warrant need not identify any particular person as the offender.

### (b) Degree of probability

The Court in *Brinegar v. U.S.* (1949) declared that "in dealing with probable cause * * * we deal with probabilities," but did not identify the degree of probability needed other than to say that "more than bare suspicion" and "less than evidence which would justify * * * conviction" was required. Some of the Supreme Court's decisions may be read as adopting a more-probable-than-not test, so that, for example, there would not be grounds to arrest unless the information at hand provided a basis for singling out but one person, e.g., *Mallory v. U.S.* (1957), though *Md. v. Pringle* (2003) can be interpreted otherwise. But the lower court cases generally do not go this far, and instead merely require that the facts permit a fairly narrow focus, so that descriptions fitting large numbers of people or a large segment of the community will not suffice. This permits an arrest to be made on the somewhat general descriptions often given by crime victims or witnesses, though courts are not inclined to be as lenient when the uncertainty goes to whether any crime has occurred, as when the police observe suspicious activity. As to this latter situation, it is commonly said that arrest and search based on events as consistent with innocent as with criminal activity are unlawful.

*Brinegar* also characterized the probable cause requirement as "the best compromise that has been found for accommodating" the often opposing interests of privacy and effective law enforcement. This raises the question of whether this "compromise" must always be struck in precisely the same way, or whether instead probable cause may require a greater or a lesser quantum of evidence, depending upon the facts and circumstances of the individual case. As discussed later herein (see §§ 2.9, 2.11), certain unique investigative techniques which involve significantly lesser intrusions into freedom and privacy are governed by a less demanding probable cause standard. Also, some investigative activities are so intrusive that more than the usual probable cause showing is needed. *Winston v. Lee* (1985) (obtaining evidence by surgery requires, inter alia, strong need for that evidence). Compare *N.Y. v. P.J. Video, Inc.* (1986) (fact First Amendment interests involved does not require higher probable cause standard). The Court has wisely declined to adopt a sliding-scale probable cause formulation which would require a weighing and balancing of the competing interests in each and every case. *Dunaway v. N.Y.* (1979).

### (c) Information which may be considered

Probative evidence may be considered in determining whether there is probable cause, without regard to whether such evidence would be admissible at trial. Thus, it is proper to consider hearsay, *Draper v. U.S.* (1959), and a prior police record, *Brinegar v. U.S.* (1949). As the Court explained in *Brinegar,* those rules of evidence at trial which exclude probative evidence because of "possible misunderstanding or misuse by the jury" have no place at the probable cause determination, where "we deal with probabilities. These are not technical; they are the factual and practical considerations of everyday life on which reasonable and prudent men, not legal technicians, act." Probable cause may not be established by showing the arresting or searching officer subjectively believed he had grounds for his action. *Beck v. Ohio* (1964).

### (d) Information from informants

Those probable cause cases that have reached the Supreme Court have dealt almost exclusively with the troublesome question of when probable cause may be established solely upon the basis of information from an informant or upon such information plus some corroborating facts. Under the traditional view, if probable cause is to be based solely upon the informant's information, then the warrant application or the testimony at the suppression hearing if there was no warrant must reveal (1) underlying circumstances showing reason to believe that the informant is a credible person, and (2) underlying circumstances showing the basis of the conclusions reached by the informant. *Aguilar v. Tex.* (1964). This "two-pronged test" of *Aguilar* was abandoned in *Ill. v. Gates* (1983), discussed below, but *Gates* declares that "veracity" and "basis of knowledge" remain "highly relevant," so it is still useful to think about those two factors.

For example, a search warrant affidavit which merely states that a credible informant reported that narcotics are concealed in certain premises (as in *Aguilar*) is defective in two respects. First, there is no disclosure of why the informant is believed to be a credible person, such as that he provided information on past occasions which investigation proved to be correct, *McCray v. Ill.* (1967), or that his statement constituted an admission against his own penal interest, *U.S. v. Harris* (1971). But such disclosure alone should not be enough, for even a credible person may reach unjustified conclusions on the basis of circumstantial evidence or information from unreliable sources. That is, even if it were established that the informant was a credible person, it would still be unclear whether he asserted that there were narcotics in the house because (a) he saw them there, (b) he assumed they were there because of defendant's suspicious conduct, or (c) he was told by someone that they were there. Probable cause cannot be reliably determined without deciding which is the case, for while an informant's direct observation of criminal conduct would suffice, *McCray v. Ill.* (1967), it cannot be decided whether the suspicious conduct is adequate unless the precise nature of that conduct is revealed to the judge, *U.S. v. Ventresca* (1965), while hearsay-upon-hearsay can hardly be adequate unless it is determined that the ultimate source of the information was also credible and in a position to know of what he speaks.

If the underlying circumstances concerning the informant's credibility are shown, but the source of his information is not disclosed, it must then be considered whether the informant's tip is "in sufficient detail that the magistrate may know that he is relying on something more substantial than a casual rumor circulating in the underworld or an accusation based merely on an individual's general reputation." *Spinelli v. U.S.* (1969). The Court in

*Spinelli* said that the detail provided in *Draper v. U.S.* (1959), "provides a suitable benchmark." There, when an informant who had given reliable information in the past indicated that one Draper was peddling narcotics and that he would return from Chicago by train on one of two days with narcotics, and also described Draper and his clothing and said he would be carrying a tan zipper bag and that he habitually walked fast, there was at that moment probable cause for arrest. The officers knew from their past experience that the informant was credible, but they did not know the exact source of his information; yet there was probable cause, for, as the Court later explained in *Spinelli,* the agents had been given so many details that they could "reasonably infer that the informant had gained his information in a reliable way." That is, the informant had given enough details to justify the conclusion that his source was reliable—either direct observation, admissions by the defendant, fair conclusions drawn from circumstantial evidence, or information given by another who was reliable and in a position to know.

This self-verifying detail analysis must be distinguished from the question whether it is significant that there has been partial corroboration of the informant's tale. The Supreme Court has relied upon corroboration when neither the informant's basis of knowledge nor his veracity was otherwise clearly established. Thus in *Ill. v. Gates* (1983), where an anonymous letter said a named couple made their living selling drugs and predicted the husband would soon fly to Florida and drive back with another supply, and later police surveillance established he did fly to Florida and then drive northward on an interstate highway, this was deemed sufficient corroboration to show probable cause. The Court stressed that "future actions of third parties ordinarily are not easily predicted," and that the observed conduct, though on its face innocent activity, was "as suggestive of a pre-arranged drug run, as it is of an ordinary vacation trip." (Some cases are much easier than *Gates* because the informer's story will prompt a surveillance by which police see actions so highly suggestive of criminal conduct that the observation itself will amount to probable cause, in which case neither the credibility of the informant nor the basis of his knowledge is important. *Adams v. Williams* (1972).)

But the greater significance of *Gates* lies in the Court's abandonment of the *Aguilar* "two-pronged test" in favor of a "totality of the circumstances analysis." Two unconvincing reasons were given for such a shift: (1) that such a "flexible" standard would be easier for laymen police and magistrates to understand and apply; and (2) that veracity and basis of knowledge should not have "independent status" because "a deficiency in one may be compensated for * * * by a strong showing as to the other." Logically, that is not so. A described basis of knowledge coming from an informant of unknown veracity does not establish veracity (as compared to detailed prevarication). Also, known veracity does not show a basis of knowledge, as is reflected by the Court's repeated holdings "that the unsupported assertion or belief of [a presumptively reliable] officer does not satisfy the probable cause requirement." *Ill. v. Gates* (1983) (White, J., conc.). Just how much *Gates* has "watered down" the probable cause standard is uncertain, but it is clear that a "bare bones" affidavit of the *Aguilar* variety is still far off the mark. *Gates* cautions: "Sufficient information must be presented to the magistrate to allow that official to determine probable cause; his action cannot be a mere ratification of the bare conclusions of others."

When probable cause is based in whole or in part upon information from an informant, his identity need not always be disclosed at the suppression hearing. Disclosure is not required when the officer has testified in full and has been cross-examined as to what the informant told him and as to why the information was believed trustworthy. *McCray v. Ill.* (1967). Although disclosure may be compelled if there is good reason to doubt the officer's credibility, many courts protect more broadly against perjury and at the same time honor the informer privilege by requiring disclosure only in camera when the defendant has fairly put into issue the existence of the informant or the correctness of the officer's report of the informer's tale or prior performance.

### (e) Information from other sources

The reliability of informants used to uncover narcotics and gambling offenses has been a matter of special concern because they are often engaged in criminal conduct themselves. Thus, when the facts are provided by a police officer, *U.S. v. Ventresca* (1965), a crime victim, an eyewitness, a cooperative citizen, *Jaben v. U.S.* (1965), or an informant not from the criminal milieu, there is no comparable need for establishing credibility. It is still necessary to show why the person giving the information has a basis for his knowledge, although the number of details which need be disclosed varies depending upon the circumstances. See *Jaben v. U.S.* (1965), pointing out that tax evasion is not a crime which one might directly observe and that therefore there need not be disclosure of the details of the investigation into defendant's income. A warrantless arrest based upon the conclusory statements or directive of another policeman (i.e., that a certain person should be arrested) is not per se illegal, but will be upheld only upon a subsequent showing that the instigating official possessed facts constituting probable cause. *Whiteley v. Warden* (1971). Inconclusive direct observations by an officer can amount to probable cause, as in *Md. v. Pringle* (2003), deeming it a "reasonable inference," where police find drugs concealed in a car, that "any or all three of the occupants had * * * exercised dominion and control" of them.

### (f) Unconstitutional statute

What if the officer has information providing probable cause to believe that the suspect has violated a criminal statute, but the statute itself is later held unconstitutional? In *Mich. v. DeFillippo* (1979), the defendant was arrested pursuant to a local ordinance, later held unconstitutional, making it a violation for a person lawfully stopped to refuse to produce evidence of his identity. Upholding the admission of drugs seized in a search incident to that arrest, the Court noted that a "prudent officer" could not be required "to anticipate that a court would later hold the ordinance unconstitutional." That rule is to be distinguished from the *Krull* doctrine (§ 6.4(c)), applying a "good faith" exception as to such reliance upon statutes conferring search power later found unconstitutional.

## § 2.4  SEARCH WARRANTS: ISSUANCE

### (a) Who may issue

Where a state attorney general, as authorized by state law, issued a search warrant in the context of an investigation of which he had taken personal charge, this procedure violated the Fourth Amendment, as he "was not the neutral and detached magistrate required by the Constitution." *Coolidge v. N.H.* (1971). But it is not necessary "that all warrant authority must reside exclusively in a lawyer or judge"; an issuing magistrate need only be "neutral and detached" and "capable of determining whether probable cause exists," and thus a clerk of court could be authorized to issue arrest warrants for municipal ordinance violations. *Shadwick v. City of Tampa* (1972). It does not necessarily follow that a clerk could be permitted to issue search warrants, as to which the probable cause issues are often much more complex.

Even a judicial officer may not issue a warrant if he has such a personal interest in the matter that his impartiality is in doubt, as where a magistrate receives a fee only when he responds affirmatively to warrant requests. *Connally v. Ga.* (1977). A magistrate's conduct may show he is not "neutral and detached," as in *Lo-Ji Sales, Inc. v. N.Y.* (1979), where the judge allowed himself to become "the leader of the search party which was essentially a police operation." If a magistrate conducts himself in such a fashion in a particular case that he is not "neutral and detached," it appears that under the *Leon* "good faith" doctrine (see § 6.4(b)) suppression is required only if the police actually knew that the magistrate had "wholly abandoned his judicial role."

### (b) Passage of time since facts gathered

If information showing probable cause that a crime was committed is gathered, and assuming no other evidence to the contrary is later uncovered, this probable cause will still be present weeks, months, or years later. The same is not true, however, as to information showing probable cause to believe that certain items are to be found at a particular place. As time passes, the chances increase that the goods have since been removed from that location. For this reason, an affidavit in support of a search warrant must contain a statement as to the time when the facts relied upon occurred.

This statement of time must be reasonably definite, but declarations that the observations were made "recently" or "within" or "during" a named period have been approved. *Rugendorf v. U.S.* (1964).

Just how long a time period may elapse without probable cause vanishing "must be determined by the circumstances of each case." *Sgro v. U.S.* (1932). Generally, a longer time will be allowed as to an ongoing criminal enterprise as compared to a one-shot criminal episode. Thus 49 days is not too long re a search for forged tax stamps being used in an elaborate and extensive counterfeiting scheme, but 4 days might be deemed too long as to a one-time illegal sale of liquor. It is also generally true that more time will be tolerated when the search is for items which have continuing utility and are not strongly incriminating. Thus, the passage of 3 months from a bank robbery is not too long as to search for clothing worn by the robber, but is too long as to search for the bank's money bag. Likewise relevant is the extent to which the criminal would have had access to the place to be searched during the time which has elapsed.

### (c) Anticipatory warrants

Somewhat the converse issue is presented by the use of an anticipatory search warrant, one based upon an affidavit showing probable cause that at some future time (but not presently) certainly evidence will be present at a specific place. In *United States v. Grubbs* (2006), the Court ruled that "when an anticipatory warrant is issued, 'the fact that the contraband is not presently located at the place described in the warrant is immaterial, so long as there is probable cause to believe that it will be there when the search warrant is executed,' " and then adopted a two-pronged probable cause standard for anticipatory search warrants. It is necessary not only (i) that upon occurrence of the triggering condition (typically a controlled delivery of a package known to contain contraband to the premises named in the warrant) "there is a fair probability that contraband or evidence will be found in a particular place," but *also* (ii) "that there is probable cause to believe the triggering condition will occur" with respect to that place. Grubbs' claim that this triggering condition must be set out in the warrant and not just in the affidavit was rejected on the ground that the Fourth Amendment identifies only two matters, the place to be searched and the things to be seized, that need to be specified in the warrant. But the Court cautioned that if "the government were to execute an anticipatory warrant before the triggering condition occurred," such execution would violate the Fourth Amendment, for then "there would be no reason to believe the items described in the warrant could be found at the searched location."

### (d) Particular description of place or person to be searched

The Fourth Amendment provides that no warrants shall issue except those "particularly describing the place to be searched." This means the description must be such that the executing officer can "with reasonable effort ascertain and identify the place intended." *Steele v. U.S.* (1925). (However, under the *Leon* "good faith" exception to the exclusionary rule, see § 6.4(b), suppression is required only if the warrant is "so facially deficient— i.e., in failing to particularize the place to be searched or the things to be seized—that the executing officers cannot reasonably presume it to be valid.")

In describing premises to be searched, more care is generally required in urban areas than in rural areas. Farm property, for example, might merely be described in a general way and identified by section, township and range number. In a city, however, a building must be identified by street and number or by an equally specific description. *Steele v. U.S.* (1925). Minor errors in description, such as an incorrect street number, will not invalidate a warrant if it is still apparent what building or what part of a building is to be searched. In multiple-occupancy structures, the particular unit to be searched must be identified by occupant, room number, or apartment number, unless the multi-unit character of the property was reasonably not known to the officers applying for or executing the warrant and was not externally apparent. Similarly, full execution of a warrant authorizing search of an apartment covering the entire third floor is lawful where the police failure to perceive at execution that there were two apartments on that floor "was objectively understandable and reasonable." *Md. v. Garrison* (1987).

If a search warrant is obtained for search of an automobile, the description must direct the executing officer to one specific vehicle, either by license number or by the make of the car and the name of the operator. As to misdescription, the question again is whether the officer could select the proper vehicle, and thus a license number is sufficient notwithstanding a mistake as to the color and model year of the car.

A valid warrant for the search of a certain person must indicate the person's name, if known. If his name is not known, an otherwise complete description, listing such facts as the individual's aliases, approximate age, height and weight, race, and clothing, is adequate.

### (e) Particular description of things to be seized

The Fourth Amendment also provides that no search warrants shall issue except those "particularly describing the * * * things to be seized." "The requirement that warrants shall particularly describe the things to be seized makes general searches under them impossible * * *. As to what is to be taken, nothing is left to the discretion of the officer executing the warrant." *Marron v. U.S.* (1927). (Here again, it must be noted that under the *Leon* rule, see § 6.4(b), suppression is necessary only if the warrant is "so facially deficient—i.e., in failing to particularize the place to be searched or the things to be seized—that the executing officers cannot reasonably presume to be valid." A somewhat different application of this "good faith" exception was involved in *Mass. v. Sheppard* (1984), holding the evidence need not be suppressed when the search warrant misdescribed the items to be seized but the police officer relied on the magistrate's representation he had corrected the description to match that officer's correct description in his affidavit.)

The degree of particularity required varies somewhat depending upon the nature of the materials to be seized. Greater leeway is permitted in describing contraband (property the possession of which is a crime), and thus during Prohibition a description merely of "cases of whiskey" would suffice. *Steele v. U.S.* (1925). By comparison, innocuous property must be described more specifically so that executing officers will not be confused between the items sought and other property of a similar nature which might well be found on the premises. The particularity requirement requires even closer scrutiny of warrants for documents because of the potential they carry for very serious intrusions into privacy. *Andresen v. Md.* (1976).

Because of First Amendment considerations, this constitutional requirement "is to be accorded the most scrupulous exactitude when the 'things' are books, and the basis for their seizure is the ideas they contain," *Stanford v. Tex.* (1965), or when they are the papers of a newsgathering organization.

*Zurcher v. Stanford Daily* (1978). Also, in obscenity cases a search warrant may not authorize the seizure of great quantities of the same publication before the owner has had an opportunity to litigate the question of obscenity, for this would be an unconstitutional prior restraint. *A Quantity of Copies of Books v. Kan.* (1964). For the same reason, seizure of even a single copy of a film may not continue if it would prevent further showing of that picture by the exhibitor. *Heller v. N.Y.* (1973).

A defective description in the warrant sometimes may be saved by an adequate description in the affidavit. But *Groh v. Ramirez* (2004) held this permissible only "if the warrant used appropriate words of incorporation, and if the supporting document accompanies the warrant," apparently on the ground that only then is there sufficient notice to the occupant when a copy of the warrant is left at the conclusion of the search. But the Court emphasized it was dealing with a case where the warrant did not describe the items to be seized "at all," and distinguished other cases, such as where a warrant description contained "a mere technical mistake or typographical error."

If a search warrant is issued to search a place for several items, but it is later determined that not all of those items are described with sufficient particularity or that probable cause does not exist as to all of them, it is often possible to severe the tainted portion of the warrant from the valid portion so that evidence found in execution of the latter will be admissible. Assume, for example, a warrant for a gun used in and money taken in a bank robbery, and assume also that there is probable cause to search for the gun and that it is particularly described but that there is either no continuing probable cause or no adequate description of the money. If the police, while looking in a desk drawer for the gun, were to find money that by its wrappings clearly came from that robbery, the money would be admissible because found in plain view in execution of the valid part of the warrant. But if the money was found after the gun was located or by looking where the gun could not be (e.g., an envelope), the money would not be admissible.

## § 2.5  SEARCH WARRANTS: EXECUTION

### (a) Time of execution

Even where statutes or court rules purport to authorize execution within a fixed period of time, e.g., 10 days, the better view is that execution even within that time is permissible only if the probable cause recited in the affidavit continues until the time of execution, giving consideration to the intervening knowledge of the officers and the passage of time. Three members of the Court have suggested that a search warrant may be executed at night only upon a special showing of a need to do so, as provided by law in several jurisdictions, because of the "Fourth Amendment doctrine that increasingly severe standards of probable cause are necessary to justify increasingly intrusive searches." *Gooding v. U.S.* (1974). A search warrant may be executed in the absence of the occupant.

## (b) Entry without notice

The common statutory requirement that police ordinarily give notice of their authority and purpose prior to making entry in the execution of a search warrant is grounded in the Fourth Amendment, *Wilson v. Ark.* (1995), for it serves to decrease the potential for violence, protect privacy, and prevent the physical destruction of property. (However, under *Hudson v. Mich.* (2006), discussed in §§ 6.3(e), 6.6(d), the exclusionary rule is inapplicable to violation of this knock-and-announce requirement.) Police are sometimes excused from the usual notice requirements, but the so-called "blanket rule," where, for example, all felony cases were deemed to involve a sufficient risk of evidence destruction to justified entry without notice, was rejected by the Supreme Court in *Richards v. Wis.* (1997) as too broad.

*Richards* held that police are excused only when, under the circumstances of the particular case, they have a "reasonable suspicion" that knocking and announcing their presence would be dangerous or futile, or that it would inhibit the effective investigation of the crime by, for example, allowing the destruction of evidence. Illustrative is *U.S. v. Ramirez* (1998), involving execution of a search warrant authorizing entry to seize a wanted person, where the Court concluded there was a reasonable suspicion giving notice would be dangerous to the police or others, as police had confirmed an informant's assertion that the wanted person might be inside, and that person was a prison escapee with a violent past, reportedly had access to a large supply of weapons, and had vowed he would not do federal time.

*U.S. v. Banks* (2003) deals with two aspects of the absence of a response to given notice: (1) police may reasonably conclude they have been refused admittance when, on the known facts, it reasonably appears the occupant has had time to get to the door; but (2) a lesser time (e.g., 15–20 seconds in *Banks*) will excuse not waiting longer if in that time the occupant could have reached readily disposable contraband.

### (c) Detention and search of persons on the premises to be searched

An individual who merely happens to be present in premises where a search warrant is being executed may not, by virtue of that fact alone, be subjected to a search of his person. This is because such a search "must be supported by probable cause particularized with respect to that person," a requirement which "cannot be undercut or avoided by simply pointing to the fact that coincidentally there exists probable cause * * * to search the premises where the person may happen to be." *Ybarra v. Ill.* (1979).

Of course, if probable cause to search that person did exist and was established when the warrant to search the premises was obtained, that warrant could also authorize search of the person. During execution of a warrant lacking such authorization, a person might be discovered within as to whom there are grounds for arrest, in which case a search of the person could be undertaken incident to arrest and without reliance upon the search warrant. *Marron v. U.S.* (1927). Or, if there are not grounds to arrest but yet probable cause that the person has in his possession the items named in the search warrant, this would appear to be an additional basis for the search, for there would not be time to seek an additional warrant. But an actual search of such a person may not be undertaken merely because of suspicion that person may have the objects named in the search warrant. *Ybarra v. Ill.* (1979). If there is some basis for thinking that the person may be armed, and if only a frisk is undertaken, this would seem proper. Cf. *Terry v. Ohio* (1968) (discussed in § 2.9).

In *Mich. v. Summers* (1981), the Court held that a resident of premises where a search warrant for contraband is to be executed may be detained there during warrant execution. The Court explained that such detention would serve three important government interests: (1) preventing flight in the event incriminating evidence was found; (2) minimizing the risk of harm to the police; and (3) facilitating the orderly completion of the search. Per *Muehler v. Mena* (2005), a *Summers* detainee may sometimes be handcuffed (as when the warrant authorizes a search for weapons and there are multiple detainees), and may be questioned about matters unrelated to the warrant if the questioning does not extend the length of the detention.

### (d) Seizure of items not named in the warrant

Even if, as required, the police look within the described place only where the described items might be located, *Harris v. U.S.* (1947), and terminate the search once those items are discovered, they may discover supposed incriminating evidence other than that named in the warrant. As to this situation, the Court stated in *Coolidge v. N.H.* (1971): "Where, once an otherwise lawful search is in progress, the police inadvertently come upon a piece of evidence [in plain view], it would often be a needless inconvenience, and sometimes dangerous—to the evidence or to the police themselves—to require them to ignore it until they have obtained a warrant particularly describing it." The requirement that the discovery be "inadvertent" was abandoned in *Horton v. Cal.* (1990), where the Court explained it disapproved of Fourth Amendment "standards that depend upon the subjective state of mind of the officer" and believed the Amendment's particularity-of-description requirement would serve "the interest in limiting the area and duration of the search that the inadvertence requirement inadequately protects." But the observed item may be seized only if there is probable cause it constitutes the fruits, instrumentalities or evidence of crime. Reasonable suspicion that the article is of such character is an insufficient basis for a closer examination of the item (e.g., picking it up to reveal a serial number) not otherwise permissible in executing the warrant. *Ariz. v. Hicks* (1987).

### (e) Notice

In *City of West Covina v. Perkins* (1999), the Supreme Court concluded "that when law enforcement agents seize property pursuant to warrant, due process requires them to take reasonable steps to give notice that the property has been taken so the owner can pursue available remedies for its return" (to be distinguished from the kind of notice required by *Groh v. Ramirez* (2004); see § 2.4(e)). In *Perkins*, police had left at the premises a notice of the warrant execution and an inventory of the property seized, so the Court did not have occasion to "decide how detailed the notice of the seizure must be or when the notice must be given" or whether violation of this 14th Amendment requirement would provide a basis for evidence suppression. The Court went on to hold that there is no constitutional requirement of "individualized notice of state-law remedies [for recovery of the property seized] established by published, generally available statute and case law."

### § 2.6    WARRANTLESS SEARCHES AND SEIZURES OF PERSONS

#### (a) Arrest

The prevailing view, as a matter of state law, is that an arrest warrant is not required in serious cases notwithstanding the practicability of obtaining one before arrest. Arrest without warrant was lawful at common law when the officer had "reasonable grounds to believe" that a felony had been committed and that the person to be arrested had committed it, and this is the prevailing rule today either as a matter of statute or court decision. This "reasonable grounds" test and the "probable cause" requirement of the Fourth Amendment "are substantial equivalents." *Draper v. U.S.* (1959). While an indictment fair on its face returned by a properly constituted grand jury supplies the requisite probable cause for issuance of an arrest warrant, the same is not true of a conclusory information sworn to by the prosecutor. *Kalina v. Fletcher* (1997).

The common law rule with respect to misdemeanors was quite different: a warrant was required except when the offense occurred in the presence of the arresting officer, and some authorities recognized a second requirement that the offense in question constitute a "breach of the peace." But because of the "divergent conclusions" reached on the latter point prior to adoption of the Fourth Amendment, as well as the longstanding state and federal practice of authorizing warrantless arrests for misdemeanors not amounting to a breach of the peace, the Court has rejected the claim that the breach-of-the-peace limitation is a part of the Fourth Amendment reasonableness requirement. *Atwater v. City of Lago Vista* (2001). *Atwater* notes there was no need in that case to speculate about whether the in presence requirement was a part of the Fourth Amendment, as to which lower courts have quite consistently answered in the negative. On the view that there may be a need to arrest for a misdemeanor *not* occurring in any officer's presence, several jurisdictions have adopted the felony warrantless arrest rule for misdemeanors as well.

With the exception of the case in which private premises must be entered to make the arrest (see § 2.7(a)), there is no constitutional requirement that an arrest warrant be obtained when it is practicable to do so. While the Court has expressed a "preference for the use of arrest warrants when feasible," see *Gerstein v. Pugh* (1975), it also has declined "to transform this judicial preference into a constitutional rule," *U.S. v. Watson* (1976). Such a rule, it noted in *Watson,* would "encumber criminal prosecutions with endless litigation with respect to the existence of exigent circumstances." On the other hand, *Gerstein v. Pugh* (1975) held that once a warrantless arrest is made, the Fourth Amendment "requires a [prompt] judicial determination of probable cause as a prerequisite to extended restraint on liberty following [the warrantless] arrest." That determination, upon a standard which "is the same as that for arrest," may be made in an ex parte proceeding (i.e., without defense participation) in the same manner as the issuance of a warrant. A probable cause determination within 48 hours of arrest is presumptively reasonable, though a particular defendant may show such a delay was unreasonable because "for the purpose of gathering additional evidence to justify the arrest, a delay motivated by ill will against the arrested individual, or delay for delay's sake." On the other hand, a later probable cause determination is presumptively unreasonable, meaning "the burden shifts to the government to demonstrate the existence of a bona fide emergency or other extraordinary circumstance." *County of Riverside v. McLaughlin* (1991). Whether an untimely probable cause determination requires suppression of the arrestee's earlier confession "remains an unresolved question." *Powell v. Nev.* (1994).

Rejecting the contention that *Watson* means the Fourth Amendment has nothing to say about *how* a seizure is made, the Court in *Tenn. v. Garner* (1985) held that the use of deadly force to arrest a fleeing felon is unreasonable unless "the suspect threatens the officer with a weapon or there is probable cause to believe that he has committed a crime involving the infliction or threatened infliction of serious physical harm." The Fourth Amendment reasonableness standard (1) applies to "*all* claims that law enforcement officers have used excessive force—deadly or not—in the course of" any seizure; (2) "requires careful attention to the facts and circumstances of each particular case, including the severity of the crime at issue, whether the suspect poses an immediate threat to the safety of the officers or others, and whether he is actively resisting arrest or attempting to evade arrest by flight"; (3) "must embody allowance for the fact that police officers are often forced to make split-second judgments * * * about the amount of force that is necessary in a particular situation"; and (4) asks "whether the officers' actions are 'objectively reasonable' in light of the facts and circumstances confronting them, without regard to their underlying intent or motivation." *Graham v. Connor* (1989). This standard applies *only* to Fourth Amendment activity, not other police conduct, which is instead governed by the due process shocks-the-conscience standard of the 14th Amendment. *Co. of Sacramento v. Lewis* (1998).

### (b) Search incident to arrest

"When an arrest is made, it is reasonable for the arresting officer to search the person arrested in order to remove any weapons that the latter might seek to use in order to resist arrest or effect his escape [and to] seize any evidence on the arrestee's person in order to prevent its concealment or destruction." *Chimel v. Cal.* (1969). Given this justification, doubt existed for some time as to whether a search could be undertaken incident to an arrest for a lesser offense, such as a minor traffic violation, where there would be no evidence to search for and a relatively lesser risk that the arrestee would be armed. But in *U.S. v. Robinson* (1973), the Court held that a full search of the person incident to a "full custody arrest" (i.e., one made for the purpose of taking the person to the station) may be undertaken without regard to "what a court may later decide was the probability in a particular arrest situation that weapons or evidence would in fact be found upon the person of the suspect," apparently on the ground that it would be unwise to have courts second-guessing such a "quick *ad hoc* judgment" by arresting officers. The limited frisk alternative of *Terry* (see § 2.9(d)) was deemed insufficient in the case of arrest, as "the danger to an officer is far greater in the case of the extended exposure which follows the taking of a suspect into custody and transporting him to the police station."

What the officer may do absent a "custodial arrest" was later reached in *Knowles v. Iowa* (1998), where the search came after an officer stopped Knowles for speeding but then issued him a citation pursuant to a statute permitting but not requiring that alternative course of action. A unanimous Supreme Court held the two search-incident-to-arrest rationales discussed in *Robinson* did not justify the search. The threat to officer safety, the Court concluded, was far less than where (as stated in *Robinson*) there is "extended exposure which follows the taking of a suspect into custody and transporting him to the police station." The concern with officer safety was thus deemed sufficiently met by the officer's authority recognized in earlier decisions: to require the driver, *Pa. v. Mimms* (1977), and passenger, *Md. v Wilson* (1997), of the stopped vehicle to get out of the car; to frisk the driver and any passenger on a "reasonable suspicion they may be armed and dangerous," *Terry v. Ohio* (1968); and to make a limited search of the passenger compartment upon reasonable suspicion "that an occupant is dangerous and may gain immediate control of a weapon," *Michigan v. Long* (1983). As for the second *Robinson* rationale, the "need to discover and preserve evidence," it was not present in *Knowles* because there was no evidence of speeding to be found. Left unresolved was the question whether, incident to citation for an offense for which there *could be* such evidence, the officer would have the search authority he would have if he instead had opted for custodial arrest, or whether instead any search would have to be justified by showing probable cause to *search*.

The Supreme Court's ruling in *Robinson* makes more significant the longstanding issue of what items are subject to seizure once discovered. Clearly seizure is not limited to the items sought; "when an article subject to lawful seizure properly comes into an officer's possession in the course of a lawful search it would be entirely without reason to say that he must return it because it was not one of the things it was his business to look for." *Abel v. U.S.* (1960). But in *Abel* there was probable cause to seize the item in question, and on this ground *Abel* was distinguished in a case where the officer seized an unlabeled bottle of pills from the pocket of a defendant arrested for public intoxication. The court, noting the absence of cases in point, concluded that the seizure was improper because the officer acted only upon suspicion that the pills might be narcotics and not upon reasonable grounds to believe that the article he has discovered is contraband. Compare the situation as to seizure of items not named in a search warrant, § 2.5(d), which likewise raises the question of how much discretion should be left to the searching officer; and consider *Warden v. Hayden* (1967), where the court, in rejecting the contention that abolition of the "mere evidence" rule would result in indiscriminate seizures, emphasized that there "must, of course, be a nexus * * * between the item to be seized and criminal behavior," and that "probable cause must be examined in terms of cause to believe that the evidence sought will aid in a particular apprehension or conviction."

### (c) Time of search; inventory

It is clear that a search cannot be justified as being "incident" to arrest if the search is conducted without arrest and at a time when a lawful arrest could not be made because sufficient grounds are lacking or because of physical inability to make an arrest at that time. But a search of the person qualifies as a search incident to arrest if "the formal arrest followed quickly on the heels" of that search and was sufficiently grounded upon facts other than those uncovered by the search. *Rawlings v. Ky.* (1980). This is a sound position, as a search before arrest when there are grounds to arrest involves no greater invasion of the person's security and privacy, and has the advantage that if the search is not productive the individual may not be arrested at all. If there was no present intent to arrest and arrest does not promptly follow the search, then the search is not properly characterized as "incident" to arrest, but it is still lawful if made upon probable cause and limited to the extent "necessary to preserve highly evanescent evidence [e.g., fingernail scrapings]." *Cupp v. Murphy* (1973).

Courts have generally upheld delayed searches of the person arrested (such as those made on the way to or at the station), either on the theory that police control of the person by arrest is so substantial that it of necessity carries with it a continuing right of search, or on the ground that the police are entitled to inventory the property found on a person before placing him in a cell. A contrary result has sometimes been reached because of a prior failure of the police to permit the defendant to exercise his right of stationhouse release. Police need not resort to less intrusive means than the inventory of all effects found on or in possession of a person arrested, provided such searches are pursuant to "standardized inventory procedures." *Ill. v. Lafayette* (1983). In *U.S. v. Edwards* (1974), the Court held that "once the defendant is lawfully arrested and is in custody, the effects in his possession at the place of detention that were subject to search at the time and place of his arrest may lawfully be searched and seized without a warrant even though a substantial period of time has elapsed between the arrest and subsequent administrative processing on the one hand and the taking of the property for use as evidence on the other," at least where such searches are not unreasonable "either because of their number or their manner of perpetration." This qualification suggests that neither *Robinson* nor *Edwards* disturb the holding in *Schmerber v.*

*Cal.* (1966) that, except where delay would threaten loss of the evidence, a search warrant is required to intrude into an arrestee's body.

### (d) "Subterfuge" and unnecessary arrests

*Robinson* has been criticized on the ground that it opens the door to "subterfuge" arrests for minor offenses made to support searches of persons for evidence of more serious offenses as to which probable cause is lacking, particularly in light of the fact that *Robinson* was applied in the companion case of *Gustafson v. Fla.* (1973) to a situation in which the officer had complete discretion as to whether to arrest or give a citation and whether to search if an arrest was made. Evidence has sometimes been suppressed upon a showing that the desire to seek such evidence was the motivation behind arrest for such minor crimes as vagrancy or a traffic violation, but some courts have overlooked strong evidence of such a "subterfuge."

More recently, however, the pretextual arrest issue appears to have been settled by *Whren v. U.S.* (1996), where it was indicated that neither the officer's subjective motivations nor his departure from usual practice could ordinarily place an otherwise-valid arrest into question. Specifically, the Court stated that with "rare exception" (later stated to be "searches and seizures conducted in an extraordinary manner, unusually harmful to an individual's privacy or even physical interests"), the reasonableness of Fourth Amendment activity "is not in doubt where the search or seizure is based on probable cause." (Although *Whren* involved a traffic stop, it was assumed to cover custodial arrests as well, as the Court later confirmed in *Ark. v. Sullivan* (2001).)

The *Whren* decision made even more significant the issue alluded to in *Gustafson*, i.e., whether the Fourth Amendment reasonableness requirement imposed some limitation upon the power of police to opt for arrest in lieu of a citation in the case of minor offenses. But in *Atwater v. City of Lago Vista* (2001), where a § 1983 plaintiff was arrested for a seat belt violation, the Court rejected 5–4 plaintiff's claim that custodial arrest was constitutionally forbidden, "even upon probable cause, when conviction could not ultimately carry any jail time and when the government shows no compelling need for immediate detention." Such a rule, the majority objected, would lack "the values of clarity and simplicity" needed for any rule intended to govern a police decision made "on the spur (and in the heat) of the moment," a price not worth paying absent any showing that "unnecessary minor-offense arrests" are at all common.

### (e)  The significance of booking

"Booking" is an administrative step taken after the arrested person is brought to the police station, which involves entry of the person's name, the crime for which the arrest was made, and other relevant facts on the police "blotter," and which may also include photographing, fingerprinting, and the like. Because booking results in a record of some of the circumstances of arrest, the question has arisen whether the entries made are relevant in determining the lawfulness of the arrest. A few courts have taken the position that an entry that the defendant was arrested "on suspicion of" or "for investigation of" a certain offense shows that the arrest was without probable cause, but in practice such entries are often made solely for the purpose of identifying those cases being referred to the detective division. It has been held that if a person was booked for one offense, his arrest may thereafter be upheld on the ground that the police had sufficient evidence of a quite different offense. Some courts required that there be a nexus between the two offenses, but a unanimous Court rejected such a limitation in *Devenpeck v. Alford* (2004).

## § 2.7  WARRANTLESS SEARCHES AND SEIZURES OF PREMISES

### (a) Entry to arrest

In *Payton v. N.Y.* (1980), the Court held that the Fourth Amendment prohibits the police from making a warrantless nonconsensual entry into a suspect's home to make a routine arrest. The Court reasoned that the "basic principle of Fourth Amendment law" that searches and seizures inside a home without a warrant are presumptively unreasonable, long applied when the purpose was to search for an object, "has equal force when the seizure of a person is involved." This is because "any differences in the intrusiveness of entries to search and entries to arrest are merely ones of degree rather than kind," and they "share this fundamental characteristic: the breach of the entrance to an individual's home." As for the argument that a warrant requirement was impractical, the Court, after noting it had been provided with no "evidence that effective law enforcement has suffered in those States that already have such a requirement," declared that "such arguments of policy must give way to a constitutional command that we consider to be unequivocal."

Prior to *Payton,* the Court had held that police may enter premises without a warrant in immediate pursuit of a person to be arrested who sought refuge therein on seeing the police approach, *U.S. v. Santana* (1976). Such an entry may also be made in hot pursuit of an offender, as in *Warden v. Hayden* (1967), where the police were informed that an armed robbery had taken place and that the suspect had entered a certain house five minutes before they reached it, as delay under these circumstances would endanger the lives of the police and others. Once inside, the Court concluded in *Hayden,* the police were justified in looking everywhere in the house where the suspect might be hiding and also (before his capture) where weapons might be hidden.

*Payton* casts no doubt on those decisions, for the Court emphasized it was dealing with in-premises arrests for which no exigent circumstances claim had been made. Thus, the Court in *Payton* had no occasion to elaborate upon what would amount to exigent circumstances. The Court did, however, place considerable reliance upon a case in which exigent circumstances were found to be present based upon these factors: (1) a crime of violence was involved; (2) the suspect was reasonably believed to be armed; (3) there was a very clear showing of probable cause; (4) there was a strong reason to believe the suspect was within the premises; (5) there was a likelihood the suspect would escape if not swiftly apprehended; and (6) the entry was made peaceably. Emphasizing the absence of the first of these factors, the Court in *Welsh v. Wis.* (1984) held illegal a warrantless entry to arrest for driving under the influence, made to ensure that defendant's blood-alcohol level was determined before it dissipated. Noting the crime was a civil offense not punishable by imprisonment, the Court found it "difficult to conceive of a warrantless home arrest that would not be unreasonable under the Fourth Amendment when the underlying offense is extremely minor."

In response to the "suggestion that only a search warrant based on probable cause to believe the suspect is at home at a given time can adequately protect the privacy interests at stake," the Court in *Payton* concluded that an arrest warrant, though affording less protection than a search warrant, would suffice: "If there is sufficient evidence of a citizen's participation in a felony to persuade a judicial officer that his arrest is justified, it is constitutionally reasonable to require him to open his doors to the officers of the law. Thus, for Fourth Amendment purposes, an arrest warrant founded on probable cause implicitly carries with it the limited authority to enter a dwelling in which the suspect lives when there is reason to believe the suspect is within." But a search warrant, issued on probable cause the person to be arrested is now present within, is needed to enter premises of a third party. *Steagald v. U.S.* (1981). Under the *Payton-Steagald* warrant requirement, police actions in executing the warrant must be "related to the objectives of the authorized intrusion," meaning that the police may not be accompanied by others, such as members of the news media, whose presence within "was not related to the objective of their authorized intrusion." *Wilson v. Layne* (1999) (a § 1983 action, meaning the Court did not discuss the exclusionary rule consequences, if any, of such a violation).

### (b) Entry without notice

The proposition that police must ordinarily give notice of their authority and purpose prior to making an entry of premises to arrest a person therein has common law credentials and is often found expressed by statute. It appears to have been viewed in *Ker v. Cal.* (1963) as a Fourth Amendment requirement, a conclusion strengthened by the Court's more recent holding that this is so as to entry to execute a search warrant, *Wilson v. Ark.* (1995). Where notice is given, the occupant must be given a reasonable opportunity to respond, except that a shorter delay will suffice if in that interval the occupant would be able to reach disposable contraband. *U.S. v. Banks* (2003), discussed in § 2.5(b). Entry without notice is permissible, however, when the officer has some reason to believe that compliance with the usual notice requirements would increase his peril, frustrate an arrest, or permit the destruction of evidence.

Some jurisdictions have followed a so-called "blanket rule" under which such exigent circumstances could be established based upon the general category of case involved, as determined by the nature of the charge for which the arrest is to be made, but the Supreme Court has rejected that approach in search warrant cases, *Richards v. Wis.* (1997), justifying the conclusion that the "blanket rule" is likewise impermissible in the present context. Rather, *Richards* teaches that what is required is that the police, based upon the circumstances of the particular case, have a "reasonable suspicion" that one of the previously mentioned risks is present. Illustrative is *U.S. v. Ramirez* (1998), an entry-to-arrest case in which, however, the police also had a search warrant, where the Court concluded there was a reasonable suspicion giving notice would be dangerous to the police or others, as police had confirmed an informant's assertion that the person to be arrested might be inside, and that person was a prison escapee with a violent past who reportedly had access to a large supply of weapons and had vowed he would not do federal time.

### (c) Search incident to and after arrest

For many years, it could be said that the right to make a warrantless search incident to arrest was one exception which came close to swallowing up the search warrant requirement. Per *Harris v. U.S.* (1947), and *U.S. v. Rabinowitz* (1950), such searches were permitted of the premises where the arrest occurred, without regard to the practicality of obtaining a search warrant. Under the *Harris-Rabinowitz* rule, the scope of the search extended to the entire premises in which the defendant had a possessory interest, and such searches were usually upheld without any showing of probable cause that the objects sought would be found there. In *Chimel v. Cal.* (1969), the Court, noting that in more recent decisions such searches had been justified solely upon the need to prevent the arrested person from obtaining a weapon or destroying evidence, overruled *Harris* and *Rabinowitz* and limited the scope of warrantless searches incident to arrest consistent with that purpose:

"When an arrest is made, it is reasonable for the arresting officer to search the person arrested in order to remove any weapons that the latter might seek to use in order to resist arrest or effect his escape. * * * In addition, it is entirely reasonable for the arresting officer to search for and seize any evidence on the arrestee's person in order to prevent its concealment or destruction. And the area into which an arrestee might reach in order to grab a weapon or evidentiary items must, of course, be governed by a like rule. A gun on a table or in a drawer in front of one who is arrested can be as dangerous to the arresting officer as one concealed in the clothing of the person arrested. There is ample justification, therefore, for a search of the arrestee's person and the area 'within his immediate control'—construing that phrase to mean the area from within which he might gain possession of a weapon or destructible evidence.'' A broader search of the place of arrest "may be made only under the authority of a search warrant.'' *Chimel* involved a search of an entire house, but the Court made it clear that the new rule would also bar more limited searches, such as the one-room search in *Rabinowitz* and the four-room search in *Harris*.

*Chimel* is not inconsistent with the notion that if it is necessary for the arrestee to put on clothing or do other things before he is taken to the station, then the police may examine closets and other places to which the arrestee is permitted to move. Such accompanying of the arrestee about the premises is always reasonable, without regard to the degree of risk in the particular case, even if the arrest took place off the premises. *Wash. v. Chrisman* (1982). Subsequent to an in-premises arrest, police may conduct a protective sweep of the area for their own protection, extending (i) to "closets and other spaces immediately adjoining the place of arrest from which an attack could be immediately launched,'' even without reasonable suspicion such a risk is present; and (ii) to other parts of the premises, on a reasonable belief "that the area to be swept harbors an individual posing a danger to those on the arrest scene." *Md. v. Buie* (1990). If a "potential accomplice" is found, he may be frisked for weapons, and the area within his immediate control may also be searched for weapons and evidence.

### (d) Plain view

As noted in *Coolidge v. N.H.* (1971), "an object which comes into view during a search incident to arrest that is appropriately limited in scope under existing law may be seized without a warrant." Thus, if an object is discovered by the officer from a place where he is lawfully present, that discovery is not illegal, and this is so even if an arrest has been made but the object itself is not within the control of the arrestee under *Chimel*. While in *Coolidge* it was indicated that the item may be seized only if its discovery was "inadvertent," that limitation was later abandoned as unnecessary in *Horton v. Cal.* (1990) (see § 2.5(d)).

Assuming no problems in the manner in which the plain view was acquired, it does not necessarily follow that the observed object may be seized. As stated in *Coolidge,* it must be "an incriminating object," meaning that there must be probable cause that the object is the fruit, instrumentality, or evidence of crime. That determination must be made by the police without exceeding their authority, and even the lesser intrusion of picking up an object and looking at it is impermissible on reasonable suspicion short of probable cause. *Ariz. v. Hicks* (1987).

## (e) Search to prevent loss of evidence

In *Agnello v. U.S.* (1925), the Court held that "belief, however well founded, that an article sought is concealed in a dwelling house furnishes no justification for a search of that place without a warrant." But in *Johnson v. U.S.* (1948), and *Chapman v. U.S.* (1961), reference was made to the possibility of a warrantless dwelling search being upheld upon a showing of a need for immediate action. This issue also took on increased importance because of the *Chimel* decision, and was not directly confronted in *Chimel* because no emergency was present there; the police had sufficient opportunity to obtain a search warrant before they tipped their hand by making an arrest.

But in *Vale v. La.* (1970), the circumstances were different; the police had come to arrest the defendant on another matter, observed what reasonably appeared to be a sale of narcotics by the defendant to a person who drove up to his house, arrested the defendant in front of his house, made a cursory inspection of the house to determine if any one else was there, and then (after the defendant's mother and brother entered the house during the inspection) made a warrantless search of the house for the additional narcotics they believed were hidden there. Yet the Court concluded that the state had not met its burden "to show the existence of such an exceptional situation" as to justify a warrantless search, as the goods seized were not actually in the process of destruction or removal from the jurisdiction. The Court also asserted that because the officers had arrest warrants for Vale, "there is thus no reason * * * to suppose that it was impracticable for them to obtain a search warrant as well," but this is a questionable conclusion in view of the fact that here (unlike *Chimel*) the probable cause for search did not exist until the officers on the scene observed the illegal transaction. *Vale,* therefore, cannot easily be squared with the search-of-vehicles cases (see § 2.8(b)), but does show that the Court is much more protective of dwellings then vehicles. Although some courts have resisted a broader formulation on the ground that the police can too easily conjure up reasons why evidence within premises might be subject to future destruction or disposal, the lower courts have generally not accepted the *Vale* formulation as controlling. They have been inclined to state the exception in broader terms, covering instances in which the police reasonably conclude that the evidence would be destroyed or removed if they delayed the search while a warrant was obtained. But the mere fact that a homicide has occurred in certain premises does not of itself establish exigent circumstances justifying a warrantless search. *Mincey v. Ariz.* (1978).

Some lower courts have held that the police may respond to the risk of evidence destruction by impounding the premises and keeping the occupants thereof under surveillance while a search warrant is being obtained. In *Segura v. U.S.* (1984), dealing with a somewhat easier case in which the 19–hour impoundment was of unoccupied premises belonging to persons then under lawful arrest, the Court held "that where officers, having probable cause, enter premises, and with probable cause, arrest the occupants who have legitimate possessory interests in its contents and take them into custody and, for no more than the period here involved, secure the premises from within to preserve the status quo while others, in good faith, are in the process of obtaining a warrant, they do not violate the Fourth Amendment's proscription against unreasonable seizures." The Court went on to hold that in any event any illegality in the initial entry would not require suppression of the evidence first discovered in the later execution of the search warrant.

Also relatively easy was the situation involved in *Ill. v. McArthur* (2001), where the defendant (who exited the premises voluntarily after his estranged wife told police standing by that he had marijuana hidden within) was told by police that while a search warrant was sought he would not be allowed to reenter unless accompanied by an officer. In finding that restriction reasonable, the Court stressed four circumstances: (i) the police had probable cause to get the warrant; (ii) the police had good reason to fear that unless restrained McArthur would have destroyed the drugs, as he probably had perceived his wife had informed police about the drugs; (iii) the police tried to reconcile their law enforcement needs with defendant's privacy by imposing a restraint less restrictive than a warrantless search of the premises; and (iv) the restraint was imposed for a limited period of time, two hours.

Entry of premises to search for evidence must be distinguished from those instances in which an immediate search of premises is necessary because of a risk of bodily harm or even death, as in *Brigham City v. Stuart* (2006). The Court there upheld officers' entry upon seeing through a screen door and window that a juvenile being held back by several adults had broken loose and struck one of them sufficiently hard that the victim was spitting blood, for they "had an objectively reasonable basis for believing both that the injured adult might need help and that the violence in the kitchen was just beginning." This objective standard, the Court added, means that if the circumstances viewed objectively justify the action, it is irrelevant whether the subjective motive of the police was to gather evidence or render assistance. Many of the lower court cases upholding entry on an emergency aid theory are based upon facts much more ambiguous than in *Stuart*; they stress the need for prompt assessment of often ambiguous information concerning potentially serious consequences.

## § 2.8    WARRANTLESS SEARCHES AND SEIZURES OF AUTOMOBILES

### (a) Search incident to arrest

Although *Chimel* involved search of premises, the more limited rule of that case was also applied for a time to a search of an automobile incident to arrest. But the need for such case-by-case assessment was largely obviated by *N.Y. v. Belton* (1981), where the

Court reasoned: (1) Fourth Amendment protections "can only be realized if the police are acting under a set of rules which, in most instances, make it possible to reach a correct determination beforehand as to whether an invasion of privacy is justified in the interest of law enforcement"; (2) "no straightforward rule has emerged from the litigated cases respecting the question involved here"; (3) this has caused the courts "difficulty" and has put the appellate cases into "disarray"; (4) the cases suggest "the generalization that articles inside the relatively narrow compass of the passenger compartment of an automobile are in fact generally, even if not inevitably, within 'the area into which an arrestee might reach in order to grab a weapon or evidentiary item' "; and thus (5) "the workable rule this category of cases requires" is best achieved by holding "that when a policeman has made a lawful custodial arrest of the occupant of an automobile, he may, as a contemporaneous incident of that arrest, search the passenger compartment of that automobile," inclusive of "the contents of any containers found within the passenger compartment."

*Belton* applies only when there has been a "custodial arrest," and thus is inapplicable when the driver has instead been given a citation; see the *Knowles* case, § 2.6(b). To maintain *Belton*'s bright-line character, *Thornton v. U.S.* (2004) held it applicable as well to the arrest of "recent occupants," those who exited the vehicle shortly before being accosted by police. Because *Belton* requires that the arrest and search be "contemporaneous," it appears that the search of the vehicle must occur at the place of arrest and not later at the station. There is disagreement as to whether *Belton* also means the search must be made before the arrestee is taken from the scene, but clearly it is unnecessary that he have continuing access to the car. The term "passenger compartment" in *Belton* has been construed to mean all areas reachable without existing the vehicle, without regard to the likelihood that such reaching actually occurred in the particular case. But *Belton* does not permit the dismantling of the vehicle to get inside door panels, the opening of sealed containers, or other searches into particular places to which the arrest unquestionably had no chance of accessing immediately preceding his apprehension or exit from the vehicle.

Some have questioned *Belton* on the ground it encourages pretext arrests to facilitate desired vehicle searches for which grounds are otherwise lacking, a contention that took on greater force when the Court later held in *Whren v. U.S.* (1996) that neither the officer's subjective motivations nor his departure from usual practice could ordinarily put in doubt an arrest made on probable cause.

### (b) Search on probable cause

In *Carroll v. U.S.* (1925), the Court upheld a warrantless search of a vehicle being operated on the highway upon probable cause that it contained contraband, because the driver was not subject to lawful arrest and thus the car could be quickly moved out of the locality. Some courts concluded

*Carroll* could not be relied upon to justify a warrantless search of the car after arrest of the driver because "exigencies do not exist when the vehicle and the suspect are both in police custody." But in *Chambers v. Maroney* (1970), the Supreme Court reached a contrary conclusion. In response to the contention that *Carroll* was not applicable on these facts because the car in which the defendant was arrested could simply be held until a search warrant was obtained, the Court in *Chambers* responded: "For constitutional purposes, we see no difference between on the one hand seizing and holding a car before presenting the probable cause issue to a magistrate and on the other hand carrying out an immediate search without a warrant." Neither *Chambers* nor later decisions of the Court (e.g., *Cardwell v. Lewis* (1974), allowing warrantless seizure and search of a car parked in a public parking lot after arrest of the driver elsewhere; *Tex. v. White* (1975), allowing search of the vehicle at the station after the driver's arrest though, unlike *Chambers,* there was no indication an immediate at-the-scene search would have been impractical) could be explained in terms of the oft-stated principle that a search warrant is required except in exigent circumstances. Finally, the Court acknowledged in *U.S. v. Chadwick* (1977) that warrantless vehicle searches are being permitted "in cases in which the possibilities of the vehicle's being removed or evidence in it destroyed were remote, if not non-existent." Why? Because, the Court explained: "One has a lower expectation of privacy in a motor vehicle because its function is transportation and it seldom serves as one's residence or as the repository of personal effects. * * *. It travels public thoroughfares where both its occupants and its contents are in plain view."

In *Cal. v. Carney* (1985), this reformulated vehicle exception was even applied to a motor home which "is being used on the highways, or if it is readily capable of such use and is found stationary in a place not regularly used for residential purposes." The majority emphasized both justifications for the vehicle exception, noting that a motor home in such circumstances is "readily mobile" and has "a reduced expectation of privacy stemming from its use as a licensed motor vehicle subject to a range of police regulation inapplicable to a fixed dwelling." One consequence of the Court's alternative reliance upon the "reduced expectation" theory, as the Court continues to emphasize, *Md. v. Dyson* (1999), *Pa. v. Labron* (1996), is that the so-called automobile exception to the Fourth Amendment's warrant requirement has *no* separate exigency requirement. This means, for one thing, that warrantless car searches are not likely to be jeopardized by more substantial delay between seizure of the vehicle and search of it than existed in *Chambers*. Cf. *U.S. v. Johns* (1985).

### (c) Search of containers and persons therein

Despite the "lesser expectation of privacy in a motor vehicle" of which the Court spoke in *Chadwick,* there is no comparable lesser expectation as to containers such as luggage, and thus they can be searched without a warrant only upon a genuine showing of exigent circumstances, *U.S. v. Chadwick* (1977). (This is so even if the police have lawful possession of the object, as "an officer's authority to possess a package is distinct from his authority to examine it." *Walter v. U.S.* (1980).) But what if the container is in an automobile? In an effort to reconcile the *Chadwick* and *Chambers-Carney* lines of authority, the Court has held that if there exists probable cause to search the entire car, then the authority to make a warrantless search of the vehicle (as with the authority to execute a search warrant for a vehicle) extends to containers within the vehicle in which the objects sought might be concealed, *U.S. v. Ross* (1982), even if the police earlier removed the container from the vehicle but still had lawful possession of it, *U.S. v. Johns* (1985). By contrast, it was once the rule that absent true exigent circumstances a search warrant was required to search a container within a car if there was probable cause only as to the container (e.g., a suitcase placed in a taxi by a passenger), *Ark. v. Sanders* (1979), but *Sanders* was later overruled because of a perceived need for "one clear-cut rule to govern automobile searches": that containers in cars may be searched without a warrant whether the probable cause is specific or general. *Cal. v. Acevedo* (1991).

Assuming a lawful warrantless search of a vehicle, may it automatically extend to the person of an occupant? No, the Supreme Court held in *U.S. v. Di Re* (1948), for the need to do so is no greater than the necessity "for searching guests of a house for which a search warrant had issued," which the government conceded would not be lawful. Some argue the *Di Re* analogy is unsound because it is too easy, while police are trying to stop a moving vehicle, for incriminating evidence to be transferred to an occupant. But *Di Re* was not overturned but merely distinguished in *Wyo. v. Houghton* (1999), where the Court held that "when there is probable cause to search for contraband in a car, it is reasonable for police officers * * * to examine packages and containers without a showing of individualized probable cause for each one," meaning that such a search may extend to a passenger's personal belongings (at least those not attached to the person) even absent information suggesting either the passenger's involvement in the criminality or the driver's placement of contraband into the passenger's effects. That conclusion, the Court explained, was justified by the reduced expectation passengers have as to their effects within vehicles, considered with the "practical realities," i.e., that it would be very difficult to sort out on a case-by-case basis whether there was a likelihood the sought contraband might be in the passenger's effects.

**(d)  Inventory**

If the police have lawfully impounded a vehicle (e.g., because it was found illegally parked in such a way as to constitute a traffic hazard), they may, pursuant to an established standard procedure, secure and inventory the vehicle's contents in order to (i) protect the owner's property while it remains in police custody, (ii) protect the police from claims or disputes over lost or stolen property, and (iii) protect the police from potential danger. *So. Dak. v. Opperman* (1976). If the driver was stopped on the street while operating the vehicle and then arrested, some lower courts have held that the police must honor the driver's request that the car instead be lawfully parked there or turned over to a friend; some cases indicate the police must even take the initiative and inquire of the driver what disposition he prefers; and some others declare that if the car is impounded, the driver must be allowed to decide between inventory and waiver of any claims against the police. But in *Colo. v. Bertine* (1987) the Court held vehicle inventory procedures are reasonable under the Fourth Amendment without regard to the existence of such "alternative 'less intrusive' means."

An inventory is unlawful if it was not undertaken pursuant to standard policy or practice in the department, but *Bertine* holds that it is not objectionable that "departmental regulations gave the police officers discretion to choose between impounding * * * and parking, * * * so long as that discretion is exercised according to standard criteria." An inventory is illegal if it appears to have been undertaken solely for some other motive (as shown, for example, by the failure to use inventory forms or to complete the inventory once contraband was discovered). In terms of scope, the inventory must be limited to areas of the car in which valuables might be found, and may not extend to examination of "materials such as letters or checkbooks, that 'touch upon intimate areas of an individual's personal affairs,' " *So. Dak. v. Opperman,* supra (Powell, J., conc.). The inventory may extend to containers (such as suitcases) found in the car. *Colo. v. Bertine,* supra. Though that case declared it "permissible for police officers to open closed containers in an inventory search only if they are following standard police procedures that mandate the opening of such containers in every impounded vehicle," more recent and seemingly conflicting dictum says police "may be allowed sufficient latitude to determine whether a particular container should or should not be opened in light of the nature of the search and characteristics of the container itself." *Fla. v. Wells* (1990).

### (e) Other seizure of vehicles

If a vehicle is itself evidence of crime, may it be seized without a warrant as evidence in plain view? Not necessarily, at least four Justices concluded in *Coolidge v. N.H.* (1971), for a warrantless seizure on a plain view theory is permissible only upon "inadvertent discovery" of the item seized. In *Horton v. Cal.* (1990), the Court abandoned the "inadvertent discovery" limitation, but then seemed to endorse the result in *Coolidge* on two other grounds: (1) the seized object's incriminating character must also be "immediately apparent," not the case in *Coolidge* because the probative value of the cars seized "remained uncertain until after the interiors were swept and examined microscopically"; and (2) the officer must also have lawful access to the vehicle, not the case in *Coolidge* because the seizure there "was accomplished by means of a warrantless trespass on the defendant's property."

It is common at both the federal and state level to find statutes authorizing the seizure and subsequent forfeiture of a vehicle because it was used in certain criminal activity. The question of whether such a seizure could be made without a warrant was settled in *Fla. v. White* (1999), upholding the warrantless seizure of a vehicle from a public place on probable cause that it constituted forfeitable contraband under a state forfeiture statute. Noting the "special considerations" recognized in the previously discussed search-of-vehicle-on-probable-cause cases, the Court concluded the need to permit warrantless action was "equally weighty when the *automobile*, as opposed to its contents, is the contraband that the police seek to secure." *White*, the Court added, was "nearly indistinguishable" from *G.M. Leasing Corp. v. U.S.* (1977), upholding warrantless seizure of vehicles from public streets and lots as part of a levy on a corporation's assets for tax deficiencies.

## § 2.9  STOP–AND–FRISK AND OTHER BRIEF DETENTION

### (a) Background

Police have long followed the practice of stopping suspicious persons on the street or other public places for purposes of questioning them or conducting some other form of investigation, and, incident to many stoppings, of searching the person for dangerous weapons. Because this investigative technique, commonly referred to as stop-and-frisk, is ordinarily employed when there are not grounds to arrest the suspect and to search him incident to arrest, it was often questioned whether the practice could be squared with the Fourth Amendment. The Supreme Court provided some answers in *Terry v. Ohio* (1968).

In *Terry,* where an officer observed three men who appeared to be "casing" a store for a robbery and then approached them for questioning and frisked them, finding weapons on two of them, the Court held "that where a police officer observes unusual conduct which leads him reasonably to conclude in light of his experience that criminal activity may be afoot and that the persons with whom he is dealing may be armed and presently dangerous; where in the course of investigating this behavior he identifies himself as a policeman and makes reasonable inquiries; and where nothing in the initial stages of the encounter serves to dispel his reasonable fear for his own or others' safety, he is entitled for the protection of himself and others in the area to conduct a carefully limited search of the outer clothing of such persons in an attempt to discover weapons which might be used to assault him."

The result in *Terry* rests upon three fundamental conclusions the Court reached concerning Fourth Amendment theory. First of all, the Court concluded that restraining a person on the street is a "seizure" and that exploring the outer surfaces of his clothing is a "search," and thus rejected "the notions that the Fourth Amendment does not come into play at all as a limitation upon police conduct if the officers stop short of something called a 'technical arrest' or a 'fullblown search.' " Secondly, after noting that the police conduct here was without a warrant and thus subject to the reasonableness rather than the probable cause part of the Fourth Amendment, the Court utilized the balancing test of the *Camara* case (see § 2.11(a)) to conclude that a frisk could be undertaken upon facts which would not support an arrest and full search. (Justice Douglas objected in dissent that the Court had in effect said that the police have more power without a warrant than with a warrant, which could have been answered—but was not—by observing that the balancing test applies in determining both the reasonableness of warrantless searches and seizures and, as in *Camara,* the probable cause for those with warrant.) Finally, in response to the defendant's observation that some stops and frisks are employed for harassment and other improper purposes, the Court noted that the exclusionary rule is ineffective when the police have no interest in prosecution and that consequently a flat prohibition of all stops and frisks would not deter those undertaken for improper objectives.

## (b) Temporary seizure for investigation

As for what Fourth Amendment evidentiary test is to be applied to temporary seizures, in *U.S. v. Cortez* (1981), the Court stated that the essence of the standard is that "the detaining officers must have a particularized and objective basis for suspecting the particular person stopped of criminal activity." The Court's emphasis in *Terry* was upon the situation "where a police officer observes unusual conduct which leads him reasonably to conclude in light of his experience that criminal activity may be afoot." If this language is compared with that usually employed to describe the evidentiary test for arrest, it appears that some difference exists in the degree of probability required. As to the probability required for arrest, it may generally be stated that it must be more probable than not that the person has committed an offense; that is, there must be a more than 50% probability that a crime has been committed, and at least sometimes a more than 50% probability that the person arrested committed it, *Wong Sun v. U.S.* (1963) (see § 2.3(b)). But for a *Terry* stop on reasonable suspicion, significantly less than a preponderance of the evidence that a crime has been or is about to be committed and that the suspect is the person who committed or is planning the offense will suffice. *U.S. v. Soko-*

*low* (1989). Thus, the stopping of a suspect near the scene of a recent robbery because he fitted the general description given by the victim is proper even if arrest would not be proper because the description would also fit several others in the area. (This is so without regard to whether a less intrusive investigative technique is available. *Sokolow*, supra.) The reasonable suspicion for a stop may differ from probable cause to arrest in a quite different way, namely, in the extent to which the information must be shown to be reliable. *Ala. v. White* (1990).

Although some lower courts have held that if the means of avoidance are sufficiently extreme they alone may justify a *Terry* stop, that conclusion is in doubt after *Ill. v. Wardlow* (2000). The majority held there were grounds for a stop where the defendant engaged in "headlong" and "unprovoked flight upon noticing the police," given the additional factor of defendant's presence in an area of heavy narcotics trafficking. Four Justices, dissenting in part, while emphasizing the majority's failure to endorse a proposed per se rule allowing a stop in all cases of unprovoked flight upon seeing an identifiable policeman, appeared to admit that flight under *some* circumstances could justify a stop, but then found the majority's conclusion unsound "because many factors providing innocent motivations for unprovoked flight are concentrated in high crime areas."

In *Adams v. Williams* (1972), the Court, 6–3, upheld a stop based upon information the suspect possessed a gun and narcotics, given by a known informant who had provided information in the past. Because the informer could have been prosecuted for making a false complaint if his tip proved false, the tip (though insufficient for arrest) was deemed to have sufficient "indicia of reliability" to justify a stop. As for an anonymous tip from an informant regarding criminal activity, such a tip (i) is insufficient standing alone when the tip gives no indication of the informant's reliability or basis of knowledge; and (ii) is also insufficient despite corroboration of part of the informant's story re innocent existing circumstances (e.g., that a certain car is presently parked at a certain location), as virtually anyone could predict such a continuing circumstance; but (iii) is sufficient when corroboration of the informant's prediction of future events (e.g., that a certain person will travel to a certain place) demonstrates "a special familiarity with" the suspect's affairs. *Ala. v. White* (1990). Many lower courts adopted a "firearms exception" to the *White* rule, so that an anonymous tip a person was illegally armed sufficed even without confirmation of predicted future events, but in *Fla. v. J. L.* (2000) the Court rejected that position because it would allow anyone wishing to harass another to set in motion a police search simply by making an anonymous phone call.

In *U.S. v. Hensley* (1985), the Court applied the *Whiteley* approach (see § 2.3(e)) in this context, and thus held that a stopping on the basis of a conclusory police bulletin was lawful provided the bulletin had been "issued on the basis of articulable facts supporting a reasonable suspicion." But in *Brown v. Tex.* (1979), where in the afternoon officers saw defendant and another man walk away from each other in an alley in an area with a high incidence of drug traffic, but there was no indication it was unusual for people to be in the alley and the police did not point to any facts supporting their conclusion the situation "looked suspicious," the Court held there were not grounds for a stop. Similarly, merely consorting with narcotic addicts does not constitute grounds for a stop. *Sibron v. N.Y.* (1968).

Although the results in *Brown* and *Sibron* may have been influenced to some degree by doubts about whether *Terry* should apply to suspicion of minor possessory offenses, the Court has recognized an offense category limitation only in the somewhat different situation presented by *U.S. v. Hensley* (1985). The Court there held a *Terry* stop was also permissible to investigate *past* criminal activity, but only as to "felonies or crimes involving a threat to public safety," where "it is in the public interest that the crime be solved and the suspect detained as promptly as possible."

A detention for investigation of a somewhat different kind was involved in *U.S. v. Van Leeuwen* (1970), where the Court, citing *Terry,* upheld the holding of mailed packages for approximately one day while the police promptly investigated the suspicious circumstances of the mailing and obtained a search warrant for the packages. Similarly, in *U.S.*

*v. Place* (1983), the Court held a traveler's luggage could be seized on reasonable suspicion for purposes of investigation, but wisely added that because such a seizure affects the suspect's travel plans the luggage may be held no longer than if the traveler himself were detained.

### (c) No seizure and arrest distinguished

If it turns out that grounds for a *Terry* stop were lacking, the police-citizen encounter is still lawful if no seizure occurred. While stopping a vehicle is a seizure, *U.S. v. Hensley* (1985), many police contacts with pedestrians are not. A person "has been 'seized' within the meaning of the Fourth Amendment only if, in view of all the circumstances surrounding the incident, a reasonable person would have believed that he was not free to leave," which means that the "subjective intention" of the police officer "is irrelevant except insofar as that may have been conveyed to the" suspect. *U.S. v. Mendenhall* (1980), followed in *Fla. v. Royer* (1983), and elaborated in *Fla. v. Bostick* (1991) as presupposing "an *innocent* person." Lower court decisions reflect the view that there is no Fourth Amendment seizure when the policeman, although perhaps making inquiries which a private citizen would not be expected to make, has otherwise conducted himself in a manner consistent with what would be viewed as a nonoffensive contact if it occurred between two ordinary citizens.

*I.N.S. v. Delgado* (1984) held a "factory survey" involved no seizure where it was apparent INS agents were only questioning workers and those questioned were obligated to remain on the premises anyway by virtue of their obligation to their employer. Similarly, in *Fla. v. Bostick,* supra, followed in *U.S. v. Drayton* (2002), the Court recognized that literal application of the "free to leave" test is inappropriate in some circumstances (e.g., where defendant was questioned on a bus he did not want to leave), and concluded that in such cases the proper question "is whether a reasonable person would feel free to decline the officers' requests or otherwise terminate the encounter."

In *Cal. v. Hodari D.* (1991), the word "seizure" in the Fourth Amendment was construed to cover "application of physical force to restrain movement, even when it is ultimately unsuccessful," as well as "*submission* to the assertion of authority," but not a "show of authority" to which "the subject does not yield." This means a suspect's act of discarding contraband is not the fruit of an illegal seizure when, at the time of that act, an officer lacking reasonable suspicion was vigorously chasing but had not yet caught the suspect.

If the dimensions of a permissible stop are exceeded when only a reasonable suspicion exists, the result is an illegal arrest. This can occur because of excessive force or threats of force, but it is not excessive for the police to draw weapons when they have reason to suspect the person is armed and dangerous. *U.S. v. Hensley* (1985). There is no per se rule that the passage of a certain time, such as

20 minutes, escalates the stop into an arrest. In determining whether the time was excessive, it is useful to ask whether the police were diligently pursuing a means of investigation likely to resolve the matter one way or another very soon. *U.S. v. Sharpe* (1985). Movement of the suspect to a nearby location to facilitate the investigation does not inevitably escalate the detention into an arrest. But, as *Fla. v. Royer* (1983) illustrates, such escalation can occur from a wrong choice of investigative techniques by the police. There, the Court held taking the suspected drug courier a mere 40 feet to an airport police office for questioning was an arrest, as resort to "the least intrusive means reasonably available" would have resulted in the summoning of a drug detection dog to the corridor. More recently, however, the Court has cautioned against "unrealistic second-guessing," and has declared that the "question is not simply whether some other alternative was available, but whether the police acted unreasonably in failing to recognize or to pursue it." *U.S. v. Sharpe* (1985).

*Terry*'s statement that a stop is reasonable only if "the officer's action * * * was reasonably related in scope to the circumstances which justified the interference in the first place," suggests a limitation on investigative techniques during a stop, as was seemingly confirmed in *Hiibel v. Sixth Judicial Dist. Ct.* (2004), holding that refusal to state one's name during a *Terry* stop could be criminalized only if "the request for identification was 'reasonably related in scope to the circumstances which justified' the stop." But in *Illinois v. Caballes* (2005), where after defendant was stopped for a minor traffic violation a drug dog was used to detect drugs within the car even absent reasonable suspicion drugs were there, the Court held an investigative technique violates *Terry*'s limits only if it (1) extends the period of custody or (2) itself constitutes a search (which use of the dog was not; see § 2.2(b)).

## (d) Protective search

*Terry* makes it clear that whether it is proper to make a protective search incident to a stopping for investigation is a question separate from the issue of whether it is permissible to stop the suspect. For a protective search, it must reasonably appear that the suspect "may be armed and presently danger-ous," which would again appear to require only a significant possibility, rather than the more than 50% probability which would surely justify an arrest and full search for carrying a concealed weapon. Although *Terry* also emphasizes that the officer frisked only after he had made some initial inqui-ries and the responses did not "dispel his reason-able fear," the frisk upheld in *Adams* was not preceded by inquiries.

*Terry* indicates that a two-step process must ordi-narily be followed: the officer must pat down first and then intrude beneath the surface of the sus-pect's clothing only if he comes upon something which feels like a weapon. In *Adams,* the Court approved the officer's conduct in reaching directly into the suspect's pocket, apparently because the informant had indicated the precise location of the weapon. But in any event, the search is limited by its recognized purpose, that is, "to an intrusion reasonably designed to discover guns, knives, clubs, or other hidden instruments for the assault of the police officer." This means that the search must be limited to those places to which the suspect has immediate access, and may not otherwise go beyond what is necessary to determine if the suspect is armed. *Minn. v. Dickerson* (1993) (prohibiting further squeezing of suspect's pocket to determine if lump was cocaine).

As for a protective search beyond the person, the Court in *Mich. v. Long* (1983) held "that the search of the passenger compartment of an automobile, limited to those areas in which a weapon may be placed or hidden, is permissible if the police officer possesses a reasonable belief based on 'specific and articulable facts which, taken together with the rational inferences from those facts, reasonably warrant' the officers in believing that the suspect is dangerous and the suspect may gain immediate control of weapons." But the Court then reached the questionable conclusion that such a risk can be present, even as to a suspect outside the car, because of the possibility he would "break away" from the police during the investigation or merely would reenter the car at its conclusion.

Absent grounds for a *Terry* frisk, an officer may still take minimally intrusive action for his own protection without *any* showing of justification based upon the facts of the individual case. The Court has thus held that where a vehicle has been lawfully stopped, the driver, *Pa. v. Mimms* (1977), or even a passenger, *Md. v. Wilson* (1997), may be required to alight from the vehicle.

### (e) Brief detention at the station

It remains unclear whether the *Terry* balancing test may be utilized to support a brief detention for investigation at the station on grounds slightly short of that required for arrest. In *Davis v. Miss.* (1969), holding fingerprints inadmissible because obtained after an illegal arrest, the Court noted it was arguable "that because of the unique nature of the fingerprinting process, such detention might, under narrowly defined circumstances, be found to comply with the Fourth Amendment even though there is no probable cause in the traditional sense," in that it "may constitute a much less serious intrusion upon personal security than other types of police searches and detentions." The Court added that a warrant would be required for such a detention, a matter which concurring Justice Harlan preferred to leave open.

*Davis* suggests that the intended investigative technique is a relevant consideration; the Court emphasized that detention for fingerprinting "involves none of the probing into an individual's private life and thoughts which marks an interrogation or search," cannot "be employed repeatedly to harass any individual," and "is an inherently more reliable and effective crime-solving tool than eyewit-

ness identifications or confessions and is not subject
to such abuses as the improper line-up and the
'third degree.' " Consistent with this, it was held in
*Dunaway v. N.Y.* (1979) that custodial questioning
at the station on less than probable cause for a full-
fledged arrest was unlawful. But there is case authority that a properly conducted lineup would be
reliable and that therefore detention to facilitate it
would be permissible on less than the grounds needed for arrest.

Statutes authorizing stationhouse detention for
other investigative purposes, such as fingerprinting
or taking voice or handwriting exemplars, have
been upheld. The status of these provisions is not
entirely clear, as *Dunaway* can be read broadly as
barring all at-the-station detention on less than full
probable cause, or narrowly as dealing only with
interrogation and allowing detention for other types
of investigation, at least if there is judicial authorization and the suspect is ordinarily given a chance
to respond to a summons. But it is noteworthy that
in more recently reasserting the *Davis* dictum, the
Court made seemingly favorable reference to those
statutes. *Hayes v. Fla.* (1985).

## § 2.10   GRAND JURY SUBPOENAS

Unlike the detentions for the purpose of collect-
ing evidence considered in *Davis* and *Dunaway,*
supra, the grand jury subpoena operates largely free
of Fourth Amendment restrictions. Insofar as the
Constitution is concerned, a subpoena directing a

person to testify or produce specific physical evidence before a grand jury need not be supported by a showing of probable cause, reasonable suspicion, or any other factual foundation. *U.S. v. Dionisio* (1973) (subpoena requiring production of voice exemplars); *U.S. v. Mara* (1973) (subpoena requiring handwriting exemplars). As the Court noted in *Dionisio,* "a subpoena to appear before the grand jury is not a 'seizure' in the Fourth Amendment sense." Unlike an arrest or an "investigative stop," it does not produce an "abrupt" detention, "effected with force or the threat of it," or result "in a record [like an arrest record] involving social stigma." A subpoena, the Court has noted "is served in the same manner as other legal process [and] involves no stigma whatever." *U.S. v. Dionisio,* supra. The Court has acknowledged that the compulsion to appear or produce evidence does require some "personal sacrifice," but that obligation is characterized as simply a "part of the necessary contribution of the individual to the welfare of the public." *Blair v. U.S.* (1919). The Court also has stressed in this connection that a person subpoenaed retains his privilege against self-incrimination (see § 8.2) and, where applicable, judicial protection against abuse of the grand jury process. A subpoena issued on the basis of "tips [or] rumors" is not abusive, however, since a grand jury has an obligation to "run down" every "available clue" in conducting its investigation. *U.S. v. Dionisio,* supra.

While the Fourth Amendment does not require a showing of some factual foundation for a subpoena, it does prohibit a subpoena duces tecum too sweeping in its terms "to be regarded as reasonable." *Hale v. Henkel* (1906). This prohibition, arguably resting more appropriately on the due process clause, has application primarily to subpoenas requesting production of numerous documents. In barring overly broad subpoenas duces tecum, courts have sought to ensure that a subpoena (1) commands production only of documents relevant to the investigation being pursued, (2) specifies the documents to be produced with reasonable particularity, and (3) includes records covering only a reasonable period of time.

## § 2.11    INSPECTIONS; REGULATORY SEARCHES

The Fourth Amendment has been held to apply to a variety of searches and inspections conducted as part of regulatory schemes. In each case, however, the standards applied have been somewhat different than those applied to searches conducted in the course of criminal investigations.

### (a) Inspection of premises

Administrative inspections of residential and commercial premises for fire, health and safety violations may not be undertaken without a search warrant unless the occupant consents to the inspection or the inspection is made in an emergency. The occupant is thus usually free to challenge the inspector's decision to search without the risk of suffering criminal penalties for his refusal. However, a search warrant for such an inspection does not require a showing of probable cause that a particular dwelling contains violations of the code being enforced, but only that reasonable legislative or administrative standards for conducting an area inspection are satisfied with respect to a particular building. This special probable cause test was arrived at "by balancing the need to search against the invasion which the search entails," considering (1) the long history of acceptance of such inspection programs; (2) the public interest in abating all dangerous conditions, even those which are not observable from outside the building; and (3) the fact that the inspections are neither personal in nature nor aimed at discovery of evidence of crime, and thus involve a relatively limited invasion of privacy. *Camara v. Mun. Ct.* (1967); *See v. City of Seattle* (1967).

The *Camara-See* warrant requirement has been held inapplicable to certain business inspection schemes. The latest case of that genre, *N.Y. v. Burger* (1987), involving warrantless inspection of an auto junkyard, stressed these factors: (1) the business was "closely regulated," considering the long tradition of regulation and its extensive nature; (2) "a 'substantial' government interest," combatting auto theft, supports the regulatory scheme; (3) warrantless inspections are "necessary to further [the] regulatory scheme," as frequent and unannounced inspections are necessary to detect stolen cars and parts; (4) the statutory scheme "provides a 'constitutionally adequate substitute for a warrant'" by informing the businessman inspections will occur regularly, of their permissible scope, and who may conduct them; and (5) the permitted inspection is "carefully limited in time, place, and scope" (business hours only, auto dismantling businesses only, of records, cars and parts only).

Entry of premises to fight a fire and thereafter find the cause may be made without a warrant, but subsequent entries on probable cause of arson require a regular criminal warrant on full probable cause. *Mich. v. Tyler* (1978). A post-fire entry merely to ascertain the cause of the fire may be made without even an administrative warrant if notice is given. *Mich. v. Clifford* (1984).

### (b) Border searches

As noted in *Carroll v. U.S.* (1925), quoted with approval in *Almeida-Sanchez v. U.S.* (1973): "Travellers may be stopped in crossing an international boundary because of national self protection reasonably requiring one entering the country to identify himself as entitled to come in, and his belongings as effects which may be lawfully brought in." Border searches are considered unique, and a person crossing the border may be required to submit to a warrantless search of his person, baggage, and vehicle without the slightest suspicion, just as is true of incoming international mail (at least if correspondence is not read). *U.S. v. Ramsey* (1977). However, some evidence short of probable cause must exist to justify more intrusive and embarrassing searches;

"a real suspicion" is said to be required for a strip search, and a "clear indication" for examination of body cavities. But vehicle searches at the border, because they do not likewise intrude upon "dignity and privacy interests of the person," may be made absent reasonable suspicion, at least if made without significant damage to the property. *U.S. v. Flores–Montano* (2004). On a reasonable suspicion of alimentary canal drug smuggling, a person may be detained at the border until the suspicion is verified or dispelled (by submission to x-ray or a bowel movement). *U.S. v. Montoya de Hernandez* (1985).

The special rules on border searches also apply to persons who have already travelled some distance into the country, if the circumstances indicate that any contraband which might be found was in the place searched at the time of entry. But, a border search must occur at the border or "its functional equivalent," and thus a car found near the border but not known to have crossed the border may not be subjected to a warrantless search for illegal aliens, either by a roving patrol or at a fixed checkpoint, in the absence of consent or probable cause. *Almeida-Sanchez v. U.S.* (1973); *U.S. v. Ortiz* (1975). Such a vehicle may be stopped briefly to enable questioning of the occupants about their citizenship and immigration status if (a) the stopping occurs at a reasonably located fixed checkpoint, *U.S. v. Martinez–Fuerte* (1976), or (b) the officer is aware of specific articulable facts which, together with rational inferences from those facts, reasonably warrant suspicion that the car contains aliens who may be illegally in the country. *U.S. v. Brignoni–Ponce* (1975).

### (c) Driver's license, vehicle registration and DWI checks

When the police observe a traffic violation, they may stop the vehicle and demand to see the driver's license and the vehicle's registration and vehicle identification number. *N.Y. v. Class* (1986). A stopping for a license-registration check is also permissible when there is articulable and reasonable suspicion that a motorist is unlicensed or that a vehicle is not registered, or that either the vehicle or occupant is otherwise subject to seizure for violation of law, but the random stopping of an auto and detaining the driver in order to check the license and registration is unreasonable. This does not preclude use of methods for spot checks that involve less intrusion or less discretion, such as stopping all traffic at a roadblock. *Del. v. Prouse* (1979). Checkpoints may also be utilized to seek out intoxicated drivers, *Mich. Dep't of State Police v. Sitz* (1990), and many lower courts have upheld such checkpoints which were carefully planned by police supervisory personnel, were operated with a minimum of discretion by on-the-scene officers, and resulted in only very brief detentions.

In *City of Indianapolis v. Edmond* (2000), holding that city-operated vehicle checkpoints, complete with drug dogs, undertaken to interdict unlawful drugs, contravened the Fourth Amendment, the

Court distinguished *Prouse* and *Sitz* because in neither of these "special need" cases "did we indicate approval of a checkpoint program whose primary purpose was to detect evidence of ordinary criminal wrongdoing." *Edmond* is not a bar to an information roadblock seeking witnesses to a recent homicide at that location, as the "stop's primary law enforcement purpose was *not* to determine whether a vehicle's occupants were committing a crime." *Ill. v. Lidster* (2004).

### (d) Airport inspections

When airport hijacker detection searches were conducted selectively by use of the government's hijacker "profile," they were upheld by reliance on *Terry v. Ohio,* § 2.9(a). Now that all passengers and carry-on luggage are checked, the program can be upheld as a form of administrative search under *Camara,* at least so long as prospective passengers retain the right to leave prior to submitting to inspection. Presumably this is also the case as to the post–9/11 screening conducted by the Transportation Security Administration, which is generally more intensive and includes random selection of some travelers for even closer scrutiny.

### (e) Supervision of prisoners, probationers and parolees

A prisoner's cell and effects are not protected by the Fourth Amendment; "the prisoner's expectation of privacy [must] always yield to what must be considered the paramount interest in institutional security." *Hudson v. Palmer* (1984). If *Hudson* does not apply to searches of a prisoner's person or to searches in pretrial detention facilities, then such searches must be undertaken on reasonable suspicion or pursuant to an established routine or plan.

Probationers and parolees may be subjected to searches without arrest or a search warrant and upon evidence which falls short of the usual probable cause requirement. In *Griffin v. Wis.* (1987), involving a warrantless search of a probationer's home, the Court explained this was because of the "special needs" of the probation system, where restrictions on freedom and privacy are necessary "to assure that the probation serves as a period of genuine rehabilitation and that the community is not harmed by the probationer's being at large." The warrant requirement was deemed inappropriate for probation officers, who "have in mind the welfare of the probationer" and must "respond quickly to evidence of misconduct." The usual probable cause standard was deemed inapplicable because it "would reduce the deterrent effect of the supervisory arrangement" and because "the probation agency must be able to act based upon a lesser degree of certainty * * * in order to intervene before a probationer does damage to himself or society." The *Griffin* standard ordinarily comes into play only if the probationer or parolee is charged with a new crime. Most lower courts have for years declined to apply the exclusionary rule at probation or parole revocation proceedings, and in *Pa. Bd. of Probation & Parole v. Scott* (1998) the Court so held as to the latter, reasoning that altering the "flexible, administrative nature" of such proceedings was not worth the "minimal" deterrence that would result, even in the case of a search by an official aware of the parolee's status.

Though "special needs" analysis (as in *Griffin*) may only be used when the interest served is other than ordinary law enforcement, *City of Indianapolis v. Edmond* (2000), that limitation can be avoided as to probation/parole searches by notifying the probationer or parolee of the search conditions of his release, which sufficiently reduces his expectation of privacy that the premises may be searched on reasonable suspicion—even if the search is by a police officer seeking evidence of a new crime. *U.S. v. Knights* (2001).

Using the *Knights* balancing approach rather than the *Griffin* "special needs" approach, the Court in *Samson v. Cal.* (2006) upheld a police search of a known parolee even absent reasonable suspicion. In support, it was asserted (i) that parolees have fewer expectations of privacy than probationers because parole is more akin to imprisonment, where the *Hudson* rule applies; (ii) that parolee Samson had signed an order submitting to the clearly-stated parole condition that he would be subject to search by any parole or police officer with or without warrant or cause; (iii) that the state has an "overwhelming interest" in supervising parolees because they "are more likely to commit future criminal offenses," as manifested by California's 60–70% recidivism rate; and (iv) the system did not give officers unbridled discretion to conduct searches, as state law prohibits "arbitrary, capricious or harassing" searches.

### (f)  Supervision of students

In *N.J. v. T.L.O.* (1985), the Court held that "the Fourth Amendment applies to searches conducted by school authorities," but that under the *Camara* balancing test neither a warrant nor full probable cause is needed. Rather, the search is reasonable if limited in scope, taking into account the age and sex of the student and the nature of the infraction, and if there are "reasonable grounds for suspecting" the search will uncover evidence of a violation of law or school regulation. *T.L.O.* left unanswered whether individualized suspicion is always necessary, whether students have an expectation of privacy in school desks and lockers, and whether a higher standard applies if there is some police involvement.

But in *Vernonia School District 47J v. Acton* (1995), the Court held on the facts presented that drug testing could be required of student athletes even absent individualized suspicion. The Court emphasized that the privacy expectations intruded upon were limited (because all school children are subject to considerable supervision and control, student athletes' expectations are "even less" because they voluntarily chose a privacy-reducing activity, the testing was under conditions like those encountered in public rest rooms, and test results were disclosed to a limited number of school officials with a need to know), and were outweighed by the legitimate government interests advanced: deterring drug use by students, and preventing harm to drug users and others involved in athletic competition. *Acton* was applied to uphold testing in much less compelling circumstances in *Bd. of Educ. v. Earls* (2002), where the random testing policy covered middle and high school students participating in *any* extracurricular activity.

## (g) Supervision of employees

Government employees have a justified expectation of privacy in certain work areas, such as individual offices and the desk and filing cabinets therein. If a search of such an area is conducted by a public employer, no warrant is needed for intrusions "for legitimate work-related reasons wholly unrelated to illegal conduct," and intrusions "for noninvestigatory, work-related purposes, as well as for investigation of work-related misconduct, should be judged by the standard of reasonableness under all the circumstances" rather than the traditional quantum of probable cause. *O'Connor v. Ortega* (1987). Public employees may be required to submit to drug testing upon individualized reasonable suspicion or, absent such suspicion, where testing is triggered by a specific event and in additional a special need for testing exists. *Skinner v. Railway Labor Executives' Ass'n* (1989) (testing of crew after train accident or violation of safety rules); *National Treasury Employees Union v. Von Raab* (1989) (testing of customs agents upon transfer or promotion to position involving drug interdiction or carrying firearms).

Compare *Chandler v. Miller* (1997), invalidating a statute requiring drug testing of candidates for public office and distinguishing *Von Raab* because there the persons tested and their work were not amenable to "day-to-day scrutiny." Compare also *Ferguson v. City of Charleston* (2001), invalidating a program for identifying and testing pregnant patients suspected of drug use and then turning the results over to law enforcement agents without the knowledge or consent of the patients, where *Skinner* and *Von Raab* were distinguished on two grounds: (i) because in those cases "there was no misunderstanding about the purpose of the test or the potential use of the test results, and there were protections against the dissemination of the results to third parties"; and (ii) because in those cases the "special need" advanced was "one divorced from the State's general interest in law enforcement," while here "the central and indispensable feature of the policy from its inception was the use of law enforcement to coerce the patients into substance abuse treatment."

## § 2.12  CONSENT SEARCHES

### (a) Background

Where effective consent is given, a search may be conducted without a warrant and without probable cause. At one time, the consent doctrine was assumed to be grounded on the concept of waiver,

*Stoner v. Cal.* (1964). But in *Schneckloth v. Busta-monte* (1973), the Court concluded that "a [tradi-tional] 'waiver' approach to consent searches would be thoroughly inconsistent with our decisions," and thus held that the issue is whether the person's consent was "voluntary." Although this voluntari-ness test would appear to focus primarily upon the state of mind of the person allegedly consenting, the Court in *Schneckloth* did not have occasion to con-sider the validity of the position taken by some courts: that because it is the Fourth Amendment prohibition against unreasonable searches which is at issue, the question is whether the officers could reasonably conclude that defendant's consent was given, in much the same way that scope-of-consent issues are to be resolved (see § 2.12(e)).

## (b) Warning of rights

*Schneckloth v. Bustamonte* (1973) holds that, while a person's knowledge of his right to refuse is a factor to be taken into account in determining (based on the totality of the circumstances) whether his consent was voluntary, the prosecution is not required to prove that he was so warned or other-wise had such knowledge where the consent was obtained while the person was not in custody. (It follows from this, the Court later held in *Ohio v. Robinette* (1996), that consent by a person who could no longer be lawfully detained is not made involuntary because of a police failure to specifically advise the person he was free to leave.) The *John-son v. Zerbst* (see § 7.4(a)) test of waiver, "an intentional relinquishment or abandonment of a known right or privilege," was distinguished as applicable only to those constitutional rights which, unlike the Fourth Amendment, are intended to protect a fair trial and the reliability of the truth-determining process; the *Miranda* requirement of Fifth Amendment warnings (see § 4.4(b)) was distinguished because it only governs interrogation of those in custody. While this latter distinction suggests that the *Miranda* analogy might be persuasive as to a consent to search given by one in custody, it was held in *U.S. v. Watson* (1976), that failure to give Fourth Amendment warnings is not controlling where, as there, the defendant "had been arrested and was in custody, but his consent was given while on a public street, not in the confines of the police station." Most courts view the *Schneckloth* totality of circumstances test as equally applicable to consent obtained from one in custody at the station.

Some courts have taken the position that a consent to search given during custodial interrogation must be preceded by *Miranda* warnings because the request to search is a request that the defendant be a witness against himself which he is privileged to refuse under the Fifth Amendment. The prevailing view, however, is to the contrary, on the ground that a consent to search is neither testimonial nor communicative in the Fifth Amendment sense. If the police first obtain statements in violation of *Miranda,* the subsequently obtained consent might be claimed to be a suppressible fruit of the earlier *Miranda* violation, but the Supreme Court's refusal to apply the fruits doctrine to certain other consequences of a *Miranda* violation (see § 6.6(g)) suggests this contention would not prevail.

### (c) Consent subsequent to a claim of authority

A search may not be justified on the basis of consent when that "consent" was given only after the official conducting the search asserted that he possessed a search warrant, but in fact there was no warrant or an invalid warrant. Such a claim of authority is, in effect, an announcement that the occupant has no right to resist the search, and thus acquiescence under these circumstances cannot be construed as consent. *Bumper v. N.C.* (1968). By comparison, the consent is valid if given in response to an officer's declaration that he will *seek* a warrant, as no false or overstated claim of authority has occurred. But if the officer said he would *obtain* a warrant, this invalidates the consent if there were not grounds on which such a warrant could issue. Even when there is no assertion of a warrant or threat to obtain one, submission to such declarations as "I am here to search your house" or "I have come to search your house" are almost certain to be viewed as coercive. *Amos v. U.S.* (1921).

### (d) Other relevant factors

The voluntariness of a consent to search is "to be determined from the totality of all the circumstances," *Schneckloth v. Bustamonte* (1973). Among the other factors to be considered in determining the effectiveness of an alleged consent to search are whether the defendant (1) had minimal schooling or was of low intelligence; (2) was mentally ill or intoxicated; (3) was under arrest at the time the consent was given; (4) was overpowered by arresting officers, handcuffed, or similarly subject to physical restrictions; (5) had seized from him by police the keys to the premises thereafter searched; (6) employed evasive conduct or attempted to mislead the police; (7) denied guilt or the presence of any incriminatory objects in his premises; (8) earlier gave a valid confession or otherwise cooperated, as by initiating the search, or at least the investigation leading to the search; (9) was hesitant in agreeing to the search; or (10) was refused his request to consult with counsel. The presence of some of these factors is not controlling, however, as each case must stand or fall on its own special facts.

### (e) Scope of consent

Assuming a valid consent, the police may not exceed the physical bounds of the area as to which consent was granted, such as by looking through private papers after a consent to allow search for narcotics. The standard for determining the scope of the consent "is that of 'objective' reasonableness—what would the typical reasonable person have understood by the exchange between the officer and the suspect." *Fla. v. Jimeno* (1991). Assuming consent to search a certain place, the police may look inside unlocked (but not locked) containers large enough to contain the object the police stated they were looking for. *Jimeno,* supra. There is disagreement as to whether a voluntary consent may be used to justify a second search of the same place after a fruitless first search; at least where there has been a significant passage of time, the second search involves re-entry of defendant's home, and defendant's status has changed from suspect to accused, the second search cannot be justified on the assumption that defendant's consent is continuing. In any event, a consent may be withdrawn or limited at any time prior to the completion of the search, though such a revocation does not operate retroactively so as to make invalid a search conducted prior to revocation.

### (f) Consent by deception

A somewhat related problem concerning the scope of the consent arises when the consent was obtained by deception, as where the suspect gives the policeman a gun on the representation that the officer will aid him in selling it, but the officer then has a ballistics test run on the weapon, or where the suspect gives a blood sample to the police on the representation that it will be tested for alcohol content but it is in fact matched with blood found at the scene of a rape. The "misplaced trust" cases, upholding the admissibility of voluntary disclosures of criminal conduct to an undercover officer or police agent, *Lewis v. U.S.* (1966), *Hoffa v. U.S.* (1966), are probably distinguishable. The above situations are more like *Gouled v. U.S.* (1921) (where an old acquaintance acting for the police obtained defendant's consent to enter his office, but then conducted an extensive search when defendant left the room), in that the officer exceeded the reasonably anticipated scope of the consensual intrusion. That is, in *Lewis* and *Hoffa* the defendant voluntarily revealed his criminal activity to another, but this was not so in *Gouled* or the above illustrations.

## § 2.13  THIRD PARTY CONSENT

### (a) Background

In the area of consent searches, courts have long recognized that certain third parties may give consent which will permit use of the seized evidence against the defendant. Various theories have been utilized to explain this result. An agency theory was relied upon in *Stoner v. Cal.* (1964), where the Court held that Fourth Amendment rights can only be waived by the defendant "either directly or through an agent." But in *Bumper v. N.C.* (1968), the Court seemed to rely upon a property theory in intimating that the grandmother's consent to search of her house for a rifle, had it been voluntary, would have been effective against the grandson who lived there because she "owned both the house and the rifle." In *Frazier v. Cupp* (1969), consent by defendant's cousin Rawls to search of a duffel bag jointly used by them was held to be effective against the defendant because he "must be taken to have assumed the risk that Rawls would allow someone else to look inside." Similarly, in *U.S. v. Matlock* (1974), the Court indicated that where two or more persons have joint access to or control of premises "it is reasonable to recognize that any of the coinhabitants has the right to permit the inspection in his own right and that the others have assumed the risk that one of their number might permit the common area to be searched." This assumption-of-risk theory is consistent with the justified-expectation-of-privacy approach to the Fourth Amendment in *Katz v. U.S.* (1967) (see § 2.2(a)).

This shift in theoretical basis may affect the result. Under the agency theory it has been held that a wife's consent is ineffective against her husband if she called the police because she was angry at him, but the contrary result is correct under the assumption-of-risk theory. By like reasoning, under the latter theory A's consent may be upheld as against B even though B instructed A not to consent, even though the police passed up the opportunity to seek B's consent, *U.S. v. Matlock* (1974) or even though B's consent was earlier sought and refused. The most difficult issue is whether A's consent is effective against co-occupant B who is then present and objecting. The majority in *Ga. v. Randolph* (2006), taking into account the "widely shared social expectations" of co-inhabitants, namely, "that a caller standing at the door of shared premises would have no confidence that one occupant's invitation was a sufficiently good reason to enter when a fellow tenant stood there saying,

'stay out,' " answered in the negative (though acknowledged that if the rights of the two occupants
were not equal, then perhaps the person with the
superior interest would prevail). The Court admitted it was "drawing a fine line," so that, in a case
like *Matlock* where the defendant "was in a squad
car not far away," the outcome would be different:
"So long as there is no evidence that the police have
removed the potentially objecting tenant from the
entrance for the sake of avoiding a possible objection, there is practical value in the simple clarity of
complementary rules, one recognizing the co-ten-
ant's permission when there is no fellow occupant
on hand, the other according dispositive weight to
the fellow occupant's contrary indication when he
expresses it." The principal dissent objected to
"such random and happenstance lines" and said a
"more reasonable approach is to adopt a rule acknowledging that shared living space entails a limited yielding of privacy to others."

## (b) Relationship of third party to defendant and place searched

Most of the third party consent cases have involved the husband-wife relationship, and the prevailing view is that when a husband and wife jointly
own or occupy the premises in question, either may
consent to a search of those premises for items
which may incriminate the other. *Coolidge v. N.H.*
(1971). Recent decisions have also upheld consents
given by paramours who actually shared the premises on a continuing basis. *U.S. v. Matlock* (1974).

If a child is living at the home of his parents, a parent may consent to a search of the child's living quarters. On the other hand, a child may not give effective consent to a full search of the parents' home, although where it is not unusual or unauthorized for the child to admit visitors into the home, the mere entry of police on the premises with the consent of the child is not improper.

A landlord may not consent to the search of rented premises occupied by a tenant, and this is so even though the landlord may have some limited right of entry for purposes of inspecting or cleaning the premises. *Chapman v. U.S.* (1961). A person who rents a hotel room is treated as any other tenant, *Stoner v. Cal.,* supra, although once the time of occupancy has expired and the guest has checked out, a hotel representative may then consent to a search for anything the guest has left behind. *Abel v. U.S.* (1960). However, the landlord or his agents (such as a building custodian or superintendent) may consent to a search of hallways, basements, and other area to which all tenants have common access. A tenant may not consent to search of the part of the premises retained by the landlord, *Weeks v. U.S.* (1914), but may consent to search of the premises rented to him for items the landlord may have hidden there. A person sharing a house or apartment with another may consent to a search of areas of common usage, and a person in lawful possession of premises may give consent to search of the premises which will be effective against a nonpaying guest or casual visitor.

An employer may consent to a search of an employee's work and storage areas on the employer's premises, but he may not consent to a search of areas in which the employee is permitted to keep personal items not connected with the employment. Whether an employee can give a valid consent to a search of his employer's premises depends upon the scope of his authority. Generally, the courts have been of the view that a lesser employee, such as a secretary, may not give consent. However, if the employee is a manager or other person of considerable authority who is left in complete charge for a substantial period of time, then the prevailing view is that such a person can waive his employer's rights.

Whether a bailee, who does not own the property but has lawful possession of it, can consent to a police search of the property which will be effective against the bailor depends upon whether the nature of the bailment is such that the bailor has assumed the risk. *Frazier v. Cupp* (1969). The risk is assumed when, as in that case, a duffel bag is turned over on the understanding that the bailee may use part of it to store his effects, but not when a locked container is involved and the bailee has no key. The extent to which the bailor has surrendered control and the length of the bailment are important; perhaps an attendant in a public garage may consent to the opening of the car door to see items on the floor of the car, but for the bailee to consent to search of the trunk it must appear that the bailee was authorized to open the trunk.

## (c) Apparent authority

In *Stoner v. Cal.* (1964), in response to the state's contention that a police search of defendant's hotel room was proper because they reasonably believed that the clerk had authority to consent, the Court emphasized "that the rights protected by the Fourth Amendment are not to be eroded by strained applications of the law of agency or by unrealistic doctrines of 'apparent authority.'" This means only that an officer's mistake as to someone's *legal* authority cannot, in effect, expand the limits of third party consent. But, because the Fourth Amendment only proscribes "unreasonable" searches, a consent search is lawful despite an officer's reasonable mistake of *fact* (e.g., that the person giving consent actually has the property interest in the premises searched which he claims to have or otherwise appears to have but in fact does not have). *Ill. v. Rodriguez* (1990). In ambiguous circumstances the police may not accept even an explicit claim of authority without further inquiry. *Rodriguez,* supra.

## (d) Exclusive control

In third party consent situations, it is necessary to consider the various relationships discussed above as they relate to the particular area or object searched. In *U.S. v. Matlock* (1974), the Court said the effectiveness of the consent depended upon whether there was "common authority" over the premises, which was said to rest on "mutual use of the property" by one "having joint access or control for most purposes." Consistent with this language is the notion that even if *A* and *B* generally share premises together, they each may still have areas therein of mutually exclusive use. Such is least likely to be true in husband-wife situations, where ordinarily the personal effects of each spouse are not thought to be "off limits" to the other, but the result may well be different in the case of friends sharing an apartment.

# CHAPTER 3

# WIRETAPPING, ELECTRONIC EAVESDROPPING, AND THE USE OF SECRET AGENTS

## § 3.1 HISTORICAL BACKGROUND; APPLICATION OF FOURTH AMENDMENT

### (a) The *Olmstead* case

In *Olmstead v. U.S.* (1928), the first wiretap case to reach the Supreme Court, the police intercepted communications by placing a tap on defendant's telephone line. In a 5–4 decision, the majority read the Fourth Amendment literally in concluding that the police conduct did not constitute a search and seizure. Two reasons were given: (1) at no time did the police trespass upon defendant's premises, so that no "place" was searched; and (2) only conversations were obtained, so that no "things" were seized.

As indicated herein, both of these grounds have since been rejected, and thus it is not surprising that in recent times the forceful dissents in *Olmstead* have more often been quoted. Justice Brandeis argued that the Amendment did cover wiretapping, and also that the government, as "the omnipresent teacher," should not be upheld in its

160

admitted violation of a state wiretapping law. Justice Holmes, dissenting on the latter ground only, characterized wiretapping in violation of state law as "dirty business" and contended that "it is a less evil that some criminals should escape than that the government should play an ignoble part."

### (b) Section 605

Congress later enacted the Federal Communications Act of 1934, which provided in § 605: "[N]o person not being authorized by the sender shall intercept any communication and divulge or publish the existence, contents, substance, purport, effect, or meaning of such intercepted communication to any person." On the basis of this language, it was held that a person with standing, i.e., a party to the conversation, *Goldstein v. U.S.* (1942), could suppress in a federal prosecution evidence obtained by state or federal officers, *Nardone v. U.S.* (1937); *Benanti v. U.S.* (1957), by wiretapping interstate or intrastate communications, *Weiss v. U.S.* (1939), unless done with the consent of one of the parties to the conversation. *Rathbun v. U.S.* (1957). The ruling that wiretap evidence gathered by state officials was admissible in state prosecutions, *Schwartz v. Tex.* (1952), was finally overruled in *Lee v. Fla.* (1968), where the Court emphasized the constitutional extension of the exclusionary rule in *Mapp v. Ohio* (1961) and the lack of other effective sanctions for violation of § 605. *Lee* was decided just two days before the Crime Control Act (see § 3.2) superceded the wiretapping prohibition of § 605.

### (c) Non-telephonic electronic eavesdropping

*Goldman v. U.S.* (1942), was the "bugging" counterpart of *Olmstead:* because federal officers had merely placed a detectaphone against the outer wall of a private office, the Court held there had been no trespass and thus no Fourth Amendment violation. Similarly, in *On Lee v. U.S.* (1952), where incriminating statements were picked up via a "wired for sound" acquaintance of defendant, a 5–4 majority rejected the contention that a trespass by fraud had occurred and thus found no constitutional violation.

In *Silverman v. U.S.* (1961), a unanimous Court held that listening to incriminating conversations within a house by inserting a "spike mike" into a party wall and making contact with a heating duct serving that house amounted to an illegal search and seizure. The opinion did not clearly indicate whether the "intrusion" by the spike into defendants' premises was a critical fact, but any remaining doubts were dispelled by *Katz v. U.S.* (1967). The issue in *Katz* was whether recordings of defendant's end of telephone conversations, obtained by attaching an electronic listening and recording device to the outside of a public telephone booth, had been obtained in violation of the Fourth Amendment. In a 7–1 decision, the Court expressly rejected the "trespass" doctrine of *Olmstead* and *Goldman,* and held that the government action constituted a search and seizure within the meaning of the Fourth Amendment because it "violated the privacy upon which [the defendant] justifiably relied while using the telephone booth."

*Katz* thus made it clear that, with the possible exception of the case in which a conversation is overheard or recorded with the consent of a party to the conversation (see § 3.3), wiretapping and electronic eavesdropping are subject to the limitations of the Fourth Amendment.

## § 3.2   CONSTITUTIONALITY OF TITLE III OF THE CRIME CONTROL ACT

### (a) Background

Under what circumstances, then, may wiretapping and electronic eavesdropping without the prior consent of a party to the conversations be conducted consistent with the Fourth Amendment? Because such surveillance is authorized in limited circumstances by Title III of the Omnibus Crime Control and Safe Streets Act of 1968, 18 U.S.C.A. §§ 2510–2520, the appropriate inquiry is into the constitutionality of that legislation. Though the Supreme Court has never passed upon the Act, guidance on the issues involved may be found in certain decisions of the Court: *Osborn v. U.S.* (1966), upholding a judicially authorized use of an undercover agent with a concealed tape recorder; *Berger v. N.Y.* (1967), holding the New York eavesdropping law unconstitutional; and *Katz v. U.S.* (1967), indicating that the limited eavesdropping undertaken there would have been constitutional if a warrant had first been obtained.

## (b) Summary of Title III

Under the Act, the Attorney General or various other officials down to a specially designated Deputy Assistant Attorney General in the Criminal Division may authorize application to a federal judge for an order permitting interception of wire or oral communications (i.e., wiretapping or electronic eavesdropping) by a federal agency having responsibility for investigation of the offense as to which application is made, when such interception may provide evidence of certain enumerated federal crimes. (Use of a "pen register" to keep a record of telephone numbers dialed is not an interception under the Act, *U.S. v. N.Y. Telephone Co.* (1977), and is not a search, *Smith v. Md.* (1979).) A comparable provision permits, when authorized by state law, application by a state or county prosecutor to a state judge when the interception may provide evidence of "murder, kidnapping, gambling, robbery, bribery, extortion, or dealing in narcotic drugs, marijuana or other dangerous drugs, or other crime dangerous to life, limb, or property, and punishable by imprisonment for more than one year."

The judge may only grant an interception order as provided in § 2518 of the Act, and evidence obtained in the lawful execution of such order is admissible in court. Other willful interception or disclosure of any wire or oral communication without the prior consent of a party thereto is made criminal, and evidence so obtained is inadmissible in any state or federal proceedings, but suppression is not required merely because of noncompliance with those requirements in the Act which do not play a "substantive role" in the regulatory system. *U.S. v. Donovan* (1977). (The Act was amended in 1986 to include electronic communications—generally, communications not constituting either a wire or an oral communication that involve transfer of information in whole or in part by a wire, radio, electromagnetic, photoelectronic or photooptical system—but the authorization required for interception of such communications is not as stringent, and violation of the statute re such communications is not grounds for suppression of the evidence obtained.)

The Act originally provided that it did not limit the constitutional power of the President to take such measures as he deems necessary to, inter alia, "obtain foreign intelligence information deemed essential to the security of the United States." Those powers do not extend to warrantless tapping in *domestic* security cases, as Fourth Amendment protections are "the more necessary" for "those suspected of unorthodoxy in their political beliefs." *U.S. v. U.S. District Court* (1972). (The matter is now dealt with in the Foreign Intelligence Surveillance Act of 1978, 50 U.S.C.A. §§ 1801–1811, which establishes a warrant procedure and also provides that the President "may authorize electronic surveillance without a court order under this subchapter to acquire foreign intelligence information for periods of up to one year" if, inter alia, the Attorney General certifies in writing under oath that the surveillance is "solely directed at" the acquisition of the contents of communications "transmitted by means of communications used exclusively between or among foreign powers" and that "there is no substantial likelihood that the surveillance will acquire the contents of any communication to which a United States person is a party.")

Under § 2518, an interception order may be issued only if the judge determines on the basis of facts submitted that there is probable cause for belief that an individual is committing, has committed, or is about to commit one of the enumerated offenses; probable cause for belief that particular communications concerning that offense will be obtained through such interception; that normal investigative procedures have been tried and have failed to reasonably appear to be unlikely to succeed if tried or to be too dangerous; and probable cause for belief that the facilities from which, or the place where, the communications are to be intercepted are being used, or are about to be used, in connection with the commission of such offense, or are leased to, listed in the name of, or commonly used by such person. Each interception order must specify the identity of the person, if known, whose communications are to be intercepted; the nature and location of the communications facilities as to which, or the place where, authority to intercept is granted (except that a so-called "roving tap" may be authorized upon a particularized showing of need); a particular description of the type of communication sought to be intercepted, and a statement of the particular offense to which it relates;

the identity of the agency authorized to intercept the communications and of the person authorizing the application; and the period of time during which such interception is authorized, including a statement as to whether or not the interception shall automatically terminate when the described communication has been first obtained. No order may permit interception "for any period longer than is necessary to achieve the objective of the authorization, nor in any event longer than thirty days." Extensions of an order may be granted for like periods, but only by resort to the procedures required in obtaining the initial order.

Interception without prior judicial authorization is permitted upon a specifically designated enforcement officer's reasonable determination that "(a) an emergency situation exists that involves (i) immediate danger of death or serious physical injury to any person, (ii) conspiratorial activities threatening the national security interest, or (iii) conspiratorial activities characteristic of organized crime, that requires a wire or oral communication to be intercepted before an order authorizing such interception can with due diligence be obtained, and (b) there are grounds upon which an order could be entered." In such a case, application for an order must be made within 48 hours after the interception commences, and, in the absence of an order, the interception must terminate when the communication sought is obtained or when the application for the order is denied, whichever is earlier.

Within a reasonable time but not later than 90 days after the filing of an application which is denied or the termination of an authorized period of interception, the judge must cause to be served on the persons named in the order or application and other parties to the intercepted communications, an inventory which shall include notice of (1) the fact of the entry of the order or application; (2) the date of the entry and the period of authorized interception, or the denial of the application; and (3) the fact that during the period communications were or were not intercepted. A similar inventory is required as to interceptions terminated without an order having been issued.

### (c) Continued surveillance

The most obvious difference between a search for tangible items and the search for wire or oral communications allowed under Title III is the time dimension of the latter kind of search. A search warrant for some physical object permits a single entry and prompt search of the described premises, while Title III permits continuing surveillance up to 30 days, with extensions possible. During the authorized time, all conversations over the tapped line or within the bugged room may be overheard and recorded without regard to their relevance.

As reflected in *Berger,* this striking difference accounts for the major constitutional obstacle to legalized electronic surveillance. In holding a New York law unconstitutional, the Court emphasized that it (1) permitted installation and operation of surveillance equipment for 60 days, "the equivalent of a series of intrusions, searches, and seizures pursuant to a single showing of probable cause"; (2) permitted renewal of the order "without a showing of present probable cause for the continuance of the eavesdrop"; and (3) placed "no termination date on the eavesdrop once the conversation sought is seized." While Title III permits extensions only upon a new showing of probable cause and requires that interception cease once "the objective of the authorization" is achieved, it does permit continued surveillance for up to 30 days upon a single showing of probable cause, and thus goes well beyond the kind of with-warrant electronic surveillance the Supreme Court has approved or indicated would be permitted.

As emphasized in *Berger,* the bugging of a secret agent upheld in *Osborn* was pursuant to an order which "authorized one limited intrusion rather than a series or a continuous surveillance. And, we note that a new order was issued when the officer sought to resume the search and probable cause was shown for the succeeding one. Moreover, the order was executed by the officer with dispatch, not over a prolonged and extended period." And in *Katz* the Court noted that the "surveillance was so narrowly circumscribed that a duly authorized magistrate * * * clearly apprised of the precise intrusion * * * could constitutionally have authorized * * * the very limited search and seizure that the Government asserts in fact took place." The surveillance was limited in that the agents had probable cause to believe defendant was using certain public telephones for gambling purposes about the same time almost every day and thus activated the surveillance equipment attached to the outside of the phone booth only when defendant entered the booth.

Decisions holding that continued surveillance may also be squared with the Fourth Amendment rely upon the analysis of Justices Harlan and White, dissenting in *Berger.* First, they contend that an electronic surveillance which is continued over a span of time is no more a general search than the typical execution of a search warrant over a described area. As Justice White argued: "Petitioner suggests that the search is inherently overbroad because the eavesdropper will overhear conversations which do not relate to criminal activity. But the same is true of almost all searches of private property which the Fourth Amendment permits. In searching for seizable matters, the police must necessarily see or hear, and comprehend, items which do not relate to the purpose of the search. That this occurs, however, does not render the search invalid, so long as it is authorized by a suitable search warrant and so long as the police, in executing that warrant, limit themselves to searching for items which may constitutionally be seized."

This analogy holds only if it may be concluded that the overhearing or recording of a series of conversations is merely a search, from which certain particularly described conversations will thereafter be seized, as Justice Harlan contended: "Just as some exercise of dominion, beyond mere perception, is necessary for the seizure of tangibles, so some use of the conversation beyond the initial listening process is required for the seizures of the spoken word." A majority of the Court has yet to speak clearly on this point, although in *Katz* there is language characterizing the "electronically listening to and recording" of defendant's words as a "search and seizure." This has not deterred lower courts from consistently holding Title III is not unconstitutional merely because it authorizes wiretaps which may last several days and encompass multiple conversations.

### (d) Lack of notice

The Court in *Berger* also found the New York law "offensive" because it "has no requirement for notice, as do conventional warrants, nor does it overcome this defect by requiring some showing of special facts. On the contrary, it permits uncontested entry without any showing of exigent circumstances. Such a showing of exigency, in order to avoid notice would appear more important in eavesdropping, with its inherent dangers, than that required when conventional procedures of search and seizure are utilized." This criticism goes to the heart of all eavesdropping practices, as the Court noted, in that success depends upon secrecy.

The *Berger* Court did not explore this matter in greater detail, and thus it is not entirely clear whether Title III might be challenged on this basis.

In decisions upholding the statute, the following arguments have been made: (1) One reason for advance notice, as emphasized by four members of the Court in *Ker v. Cal.* (1963), is to guard the entering officer from attack on the mistaken belief he is making a criminal entry, and this danger is not present in most eavesdropping cases—including all which do not require a trespass. (2) Another reason for notice is so that the individual will be aware that a search was conducted, but in the more typical search case this notice may come only after the event by discovery of the warrant and a receipt at the place searched, which is comparable to the Title III requirement of service of an inventory within 90 days. (3) Prior notice is not required when there is reason to believe it would result in destruction of the evidence sought (see § 2.5(b)), and while the Court in *Berger* may have been unwilling to uphold all eavesdropping without notice on this ground, this "exigency" is sufficiently established upon a showing that "normal investigative procedures have been tried and have failed or reasonably appear to be unlikely to succeed if tried or to be too dangerous," as required by Title III. An extensive footnote (n. 16) on the subject in *Katz* suggests that the Court finds these arguments compelling.

### (e) Other considerations

An exhaustive analysis of Title III would reveal a number of other problems, primarily going to how the Act must be construed in light of the Fourth

Amendment. Four of these problems deserve brief mention here. First of all, what meaning is to be given to the "probable cause" requirement in this context? If, as discussed earlier, the Fourth Amendment has some flexibility, so that somewhat less evidence is needed to justify such lesser intrusions as a building inspection, stop-and-frisk, or brief seizure for fingerprinting (see §§ 2.9, 2.11), then it might be equally true that more evidence than usual is required to establish probable cause for the unusual degree of intrusion which results from electronic surveillance. Justice Stewart, concurring in *Berger,* took this approach and thus found the affidavits in that case adequate for a "conventional search or arrest" but insufficient for a 60–day eavesdrop. However, defendants who have made this type of argument in the lower courts have not prevailed.

Title III requires a particular description of the "type of communication sought to be intercepted, and a statement of the particular offense to which it relates," but it is unclear how this language is to be interpreted. The statute in *Berger* merely required the naming of "the person or persons whose communications * * * are to be overheard or recorded"; the Court held this did not meet the Fourth Amendment requirement that the things to be seized be particularly described and declared that the "need for particularity * * * is especially great in the case of eavesdropping [because it] involves an intrusion on privacy that is broad in scope." Yet, as Justice Harlan noted in dissent, the cases on search for tangible items make it clear that the particularity requirement of the Amendment is a flexible one, depending upon the nature of the described things and whether the description readily permits identification by the executing officer (see § 2.4(d)). From this it might be concluded, as the lower courts have rather consistently held, that specification of conversations as relating to a certain kind of criminal activity should suffice.

Next, there is the question whether an interception order may be executed by covert entry in the absence of specific judicial authorization for such execution based upon a showing of necessity therefor. In *Dalia v. U.S.* (1979), the Court held that neither Title III nor the Fourth Amendment required such specific authorization. The latter holding was based upon the conclusion that nothing in the Amendment suggests "search warrants also must include a specification of the precise manner in which they are to be executed."

Finally, there is the provision in Title III which permits interception without prior judicial approval when there are grounds for an interception order but an emergency exists with respect to "(i) immediate danger of death or serious physical injury to any person, (ii) conspiratorial activities threatening the national security interest, or (iii) conspiratorial activities characteristic of organized crime" that require interception before an order could with due diligence be obtained. If strictly construed to ensure that warrantless interceptions are not being upheld after the fact on the basis of what was discovered, this provision is consistent with Fourth Amendment decisions on search for physical evidence without warrant to prevent loss of the evidence (see § 2.7(e)). *Katz* condemned the warrantless eavesdropping challenged in that case, but the facts make it clear that there was ample time to secure a warrant.

## § 3.3  THE USE OF SECRET AGENTS TO OBTAIN INCRIMINATING STATEMENTS

### (a) "Wired" agents: *On Lee* and *Lopez*

In *On Lee v. U.S.* (1952), a wired-for-sound informant entered the laundry of the defendant, an old acquaintance, and engaged him in conversation, resulting in defendant's incriminating statements being transmitted to a narcotics agent outside. At trial, the agent testified as to these statements, but the informer was not called as a witness. A 5–4 majority rejected the claim that the informant committed a trespass by fraud, dismissed as "verging on the frivolous" the contention that the narcotics agent was trespassing by use of the transmitter and receiver, and concluded that in the absence of a trespass there was no Fourth Amendment violation.

*Lopez v. U.S.* (1963) concerned an internal revenue agent who, after receiving a bribe offer from the defendant, engaged defendant in subsequent incriminating conversations in the agent's office while equipped with a pocket recorder. The recordings were admitted at trial in support of the agent's testimony. In a 6–3 decision, the Court held no eavesdropping had occurred, in that there had been no invasion of the defendant's premises and the recording revealed only what the defendant willingly disclosed to the agent and what the agent in turn was entitled to disclose to others. The Chief Justice, concurring specially, asserted that *On Lee* was "wrongly decided" and was distinguishable from *Lopez* because in *On Lee* the eavesdropping deprived the defendant of an opportunity to cross-examine the informer. The three dissenters saw no difference between the two cases, and asserted that the Fourth Amendment should protect a person against the risk that third parties may give independent evidence of conversations engaged in with another.

## (b) Without "bugging": *Lewis* and *Hoffa*

In *Lewis v. U.S.* (1966), a federal narcotics agent misrepresented his identity and expressed a willingness to purchase narcotics, which resulted in his being invited into defendant's home, where an unlawful narcotics sale occurred. Because the agent did not "see, hear, or take anything that was not contemplated and in fact intended by petitioner as a necessary part of his illegal business," but merely entered a home "converted into a commercial center to which outsiders are invited for purposes of transacting unlawful business," the Court found no Fourth Amendment violation. *Gouled v. U.S.* (1921), was distinguished in that there a business acquaintance, acting on police order, gained entry to defendant's office as a social visitor and then searched for and seized papers in the defendant's absence.

In *Hoffa v. U.S.* (1966), the defendant unsuccessfully challenged on Fourth, Fifth, and Sixth Amendment grounds the admission of evidence obtained by a Teamsters official who at government instigation visited Hoffa during the latter's earlier trial and overheard conversations between Hoffa and his associates concerning an attempt to bribe jurors. As to the contention that the failure of the informer to disclose his role vitiated the consent to his entry of a constitutionally protected area, Hoffa's hotel suite, the Court noted that Hoffa "was not relying on the security of the hotel room [but rather] upon his misplaced confidence that [the informer] would not reveal his wrongdoing," which is not protected by the Fourth Amendment. The Fifth Amendment claim was summarily dismissed with the observation that "a necessary element of compulsory self-incrimination is some kind of compulsion," absent here because Hoffa's conversations with and in the presence of the informer were "wholly voluntary." As to the Sixth Amendment claim that the informer had intruded upon the confidential attorney-client relationship, the Court concluded that, at least on these facts, such a violation of Sixth Amendment rights in one trial does not render evidence obtained thereby inadmissible in a different trial on other charges. (It was later held in *Weatherford v. Bursey* (1977), that if an informer was present at pretrial attorney-client meetings, but he never communicated what he learned thereby, no Sixth Amendment violation has occurred.) Another Sixth Amendment argument, that from the time when there was evidence for arrest Hoffa was entitled to the same protection afforded an arrested person under *Massiah* and *Escobedo* (see § 4.3), was quickly disposed of on the ground that "there is no constitutional right to be arrested," for otherwise the police would be in the perilous position of having to guess at the precise moment they had probable cause.

### (c) The impact of *Katz*

The thrust of these four cases is that such uses of secret agents, with or without listening or recording devices, are not covered by the Fourth Amendment. It is apparently on this basis that the electronic eavesdropping provisions of Title III expressly exclude from the warrant requirement the interception of communications with the consent of a party to the conversation. However, doubts about the continued vitality of *On Lee, Lopez, Lewis,* and *Hoffa* emerged when the Court in *Katz v. U.S.* (see § 2.2(a)), rejected the old trespass-into-constitutionally-protected-areas analysis in favor of an expectation-of-privacy approach to Fourth Amendment issues.

The question reached the Court in *U.S. v. White* (1971), where an informer, carrying a concealed transmitter, engaged the defendant in conversations in a restaurant, defendant's home and the informer's car. The informer did not testify at the trial, but the narcotics agents who electronically overheard the conversations did, resulting in defendant's conviction. In a 4–man plurality opinion by White, J., it was concluded (1) that one may not have a "justifiable" expectation that his trusted associates neither are nor will become police agents, and (2) that a different result is not called for when the agent has recorded or transmitted the conversations: "Given the possibility or probability that one of his colleagues is cooperating with the police, it is only speculation to assert that the defendant's utterances would be substantially different or his sense of security any less if he also thought it possible that the suspected colleague is wired for sound." Black, J., concurred on the basis of his *Katz* dissent, which contended the Fourth Amendment did not apply to intangibles.

Brennan, J., concurred in the result in *White* on the ground that *Katz* should not be applied retroactively, but contended that *On Lee* and *Lopez* both should be viewed as overruled by *Katz,* the position apparently taken in each of the three dissenting opinions. None of the dissenters specifically questioned the status of *Lewis* and *Hoffa,* and Harlan, J., in particular, emphasized the difference between the practices involved in those cases and the instant case: "The interest *On Lee* fails to protect is the expectation of the ordinary citizen, who has never engaged in illegal conduct in his life, that he may carry on his private discourse freely, openly, and spontaneously without measuring his every word against the connotations it might carry when instantaneously heard by others unknown to him and unfamiliar with his situation or analyzed in a cold, formal record played days, months, or years after the conversation."

## § 3.4  DISCLOSURE OF ELECTRONIC SURVEILLANCE RECORDS

### (a) The "fruits" of surveillance

If conversations have been overheard or recorded by electronic surveillance in violation of the Fourth Amendment, testimony concerning or recordings of these conversations may be suppressed by a defendant with standing. Under the "fruit of the poisonous tree" doctrine (see § 6.6(a)), other evidence which was the product of illegal surveillance is also subject to suppression. This has given rise to the issue of what procedures are required to facilitate a determination whether other evidence is in fact the fruit of such a surveillance.

### (b) The *Alderman* disclosure requirement

This issue was decided in *Alderman v. U.S.* (1969), involving convictions for conspiring to transmit murderous threats in interstate commerce and two other cases of convictions for transmitting national defense information to the Soviet Union. The defendants sought disclosure of all surveillance records so that they might show that some of the evidence admitted against them grew out of illegally overheard conversations. The government urged that in order to protect innocent third parties participating or referred to in irrelevant conversations overheard by the government, surveillance records should first be subjected to in camera inspection by the trial judge. He would then turn over to defendants and their counsel only those materials "arguably relevant" to defendants' convictions, in the sense that the overheard conversations arguably underlay some item of evidence offered at trial.

The Court, in a 5–3 decision, held that a defendant should receive all surveillance records as to which he has standing. The government's proposal was rejected on the ground that the trial judge often would not be in a position to determine what conversations were relevant: "An apparently innocent phrase, a chance remark, a reference to what appears to be a neutral person or event, the identity of a caller or the individual on the other end of a telephone, or even the manner of speaking or using words may have special significance to one who knows the more intimate facts of an accused's life. And yet that information may be wholly colorless and devoid of meaning to one less well acquainted with all relevant circumstances. Unavoidably, this is a matter of judgment, but in our view the task is too complex, and the margin for error too great, to rely wholly on the in camera judgment of the trial court to identify those records which might have contributed to the Government's case." To protect innocent third parties, the Court added, the trial court could place defendants and counsel under enforceable orders against unwarranted disclosure of the materials they would be entitled to inspect.

In *Giordano v. U.S.* (1969), the Court emphasized that the disclosure required in *Alderman* was expressly limited to situations where the surveillance had been determined to be in violation of the Fourth Amendment. Justice Stewart, concurring, suggested that this preliminary determination might sometimes be made in ex parte, in camera proceedings. And in *Taglianetti v. U.S.* (1969), the Court rejected defendant's contention that he was entitled to examine additional surveillance records to establish that he might be a party to some other conversations. Distinguishing *Alderman,* the Court concluded that the trial judge could be expected to identify defendant's voice without the defendant's assistance.

## (c) The statutory limitation

By Title VII of the Organized Crime Control Act of 1970, 18 U.S.C.A. § 3504, Congress has attempted to limit the impact of *Alderman* in the federal courts. For one thing, records of an unlawful surveillance which occurred prior to June 19, 1968, (the date that the Omnibus Crime Control and Safe Streets Act of 1968 became law) need not be disclosed "unless such information may be relevant to a pending claim of * * * inadmissibility," which presumably is to be determined by the judge in camera. For another, on the legislative finding that "there is virtually no likelihood" that evidence offered to prove an event would have been obtained by exploitation of an unlawful surveillance occurring more than five years prior to that event, no such claim is to be considered. The constitutionality of these provisions is open to some doubt, considering the fact that the *Alderman* decision was cast in terms of "the scrutiny which the Fourth Amendment exclusionary rule demands."

## § 3.5   THE USE OF SECRET AGENTS TO "ENCOURAGE" CRIMINAL CONDUCT

### (a) Entrapment

Secret agents—sometimes undercover police officers but very often private citizens acting as informants—are frequently utilized to "encourage" others to engage in criminal conduct. Such tactics are for the most part confined to the crimes of prostitution, homosexuality, liquor and narcotic sales, and gambling; normal detection methods are virtually impossible as to these offenses, as they are committed privately with a willing victim who will not complain. The encouragement very frequently involves little more than a feigned offer by the agent to purchase criminal services from the suspect, but on occasion the agent may use considerably more pressure to gain the suspect's agreement to commit an offense.

The Supreme Court has held that techniques of encouragement may not reach the point where they constitute "entrapment"; if they do, the presence of entrapment constitutes a defense to the defendant's otherwise criminal act. The exact definition of entrapment is a matter of dispute, but it clearly includes the situation in which "the criminal design originates with the [police agents] and they implant in the mind of an innocent person the disposition to commit the offense and induce its commission in order that they may prosecute." *Sorrells v. U.S.* (1932). The prosecution, which has the burden of proof, can defeat the defense by showing defendant's predisposition to such criminality was independent of any government contacts with him. *Jacobson v. U.S.* (1992). So far, the Court has based the defense upon other than constitutional grounds; some of the Justices have relied upon general principles of substantive criminal law and others upon the supervisory power of the Court over the administration of justice in federal courts. *U.S. v. Russell* (1973); *Sherman v. U.S.* (1958).

### (b) Possible constitutional bases

While the entrapment defense is also recognized in the state courts, which for the most part purport to use the *Sorrells-Sherman* test, state convictions are sometimes affirmed notwithstanding evidence of what would constitute entrapment under those decisions. This has given rise to the question of whether freedom from entrapment is a federal constitutional right for which relief may be granted upon federal habeas corpus, to which the courts have so far responded in the negative.

In support of the contention that freedom from entrapment is a right protected under the due process clause, commentators have suggested that: (1) by analogy to the Fourth Amendment protection against unreasonable searches or by application of the penumbral "right of privacy," *Griswold v. Conn.* (1965), secret agents may encourage only those individuals as to whom there exists "probable cause" (under the balancing approach, see §§ 2.9, 2.11, a lesser quantum of evidence than would be required for arrest); (2) by analogy to the constitutional prohibition on illegally obtained confessions, under which ruses and appeals to sympathy are relevant considerations, *Spano v. N.Y.* (1959), secret agents may not overbear a person's will to get him to perpetrate a crime; (3) by analogy to the doctrine that it is cruel and unusual punishment to convict for mere status and without the proof of any act, *Robinson v. Cal.* (1962), the acts which serve as the basis for conviction must be attributable to the defendant rather than to the police or their agents; (4) by analogy to the constitutional limitation on abolition of *mens rea, Lambert v. Cal.* (1957), the necessary mental element for the crime may not be implanted by entrapment; and (5) by analogy to the constitutional defense of estoppel, which bars conviction for actions undertaken upon official advice that such conduct would not violate the law, *Cox v. La.* (1965), secret agents may not induce actions in which the defendant was not predisposed to engage.

In *U.S. v. Russell* (1973), the Supreme Court, while noting that the entrapment defense "is not of a constitutional dimension," acknowledged that there might be "a situation in which the conduct of law enforcement agents is so outrageous that due process principles would absolutely bar the government from invoking judicial processes to obtain a conviction." Due process does not bar conviction of a defendant for sale of narcotics supplied to him by a government agent. *Hampton v. U.S.* (1976). Lower courts have but seldom found government "over-involvement" to violate due process, and have indicated that for such a violation it must appear that (a) the plan did not originate with the defendant, (b) the defendant was not reasonably suspected of criminal conduct or design, and (c) a government agent supplied indispensible and not otherwise readily available goods or services to the illegal enterprise.

# CHAPTER 4

# POLICE INTERROGATION AND CONFESSIONS

## § 4.1 INTRODUCTION

### (a) The confession dilemma

No area of constitutional criminal procedure has provoked more debate over the years than that dealing with police interrogation. In large measure, the debate has centered upon the extent of police abuse in seeking confessions and the importance of confessions in obtaining convictions—two matters on which conclusive evidence is lacking.

Because the questioning of suspects has traditionally been undertaken behind station-house doors (for some, a sufficient indication in itself of abuse), there is not sufficient empirical evidence to assert with confidence what always, usually, or often occurs in the course of police interrogation. Attention thus has often turned to celebrated cases of confessions later proved false or to judicial opinions (including many Supreme Court cases, see § 4.2) revealing outrageous police tactics. Those who assert that police abuses have been widespread contend that these cases are fairly representative, while those of a contrary persuasion claim that these are unusual cases having no relation to day-to-day police work. There is similar disagreement as to what may be logically presumed from the nature of the police and their task: whether it is proper to presume that policemen usually abide by their sworn duty to comply with the law in enforcing the law; or whether the correct assumption is that the police are so caught up in the difficult task of fighting crime that they believe anything goes.

Hard facts about the need for confessions are also lacking. It may be true, as Justice Frankfurter declared in *Culombe v. Conn.* (1961), that "despite modern advances in the technology of crime detection, offenses frequently occur about which things cannot be made to speak," but just how frequently they occur is uncertain. Statistics have been offered to establish that confessions are seldom utilized in serious criminal cases and also to show the contrary. The former are challengeable on the ground that they fail to take account of the overwhelming majority of cases disposed of by pleas of guilty, while the latter are contested because they may only demonstrate that the police often fail to use other investigative techniques.

Assuming other techniques are available, there is still disagreement as to whether interrogation is nonetheless desirable. Some hold to the view, as expressed by Justice Goldberg in *Escobedo v. Ill.* (1964), that "a system of criminal law enforcement which comes to depend on the 'confession' will, in the long run, be less reliable and more subject to abuses than a system which depends on extrinsic evidence independently secured through skillful investigation." Others question this assumption and suggest that greater use of certain "extrinsic evidence," such as eyewitness identifications (see ch. 5), would result in even less reliability.

## (b) The Supreme Court's response

From 1936 to nearly 30 years later, the Court dealt with confessions admitted in state criminal proceedings in terms of the fundamental fairness required by the Fourteenth Amendment due process clause (see § 1.2(b)). A so-called "voluntariness" test, which depended upon the "totality of the circumstances," was used to determine whether the Constitution required exclusion of a confession (see § 4.2). Over the years, it became increasingly apparent that this test was most difficult to administer because it required a finding and appraisal of all relevant facts surrounding each challenged confession.

Essentially the same approach was used by the Court during this period on the infrequent occasions when confessions admitted in federal prosecutions were reviewed. In such instances, it might logically be thought that the Court was then relying upon the due process clause of the Fifth Amendment, although the tendency was to refer to earlier holdings in which the basis of exclusion was the Fifth Amendment privilege against self-incrimination or a common law rule of evidence. *U.S. v. Carignan* (1951). Beginning in 1943, a confession obtained by federal officers and offered in a federal prosecution could also be excluded on the ground that it was received during a period of "unnecessary delay" in taking the arrested person before a judicial officer. *McNabb v. U.S.* (1943); *Mallory v. U.S.* (1957). Although these decisions were grounded upon the Court's supervisory power over the federal courts (see § 1.2(e)), most commentators viewed them as attempts by the Court to avoid the tremendous problems inherent in the due process voluntariness test, and thus there was some expectation that the *McNabb-Mallory* rule (finally abolished or severely limited by Title II of the Omnibus Crime Control and Safe Streets Act of 1968; see *U.S. v. Alvarez–Sanchez* (1994), noting but not resolving division in the lower courts re this ambiguous legislation) would ultimately be rested upon a constitutional foundation and applied to the states.

This did not come to pass, perhaps because subsequent decisions holding that there was a constitutional right to counsel at certain pretrial "critical stages" provided a better stepping stone. (However, several states follow the *McNabb-Mallory* approach in some respect, some utilizing a per se rule of exclusion and others requiring a showing of a causal connection between the illegal delay and the challenged confession.) The anticipated move away from sole reliance upon the voluntariness test occurred in *Escobedo v. Ill.* (1964), suppressing the defendant's confession because it was obtained in violation of his right to counsel at the time of interrogation. *Escobedo* was a cautious step, for the holding was carefully limited to the unique facts of the case (see

§ 4.3(b), (c)), but it was generally assumed that this newly established right to counsel in the police station would thereafter be expanded on a case-by-case basis. Instead, the Court just two years later decided *Miranda v. Ariz.* (1966), which was grounded upon the Fifth Amendment privilege against self-incrimination and prescribed a specific set of warnings as prerequisites to all future custodial interrogations (see § 4.4).

It is *Miranda* which is of major current significance, and thus the emphasis in this chapter is upon the basis and meaning of that decision. But the voluntariness approach also deserves further attention, for it has significance even after *Miranda* because it can be used to challenge interrogation techniques used subsequent to a *Miranda* waiver, as in *Colo. v. Connelly* (1986). Added attention is also given herein to the right to counsel approach, which the Court has utilized in certain cases not amenable to easy resolution under *Miranda,* e.g., *Brewer v. Williams* (1977).

## § 4.2   THE "VOLUNTARINESS"— "TOTALITY OF CIRCUM-STANCES" TEST

### (a) Objectives of the test

Although the Supreme Court earlier had occasion to review the admissibility of confessions in the federal courts, first under the common law rule of evidence barring confessions obtained by threats or promises, *Hopt v. Utah* (1884), and later—at least in one case—under a voluntariness test apparently derived from the Fifth Amendment privilege against self-incrimination, *Bram v. U.S.* (1897), it was not until *Brown v. Miss.* (1936) that the Court barred the use of a confession in the state courts. It could not, of course, dispose of the state confession on the same grounds as were resorted to in the earlier cases; under our federal system, the Supreme Court could not proscribe mere rules of evidence for the states, and the Fifth Amendment privilege was then not applicable to the states, *Twining v. N.J.* (1908), overruled by *Malloy v. Hogan* (1964). Thus the confessions in *Brown,* obtained by brutally beating the suspects, were struck down on the notion that interrogation is part of the process by which a state procures a conviction and thus subject to the requirements of the Fourteenth Amendment due process clause. (Today, however, the Court describes the voluntariness standard in terms of both due process and self-incrimination; see § 8.1(c).)

The interests to be protected under the due process test, and thus the true dimensions of that constitutional protection, remained somewhat obscure in the earlier cases. In *Brown,* the confessions clearly were of doubtful reliability, and thus that case might be read as announcing a due process test for excluding confessions obtained under circumstances presenting a fair risk that the statements are false. Concern with this risk was emphasized in subsequent cases, such as *Chambers v. Fla.* (1940); *Ward v. Tex.* (1942); and *Lyons v. Okla.* (1944), and this led many state courts to the conclusion that unfairness in violation of due process exists when a confession is obtained by means of pressure exerted upon the accused under such circumstances that it affects the testimonial trustworthiness of the confession.

While it is fair to say that ensuring the reliability of confessions is a goal under the due process voluntariness standard, it is incorrect to define the standard in terms of that one objective. In *Rogers v. Richmond* (1961), defendant's confession was obtained after the police pretended to order his ailing wife arrested for questioning, and the state court had ruled that the statement need not be excluded "if the artifice or deception was not calculated to procure an untrue statement." The Supreme Court disagreed, emphasizing that convictions based upon coerced confessions must be overturned "not because such confessions are unlikely to be true but because the methods used to extract them offend an underlying principle in the enforcement of our criminal law: that ours is an accusatorial and not an inquisitorial system." *Rogers* thus made certain what was strongly intimated in several earlier cases, e.g., *Ashcraft v. Tenn.* (1944); *Haley v. Ohio* (1948), namely, that the exclusionary rule for confessions (in much the same way as the Fourth Amendment exclusionary rule, see § 6.3(d)) is also intended to deter improper police conduct. See § 6.2(c).

In *Townsend v. Sain* (1963), the ailing defendant had been given a drug with the properties of a truth serum, after which he gave a confession in response to questioning by police who were unaware of the drug's effect. Although the confession was not obtained by conscious police wrongdoing and apparently was reliable, the Court nonetheless held its use impermissible: "Any questioning by police officers which *in fact* produces a confession which is not the product of free intellect renders that confession inadmissible." *Townsend* thus highlights another theme which runs through many of the earlier cases, e.g., *Lisenba v. Cal.* (1941); *Watts v. Ind.* (1949): the confession must be a product of the defendant's "free and rational choice." This phrase, however, was not used in an absolute sense, but rather in conjunction with a recognized need to exert some pressure to obtain confessions. As the Court seems to have acknowledged in *Miranda,* the question of whether a confession was "voluntary" had theretofore been determined by a lesser standard than, say, the question of whether a testator's will was his voluntary act.

Viewing the voluntariness test in terms of its objectives, then, it could until more recently be said that the test was designed to bar admission of those confessions which: (a) were of doubtful reliability because of the practices used to obtain them; (b) were obtained by offensive police practices even if reliability was not in question (e.g., where there is strong corroborating evidence); or (c) were obtained under circumstances in which the defendant's free choice was significantly impaired, even if the police did not resort to offensive practices. But in *Colo. v. Connelly* (1986) the Court refuted the existence of the last category in holding the state court had erred in excluding a confession volunteered to police by a defendant who suffered from a psychosis that interfered with his ability to make free and rational choices. The "crucial element of police over-reaching" was absent, the Court reasoned, and thus "there is simply no basis for concluding that any state actor has deprived a criminal defendant of due process." *Townsend* was distinguished as a case involving "police wrongdoing" in questioning a person who had been given a truth serum, though in fact the Court in that earlier case had proceeded on the assumption that neither the police doctor who administered the painkiller nor the police who interrogated were aware of the drug's truth serum character.

*Connelly* also emphasized the narrow reading which must be given to the first category listed above. The Court conceded that a "statement rendered by one in the condition of respondent might be proved to be quite unreliable," but then declared that "this is a matter to be governed by the evidentiary laws of the forum * * * and not by the Due Process Clause of the Fourteenth Amendment." This is so, the Court explained, because the aim of the due process requirement "is not to exclude presumptively false evidence, but to prevent fundamental fairness in the use of evidence, whether true or false."

## (b) The relevant circumstances

Under the voluntariness test, the Supreme Court undertook a continuing re-evaluation on the facts of each case of how much pressure on the suspect was permissible. The rule required examination of the "totality of circumstances" surrounding each confession. *Haynes v. Wash.* (1963). The factors deemed most important were: (1) physical abuse, *Lee v. Miss.* (1948); (2) threats, *Payne v. Ark.* (1958); (3) extensive questioning, *Turner v. Pa.* (1949); (4) incommunicado detention, *Davis v. N.C.* (1966); (5) denial of the right to consult with counsel, *Fay v. Noia* (1963); and (6) the characteristics and status of the suspect, such as his lack of education, *Culombe v. Conn.* (1961), emotional instability, *Spano v. N.Y.* (1959), youth, *Gallegos v. Colo.* (1962), or sickness, *Jackson v. Denno* (1964). (Also, a foreign national can raise, "as part of a broader challenge to the voluntariness of his statements to police," the violation of his right under treaty to have consular notified of his detention. *Sanchez-Llamas v. Ore.* (2006).) However, the voluntariness test is by its nature imprecise, and thus it could rarely be said that the presence of any one of these factors or any fixed combination of them clearly required exclusion of a confession. While *Connelly,* discussed above, makes it clear that item (6), in isolation, cannot "ever dispose of the inquiry into constitutional 'involuntariness,' "the propriety of the investigative and interrogation techniques used must be judged in light of what the police knew or should

have known about defendant's ability to comprehend the events and circumstances.

*Connelly* also highlights the fact that coercive
tactics utilized by private persons cannot alone produce a confession that is involuntary in the constitutional sense. However, the "police overreaching"
language of *Connelly* should not be taken literally,
for a government employee need not be a law enforcement official for his questioning to implicate
the strictures of the Fifth Amendment.

### (c) Administration of the test

Although the *Miranda* dissenters saw the voluntariness test as "a workable and effective means of
dealing with confessions in a judicial manner,"
many critics of the totality-of-circumstances approach had long been of the contrary view. The
amorphous character of the test, together with the
seeming reluctance of some courts to overturn the
conviction of an apparently guilty defendant, led to
divergent results in the lower courts. Not infre-
quently, confessions were upheld although they
quite clearly appeared to have been obtained under
circumstances previously condemned by the Supreme Court. For example, in *Davis v. N.C.* (1966)
it was uncontested that no one other than the police
had spoken to the defendant during the 16 days of
detention and interrogation which preceded his confessions. The Court reversed, noting it had "never
sustained the use of a confession obtained after
such a lengthy period of detention and interrogation," but two state courts and two federal courts

had previously upheld the confession notwithstanding these objective facts.

*Davis* was unique in that the relevant circumstances were revealed by police records; usually, an attempt at the trial level to ascertain the "totality of circumstances" has resulted in what has been commonly referred to as a "swearing contest" between the defendant and the police. The ultimate determination of whether the confession should be excluded, therefore, typically had to be made upon the basis of several hotly disputed questions of fact.

## § 4.3   THE RIGHT TO COUNSEL

### (a) Pre-*Escobedo* developments

Several developments in the late 1950's and early 1960's enhanced the prospect that the Supreme Court might ultimately resolve the confession issue in terms of the right to counsel. In *Crooker v. Cal.* (1958), where defendant's confession was obtained following denial of his request to call an attorney, the Court held the confession voluntary and also rejected defendant's separate contention that he had a right to counsel at the police station. But the four dissenters asserted that under due process "the accused who wants a counsel should have one at any time after the moment of arrest." *Crooker* was followed in *Cicenia v. La Gay* (1958), where defendant's requests to see his attorney were refused and his counsel turned away at the station, but again there was a strong dissent. The confession in *Spano v. N.Y.* (1959), was found involuntary on traditional grounds, but four concurring justices accepted defendant's contention that his absolute right to counsel in a capital case attached at the time he was indicted (which was prior to his confession).

In *White v. Md.* (1963), the absolute right to counsel in a capital case was held applicable to a pretrial "critical stage," a preliminary arraignment at which a guilty plea later introduced into evidence was obtained. Some commentators suggested that if, as in *White,* an uncounseled guilty plea could not be admitted as evidence of guilt at trial, then it followed that the same should be true of an uncounseled confession. *White* took on greater significance when the *Betts* rule (§ 7.1(b), relied upon in *Crooker*) was overruled in *Gideon v. Wainwright* (1963), holding that the absolute right to counsel for indigent state defendants existed as to all felonies and not merely capital cases.

The argument that the right to counsel attaches when the defendant is indicted and his status thereby changes from "suspect" to "accused," not reached by the majority in *Spano,* was accepted in a somewhat different context in *Massiah v. U.S.* (1964). After defendant's indictment, he was engaged in an incriminating conversation by a bugged codefendant-turned-informer, about which the overhearing agent testified at trial. The Court held, 6–3, that the Sixth Amendment prohibits extraction of incriminating statements from an indicted person without presence of counsel. The majority indicated this would be equally true had the incriminating statements been obtained by police interrogation. *Massiah* was not limited to federal prosecutions or to cases in which the defendant had already retained counsel, *McLeod v. Ohio* (1965), but most lower courts refused to extend *Massiah* back to the point of earlier tentative charges.

### (b) The *Escobedo* case

The confession in *Escobedo v. Ill.* (1964) was obtained after defendant's repeated requests to consult with retained counsel were refused and after his attorney had actually been turned away at the station. The Court, 5–4, concluded that this pre-indictment interrogation was just as much a "critical stage" as the preliminary hearing in *White,* in that what happened then could "affect the whole trial," and that *Massiah* was apposite because "no meaningful distinction can be drawn between interrogation of an accused before and after formal indictment." Yet the Court did not announce a broad right-to-counsel-at-the-station rule, but instead cautiously limited the holding to the facts of the case:

"We hold * * * that where, as here, [1] the investigation is no longer a general inquiry into an unsolved crime but has begun to focus on a particular suspect, [2] the suspect has been taken into police custody, [3] the police carry out a process of interrogations that lends itself to eliciting incriminating statements, [4] the suspect has requested and been denied an opportunity to consult with his lawyer, and [5] the police have not effectively warned him of his absolute constitutional right to remain silent, the accused has been denied 'the Assistance of Counsel' in violation of the Sixth Amendment to the Constitution as 'made obligatory upon the States by the Fourteenth Amendment,' * * * and that no statement elicited by the police during the interrogation may be used against him at a criminal trial.''

### (c) The meaning of *Escobedo*

Because the much broader *Miranda* decision was not applied retroactively (see § 1.4(a)), the precise meaning of *Escobedo* became a matter of significance only as to confessions admitted at trials occurring between the two decisions. This matter of interpretation largely fell upon the lower courts, which usually attributed significance to each of the five "elements" in the *Escobedo* holding.

Thus: (1) While the Court said in *Miranda* that the focus requirement of *Escobedo* was really intended to mean deprivation of freedom in a significant way, this requirement has been utilized to find *Escobedo* inapplicable where the suspect was in custody on another charge and the interrogation was undertaken while the case was in the investigatory rather than accusatory stage. (2) *Escobedo* does not apply when the suspect is not in police custody, although custody may be present without a formal arrest. (3) *Escobedo* does not govern volunteered statements or even interrogation undertaken primarily for another purpose, such as to locate a kidnap victim. (4) *Escobedo* does not require a warning of the right to counsel, but applies only if the suspect makes a clear and unambiguous request for counsel. *Frazier v. Cupp* (1969). (5) *Escobedo* is inapplicable if the police have warned the suspect of his right to remain silent.

Consider also *Kirby v. Ill.* (discussed in §§ 5.2(e), 7.1(d)), where the Court concluded that the Sixth Amendment right to counsel attaches "only at or after the time that adversary judicial proceedings have been initiated." Because *Escobedo* was the "only seeming deviation" from a long line of cases accepting this starting point, the Court "in retrospect concluded that the 'prime purpose' of *Escobedo* was not to vindicate the constitutional right to counsel as such, but, like *Miranda* 'to guarantee full effectuation of the privilege against self-incrimination.'" Moreover, *Kirby* noted, *Escobedo* is now limited in its "holding * * * to its own facts."

### (d) The *Williams* case

More than ten years following the *Miranda* decision, the Court "resurrected" the *Massiah* rule in *Brewer v. Williams* (1977). Williams was arraigned in Davenport, Iowa, on an outstanding arrest warrant prior to his transportation to Des Moines on a murder charge. Though the police had assured Williams' lawyer that he would not be interrogated during the trip, a detective made a "Christian burial speech," to the effect that because of the worsening weather it would be necessary to find the body now to ensure the victim a Christian burial, after which Williams directed the police to the body. The

Supreme Court, noting (i) that the right to counsel attaches when "judicial proceedings have been initiated" against the defendant, clearly the case here in light of the warrant issuance, arraignment on the warrant, and commitment to jail by the court, and (ii) that the detective "set out to elicit information from Williams" by a means "tantamount to interrogation," concluded the case fell within "the clear rule of *Massiah* * * * that once adversary proceedings have commenced against an individual, he has a right to legal representation when the government interrogates him." Though declining to hold that the right to counsel could be waived only upon notice to counsel, the Court rejected the state court's conclusion that waiver had occurred here merely because during the trip Williams did not assert that right or a desire not to talk in the absence of counsel.

### (e) When the right attaches

In *Williams,* supra, the Court declared that "the right to counsel granted by the Sixth and Fourteenth Amendments means at least that a person is entitled to the help of a lawyer at or after the time that judicial proceedings have been initiated against him—'whether by way of formal charge, preliminary hearing, indictment, information, or arraignment.'" Later, in *Mich. v. Jackson* (1986), the Court elaborated that arraignment (in the sense of the initial appearance, not the pleading stage) "signals the initiation of adversary judicial proceedings" without regard to whether it has the particular characteristics which would make "the arraignment itself * * * a critical stage requiring the presence of counsel." The right to counsel does not attach merely because the defendant has been arrested without a warrant, nor is it sufficient that the investigation has "focused" on him. *Hoffa v. U.S.* (1966). There is a split of authority as to whether the filing of a complaint or such filing plus the issuance of an arrest warrant suffices. Considering the teaching of *Kirby v. Ill.* (1972) that the right attaches once the government has "committed itself to prosecute, and * * * the adverse positions of government and defendant have solidified," it may make a difference whether the complaint-warrant process manifests a charging decision or serves some other purpose (e.g., to justify an in-premises arrest; see § 2.7(a)).

If the necessary stage in the proceedings has been reached, then the right to counsel attaches even if, unlike the *Williams* case, defendant is not yet represented by an attorney. *U.S. v. Henry* (1980). If that stage has not been reached, then the right does not attach even if defendant has already retained counsel, for "it makes little sense to say that the Sixth Amendment right to counsel attaches at different times depending on the fortuity of whether the suspect or his family happens to have retained counsel." *Moran v. Burbine* (1986). What then if the requisite stage in the proceedings has been reached as to one offense, but the police are thereafter engaged in an investigation of some new or different offense involving the same person? In *Me. v.*

*Moulton* (1985), the Court concluded that "to exclude evidence pertaining to charges as to which the Sixth Amendment right to counsel had not attached at the time the evidence was obtained, simply because other charges were pending at that time, would unnecessarily frustrate the public's interest in the investigation of criminal activities." The dissenters argued it followed from this that evidence obtained in that investigation bearing on the charged offense should be admissible in the prosecution of that offense, but the *Moulton* majority rejected that approach because it "invites abuse by law enforcement personnel in the form of fabricated investigations."

*Moulton* did not settle that the right to counsel always attached *only* to the charged offense, and thereafter many lower courts took the view that the Sixth Amendment right also carried over to offenses uncharged but closely related to the charged offense. But one such case, where the charged offense was burglary and the uncharged offenses were murder of the occupants of the burglarized premises, finally reached the Supreme Court, which reversed 5–4. In *Tex. v. Cobb*, (2001), the Court rejected the claim that an offense-specific limitation would permit police almost total license to conduct unwanted and uncounseled interrogations, and in doing so stressed both the protections of *Miranda* and the societal interest in police talking with those charged with other crimes. The *Cobb* majority then concluded that "offense" under the Sixth Amendment means the same as in the double jeopardy clause, so that per *Blockburger v. U.S.,* see § 9.11(b), "the test to be applied to determine whether there are two offenses or only one, is whether each provision requires proof of a fact which the other does not."

## (f) Waiver of counsel

The Court in *Williams,* supra, acknowledged that the right to counsel could be waived and that, because it is the right of the client rather than the attorney, waiver by the client-defendant is possible without the lawyer's participation. Seemingly inconsistent with that conclusion is the statement in *Escobedo,* supra, that the conduct of the police in turning away the lawyer was by itself "a violation of the Sixth Amendment." But in *Escobedo* the defendant was aware of that police conduct, which certainly should cast a heavy cloud over any subsequent "waiver" by the defendant. When the defendant is not aware, however, it appears the police conduct has no bearing upon the validity of the waiver. Such a conclusion, already reached by the Court in a *Miranda* context, *Moran v. Burbine* (1986), is also appropriate here unless a much more demanding waiver standard applies in a *Williams* Sixth Amendment context. That is not the case; "because the role of counsel at questioning is relatively simple and limited," the waiver standard here is the same as under *Miranda* (see § 4.9), in contrast to the relatively high at-trial standard (see § 7.4(a)). *Patterson v. Ill.* (1988). In any event, it is apparent that "the concept of a knowing and voluntary waiver of Sixth Amendment rights does not apply in the context of communications with an undisclosed undercover informant acting for the government." *U.S. v. Henry* (1980).

The special waiver-after-assertion-of-rights rules which govern in the *Miranda* area as to a defendant who has invoked his right to counsel, see § 4.9(c), also apply to the Sixth Amendment right. Thus, when that right has attached, "if police initiate interrogation after a defendant's assertion, at an arraignment or similar proceeding, of his right to counsel, any waiver of the defendant's right to counsel for that police-initiated interrogation is invalid." *Mich. v. Jackson* (1986). The Court added this is so even though the request for counsel at arraignment was not specifically tied to the matter of police questioning and even if the police were unaware of that invocation of the right. But because this Sixth Amendment right is "offense-specific" and "cannot be invoked once for all future prosecutions," the *Jackson* rule is likewise offense-specific, so that if a defendant exercises his Sixth Amendment right to counsel when brought into court on a robbery charge, that is no bar to police-initiated questioning about an unrelated murder. *McNeil v. Wis.* (1991).

## (g) Infringement of the right

In *Massiah,* supra, the violation of the right to counsel occurred when the police, using a cooperating and wired-for-sound codefendant, "deliberately elicited" incriminating statements from the defendant. Similarly, in *Williams* the Christian burial speech infringed upon the right because the detective "deliberately and designedly set out to elicit information from Williams." But these cases, which indicate that they extend to police conduct other than interrogation in the narrow sense of that word, *Fellers v. U.S.* (2004), do not require that the police have initiated the contact. Though the Sixth Amendment is not violated when the state obtains incriminating statements by mere "luck or happenstance," "knowing exploitation by the State of an opportunity to confront the accused without counsel being present is as much a breach of the State's obligation not to circumvent the right to assistance of counsel as is the intentional creation of such an opportunity." *Me. v. Moulton* (1985).

Though *Massiah* and *Williams* seem to require "action undertaken with the specific intent to evoke an inculpatory disclosure," *U.S. v. Henry* (1980) (Blackmun, J., diss.), whether that is still so after the "jail plant" *Henry* case is unclear. The conduct of the police in asking the cellmate to report back defendant's incriminating comments, the Court held, met the "deliberately elicited" test by virtue of the government "intentionally creating a situation likely to induce Henry to make incriminating statements." Though that language, if read literally, would seem to cover even negligent triggering of events resulting in an incriminating response by the defendant, the *Henry* majority appears to have viewed the case as a true "deliberately elicited" type of case. That is, they deem the government's instructions to the informant not to question Henry about the robbery, in light of all the circumstances, as not manifesting a lack of intent to obtain incriminating statements or to have the informant take some affirmative steps to achieve that result. It is apparently still true, therefore, that there is no *Massiah-Williams* violation if the person acting with the intention of eliciting an incriminating statement is not a government agent, or if the government agent who elicits an incriminating response does so exclusively for some other legitimate purpose.

Because the majority in *Henry* did not think it was dealing with a truly "passive" situation in terms of the actions of the government's informant, the Court did not have occasion to decide whether the *Massiah-Williams* doctrine applies to both active and passive efforts to obtain incriminating statements. But in *Kuhlmann v. Wilson* (1986), on the ground that "the primary concern of the *Massiah* line of decisions is secret interrogation by investigatory techniques that are the equivalent of direct police interrogation," the Court ruled that it was not a violation of defendant's right to counsel for police merely to arrange for an informant to report back to police any overheard incriminating comments of the defendant. But *Kuhlmann* illustrates the difficulty of drawing the line between active and passive efforts; defendant's incriminating comments followed the informant's assertion that his original nonincriminating version "didn't sound too good," but the majority felt this was not enough under all the circumstances to bring the case within the "deliberately elicited" test. That problem is not present when the police " 'listening post' is an inanimate electronic device"; its use clearly does not infringe upon the right to counsel, as it "has no capability of leading the conversation into any particular subject or prompting any particular replies." *U.S. v. Henry* (1980).

### (h) Critique of counsel approach

Opinions differ as to whether the *Massiah* rule, as elaborated and extended in such cases as *Williams* and *Henry*, is a sensible one. Some claim the rule is unnecessary because *Miranda* protects against the coercive pressures of custodial interrogations while the due process voluntariness test affords sufficient protection in noncustodial situations. But others find offensive certain police practices likely to be reached only by the *Massiah* rule, such as use of an undercover agent to elicit incriminating remarks, and for them the problem with the rule is that it does not extend to similar conduct that occurs after formal arrest. As for the latter criticism, the basic issue is whether and when the Sixth Amendment should function as a shield, enabling the defendant to frustrate the state's efforts to obtain evidence directly from him. One question is whether the right to counsel rule turns on distinctions that are unresponsive to the government's need for evidence. It thus might be asked whether *Massiah*, which erected a Sixth Amendment shield around a defendant who had been arrested and indicted many months earlier, is more understandable than *Williams*, where such a shield was erected around a defendant shortly after his arrest and apparently before even the magnitude of the crime had been ascertained by the authorities.

### (i) The Crime Control Act

In the Crime Control Act of 1968, Congress purported to "repeal" the *Massiah* rule for federal prosecutions by providing that a confession is admissible if voluntary and that whether or not the defendant was without the assistance of counsel at the time "need not be conclusive on the issue of voluntariness." This legislation has been largely ignored, and properly so, for to the extent it purports to nullify the Sixth Amendment right to counsel as recognized in *Massiah* and subsequent Supreme Court decisions it is most certainly unconstitutional.

## § 4.4  THE PRIVILEGE AGAINST SELF–INCRIMINATION

### (a) The privilege in the police station

The Fifth Amendment provides that no person "shall be compelled in any criminal case to be a witness against himself." Although a literal reading of this language suggests that the privilege against self-incrimination has no application to unsworn statements obtained by station-house interrogation, in *Bram v. U.S.* (1897) the Court asserted that "in criminal trials, in the courts of the United States, wherever a question arises whether a confession is incompetent because not voluntary, the issue is controlled by that portion of the Fifth Amendment." The Court's conclusion that there was a historical connection between the privilege and the confession doctrine appears incorrect, and was subsequently challenged by many commentators. The privilege was not expressly relied upon in later cases concerning the admissibility of confessions in federal courts, while the Court dealt with confessions used in state courts solely in terms of the due process voluntariness test (see § 4.2). But in *Malloy v. Hogan* (1964), which did not involve a confession, the Court held the privilege applicable to the states, and in support of this result noted that the admissibility of a confession in a state trial had long been tested by the same standard as applied to federal prosecutions by *Bram*. Promptly thereafter, the Court decided the *Escobedo* case (see § 4.3(b)), which, while grounded upon the Sixth Amendment right to counsel, spoke of "the right of the accused to be advised by his lawyer of his privilege against self-incrimination."

Any remaining doubts were dispelled by *Miranda v. Ariz.* (1966), holding that the privilege against self-incrimination "is fully applicable during a period of custodial interrogation." Although the apparent assumption of the *Miranda* majority that this proposition was "settled" in the precedents is subject to question, this of course does not compel the conclusion that the *Miranda* holding was in error. Even the dissenters in *Miranda* conceded that the Fifth Amendment privilege "embodies basic principles always capable of expansion," although they forcefully argued that those principles would not be served by extending the privilege to the police station. See also § 8.1(a).

### (b) The *Miranda* rules

Apart from this reliance upon the Fifth Amendment rather than the Sixth, *Miranda* is striking in its contrast to *Escobedo*. The latter holding was carefully limited to the facts of the case before the Court, while *Miranda* sets forth what the dissenters called a "constitutional code of rules for confessions":

(1) These rules are required to safeguard the privilege against self-incrimination, and thus must be followed in the absence of "other procedures which are at least as effective in apprising accused persons of their right of silence and in assuring a continuous opportunity to exercise it."

(2) These rules apply "when the individual is first subjected to police interrogation while in custody at the station or otherwise deprived of his freedom of action in any significant way," and not to "general on-the-scene questioning as to facts surrounding a crime or other general questioning of citizens in the fact-finding process" or to "volunteered statements of any kind."

(3) Without regard to his prior awareness of his rights, if a person in custody is to be subjected to questioning, "he must first be informed in clear and unequivocal terms that he has the right to remain

silent," so that the ignorant may learn of this right and so that the pressures of the interrogation atmosphere will be overcome for those previously aware of the right.

(4) The above warning "must be accompanied by the explanation that anything said can and will be used against the individual in court," so as to ensure that the suspect fully understands the consequences of foregoing the privilege.

(5) Because this is indispensable to protection of the privilege, the individual also "must be clearly informed that he has the right to consult with a lawyer and to have the lawyer with him during interrogation," without regard to whether it appears that he is already aware of this right.

(6) The individual must also be warned "that if he is indigent a lawyer will be appointed to represent him," for otherwise the above warning would be understood as meaning only that an individual may consult a lawyer if he has the funds to obtain one.

(7) The individual is always free to exercise the privilege, and thus if he "indicates in any manner, at any time prior to or during questioning, that he wishes to remain silent, the interrogation must cease"; and likewise, if he "states that he wants an attorney, the interrogation must cease until an attorney is present."

(8) If a statement is obtained without the presence of an attorney, "a heavy burden rests on the Government to demonstrate that the defendant

knowingly and intelligently waived his privilege against self-incrimination and his right to retained or appointed counsel," and such waiver may not be presumed from the individual's silence after the warnings or from the fact that a confession was eventually obtained.

(9) Any statement obtained in violation of these rules may not be admitted into evidence, without regard to whether it is a confession or only an admission of part of an offense or whether it is inculpatory or allegedly exculpatory.

(10) Likewise, exercise of the privilege may not be penalized, and thus the prosecution may not "use at trial the fact that [the defendant] stood mute or claimed his privilege in the face of accusation."

The Supreme Court has more recently asserted that *Miranda* "recognized that these procedural safeguards were not themselves rights protected by the Constitution but were instead measures to insure that the right against compulsory self-incrimination was protected. * * * The suggested safeguards were not intended to 'create a constitutional straightjacket,' but rather to provide practical reinforcement for the right against compulsory self-incrimination." *Mich. v. Tucker* (1974). This approach is reflected generally in the cases interpreting *Miranda* (see §§ 4.5–4.9). See also § 1.3(e).

### (c) Criticism of *Miranda*

Not unexpectedly, the *Miranda* decision was greeted with criticism from many quarters. It was contended that police abuse was not so widespread as to call for such a far-reaching decision, and that confessions were essential to law enforcement but would be unobtainable under the new rules (see § 4.1(a)). Recent empirical studies, however, have concluded that the impact of *Miranda* has been quite different than predicted by the Court's critics. In most instances the *Miranda* warnings have not appreciably reduced the amount of talking by a suspect, and the police are now obtaining about as many confessions as before *Miranda*. Moreover, as the Court emphasized in reaffirming *Miranda* in *Dickerson v. U.S.* (2000), while under *Miranda* it may sometimes be the case that "a guilty defendant go[es] free," that is a lesser disadvantage than trying to operate exclusively under a totality-of-the-circumstances test, which "is more difficult than *Miranda* for law enforcement officers to conform to, and for courts to apply in a consistent manner."

These conclusions lend some support to the views of another group of critics, those who find a fundamental inconsistency in the majority's reasoning. They claim that the heavy emphasis on the inability of an uncounseled defendant to decide whether to incriminate himself when subject to the inherent pressures of custody is inconsistent with the conclusion that the decision whether to dispense with counsel can be voluntary in the same circumstances. As stated in one of the *Miranda* dissents: "But if the defendant may not answer without a warning a question such as 'Where were you last night?' without having his answer be a compelled one, how can the court ever accept his negative answer to the question of whether he wants to consult his retained counsel or counsel whom the court will appoint?''

### (d) The Crime Control Act

Title II of the Omnibus Crime Control and Safe Streets Act of 1968 amends existing legislation by adding 18 U.S.C.A. § 3501, which purports to "repeal" *Miranda* in federal prosecutions. The Act states that a confession is admissible in the federal courts if voluntarily given, and that whether the defendant was advised of his right to remain silent or his right to counsel and whether he was without counsel when he confessed are merely to be taken into consideration as circumstances bearing on the issue of voluntariness.

In *Dickerson v. U.S.* (2000), the Court noted that because Congress "may not legislatively supersede our decisions interpreting and applying the Constitution," the validity of the above provision depends upon "whether the *Miranda* Court announced a constitutional rule or merely exercised its supervisory authority to regulate evidence in the absence of congressional direction." In deciding it was the former, the 7–2 majority in *Dickerson* emphasized: (i) that *Miranda*, two of its companion cases, and many of the cases in which the Court later applied *Miranda* involved state prosecutions, as to which the Supreme Court's authority "is limited to enforcing the commands of the United States Constitution"; (ii) that the *Miranda* majority opinion "is replete with statements indicating that the majority thought it was announcing a constitutional rule"; and (iii) that the contrary is not shown by later decisions narrowing *Miranda*, for those decisions and others broadening *Miranda* in other respects merely show "that no constitutional rule is immutable." And while the Court in *Miranda* stated there could be a legislative alternative if it was "equally as effective in preventing coerced confessions," § 3501 did not meet that test, as it merely "reinstates the totality test as sufficient."

## § 4.5  *MIRANDA:* WHAT OFFENSES ARE COVERED?

### (a)  Traffic and other minor offenses

Although a number of lower courts held *Miranda* inapplicable to traffic and other minor crimes, a unanimous Court held otherwise in *Berkemer v. McCarty* (1984). The Court concluded that such an exception would undermine *Miranda*'s clarity (especially when a misdemeanor investigation escalated into or was a pretext for a felony investigation), and that the purposes of *Miranda* are served even as to minor traffic offenses.

### (b)  Tax investigations

In *Mathis v. U.S.* (1968), statements were obtained by an internal revenue agent from a defendant incarcerated in jail on another matter. The government contended that the *Miranda* warnings were not required because the questions were asked as "part of a routine tax investigation where no criminal proceedings might even be brought," but the Court ruled otherwise because there is always the possibility that criminal prosecution will result.

### (c) Proceeding at which confession offered

Because *Miranda* is grounded in the privilege against self-incrimination, it protects only against compulsion "in any criminal case." Thus the *Miranda* exclusionary rule applies in criminal cases at stages of the proceedings having to do with guilt or punishment. *Estelle v. Smith* (1981). It does not apply, however, *Estelle* concluded, at a hearing to ascertain defendant's competence to stand trial. Nor does it apply in such noncriminal contexts as prison discipline hearings, *Baxter v. Palmigiano* (1976), see § 8.4(b), or in a civil sexually dangerous persons proceeding which was not "punitive either in purpose or effect," *Allen v. Ill.* (1986).

## § 4.6   *MIRANDA:* WHEN IS INTERROGATION "CUSTODIAL"?

### (a) "Custody" vs. "focus"

In defining that interrogation which is "custodial," the *Miranda* Court dropped a footnote stating that was "what we meant in *Escobedo* when we spoke of an investigation which had focused on an accused." Though this might be taken to mean that custody and focus are alternative grounds for requiring the warnings, a more likely explanation for this footnote is that the Court was attempting to maintain some continuity between *Escobedo* and the new approach of *Miranda,* while in fact making a fresh start in describing the point at which the constitutional protections begin. The Court has since rejected the claim that "focus" involves psychological restraints equivalent of custody, necessitating the *Miranda* warnings. *Beckwith v. U.S.* (1976).

### (b) Purpose of the custody

*Mathis v. U.S.* (1968) posed the question whether *Miranda* applies when the purpose of the custody is unrelated to the purpose of the interrogation, as there the defendant was in jail serving a state sentence when questioned by a revenue agent about his tax returns. The Court, 5–3, answered in the affirmative, asserting that a contrary result would go "against the whole purpose of the *Miranda* decision." The dissenters were unwilling to accept this conclusion, for they read *Miranda* as resting "not on the mere fact of physical restriction but on a conclusion that coercion—pressure to answer questions—usually flows from a certain type of custody, police station interrogation of someone charged with or suspected of a crime."

### (c) Subjective vs. objective approach

A most fundamental question concerning the "custody" element of *Miranda* is whether it is to be determined by (1) the subjective state of mind of the suspect, which would square with the "potentiality for compulsion" concern expressed in *Miranda* but would make it difficult for police to ascertain when warnings are required; (2) the subjective state of mind of the officer, the approach used in *Orozco v. Tex.* (1969), which would be easy for the police to apply but would not square with the "potentiality for compulsion" to the extent that it made the unstated intentions of the officer determinative; or (3) an objective approach. The first two have the added defect that the "custody" issue would be decided by swearing contests concerning intentions, and thus the Court wisely concluded in *Berkemer v. McCarty* (1984) that an objective standard should be used. The Court thus rejected the argument that "custody" existed because of the officer's uncommunicated intention to make an arrest, and reasoned that a "policeman's unarticulated plan has no bearing on the question whether a suspect was 'in custody' at a particular time; the only relevant inquiry is how a reasonable man in the suspect's position would have understood his situation." That view was reaffirmed in *Stansbury v. Cal.* (1994).

This objective approach will often require a careful examination of all the circumstances of the particular case. Account must be taken of those facts intrinsic to the interrogation: when and where it occurred, how long it lasted, how many police were present, what the officers and the defendant said and did, the presence of physical restraint or the equivalent (e.g., drawn weapons, a guard at the door), and whether the defendant was being questioned as a suspect or as a witness. Events before the interrogation, such as how the defendant got to the place of questioning, are also relevant. The Supreme Court has also taken into account events after the questioning, e.g., in *Ore. v. Mathiason* (1977), that defendant was then permitted to depart, though such facts would seem to have nothing to do with how a reasonable person would have perceived the situation at the time of the questioning. The *Berkemer* test probably requires consideration of obvious unique characteristics of the suspect (e.g., his youth), notwithstanding *Yarborough v. Alvarado* (2004), reaching a contrary result in a deferential-review habeas corpus case as to a petitioner almost 18 when questioned.

### (d) Presence at station

Though *Miranda* expressly covers the case of a person "in custody at the station," not all presence at a police station is custodial. Thus in *Ore. v. Mathiason* (1977), where the defendant came to the station in response to the written request of a police officer that he come by to "discuss something," the Court correctly concluded defendant "came voluntarily to the police station." The Court's other conclusion that the situation did not later become custodial when the defendant, a parolee, was told his fingerprints had been found at a burglary scene, is open to question. A supposed "invitation" which involves the suspect going to the station in the company of a police officer, at least when the officer has not unequivocally advised the defendant he is free to leave at any time, is much more likely to support a finding of "custody" for *Miranda* purposes. Cf. *Dunaway v. N.Y.* (1979).

### (e) Presence elsewhere

Courts are much less likely to find the circumstances custodial when the interrogation occurs in familiar or at least neutral surroundings. See, e.g., *Beckwith v. U.S.* (1976) (questioning in suspect's home noncustodial). But, the circumstances of each case must be carefully examined. See, e.g., *Orozco v. Tex.* (1969) (questioning at suspect's home custodial where four police entered defendant's bedroom at 4 a.m.). In *Minn. v. Murphy* (1984), concluding defendant's meeting with his probation officer at her office and pursuant to her order was not custodial, the Court emphasized that such interviews were "arranged by appointment at a mutually convenient time" and that Murphy, by virtue of past interviews, was familiar with the officer and that environment.

Although the Court in *Miranda* excluded "general on-the-scene questioning" from the holding in that case, this does not mean crime scene interrogation is never custodial. As stated in *N.Y. v. Quarles* (1984), "the ultimate inquiry is simply whether there is a 'formal arrest or restraint on freedom of movement' of the degree associated with a formal arrest." Such was the case in *Quarles,* where the questioning occurred in a supermarket minutes after defendant had been arrested by four officers with guns drawn and then handcuffed. But such was not the case in *Berkemer v. McCarty* (1984), involving roadside questioning during a routine traffic stop. Thus a *Terry* type of stop, see § 2.9, though a seizure for Fourth Amendment purposes, is not ordinarily an "in custody" situation for purposes of *Miranda*, at least absent a physical restraint such as handcuffing, drawing a gun, holding by the arm, or placing in a police car.

## § 4.7  *MIRANDA:* WHAT CONSTITUTES "INTERROGATION"?

### (a) "Volunteered" statements

The *Miranda* Court emphasized that "there is no requirement that police stop a person who enters a police station and states that he wishes to confess to a crime, or a person who calls the police to offer a confession or any other statement he desires to make. Volunteered statements of any kind are not barred by the Fifth Amendment and their admissibility is not affected by our holding today." Thus, it is clear that a statement not preceded by the *Miranda* warnings will be admissible when, for example, the defendant walks into a station and confesses or blurts out an admission when approached by an officer near a crime scene. Also, because the *Miranda* Court found custody-plus-interrogation coercive, rather than mere custody, it likewise seems clear that a statement may qualify as "volunteered" even though made by one in custody.

## (b) Follow-up questioning

Assuming a truly volunteered statement, may the police follow up that statement with some questions? *Miranda* is not entirely clear on this issue; at one point custodial interrogation is defined as "questioning initiated by law enforcement officers," suggesting that police questioning designed to clarify or amplify a volunteered statement is permissible, but elsewhere it is said that the suspect must be warned "prior to any questioning." So far, courts have been quite willing to admit the answers to follow-up questions on the ground that these answers are a continuation of the volunteered statement. It may well be, however, that a distinction should be drawn between questions designed to clarify an ambiguous statement (e.g., "did what"? in response to "I did it"), and those which seek to enhance the defendant's guilt or raise the offense to a higher degree (e.g., "why did you do it?").

## (c) The "functional equivalent" of questioning

What if the police have done something (other than questioning the suspect) which appears to have prompted his statement, such as showing him incriminating physical evidence or confronting him with a confessing accomplice or the accusing victim? Such actions will usually fall within the Court's holding in *R.I. v. Innis* (1980):

"We conclude that the *Miranda* safeguards come into play whenever a person in custody is subjected to either express questioning or its functional equivalent. That is to say, the term 'interrogation' under *Miranda* refers not only to express questioning, but also to any words or actions on the part of the police (other than those normally attendant to arrest and custody) that the police should know are reasonably likely to elicit an incriminating response from the suspect. The latter portion of this definition focuses primarily upon the perceptions of the suspect, rather than the intent of the police. This focus reflects the fact that the *Miranda* safeguards were designed to vest a suspect in custody with an added measure of protection against coercive police practices, without regard to objective proof of the underlying intent of the police. A practice that the police should know is reasonably likely to evoke an incriminating response from a suspect thus amounts to interrogation. But, since the police surely cannot be held accountable for the unforeseeable results of their words or actions, the definition of interrogation can extend only to words or actions on the part of police officers that they *should have known* were reasonably likely to elicit an incriminating response."

In *Innis,* the defendant, who had already asserted his *Miranda* rights, made incriminating statements after one officer said to another, as they took defendant to the station after his arrest, that the missing shotgun might fall into the hands of students at a nearby school for handicapped children. The majority concluded this was a dialog between the police rather than questioning, and that it was not the "functional equivalent" of questioning because there was nothing in the record to suggest the officers "should have known" the brief conversation would prompt defendant to make an incriminating response. (This is not to suggest that comments directed at the suspect are inevitably interrogation; under the *Innis* test, it is not interrogation for the police to ask the suspect to perform physical sobriety tests, *Pa. v. Muniz* (1990), or take a blood alcohol test, *So. Dak. v. Neville* (1983).) The Court in *Innis* then confused matters further by a footnote assertion that the intent of the police was not irrelevant on the question of what they "should have known." But neither the probability of an incriminating response nor the undisclosed intentions of the police is directly relevant to the concerns underlying *Miranda,* and thus a much more appealing interpretation of *Innis* is that the test is whether an objective observer of the officer's actions would conclude they were designed to elicit an incriminating response. This avoids the fact-finding difficulties of a subjective test, but yet for the most part identifies those situations in which the suspect may have experienced the *Miranda* "potentiality for compulsion" by perceiving that the police were trying to get him to make an incriminating response.

Notwithstanding the language in *Innis, Ariz. v. Mauro* (1987) indicates that it is not inevitably interrogation for police to allow a scenario to occur which they know will likely prompt the defendant to incriminate himself. The Court there held, 5–4, that it was not interrogation for police to accede to the request of defendant's wife, also a suspect in the death of their son, to speak with defendant and then to have a police officer and tape recorder conspicuously present at the meeting. Stressing that "Mauro was not subjected to compelling influences, psychological ploys, or direct questioning," the majority concluded the police action did not implicate the purpose underlying *Miranda:* "preventing government officials from using the coercive nature of confinement to extract confessions that would not be given in an unrestrained environment."

It must be remembered that conduct which does not constitute "interrogation" under *Innis* may still amount to the eliciting of an incriminating statement in violation of defendant's right to counsel; see § 4.3(g). Such is the case as to questioning by an undercover "jail plant." Though such conduct in a post-charge setting violates defendant's Sixth Amendment rights, see § 4.3(g), it does not violate *Miranda,* for it is the impact on the suspect's mind of the interplay between police interrogation and police custody—each reinforcing the pressures and anxieties produced by the other—that the Court in *Miranda* correctly discerned makes "custodial police interrogation" so devastating. *Ill. v. Perkins* (1990).

### (d) Purpose of the questioning

The Supreme Court has held that the privilege against self-incrimination offers no protection against requiring a suspect to appear in a lineup, to give a handwriting sample, or to speak for identification the words uttered by the offender at the scene of the crime (see § 5.1). Thus, *Miranda*-type warnings are not a prerequisite to these procedures. The claim that a psychiatric examination to determine a defendant's prior state of mind is like taking handwriting exemplars and thus is not covered by *Miranda* was rejected in *Estelle v. Smith* (1981), but the Court went on to indicate that a defendant who asserted an insanity defense and introduced supporting psychiatric testimony could be required to submit to examination by a government psychiatrist. Following *Smith,* the Court held in *Buchanan v. Ky.* (1987) that "if a defendant requests [a psychiatric] evaluation or presents psychiatric evidence [here, to make out the affirmative defense of extreme emotional disturbance], then, at the very least, the prosecution may rebut this presentation with evidence from the reports of the examination that the defendant requested."

*Pa. v. Muniz* (1990) illustrates the point that *Miranda* requirements are inapplicable to questioning which produces an incriminating response other than a "testimonial" one (see § 8.1(d)). The defendant, under arrest for driving under the influence, was asked a series of questions about his name, address, birthday, age, etc. The absence of *Miranda* warnings did not require suppression of the video-tape of his slurred-speech responses, as requiring one to reveal the physical manner in which he speaks is not testimonial in character. But the content of one of defendant's answers, that he did not know the date of his sixth birthday, was incriminating, as the inference his mental state was confused was derived from a "testimonial act," that is, one in which the defendant was required "to communicate an express or implied assertion of fact or belief." *Muniz* supports those lower court decisions holding that routine inquiries during booking are lawful even absent *Miranda* warnings. Indeed, it may well be that questions asked for purposes of identification (e.g., "what is your name?", "where do you live?") on other occasions are likewise outside the privilege, and that therefore they may be put to a suspect in custody without first giving him the *Miranda* warnings. Cf. *Cal. v. Byers* (§ 8.3(f)), holding that a statute requiring a driver of a car involved in an accident to stop and give the driver of the other car his name and address does not violate the privilege; and *Hiibel v. Sixth Judicial Dist. Ct.* (§ 8.2(c)), asserting that "answering a request to disclose a name is likely to be so insignificant in the scheme of things as to be incriminating only in unusual circumstances." This conclusion is consistent with the *Innis* definition of "interrogation," supra.

Still another type of case is that in which the authorities claim that they were questioning for the purpose of protecting themselves or others from weapons by asking the defendant whether he had a gun or where a gun was located. In *N.Y. v. Quarles* (1984) the Court recognized "a 'public safety' exception to the requirement that *Miranda* warnings be given," reasoning that "the need for answers to questions in a situation posing a threat to the public safety outweighs the need for the prophylactic rule protecting the Fifth Amendment's privilege against self-incrimination." Somewhat similar is the so-called "rescue doctrine," under which it has been held that *Miranda* warnings are unnecessary before custodial questioning undertaken to save life (e.g., in an effort to locate a kidnap victim).

### (e) Questioning by non-police

In *Miranda,* the Court defined interrogation as "questioning initiated by law enforcement officers." This language has been relied upon by courts in holding *Miranda* inapplicable to questioning by such persons as a private investigator, a high school principal, and the victim. It has also been held that *Miranda* is not applicable to interrogation by the defendant's parole or probation officer, although the Supreme Court has intimated the contrary because such an official "is a peace officer, and as such is allied, to a greater or lesser extent, with his fellow peace officers." *Minn. v. Murphy* (1984), quoting *Fare v. Michael C.* (1979). Also, the Court has on other occasions held *Miranda* applicable to questioning by persons not primarily responsible for criminal law enforcement. *Estelle v. Smith* (1981) ("a psychiatrist designated by the trial court"); *Mathis v. U.S.* (1968) (IRS "civil investigator," where a possibility "his work would end up in a criminal prosecution").

## § 4.8  *MIRANDA*: WHAT WARNINGS ARE REQUIRED?

### (a)  Adequacy of the warnings

*Miranda* does not require slavish adherence to the precise words used therein for the necessary warnings; the warnings given are adequate if they convey the substance of the *Miranda* requirements. *Cal. v. Prysock* (1981). Thus, it is sufficient that the police told the defendant that "he didn't have to make any statement" (instead of that he had a right to remain silent). Warnings that anything the suspect says "might," "may," "can," or "could" be used against him have been sustained, but a warning that the statement may be used "for or against" the suspect contains an improper inducement to speak.

Failure to advise the defendant of his right to have counsel appointed is fatally defective. A contrary result has sometimes been reached where the defendant later had retained counsel at trial and on appeal, which seems inconsistent with footnote 43 in *Miranda:* "While a warning that the indigent may have counsel appointed need not be given to the person who is known to have an attorney or is known to have ample funds to secure one, the expedient of giving a warning is too simple and the rights involved too important to engage in *ex post facto* inquiries into financial ability when there is any doubt at all on that score." Informing a defendant of "his right to have a lawyer present prior to and during interrogation" and of "his right to have a lawyer appointed at no cost if he could not afford one" is sufficient, as collectively it indicates the right to appointed counsel prior to and during interrogation. *Cal. v. Prysock* (1981). Indeed, even a warning of a right to counsel before and during questioning accompanied by a statement that appointment of counsel will only occur "if and when you go to court" is sufficient, as *Miranda* does not require "that attorneys be producible on call," but only that police not interrogate if they cannot provide appointed counsel. *Duckworth v. Eagan* (1989).

### (b) "Cutting off" the warnings

What if the warning officer never completes his task because the suspect cuts him off with the assertion that the warnings are unnecessary because he is fully aware of all of his rights? The view that this is no excuse for not completing the warnings is consistent with the language in *Miranda* which emphasizes that the expedient of giving adequate warnings is so simple that "we will not pause to inquire in individual cases whether the defendant was aware of his rights without a warning being given."

### (c) Multiple interrogation sessions

Once the warnings have been completely given and the defendant has given an effective waiver, must the warnings be repeated again at the outset of a subsequent interview? The courts have quite consistently answered in the negative, both when the later interview follows promptly after the first and when several days have intervened. It might be argued, however, that the *Miranda* concern with the suspect's continuing right to invoke the privilege means that a substantial interval or change in interrogators calls for repetition of the warnings, particularly so that the "warning will show the individual that his interrogators are prepared to recognize his privilege should he choose to exercise it."

As for the increasingly popular "police protocol * * * that calls for giving no warnings of the rights * * * until interrogation has produced a confession," which "could lead to an entirely reasonable inference [by the defendant] that what he had just said will be used, with subsequent silence being of no avail," *Mo. v. Seibert* (2004) holds a post-warnings confession must also be suppressed when the circumstance in which the *Miranda* warnings were given shows they could not "function 'effectively.' " Relevant factors are: (1) the extent of the questions and answers in the first round of questioning; (2) the overlapping content of the two statements; (3) the timing and setting of the first and second interrogations; (4) the continuity of police personnel; and (5) the degree to which the interrogator's questions treated the second round as continuous with the first.

### (d) Additional admonitions

Because *Miranda* stresses that many suspects will assume that "silence in the face of accusation is itself damning and will bode ill when presented to a jury," it has been argued that suspects should be warned about another important part of the *Miranda* holding—that the "prosecution may not * * * use at trial the fact that he stood mute or claimed his privilege in the face of accusation." But the courts have not mandated the giving of such a warning.

Likewise, there is no requirement that the suspect be advised of the nature of the crime about which the police wish to interrogate, and this is so even when the circumstances suggest the desired questioning is about a matter quite different from that later encompassed by the interrogation. *Colo. v. Spring* (1987) (arrest by federal ATF agents for firearms violations, questioning about an unreported homicide in another state). The Court reasoned that since the defendant had been told he had a right to remain silent and that *anything* he said could be used against him, he had all the information necessary for a knowing and intelligent waiver of his Fifth Amendment rights; "the additional information could affect only the wisdom of a *Miranda* waiver, not its essentially voluntary and knowing nature." As for the statement in *Miranda* that "any evidence that the accused was threatened, tricked, or cajoled into a waiver will * * * show that the defendant did not voluntarily waive his privilege," the Court in *Spring* responded that mere "official silence" about the desire to question about the murder did not constitute trickery, and cautiously left unresolved whether a waiver of *Miranda* rights would be valid had there been "an affirmative misrepresentation by law enforcement officials as to the scope of the interrogation."

The U.S. is party to a treaty providing that if a foreign national is detained in this country, he must be advised of his right under the treaty to have the consular post of his country informed "without delay" of his detention. Police failure to give such an admonishment does not require suppression of a confession thereafter obtained, as the treaty does not provide such a remedy but leaves implementation to domestic law, and in this country the exclusionary rule has been used primarily with respect to Fourth and Fifth Amendment violations, while the treaty provision "has nothing whatsoever to do with searches or interrogations." *Sanchez-Llamas v. Ore.* (2006).

## § 4.9  *MIRANDA*: WHAT CONSTITUTES WAIVER?

### (a) Express or implied

In *N.C. v. Butler* (1979), it was held: "An express written or oral statement of waiver [of *Miranda* rights] is usually strong proof of the validity of that waiver, but is not inevitably either necessary or sufficient to establish waiver. The question is not one of form, but rather whether the defendant in fact knowingly and voluntarily waived [the *Miranda* rights]. The courts must presume that a defendant did not waive his rights; the prosecution's burden is great; but in at least some cases waiver can be clearly inferred from the actions and words of the person interrogated." But this does not mean waiver is established merely by the fact that the defendant thereafter answered questions, *Tague v. La.* (1980), as *Miranda* cautions that "a valid waiver will not be presumed simply from the silence of the accused after warnings are given or simply from the fact that a confession was in fact eventually obtained."

## (b) Facts bearing on the waiver

*Butler* instructs that the waiver issue is to be decided on "the particular facts and circumstances surrounding that case, including the background, experience, and conduct of the accused." However, the voluntariness of a *Miranda* waiver depends upon the absence of police overreaching, not of "free choice" in the broad sense of that term, and thus a waiver is voluntary though produced by moral and psychological pressures emanating from sources other than official coercion. *Colo. v. Connelly* (1986). As for police overreaching, courts have held waivers involuntary when obtained by threats or promises or only after extended detention or persistent questioning. A waiver is not invalid merely because police withheld from the defendant information that an attorney had sought to consult him, as "events occurring outside the presence of the suspect and entirely unknown to him" have no bearing on whether the waiver was "knowing and intelligent." *Moran v. Burbine* (1986). The *Connelly* rule that police overreaching is a prerequisite to finding a waiver involuntary does not apply to the second requirement of waiver, as stated in *Colo. v. Spring* (1987), that it be "made with full awareness both of the nature of the right being abandoned and the consequences of the decision to abandon it."

If the defendant requests an attorney, this is per se an invocation of his Fifth Amendment rights, requiring that all interrogation cease. This is because of the "pivotal role" of counsel in the criminal process, and thus a comparable per se approach is not applicable to a request for a probation officer, clergyman, or close friend. *Fare v. Michael C.* (1979). If the defendant's invocation of his right to counsel is limited in some way, it does not prohibit further police contact with the defendant consistent with that limitation. *Conn. v. Barrett* (1987) (counsel invoked only as to giving of written statement; police could still seek oral statement).

On the question of whether an effective waiver can be established in the face of defendant's refusal to sign a waiver-of-rights form, or to have his confession reduced to writing, the prevailing view is yes. That position is supported by the Supreme Court's approach in *N.C. v. Butler,* discussed above. However, it does seem that under such circumstances no waiver should be found if other indications of the suspect's intentions to waive are at all ambiguous. In *Barrett,* supra, the Court stressed that the defendant had "made clear his intentions."

Another type of scope-of-waiver issue was presented in *Wyrick v. Fields* (1982), where Fields after consultation with counsel agreed to take a polygraph test, which was preceded by a *Miranda* waiver. After the test, Fields was asked to explain why his answers indicated deceit, and he made an incriminating response. The Court held the waiver extended to that questioning, as neither Fields nor his attorney could have reasonably assumed "that Fields would not be informed of the polygraph readings and asked to explain any unfavorable result."

## (c)  Waiver after assertion of rights

A suspect who has once refused to waive his *Miranda* rights may in some circumstances execute an effective waiver at a subsequent interrogation session. In *Mich. v. Mosley* (1975), the Court rejected the claim that assertion of *Miranda* rights creates "a per se proscription of indefinite duration upon any further questioning by any police officer on any subject," and concluded that instead the test is whether the defendant's right to cut off questioning was "scrupulously honored." In *Mosley,* the defendant, after receiving the *Miranda* warnings, declined to discuss the robberies for which he was arrested, but two hours later waived his *Miranda* rights to a different officer with respect to an unrelated homicide. In holding his incriminating statements admissible, the Court stressed that this was not a case "where the police failed to honor a decision of a person in custody to cut off questioning, either by refusing to discontinue the interrogation upon request or by persisting in repeated efforts to wear down his resistance and make him change his mind." Rather, "the police here [i] immediately ceased the interrogation, [ii] resumed questioning only after the passage of a significant period of time and the provision of a fresh set of warnings, and [iii] restricted the second interrogation to a crime that had not been a subject of the earlier interrogation." Lower courts have not read *Mosley* as limited to instances where, as in that case, the interrogator and subject matter were different at the resumed interrogation.

The *Mosley* "scrupulously honored" test applies when the defendant has invoked his right to silence, but is insufficient when the defendant has invoked his right to counsel; "an accused, * * * having expressed his desire to deal with the police only through counsel, is not subject to further interrogation by the authorities until counsel has been made available to him, unless the accused himself initiates further communication, exchanges or conversations with the police." *Edwards v. Ariz.* (1981). The "available to him" part of *Edwards* means "that when counsel is requested, interrogation must cease, and officials may not reinitiate interrogation without counsel present, whether or not the accused has consulted with his attorney" in the interim. *Minnick v. Miss.* (1990). When *Edwards* applies, a two-step analysis must be used: it must be determined (i) whether the defendant "initiated" the further conversation and, if so, (ii) whether he thereafter waived his right to silence and to counsel. *Ore. v. Bradshaw* (1983). The Court in *Bradshaw* was divided as to just what "initiation" means (e.g., whether defendant's inquiry of "what is going to happen to me now?" should suffice).

Uncertainties about whether *Edwards* applies occur when the defendant's actions or statements preceding or contemporaneous with the purported request for counsel make that request ambiguous or equivocal. Courts have dealt with such situations in various ways: requiring that all questioning cease notwithstanding the equivocal or ambiguous nature of the request; requiring a specified degree of clarity to trigger the right to counsel; or permitting only that interrogation designed to clarify the earlier statement. But then, in *Davis v. U.S.* (1994), the Court held, only with respect to a post-waiver setting, that *Edwards* would not be extended so as to "require law enforcement officers to cease questioning immediately upon the making of an ambiguous or equivocal reference to an attorney." The Court recognized its holding "might disadvantage some suspects who—because of fear, intimidation, lack of linguistic skills, or a variety of other reasons—will not clearly articulate their right to counsel although they actually want to have a lawyer present," but deemed that consideration outweighed by the fact that the "clarity and ease of application" of the bright-line *Edwards* rule otherwise "would be lost." *Davis*, which lower courts have applied as well to ambiguous references to the right to remain silent, does not affect the holding in *Smith v. Ill.* (1984) that a defendant's "post-request responses to further interrogation may not be used to cast retrospective doubt on the clarity of the initial request itself."

*Edwards* presents no bar to a police-initiated waiver of the *Miranda* right to counsel occurring subsequent to that defendant's assertion of his *Sixth Amendment* right to counsel at a court proceeding. Such invocation of the Sixth Amendment right (which is offense-specific) does not also constitute invocation of *Miranda* as to other, uncharged offenses, for a defendant "might be quite willing to speak to the police without counsel present concerning many matters, but not the matter under prosecution." *McNeil v. Wis.* (1991). On the other hand, *Edwards* does apply when the defendant has invoked his *Miranda* right to counsel even when the later interrogation concerns a wholly unrelated crime. This conclusion maintains *Edwards* as "a bright-line rule" without qualification or exceptions, and is grounded in the notion that a defendant's claim he does not want to submit to custodial interrogation without counsel is no more limited to a particular offense than a waiver of *Miranda* rights. *Ariz. v. Roberson* (1988).

# CHAPTER 5

# LINEUPS AND OTHER PRE-TRIAL IDENTIFICATION PROCEDURES

## § 5.1 THE PRIVILEGE AGAINST SELF–INCRIMINATION

### (a) The *Schmerber* case

In *Schmerber v. Cal.* (1966), the Court upheld the admission into evidence of a blood sample taken by a physician at police direction from a defendant over his objection after his arrest for drunken driving. The Court, in a 5–4 decision, rejected the defendant's contention that admission of the sample violated his Fifth Amendment privilege not to "be compelled in any criminal case to be a witness against himself." The majority reasoned that "the privilege protects an accused only from being compelled to testify against himself, or otherwise provide the State with evidence of a testimonial or communicative nature." As the Court later put it, the privilege only protects one from being compelled to express the "contents of his mind." *Doe v. U.S.* (1988), discussed in § 8.1(d).

In defining the scope of the privilege, the *Schmerber* majority noted that many identification procedures were not protected by the Fifth Amendment.

*Holt v. U.S.* (1910), holding that a defendant could be compelled to model a blouse, was cited as the "leading case," and it was observed that "both federal and state courts have usually held that it offers no protection against compulsion to submit to fingerprinting, photographing or measurements, to write or speak for identification, to appear in court, to stand, to assume a stance, to walk, or to make a particular gesture."

## (b) Application to pretrial identification

It is thus not surprising that the Court subsequently relied upon *Schmerber* in holding that several identification practices do not conflict with the privilege: requiring the defendant to appear in a lineup and to speak for identification, *U.S. v. Wade* (1967); or to provide handwriting exemplars, *Gilbert v. Cal.* (1967). In both cases the Court split 5–4 on this issue. The majority relied upon the *Schmerber* distinction between an accused's "communications" in whatever form, vocal or physical, and "compulsion which makes a suspect or accused the source of 'real or physical evidence.' " The dissenters argued that *Schmerber* was wrongly decided, in that the privilege is designed to bar the government from forcing a person to supply proof of his own crime, and that even assuming the correctness of *Schmerber* the instant cases were distinguishable because each defendant was required "actively to cooperate—to accuse himself by a volitional act." Other courts have followed the majority view (see § 8.1(d)) and have thus held the privilege inapplicable to such other identification procedures as finger-printing or examination by ultraviolet light.

### (c) Consequences of failure to cooperate

Although not protected by the Fifth Amendment, some identification procedures (such as speaking or writing for identification) require the active partic-ipation of the suspect. But, what if the suspect will not cooperate? One possibility, feared the dissenters in *Wade,* is that "an accused may be jailed—indefi-nitely—until he is willing to" cooperate. Indeed, some courts have utilized civil contempt and crimi-nal contempt as a means to coerce or punish the suspect who failed to comply with a court order to participate in some identification proceeding. An-other possibility is that the prosecution may be permitted to comment at trial on the lack of cooper-ation. Cf. *So. Dak. v. Neville* (1983), holding refusal to give a blood sample is admissible at a criminal trial, as the refusal "is not an act coerced by the officer." But comment on the defendant's refusal to speak for identification is improper if it was the direct result of a prior police warning of the right to remain silent, for then the silence is insolubly am-biguous.

### (d) Change in appearance

If a suspect drastically alters his appearance be-tween the time of the crime and of identification procedures, this is admissible at trial as an indica-tion of consciousness of guilt. Also, the identifica-tion procedure may be conducted in such a way as to simulate the defendant's prior appearance (e.g., by having him wear a false beard), but interference with the suspect's due process right to determine his personal appearance (e.g., by having him shave off a beard) requires a showing of substantial justification.

## § 5.2 THE RIGHT TO COUNSEL AND CONFRONTATION: LINEUPS

### (a) Procedures required

At least after the accused has been indicted, ruled the Court in *U.S. v. Wade* (1967) and *Gilbert v. Cal.* (1967), he should not be exhibited to witnesses in a lineup conducted for identification purposes without notice to and in the absence of his counsel. Rather, both the accused and his counsel must be notified of the impending lineup, and the lineup must not be conducted until counsel is present (expressly left open was the possibility that the presence of substitute counsel might suffice where notification and presence of the suspect's own counsel would result in prejudicial delay). In the absence of "legislative or other regulations * * * which eliminate the risks of abuse and unintentional suggestion at lineup proceedings," the Court emphasized in *Wade,* the above procedures are required by virtue of the defendant's constitutional right to confrontation and his right to counsel at a critical stage of the proceedings. (Apparently no court has yet held any set of regulations to be adequate.)

As explained by the Court, the right to counsel in this context is supportive of another right—here, the right to confrontation—in much the same way that the *Miranda* counsel requirement rests upon the privilege against self-incrimination. (But see *Kirby v. Ill.,* discussed in § 5.2(e).) Under past lineup practices, the defense was often unable "meaningfully to attack the credibility of the witness' courtroom identification" because of several factors which militate against developing fully the circumstances of a prior lineup identification by that witness: (a) other participants in the lineup are often police officers, or, if not, their names are rarely recorded or divulged at trial; (b) neither witnesses nor lineup participants are apt to be alert for or schooled in the detection of prejudicial conditions; (c) the suspect (often staring into bright lights) may not be in a position to observe prejudicial conditions, and, in any event, might not detect them because of his emotional tension; (d) even if the suspect observes abuse, he may nonetheless be reluctant to take the stand and open up the admission of prior convictions; and (e) even if he takes the stand, his version of what transpired at the lineup is unlikely to be accepted if it conflicts with police testimony. Moreover, the Court pointed out, the need to learn what occurred at the lineup is great; the risk of improper suggestion is substantial, and once the witness has picked out the accused in a lineup, he is unlikely to go back on his word in court.

The three dissenters to this aspect of *Wade* and *Gilbert* saw no need for the imposition of such a "broad prophylactic rule" in the absence of evidence that improper police practices at lineups were widespread. They also expressed concern that the delays required to comply with the procedures prescribed by the majority would make prompt and certain identification impossible.

Although there are cases to the contrary, the better view is that *Wade* and *Gilbert* apply at the moment of actual identification and not merely the moment of viewing, as it is important for counsel to be able to reconstruct the former at trial. The contrary position is bolstered to some extent by the *Ash* decision (see § 5.3(a)). *Wade* and *Gilbert* apply to a one-on-one identification procedure as well, even if conducted in the course of a judicial proceeding. *Moore v. Ill.* (1977).

### (b) Waiver or substitution of counsel

The Court in *Wade* indicated that there might be an "intelligent waiver" of counsel, in which case notice to and presence of an attorney would not be required. Although this may seem consistent with the waiver permitted in *Miranda* (see § 4.4(b)), some have questioned whether the right to counsel at the lineup should be subject to waiver. The argument is that while waiver of counsel under *Miranda* serves the legitimate objective of permitting the suspect to bear witness to the truth, no comparable value is served by waiver under *Wade*.

The *Wade* opinion does not dwell upon the question of what is required to show an effective waiver, although it seems likely that the approach in *Miranda* is to be followed here. This means the defendant must be advised that he has a right to counsel for this particular purpose and that counsel will be provided for him if he is indigent, and "a heavy burden" rests upon the government to show an express waiver following the warnings. Moreover, waiver of counsel for another purpose will not suffice, and thus a waiver of counsel following the *Miranda* warnings does not carry over to the lineup.

The Court in *Wade*, in response to the argument that a counsel requirement would "forestall prompt identifications," deliberately opted to "leave open the question whether the presence of substitute counsel might not suffice where notification and presence of the suspect's own counsel would result in prejudicial delay." Given the state's interest in a prompt lineup, it would seem that substitute counsel would suffice where he was sufficiently apprised of the circumstances so as to be able effectively to represent the defendant.

### (c) Consequences of violation

If the required lineup procedures are not followed, then testimony as to the fact of identification at the lineup is inadmissible at trial. "Only a *per se* exclusionary rule as to such testimony can be an effective sanction to assure that law enforcement authorities will respect the accused's constitutional right to the presence of his counsel at the critical lineup." If such testimony is admitted, the defendant is entitled to a new trial unless it is determined that the error was harmless beyond a reasonable doubt (see § 9.10). *Gilbert v. Cal.* (1967).

But, what of subsequent in-court identification by a witness who earlier identified the defendant at an improperly conducted lineup? This presents a "fruit of the poisonous tree" problem, and consistent with the general approach to that kind of issue (see § 6.6(a)), it must be determined "whether, granting establishment of the primary illegality, the evidence to which instant objection is made has been come at by exploitation of that illegality or instead by means sufficiently distinguishable to be purged of the primary taint." Thus, the government will be afforded the opportunity to establish by clear and convincing evidence that the in-court identifications were based upon observations of the suspect other than the lineup identification. Relevant factors are "the prior opportunity to observe the alleged criminal act, the existence of any discrepancy between any pre-lineup description and the defendant's actual description, any identification prior to lineup of another person, the identification by picture of the defendant prior to the lineup, failure to identify the defendant on a prior occasion, and the lapse of time between the alleged act and the lineup identification," in addition to "those facts which, despite the absence of counsel, are disclosed concerning the conduct of the lineup." *U.S. v. Wade* (1967).

Justice Black, dissenting in part in *Wade,* argued that this "tainted fruit" determination is "practically impossible," in that the witness will be unable "to draw a sharp line between a courtroom identification due exclusively to an earlier lineup and a courtroom identification due to memory not based on the lineup." The majority rejected his contention that therefore all in-court identifications should be admissible, noting that if this were the case then the state could easily circumvent the lineup requirements by resting upon the witnesses' courtroom identification and thus leave the defendant in the same predicament as before. However, some have taken note of the difficulty in making the "tainted fruit" determination in questioning whether the Court went far enough; they fear that trial judges, inevitably left with considerable discretion in making this decision, will readily find an "independent source" for in-court identifications and in that way free the police from the necessity of complying with the *Wade-Gilbert* formula. Several commentators, upon review of lower court decisions, suggest that experience has shown this to be the case.

18 U.S.C.A. § 3502, a part of the Omnibus Crime Control and Safe Streets Act of 1968, provides that the "testimony of a witness that he saw the accused commit * * * the crime" is admissible in a federal court. This appears to be a patently unconstitutional attempt to "repeal" *Wade.* Though the Court in *Wade* said the need for counsel could be removed by statutes "which eliminate the risks of abuse and

unintentional suggestion at lineup proceedings and the impediments to meaningful confrontation at trial," this statute hardly does that.

### (d) Role of counsel

What, exactly, is the role of defense counsel at the lineup? *Wade* stresses the need to protect the defendant's "right meaningfully to cross-examine the witnesses against him and to have effective assistance of counsel at the trial itself," which most clearly suggests that counsel should function as an observer at the lineup. On the basis of his observations, he would then be in a position at trial to decide whether it is tactically wise to bring out the lineup identification in order to cast doubt upon an in-court identification. And, if he decides to do so, he will better know what questions to ask the witness about the circumstances of the lineup. The observer-counsel may also have to become a witness at the trial, for the Court in *Wade* emphasized that the suspect, other participants in the lineup, and the witnesses at the lineup are unlikely to observe or recognize prejudicial circumstances. Rule 3.7 of the ABA Model Rules of Professional Conduct, however, provides that if a lawyer learns he will be required to be a witness for his client, except as to merely formal or uncontested matters, he should withdraw from the case unless doing so "would work substantial hardship on the client."

The majority in *Wade* implies that counsel might also take a more active role at the lineup; they say that "presence of counsel itself can often avert prejudice" and assist law enforcement "by preventing the infiltration of taint in the prosecution's identification evidence." The dissenters find in *Wade* "an implicit invitation to counsel to suggest rules for the lineup and to manage and produce it as best he can." Defense counsel obviously cannot compel the police to conduct the lineup in a certain way, although he might point out unfair features of the identification process and even suggest corrective measures. As a matter of tactics, however, counsel may prefer simply to allow the prejudicial practices so that he might bring them out in cross-examination. But if, as at least one court has suggested, such a tactic should be treated as a waiver of any suggestive procedure not objected to by counsel at the time of the lineup, counsel would be confronted with some very hard choices at a very early stage of the case. If that is to be the consequence, then the notion of defense counsel playing an active role at the identification proceeding is unsound. (The situation is different as to a later in-court identification, and thus in *Moore v. Ill.* (1977), the Court quite correctly said that if counsel had been present at the preliminary hearing he could have acted in such a way as to avoid "some or all of this suggestiveness.")

### (e) Pre-indictment identifications

Because both *Wade* and *Gilbert* involved lineups held after indictment and appointment of counsel, lower courts were in disagreement as to whether counsel was required at any pre-indictment identifications. In *Kirby v. Ill.* (1972), the Court held that the *Wade-Gilbert* rule applies only to lineups occurring "at or after the initiation of adversary judicial criminal proceedings—whether by way of formal charge, preliminary hearing, indictment, information, or arraignment." The rationale was that the constitutional right to counsel has traditionally been so limited, and with good reason, in that only after such initiation is a defendant "faced with the prosecutorial forces of organized society, and immersed in the intricacies of substantive and procedural criminal law." This conclusion, the three dissenters cogently pointed out, is based upon a misreading of *Wade* and *Gilbert* as purely right to counsel cases, rather than cases concerned with protecting the right to confrontation at trial, and ignores the fact that the practices condemned in those cases may just as easily occur during a pre-indictment lineup.

Except for the language quoted above, *Kirby* does not explore what it takes to "initiate" adversary judicial criminal proceedings, but that language was later relied upon in holding that a preliminary hearing suffices. *Moore v. Ill.* (1977). It is generally agreed that a warrantless arrest is not sufficient, but the courts are not in agreement as to whether proceedings are initiated by issuance of an arrest warrant upon information and oath. At least where the warrant is not connected with a decision to charge and serves only purposes relating to arrest, it would seem that neither issuance nor execution of the warrant should be sufficient. Compare *Brew-*

*er v. Williams* (1977) (concluding that adversary judicial proceedings clearly had been initiated where a warrant had been issued and defendant had been arraigned on the warrant and committed to jail).

## § 5.3    THE RIGHT TO COUNSEL AND CONFRONTATION: OTHER IDEN- TIFICATION PROCEDURES

### (a) The use of pictures

Does it follow from *Wade* and *Gilbert* that an accused in custody has a right to have his counsel present while witnesses view still or motion pictures of him for purposes of identification? No, the Court concluded in *U.S. v. Ash* (1973). Throughout the expansion of the constitutional right to counsel to certain pretrial proceedings, said the majority, "the function of the lawyer has remained essentially the same as his function at trial," namely, to give the accused "aid in coping with legal problems or assistance in meeting his adversary." This being so, there is no such right at photo-identification, as unlike a lineup, there is no "trial-like confrontation" involving the "presence of the accused." Moreover, even if a broader view were taken of the right to counsel, it need not extend "to a portion of the prosecutor's trial-preparation interviews with witnesses," given "the equal ability of defense counsel to seek and interview witnesses himself." Stewart, J., concurring, while objecting to the majority's distinction of *Wade* as a situation where the lawyer is giving advice or assistance to the defendant at the lineup, concluded that the lawyer's role "as an observer" need not be extended to photo identification, where "there are few possibilities for unfair suggestiveness."

The three dissenters in *Ash* objected that the risk of "impermissible suggestiveness" which led to *Wade* and *Gilbert* was equally present in the case of identification by pictures, and that because the defendant is not personally present for such identification there is less "likelihood that irregularities in the procedure will ever come to light" if counsel has not observed the identification. As for the majority's characterization of the right to counsel, the dissenters argued that historically the right to counsel attached at certain pretrial procedures not because of the assistance the attorney could immediately render at that time, but rather "to protect the fairness of the trial itself."

## (b) Scientific methods

In *Wade,* the government argued that a lineup is no different from other identification procedures, such as taking and analyzing "the accused's fingerprints, blood sample, clothing, hair, and the like," apparently in an attempt to bring the instant case within the ruling of *Schmerber v. Cal.* (1966). The majority in *Schmerber* held that the taking of a blood sample was not covered by the Fifth Amendment, and thus found "no issue of counsel's ability to assist petitioner in respect of any rights he did possess." The Court in *Wade* distinguished the other procedures listed by the government on the

ground that they do not present the risks attendant
lineups: "Knowledge of the techniques of science
and technology is sufficiently available, and the
variables in techniques few enough, that the accused has the opportunity for a meaningful confrontation of the Government's case at trial through the
ordinary processes of cross-examination of the Government's expert witnesses and the presentation of
the evidence of his own experts." On this basis, the
Court held in *Gilbert* that the taking of handwriting
exemplars is not a critical stage entitling the suspect to the assistance of counsel. Thus, while the
suspect might benefit from counsel's advice as to
whether to give the exemplars or refuse and suffer
the consequences (see § 5.1(c)), this does not involve a constitutional right to which the right to
counsel might be linked.

## § 5.4    DUE PROCESS: "THE TOTALITY OF THE CIRCUMSTANCES"

### (a) Generally

An identification made under circumstances in
which counsel is not required, or perhaps even one
made in the presence of counsel, might be challenged on yet another ground. A "recognized
ground of attack upon a conviction independent of
any right to counsel claim" is that the defendant's
identification was "so unnecessarily suggestive and
conducive to irreparable mistaken identification
that he was denied due process of law." *Stovall v.
Denno* (1967). (The later congressional declaration

that testimony of an identification witness "shall be admissible in evidence in a criminal prosecution," 18 U.S.C.A. § 3502, cannot "repeal" a defendant's right under *Stovall* not to be convicted on the basis of an identification so unreliable as to violate due process.)

If an identification was "suggestive" (e.g., a one-on-one confrontation) and also "unnecessarily" so (i.e., there was no good reason for foregoing more reliable procedures), that alone does not require the exclusion of evidence. The Court declined to hold otherwise as to an identification which predated the *Stovall* decision. *Neil v. Biggers* (1972). If there has been suggestiveness, a subsequent in-court identification is inadmissible only if there is "a very substantial likelihood of irreparable misidentification," and "with the deletion of 'irreparable', [that test] * * * serves equally well as a standard for the admissibility of testimony concerning the out-of-court identification itself." *Neil v. Biggers,* supra. The Court later refused to apply a per se rule to post-*Stovall* identifications, and instead adhered to the "totality of the circumstances" test. *Manson v. Brathwaite* (1977). Under *Manson,* the factors to be considered in evaluating the likelihood of misidentification "include the opportunity of the witness to view the criminal at the time of the crime, the witness' degree of attention, the accuracy of his prior description of the criminal, the level of certainty demonstrated at the confrontation, and the time between the crime and the confrontation."

In the *Wade-Gilbert* context, these same factors bear on the question of whether an in-court identification is a "fruit of the poisonous tree," as to which the government has the burden of proof (see § 5.2(c)). But in the context of the *Stovall* rule, these factors bear directly upon the question of whether there has been a violation of due process, which suggests the burden is on the defendant. But courts have been inclined to place the burden on the government here as well; the asserted justification is that the government gave rise to the issue by using unfair procedures.

### (b)  Lineups

An apt illustration of a due process violation in a lineup identification is provided by *Foster v. Cal.* (1969). The Court concluded it was "all but inevitable" that the victim of a robbery would identify defendant "whether or not he was in fact" the robber, as: (1) defendant was placed in a lineup with two other men who were half a foot shorter; (2) only he wore a jacket similar to that worn by the robber; (3) when this did not lead to positive identification, the police permitted a one-to-one confrontation; and (4) because the witness' identification was still tentative, some days later another lineup was arranged, but defendant was the only person in this lineup who had also appeared in the first lineup.

### (c)  The use of pictures

In *Simmons v. U.S.* (1968), FBI agents identified a bank robbery suspect on the basis of his use of a car which was similar to that used in the robbery. From a relative of the suspect they obtained six snapshots, mostly group pictures, in which the suspect appeared, from which five bank employees separately identified the suspect the day after the robbery. Balancing the need against the risks, the Court concluded that this procedure was not "unnecessarily suggestive." The use of the photos was justified, in that a serious felony had occurred, the perpetrators were still at large, inconclusive clues led to the suspect, and it was important for the FBI swiftly to determine whether they were on the right track so that they could properly deploy their forces. Also, there was little risk of misidentification, as the employees had all gotten a good look at the robber, they examined the pictures while their memories were still fresh, each witness examined the pictures separately, and the FBI agents disclosed nothing about the progress of the investigation or suggesting which persons in the pictures were under suspicion.

### (d) One-man showups

In contrast to a properly conducted lineup, the display of a single suspect to a witness carries with it a considerable risk of misidentification: the witness may well conclude that the individual displayed must be the offender, for otherwise he would not be in custody and singly displayed. In *Stovall v. Denno* (1967), the Court noted that "the practice of showing suspects singly to persons for the purpose of identification, and not as part of a lineup, has been widely condemned," but held that under the unique circumstances of the case the one-man showup was justified. The defendant was arrested because keys found at the scene of the murder were traced to him. The wife of the murder victim, who herself had been repeatedly stabbed while defending her husband, was hospitalized for major surgery to save her life. Two days after the crime, defendant was brought to her hospital room, where she identified him after he spoke a few words. Defendant was handcuffed to one of the five police officers who were present with two members of the prosecutor's staff, and he was the only black in the room. The Court concluded that "an immediate hospital confrontation was imperative," as no one knew how long the witness might live, she could not visit the jail, and she was the only person who could have exonerated the defendant.

While *Stovall* thus rests upon a rather unique showing of need for the one-man showup—the fact that the sole eye witness was near death—there may be other reasons why this less reliable procedure is sometimes "imperative." For example, if *Stovall* is considered with *Simmons,* where the recognized need was for the police "swiftly to determine whether they were on the right track," it might be said that an on-the-scene one-man showup of a suspect who has just been arrested or detained for investigation does not violate due process. This is the conclusion that has been reached by the lower courts, who have also stressed the increased reliability of identifications made promptly after the event. Similarly, some courts have upheld a one-man showup where it was the suspect who was seriously injured. But failure to use a lineup is not excused merely because it would be inconvenient or difficult to assemble a group of persons physically comparable to the suspect. *Neil v. Biggers* (1972).

## (e) In-court identifications

A one-on-one confrontation in court would seem even more suggestive, for the witness is given even a stronger impression that the authorities are satisfied they have the right man. As stated in *Moore v. Ill.* (1977), it "is difficult to imagine a more suggestive manner in which to present a suspect to a witness for their critical first confrontation." The Court in *Moore* stated defense counsel might have avoided such suggestiveness by seeking to have the court proceeding postponed until a lineup was conducted or by asking that the defendant be allowed to be seated in the audience before the identifying witness was called. But the lower courts often say that whether to require such safeguards is a matter left to the trial judge's discretion. Defense counsel's resort to self-help, such as by placing a "decoy" at his side in lieu of the defendant, has been viewed as unethical.

# CHAPTER 6

# THE EXCLUSIONARY RULES AND THEIR APPLICATION

## § 6.1 INTRODUCTION

A violation of the constitutional restraints discussed in chapters 2–5 can lead to a tort suit, the issuance of an injunction, or the imposition of administrative sanctions. But within the criminal justice process itself, such violations have their most direct impact in the exclusion of evidence. Indeed, the very issue of whether a particular police practice does constitute a violation is almost invariably raised by a defense motion challenging the prosecution's attempt to introduce at trial evidence obtained through that police practice. The constitutionality of a search will be raised by a motion seeking suppression of evidence obtained in that search. The constitutionality of an arrest ordinarily will be presented by a motion seeking suppression of evidence obtained through a search of the person or a place incident to that arrest. The legality of electronic surveillance (including, but not limited to, its constitutionality) will be raised by a motion under § 2515 of Title III of the Crime Control Act, which states that no illegally intercepted communication and "no evidence derived therefrom may be received in evidence in any trial, hearing, or other proceeding." The constitutionality of a police interrogation will be challenged via a motion to exclude from evidence statements of the accused that were the fruits of that interrogation. Claims that an identification procedure violated constitutional limits will be presented via a motion to exclude identification evidence obtained through that procedure.

In the context of the Fourth Amendment, the prohibition against admission at trial of unconstitutionally obtained evidence has come to be known as the "exclusionary rule." The barring of evidence under the other constitutional limitations discussed in chapters 2–5 is less often described as resting on an "exclusionary rule," but references to a Sixth Amendment, due process, or even a self-incrimination "exclusionary rule" are found in occasional judicial opinions. Several common issues are presented in the exclusion of evidence under each of the different constitutional guarantees, and that explains why we discuss the different exclusionary requirements in the same chapter. It should be kept in mind, however, that each guarantee provides a separate grounding for its exclusionary requirement, which may give that requirement a somewhat different scope than the exclusionary requirements of the other guarantees. Thus, the title of this chapter refers in the plural to the "exclusionary rules" rather than to the more common singular phrasing of "exclusionary rule."

## § 6.2  FIFTH AMENDMENT, SIXTH AMENDMENT, AND DUE PROCESS EXCLUSION

### (a)  Fifth Amendment exclusion

As the Supreme Court has noted in several contexts, but most notably in its rulings sustaining immunity grants (§ 8.2(e)), the crux of a violation of the Fifth Amendment's self-incrimination clause lies in the prosecution's use in a criminal trial of a statement obtained from the defendant through governmental compulsion. Thus, as Justice Black noted in his separate opinion in *Coolidge v. N.H.* (1971), "the Fifth Amendment in and of itself directly and explicitly commands its own exclusionary rule." If the statement of the defendant was obtained through methods that constitute "compulsion" under the self-incrimination clause, the trial court must bar admission of that statement to prevent a violation of the Fifth Amendment. See also § 8.1(e).

*Miranda*'s requirement of exclusion of statements obtained through custodial interrogation that failed to follow the *Miranda* rules (see § 4.4(b)) apparently also is based upon the Fifth Amendment's command of absolute exclusion. *Dickerson v. U.S.* (2000). However, the "*Miranda* exclusionary rule" is said to "sweep more broadly than the Fifth Amendment itself," triggering exclusion of defendant's statements "even in the absence of a Fifth Amendment violation" on the basis of a "prophylactic," "irrebuttable presumption" of compulsion.

*Ore. v. Elstad* (1985). As will be seen, this distinction has lead to differences in the applicable scope of *Miranda*'s exclusionary rule and the core Fifth Amendment exclusionary rule. See §§ 1.3(e), 6.6(g), 6.7(b), 8.1(e).

### (b) Sixth Amendment exclusion

An accused is entitled to the assistance of counsel at all critical stages of criminal process. See § 7.1(e). If the state obtains evidence at such a critical stage without counsel being present, and without a waiver of counsel, that evidence will not be admitted at trial. Thus, where an accused is subjected to a lineup without the Sixth Amendment protection required under *Wade* (§ 5.2), evidence of his identification at that lineup is inadmissible. So too, where the police deliberately elicit a statement from an accused without his waiver of counsel, that statement must be excluded under *Massiah* and its progeny (§ 4.3). *White v. Md.* (1963) similarly barred prosecution evidence of the defendant having entered a non-binding guilty plea at his first appearance because he had not received (or waived) the assistance of counsel at that proceeding. The Court has not offered any extensive explanation of why the Sixth Amendment requires a remedy of excluding evidence in such cases, but its opinions have suggested two quite different rationales for the Sixth Amendment's exclusionary rule.

Initially, exclusion under the Sixth Amendment, akin to exclusion under the Fifth Amendment, may rest on the premise that the crux of the Sixth

Amendment violation lies in the admission at trial of the evidence obtained without affording the accused the assistance of counsel. The Court has noted in other contexts that a Sixth Amendment violation is not present unless the action alleged to have constituted the violation, whether it be state interference with the lawyer-client relationship or ineffective assistance by counsel, has resulted in prejudice to the defendant at trial. See § 7.7(c). Applying this analysis to cases where the state has obtained evidence by undercutting the lawyer-client relationship, the Sixth Amendment violation comes into play only with the state's use of that evidence. *Massiah*, for example, described the violation there as the introduction of the statement after it had been deliberately elicited. Under this view, the evidence must be excluded to prevent the critical element of the violation (i.e., the trial prejudice) from occurring. See also § 6.7(c) (noting the rationale of the dissent in *Mich. v. Harvey*). But consider *Me. v. Moulton* (1985) (suggesting the *Massiah* violation occurs with elicitation of the statement in itself).

The Court's opinions at times also have suggested that exclusion under the Sixth Amendment is based on a deterrence rationale similar to that offered in support of the Fourth Amendment's exclusionary rule. Thus, *Gilbert v. Cal.* (1967) held that violation of the *Wade* requirements would result in automatic exclusion of the subsequent lineup identification because, though the lineup without counsel may have been fairly conducted and a counsel who was not present may nonetheless be able to mount an adequate challenge at trial to an unfair identification, "only a per se exclusionary rule" could constitute "an effective sanction to assure that law enforcement authorities will respect the accused's constitutional right to the presence of his counsel at the critical lineup." Similarly, *Nix v. Williams* (1984), in dealing with the admissibility of secondary evidence discovered through a Sixth Amendment violation, justified applying an inevitable discovery exception (see § 6.6(c)) by reference to the traditional "deterrence rationale" of "the exclusionary rule." The defendant there contended that the "Sixth Amendment exclusionary rule" played a role different than the "Fourth Amendment exclusionary rule" and therefore did not permit the approach adopted in Fourth Amendment cases (see § 6.3(d)) of balancing the incremental deterrence provided by expanding exclusion against the cost of keeping from the factfinder reliable and relevant evidence. However, at least as to the secondary evidence issue considered in *Nix v. Williams,* the Court did not find that contention persuasive, and looked to that balancing approach.

### (c) Due process exclusion

Where the Court holds a particular police practice to violate due process because it presents a grave potential for producing untrustworthy evidence, exclusion of that evidence follows logically from the grounding of the violation. Thus, the Court has held that identification evidence must be excluded where it is the product of identification procedures so suggestive as to violate due process. See § 5.4. Indeed, in this situation, it presumably is the use of the evidence rather than the identification procedure itself that violates due process. In contrast, in the case of prohibited interrogation techniques which are likely to produce an untrustworthy confession (e.g., police brutality), the offensive police practice presumably violates due process in itself. Nonetheless, exclusion of the confession here too is mandated, apart from any attempt to remedy the deprivation of personal dignity inflicted by the prohibited police practice, by the danger to a fair trial posed by prosecution use of the potentially unreliable confession.

While the condemnation of police interrogation practices under the "voluntariness" standard of due process often rests at least in part on the potential for producing untrustworthy confessions, not all practices held to violate that standard have that characteristic. Police interrogation practices have been held to be "so offensive to a civilized system that they must be condemned," *Miller v. Fenton* (1985), even though the evidence produced is likely to be most reliable. See § 4.2(a). Indeed, in *Rochin v. Cal.* (1952), this concept was applied outside the area of "involuntary" confessions to require exclusion of evidence extracted from the body of a suspect. Decided at a time when the Fourth Amendment exclusionary rule did not apply to the states (see § 6.3(a)), *Rochin* held that the use of stomach pumping to obtain two morphine tablets the suspect had swallowed so "shock[ed] the conscience" of a "civilized society" as to violate due process and bar the state's use of those tablets in evidence. Though *Rochin* involved a search and today would be decided under the Fourth Amendment, *Rochin*'s "shock the conscience" standard (and its accompanying exclusionary rule) remain applicable to police practices that do not fall within the Fourth Amendment. See *Co. of Sacramento v. Lewis* (1998) (since high-speed chase did not constitute a seizure, Fourth Amendment did not apply; practice was subject to review under *Rochin* standard, but police recklessness did not violate that standard).

*Rochin* and several other due process rulings clearly have carried the exclusionary remedy beyond the scope of a "reliability analysis." Insofar as such due process rulings have relied on the principle that "ours is an accusatorial and not an inquisitorial system," as noted in several involuntary confession cases, e.g., *Rogers v. Richmond* (1961), the due process exclusionary remedy may be explained in much the same manner as exclusion under the self-incrimination privilege. However, due process violations leading to exclusion also often have been characterized as offensive because of the character of the police practice itself, rather than the prosecution's use of evidence forced from the accused. Here, the due process exclusionary rule apparently is designed largely to deter police from engaging in such offensive conduct, as the Supreme Court recognized in *Colo. v. Connelly* (§ 4.2(a)).

## § 6.3   FOURTH AMENDMENT EXCLUSION

### (a) From *Weeks* to *Mapp*

The Fourth Amendment exclusionary rule dates back to a period marked generally by relatively narrow readings of the Fourth Amendment, but it remains today, even after the adoption of a far more expansive view of the Amendment. The 1914 decision in *Weeks v. U.S.* established the exclusionary rule as the governing standard for federal courts. *Weeks* held that evidence obtained by federal officials in violation of the Fourth Amendment would be barred from a federal prosecution. To rule otherwise, the Court noted, would be "to affirm by judicial decision a manifest neglect if not an open defiance of the prohibitions of the Constitution." Six years later, in *Silverthorne Lumber Co. v. U.S.* (1920), Justice Holmes added that without the remedy of exclusion, the Fourth Amendment would be reduced to "a form of words." Despite this strong language, the *Weeks* rule reflected at the time a distinctly minority position in the interpretation of fundamental law governing searches and seizures. A substantial majority of state courts, interpreting state constitutional provisions identical to the Fourth Amendment, refused to adopt an exclusionary rule. The most widely cited criticism of the "federal position," that by Justice Cardozo (then a state court judge), characterized *Weeks* as permitting the "criminal * * * to go free because the constable has blundered."

Since the Fourth Amendment did not apply to the states, the state courts could reject the exclusionary rule so long as their admission of illegally seized evidence did not violate due process under the then prevailing "fundamental rights" interpretation of the Fourth Amendment. See § 1.2(b). Although the Court was moving at the time toward a broader reading of the fundamental rights concept, and although it acknowledged that Fourteenth Amendment due process encompassed the "security of one's privacy which is at the core of the Fourth Amendment," *Wolf v. Colo.* (1949) held that the Fourteenth Amendment did not require states to exclude evidence obtained through an unconstitutional search. The *Wolf* opinion noted that the *Weeks* exclusionary rule was "not derived from the explicit requirements of the Fourth Amendment," was not followed in "most of the English-speaking world," and had been expressly rejected in 30 states. In 1961, with the Court moving toward the adoption of the selective incorporation doctrine (see § 1.2(d)), *Wolf* was overruled in *Mapp v. Ohio* (1961). A case marked like *Wolf* itself with sharp dissents, *Mapp* held that "all evidence obtained by searches and seizures in violation of the Constitution is, by that same authority, inadmissible in a state court."

Justice Clark's opinion for the Court in *Mapp* contained an extensive discussion of the justifications for requiring exclusion of unconstitutionally seized evidence even though that evidence was likely to be reliable and relevant to proof of guilt. Prior to *Mapp,* Supreme Court opinions had suggested as many as five different justifications for the *Weeks* rule, and each of these found at least oblique support somewhere in the *Mapp* opinion. The five justifications argued for exclusion on the basis of: (1) the implications of the Fifth Amendment; (2) the need to prevent a continued violation of the individual's privacy through the introduction of the evidence; (3) the natural implications of the law of remedies; (4) the imperative of judicial integrity; and (5) the need to deter future violations. Since *Mapp,* the first three of those justifications have been flatly rejected by the Court, and the fourth has been given a clearly subordinate status. The fifth, the deterrence rationale, has emerged as the crucial justification, the one that controls the scope of the exclusionary rule.

### (b) Rejected theories

In *Boyd v. U.S.* (1886), a pre-*Weeks* ruling, the Court held that the forced disclosure of papers through a court order violated the Fourth Amendment and that those papers therefore could not be used by the government as incriminatory evidence. The Court reached this result through a linking of the Fourth and Fifth Amendments, noting that it had "been unable to perceive that the seizure of a man's private books and papers to be used in evidence against him is substantially different from compelling him to be a witness against himself." The extension of this rationale to all forms of searches was questionable from the outset; searches generally result in the seizure of physical evidence, rather than documents, and the Fifth Amendment traditionally has been limited to compelled production of evidence of a "testimonial or communicative nature." See § 5.1(a). While the *Mapp* opinion did discuss *Boyd* and did at one point draw an analogy between the exclusion of unconstitutionally seized evidence and the exclusion of coerced confessions, it focused on exclusion as a remedy required under the Fourth Amendment standing alone. Subsequently, in *Andresen v. Md.* (1976), the Court rejected the possible application of the Fifth Amendment even as to a search for documents. It reasoned that the self-incrimination clause protects only against compelling the individual to himself produce the documents, as occurs with a subpoena (see § 8.3(a)-(b)), but not with a governmental search and seizure. See § 2.2(g).

Language in *Weeks* and other early exclusionary rule cases could be read to suggest that the admission into evidence of unconstitutionally seized items in itself constituted a violation of the Fourth Amendment. The underlying theory, developed more by commentators than judicial opinions, was that the admission of such evidence constitutes a further invasion of privacy and thereby exacerbates the Fourth Amendment violation. Exclusion under this theory, as exclusion under the Fifth Amendment, is designed to prevent the basic violation that would occur with the act of introducing the evidence. The Supreme Court found no need to consider the validity of this theory, apart from the other justifications for the exclusionary rule, until the theory was presented in a rather unusual context in *U.S. v. Calandra* (1974). There, a grand jury witness argued that he could not be asked questions based on information obtained through an unconstitutional police search because this further invasion of his privacy constituted a "distinct violation of his Fourth Amendment rights." Rejecting this contention, the Court reasoned that "the wrong condemned" by the Fourth Amendment, the "unreasonable governmental intrusion into the privacy of one's person, house, papers, or effects," was "fully accomplished by the original search without probable cause." Therefore, the questions based on the illegally obtained evidence "work[ed] no new Fourth Amendment wrong." What was at stake here was simply "the derivative use of the product of a past unlawful search," presenting "a question, not of rights, but of remedies."

Several of the earlier Supreme Court opinions also lent support to the view that the exclusion of evidence is a remedy inherent in the Fourth Amendment. Justice Holmes, for example, noted that "the essence of a provision forbidding the acquisition of evidence in a certain way" is that "evidence so acquired shall not be used." *Silverthorne Lumber Co. v. U.S.* (1920). The theory here is that concomitant to any prohibition is the requirement that the judiciary respond to a violation of that prohibition by providing such relief as will cure the violation, by restoring the status quo ante, if that is possible. In the case of an unconstitutional search and seizure, the exclusionary rule was seen as providing such relief, placing both the defendant and the government in the positions that they would have occupied had there not been an unconstitutional search and seizure. *Wolf v. Colo.* (1949), however, clearly rejected this view of the exclusionary remedy, and while *Wolf* itself was later overruled, that part of its analysis continues to have majority support.

*Wolf* viewed the invasion of privacy as the crux of the Fourth Amendment violation, and the exclusion of the seized evidence, as it noted, does not restore that privacy. Indeed, exclusion is not even an available remedy for the victim of an unconstitutional search which produced no incriminating evidence. Moreover, even as to the unlawfully seized evidence, the exclusionary rule falls short of restoring the victim to the status quo ante in some instances (e.g., illegally seized contraband need not also be returned to the search victim) and gives even greater protection in others (e.g., where exclusion is required because the government lacked a warrant, the government cannot now obtain the warrant based on the probable cause it always had and simply reseize and use the evidence). Thus, *Wolf* viewed exclusion as a less than perfect remedy, no more the natural or inherent remedy of the Fourth Amendment than any of the other remedies commonly provided (e.g., the tort remedy). Although *Mapp* overruled *Wolf,* and extolled the virtues of the exclusionary rule remedy, it fell short of describing exclusion as a remedy that cured the constitutional violation. Later cases, noting the limitations of the exclusionary rule, have more clearly characterized it as something other than such a natural remedy. Thus, the Court has noted that the exclusionary rule is "neither intended nor able to cure the invasion of the defendant's rights which he has already suffered." *U.S. v. Leon* (1984). It is "a judicially-created remedy designed to safeguard Fourth Amendment rights generally through its deterrent effect, rather than a personal constitutional right of the party aggrieved." *U.S. v. Calandra* (1974).

### (c) The "imperative of judicial integrity"

The primary justification for the exclusionary rule offered in *Weeks* was the need to avoid judicial affirmance of the unconstitutional actions of the police. This rationale was later characterized as resting upon the "imperative of judicial integrity," the need that courts not become "accomplices in the willful disobedience of a Constitution they are sworn to uphold." *Elkins v. U.S.* (1960). This concern relates not only to the responsibilities of the judiciary but also to maintaining public confidence in the willingness of government to abide by "the charter of its own existence." *Mapp v. Ohio* (1961). Excluding illegally seized evidence "assure[s] the people—all potential victims of unlawful government conduct—that the government [will] not profit from its lawless behavior, thus minimizing the risk of seriously undermining popular trust in government." *U.S. v. Calandra* (1974) (Brennan J., dis.)

The judicial integrity rationale was cited as one of the primary underpinnings of the exclusionary rule in *Mapp,* but subsequent majority opinions gave it considerably less weight. In *Stone v. Powell* (1976), the Court majority contended that various aspects of the law governing the exclusionary rule "demonstrate the limited role of this [judicial integrity] justification in the determination whether to apply the rule in a particular context." The Court noted that the judicial integrity rationale was inconsistent with the restriction of exclusion to cases in which a timely objection was made by a party having standing to object to the unconstitutional search (§ 6.8), with the inapplicability of the rule to grand jury proceedings (§ 6.5(b)), with the permissible use of illegally seized evidence for impeachment (§ 6.7), and with the rule of *Frisbie v. Collins* (1952) (holding that even the most egregiously unconstitutional arrest of the defendant does not bar retaining jurisdiction over the person so that he can be tried on a properly founded charge). Subsequently, *U.S. v. Leon* (1984) concluded that what is required of the exclusionary remedy to serve the judicial integrity rationale "is essentially the same as the inquiry into whether exclusion would serve a deterrent purpose."

### (d) The deterrence rationale

Ever since *Wolf,* the deterrence rationale for the exclusionary rule has been on the ascendancy. That rationale was set forth quite succinctly in *Elkins v. U.S.* (1960): "[The exclusionary rule's] purpose is to deter—to compel respect for the constitutional guarantee in the only effectively available way—by removing the incentive to disregard it." The *Wolf* opinion looked primarily to the deterrence rationale in holding that the exclusionary rule was not applicable to the states under a fundamental rights interpretation of the Fourteenth Amendment. *Mapp* rejected *Wolf's* factual premise that other remedies (e.g., tort actions) served as an effective deterrent, but *Mapp* also stressed other justifications for the exclusionary rule, particularly the "imperative of judicial integrity." Subsequent opinions, however, characterized the deterrence rationale as the critical grounding for requiring exclusion of evidence seized in violation of the Fourth Amendment. In *U.S. v. Janis* (1976), the Court stated that "the 'prime purpose' of the [exclusionary] rule, if not the sole one, 'is to deter unlawful police conduct.' " *U.S. v. Calandra* (1974) characterized the exclusionary rule as a "judicially-created remedy designed to safeguard Fourth Amendment rights generally through its deterrent effect, rather than a personal right of the party aggrieved." This characterization has been repeated by the Court majority in almost every subsequent major discussion of the exclusionary rule. See e.g., *U.S. v. Leon* (1984).

Reliance upon the deterrence rationale as the primary grounding for the exclusionary rule has had its greatest impact in the Court's determination of the scope of the rule. Since the exclusionary remedy under this rationale is "calculated to prevent, not to repair," *Elkins,* exclusion need not

follow automatically from the establishment of a
Fourth Amendment violation. "As with any remedial device, the application of the rule * * * [will be]
restricted to those areas where its remedial objectives are thought most officiously served." *Calandra.* Thus, where the particular setting of a limited
class of illegal searches suggests that exclusion
would have no deterrent impact, the Court has held
the remedy not to apply. See § 6.4. So too, when
extension of the remedy to new proceedings or
different aspects of the criminal trial would have
some deterrent impact, but that deterrence will
only add marginally to the basic deterrence that
stems from excluding evidence from the prosecution's case-in-chief, the Court will weigh the benefits of that additional deterrence against the costs of
further exclusion. See e.g., § 6.5.

While willing to reassess the potential for deterrence in some settings, and to apply a cost/benefit
analysis as to exclusion beyond the prosecution's
case-in-chief, the Court has not been willing to
reopen its basic assumption that exclusion from
that case-in-chief is necessary to deter most unconstitutional searches. Empirical studies, the Court
has noted, are too frequently flawed to furnish a
conclusive answer as to whether the exclusionary
remedy is in fact an effective deterrent. *U.S. v.
Janis* (1976). Moreover, the critical question is not
whether there exists "specific deterrence" as to a
particular case or particular police department.
"Over the long term," the Court has noted, "this
demonstration [through exclusion] that our society

attaches serious consequences to violation of constitutional rights is thought to encourage those who formulate law enforcement policies, and the officers who implement them, to incorporate Fourth Amendment ideals into their value system." *Stone v. Powell* (1976).

### (e) Deterrence outweighed by costs

Relying upon the notion, as stated in *Scott* (§ 3.5(c)), that the exclusionary rule is applicable only "where its deterrence benefits outweigh its 'substantial social costs,' " *Hudson v. Mich.* (2006) held the exclusionary rule inapplicable to evidence obtained in execution of a search warrant where the violation was a failure to comply with the "knock-and-announce" doctrine. The stated "costs," (i) "a constant flood" of suppression motions claiming violation of the doctrine, which could not be "readily determined" because of the "difficult" issues of whether the police waited long enough or had a justification for not waiting, and (ii) "police officers' refraining from timely entry after knocking and announcing," "producing preventable violence against officers in some cases, and the destruction of evidence in many others," were deemed to outweigh "the deterrence benefits," said to be minimal because (iii) there was no incentive to violate the rule, since violation would not likely produce "incriminating evidence that could not otherwise be obtained," and (iv) there would be deterrence without suppression because of such post-*Mapp* developments as the "slow but steady expansion" of the civil-rights action remedy, for which "Congress has authorized attorney's fees," and "increasing professionalism of police forces, including a new emphasis on internal police discipline." The four dissenters objected that the stated costs were "those that typically accompany *any* use of the Fourth Amendment's exclusionary principle," and that remedies "which the Court found inadequate in *Mapp*" were still insufficient—so that the majority's position "is an argument against the Fourth Amendment's exclusionary principle itself."

## § 6.4   THE "GOOD FAITH" EXCEPTION

### (a) An exclusively Fourth Amendment doctrine

Justice White, dissenting in *Stone v. Powell* (1976), expressed the view that the Fourth Amendment exclusionary rule "should be substantially modified so as to prevent its application in those many circumstances where the evidence at issue was seized by an officer acting in the good-faith belief that his conduct comported with existing law and having reasonable grounds for this belief." There was no justification for keeping relevant and reliable evidence from the factfinder under such circumstances, Justice White argued, for where there is good faith and reasonable reliance by the police, "the exclusion can have no deterrent effect."

Justice White's proposal, based as it was on a deterrence rationale, would have no bearing on exclusionary rules having other groundings. Certainly, the presence of good faith and reasonable belief in legality could not justify allowing into evidence a statement obtained through what a court later deems to be "compulsion" under the Fifth Amendment. Nor would good faith and reasonable reliance justify admission of the fruits of a lineup so inherently suggestive as to violate due process.

There was a single attempt to develop a good faith exception as to a Sixth Amendment exclusionary rule, which arguably finds support in a deterrence rationale (§ 6.2(b)), but it drew little support. Chief Justice Burger, dissenting in *Brewer v. Williams* (§ 4.3(d)), argued for a form of good faith exception in that case (contending that the officer could not have anticipated the extension of *Massiah* to his "Christian burial speech"), but the majority did not even speak to that possibility. As for exclusion pursuant to the voluntariness test of due process (see § 6.3(b)), police practices rejected due to their offensiveness are by their very nature not good candidates for claiming police good faith along the lines suggested by Justice White. Thus, adoption of any sort of good faith exception apart from the Fourth Amendment context discussed by Justice White appears unlikely. As for the Fourth Amendment, the Court majority has so far adopted limited versions of Justice White's approach for three special situations.

### (b) Police reliance upon a warrant

In *U.S. v. Leon* (1984), the Supreme Court, with Justice White writing for the majority, held that "the Fourth Amendment exclusionary rule should be modified so as not to bar the use in the prosecution's case-in-chief of evidence obtained by officers acting in reasonable reliance on a search warrant issued by a detached and neutral magistrate but ultimately found to be unsupported by probable cause." Because the search warrant affidavit in *Leon* "provided evidence sufficient to create disagreement among thoughtful and competent judges as to the existence of probable cause," the Court concluded that the "officers' reliance on the magistrate's determination of probable cause was objectively reasonable, and application of the extreme sanction of exclusion * * * [was therefore] inappropriate." The Court added in this regard that what was "objectively reasonable" would be determined in light of what a "reasonably well-trained officer would have known." Moreover, where a case falls within the good-faith exception, that should not preclude judicial "resolution of [the] particular Fourth Amendment question * * * [where needed] to guide future action by law enforcement officers and magistrates."

In evaluating the costs and benefits of requiring exclusion in the search-with-warrant case, the *Leon* majority noted initially that exclusion to deter magistrates is inappropriate, as (i) "the exclusionary rule is designed to deter police misconduct rather than to punish the errors of judges," (ii) "there exists no evidence suggesting that judges and magistrates are inclined to ignore or subvert the Fourth Amendment," and (iii) there is no basis "for believing that exclusion of evidence seized pursuant to a warrant will have a significant deterrent effect on the issuing judge or magistrate." As to the police, in a with-warrant case, exclusion ordinarily also is inappropriate, for usually, with the officer justifiably relying upon the prior judgment of the magistrate, "there is no police illegality and thus nothing to deter." Accordingly, "the marginal or nonexistent benefits produced by suppressing evidence obtained in objectively reasonable reliance on a subsequently invalidated search warrant" could not "justify the substantial costs of exclusion," which include "interference with the criminal justice system's truth-finding function" and thereby allowing "some guilty defendants * * * [to] go free or receive reduced sentences as a result of favorable plea bargains."

*Leon,* it should be noted, does not hold that the exclusionary rule is totally inapplicable whenever a warrant had been obtained. Fourth Amendment violations relating to execution of the warrant are untouched by *Leon,* as reflected in the majority's caution that its discussion "assumes, of course, that the officers properly executed the warrant and searched only those places for those objects that it was reasonable to believe were covered by the warrant." The *Leon* Court also emphasized it was not suggesting "that exclusion is always inappropriate in cases where an officer has obtained a warrant and abided by its terms," and that exclusion is still called for whenever the officer lacks "reasonable grounds for believing that the warrant was properly issued." This limitation encompasses at least four situations.

First, the Court expressly left untouched the *Franks* doctrine, providing that a warrant facially sufficient is invalid if based upon knowingly or recklessly made falsehoods in the affidavit (§ 2.3(a)). Second, there is the situation in which the officer knows that the magistrate has "wholly abandoned his judicial role." As an illustration of such a case, the Court cited the situation in *Lo-Ji Sales* (§ 2.4(a)), where the magistrate "allowed himself to become a member, if not the leader of the search party." Third, the Court said "a warrant may be so facially deficient—i.e., in failing to particularize the place to be searched or the things to be seized—that the executing officers cannot reasonably presume it to be valid." See § 2.4(d), (e), and consider *Groh v. Ramirez* (2004) (good faith lacking where officer failed to put affidavit's list of things to be seized into warrant he prepared and to notice this "glaring deficiency"). Lastly, the officer cannot rely on the magistrate's issuance of the warrant when the warrant was issued on an affidavit "so lacking in indicia of probable cause as to render official belief in its existence entirely unreasonable." See § 2.3(a).

### (c) Police reliance upon a statute

In *Ill. v. Krull* (1987), the Court held that a "good faith exception to the exclusionary rule also should be recognized when officers act in objectively reasonable reliance upon a statute authorizing [the search in question], but where the statute is ultimately found to violate the Fourth Amendment." Held admissible under this standard was evidence seized pursuant to a state statute, subsequently ruled to be unconstitutional, that authorized warrantless administrative searches of the premises of licensed automobile-parts dealers. The *Krull* majority concluded that "[t]he approach used in *Leon* is equally applicable to the present case" because (i) application of the exclusionary rule when the police reasonably relied on a statute would "have as little deterrent effect on the officers' actions" as in the *Leon* situation, and (ii) "legislators, like judicial officers, are not the focus of the [exclusionary] rule," as there "is nothing to indicate that applying the exclusionary rule to evidence seized pursuant to the statute prior to the declaration of its invalidity will act as a significant, additional deterrent" to the occasional enactment of statutes later held to confer unconstitutional search authority. The dissenters, though conceding the good faith of the police who relied on the statute, stressed that statutes "authorizing unreasonable searches were the core concern of the Framers of the Fourth Amendment." Responding to this criticism, the majority noted that "a statute cannot support objectively reasonable reliance if, in passing the statute, the legislature wholly abandoned its responsibility to enact constitutional laws" and an officer cannot "be said to have acted in good-faith reliance upon a statute if its provisions are such that a reasonable officer should have known the statute was unconstitutional."

### (d) Police reliance on civil authorities

While "the Fourth Amendment [is] applicable to the activities of civil as well as criminal authorities," *N.J. v. T.L.O.* (1985), in *Ariz. v. Evans* (1995) the Court concluded that some government searches covered by the Fourth Amendment are nonetheless inappropriate occasions for use of the exclusionary rule, considering the kind of government official who was at fault. In *Evans*, where the defendant was arrested on the basis of an erroneous computer indication of an outstanding warrant, attributable to a court clerk's failure to advise the police that the warrant had been quashed, the Court used *Leon*-style reasoning to conclude the exclusionary rule should not apply: the arrest officer acted reasonably in relying on the computer record and thus was not in need of deterrence, and exclusion would not deter such errors by court clerks, who "have no stake in the outcome of particular criminal prosecutions."

## § 6.5   APPLICATION TO PROCEEDINGS OTHER THAN THE TRIAL

### (a)   Introduction

Decisions dealing with exclusion of unconstitutionally obtained evidence from proceedings other than the criminal trial have dealt primarily with the Fourth Amendment exclusionary rule. In part, this is because evidence of the kind typically obtained through practices other than searches (e.g., identification procedures) is less likely to have much bearing in related civil or quasi-criminal proceedings. So too, the Fifth Amendment by its very terms eliminates certain scope-issues left unresolved in the Fourth Amendment's exclusionary rule; the self-incrimination clause bars the use of compelled testimony only in a "criminal case." See §§ 4.5(c), 8.1(f). As for the Fourth Amendment exclusionary rule, the overall approach of the Court majority has remained consistent from one area of possible application to another. The Court has relied upon what it has described as a "pragmatic analysis of the exclusionary rule's usefulness in the particular context," weighing the additional deterrence that would stem from the rule's application against the costs that would be entailed. *Stone v. Powell* (1976).

### (b)   Grand jury proceedings

It is the settled federal practice, sustained against constitutional attack in *Costello v. U.S.* (1956), that "an indictment returned by a legally constituted and unbiased grand jury, * * * if valid on its face, is enough to call for trial of the charge on the merits." This means that a defendant cannot challenge an indictment on the ground that the grand jury considered unconstitutionally obtained evidence. *Lawn v. U.S.* (1958). The defendant has a sufficient remedy in being able to challenge the introduction of such evidence if it should be used at trial. *U.S. v. Blue* (1966). Of course, a grand jury witness who will not later be indicted lacks that remedy, and that is almost certainly the situation where the witness has been given immunity, as was the case in *U.S. v. Calandra* (1974). Nonetheless, *Calandra* held that a grand jury witness could not refuse to answer questions even though those questions were based on evidence obtained from an unlawful search of his premises. The *Calandra* majority concluded that the "speculative and undoubtedly minimal advance in the deterrence of police misconduct" that might result from allowing the witness' objection was outweighed by the deleterious impact such a ruling would have upon the effective and expeditious discharge of the grand jury's duties. But cf. *Gelbard v. United States* (1972) (Title III prohibition as to evidence derived from illegal electronic interception (see § 3.2) applies to all proceedings, allowing grand jury witness to refuse to answer questions derived from an illegal interception).

### (c) Parole revocation proceedings

*Pa. Board of Probation and Parole v. Scott* (1998) held the Fourth Amendment exclusionary rule inapplicable to parole revocation proceedings on reasoning that appears to govern probation revocation proceedings as well. The Court there concluded that the cost of applying the exclusionary rule, altering "the traditional flexible, administrative nature of parole revocation proceedings" was not worth the "minimal" additional deterrence that would result. As for searches conducted by police officers, even if the officers are aware that the suspect is a parolee and the evidence discovered can be used in a parole revocation proceeding, their "primary" interest "is in criminal investigation and adequate deterrence therefore is provided by exclusion at the criminal trial. As for searches by parole officers, who admittedly are" not engaged in the competitive enterprise of ferreting out crime, sufficient deterrence there is provided by "departmental training and discipline and the threat of damage actions."

## (d) Related civil or quasi-criminal proceedings

In *One 1958 Plymouth Sedan v. Pa.* (1965), the Fourth Amendment exclusionary rule was held applicable to a proceeding for the forfeiture of an automobile as having had been used in the illegal transportation of alcohol. The Court emphasized that the proceeding was "quasi-criminal in character" because its object was to "penalize for the commission of an offense against the law." In *U.S. v. Janis* (1976), the Court refused to extend *Plymouth Sedan* to a civil tax proceeding. In that case, local police seized Janis' wagering records and cash in an unconstitutional search, and then notified federal authorities, who imposed an assessment against Janis for wagering excise taxes and levied upon the seized cash. The majority opinion suggested that it would take strong evidence of a substantial additional deterrent effect before it would consider extending the exclusionary rule to what was simply a civil suit for liability that existed without regard to the criminality of defendant's wagering activities. Here, such evidence was lacking: "Working, as we must, with the absence of convincing empirical data, common sense dictates that the deterrent effect of the exclusion of relevant evidence is highly attenuated when the 'punishment' imposed upon the offending criminal enforcement officer is the removal of that evidence from a civil suit by or against a different sovereign."

### (e) Administrative proceedings

*I.N.S. v. Lopez–Mendoza* (1984) concluded that the Fourth Amendment exclusionary rule should not be applied in civil deportation hearings. The deterrent value of excluding evidence seized by INS officers in the course of arresting illegal aliens was deemed to be reduced in this setting even though, as the dissent pointed out, the evidence was not being used in a "collateral" proceeding, but in the very proceeding "for which the evidence was gathered." Deterrence here was less effective because (i) "deportation will still be possible when evidence not derived directly from the arrest is sufficient to support deportation," and (ii) INS agents know "that it is highly unlikely that any particular arrestee will end up challenging the lawfulness of his arrest." Deterrence also was less needed because (i) "the INS has its own comprehensive scheme for deterring Fourth Amendment violations" by training and discipline, and (ii) "alternative remedies" including the "possibility of declaratory relief" are available for institutional practices violating the Fourth Amendment. On the cost side, the Court found that (i) application of the exclusionary rule "in proceedings that are intended not to punish past transgressions but to prevent their continuance or renewal would require courts to close their eyes to ongoing violations of the law," (ii) invocation of the exclusionary rule at deportation hearings, where "neither the hearing officers nor the attorneys * * * are likely to be well versed in the intricacies of Fourth Amendment law," "might significantly change and complicate the character of these proceedings," and (iii) because many INS arrests "occur in crowded and confused circumstances," application of the exclusionary rule "might well result in the suppression of large amounts of information that had been obtained entirely lawfully."

## (f)  Habeas corpus

Although the issue posed in federal habeas corpus review of Fourth Amendment claims is not one of applying the exclusionary rule to a proceeding other than the trial, as the habeas petitioner's challenge is to the allegedly erroneous admission of seized evidence at trial, the Court has applied the same basic balancing approach in sharply limiting the cognizability of Fourth Amendment claims on habeas review. *Stone v. Powell* (1976) held that, "where the State has provided an opportunity for full and fair litigation of a Fourth Amendment claim, the Constitution does not require that a state prisoner be granted federal habeas corpus relief on the ground that the evidence obtained in an unconstitutional search and seizure was introduced at his trial." In reaching this result, the *Stone* Court proceeded from the premise that the deterrent function of the exclusionary rule was effectively served by exclusion at trial and the subsequent review of a failure to exclude on direct appeal. There was no reason to assume that "any specific disincentive already created by [these proceedings] * * * would be enhanced if there were the further risk that a conviction obtained in a state court and affirmed on direct review might be overturned in collateral proceedings often occurring years after the incarceration of the defendant." Moreover, on the other side of the cost/benefit ledger was the combination of both the basic "costs of applying the exclusionary rule even at trial" and the additional costs of habeas corpus review. Those additional costs included the consumption of scarce federal judicial resources in providing a second review of exclusionary rule claims, and the delayed finality of the criminal process through collateral proceedings that could be brought long after the original proceedings were completed.

Subsequent rulings have stressed the special character of the Fourth Amendment exclusionary rule and have refused to extend *Stone* to other exclusionary rules. Habeas review has been held fully applicable to claims resting on the admission of evidence at trial in violation of the due process prohibition of unduly suggestive identification procedures, *Manson v. Brathwaite* (1977), the self-incrimination prohibition against use of compelled statements, *Estelle v. Smith* (1981), the due process "voluntariness" test, *Miller v. Fenton* (1985), and admission of statements obtained in violation of *Miranda, Withrow v. Williams* (1993). *Withrow,* in distinguishing *Miranda* violations, noted that *Miranda,* " 'prophylactic' though it may be, in protecting a defendant's Fifth Amendment privilege, * * * safeguards a fundamental trial right." Moreover, unlike *Mapp*'s exclusionary rule, that right did not serve only "some value necessarily divorced from the correct ascertainment of guilt"; by "bracing against the possibility of unreliable statements in every instance of in-custody interrogation, *Miranda* serves to guard against the use of unreliable statements at trial." "Finally and most importantly, eliminating [habeas] review of *Miranda* claims would not significantly benefit the federal courts in their exercise of habeas jurisdiction, or advance the cause of federalism in any substantial way, * * * as [it] would not prevent a state prisoner from simply converting his barred *Miranda* claim into a due process [voluntariness] claim" that would still be cognizable on habeas review.

## § 6.6  DERIVATIVE EVIDENCE

### (a) Fruits of the poisonous tree

In *Silverthorne Lumber Co. v. U.S.* (1920), the Court held invalid a subpoena that had been issued on the basis of information acquired through an illegal search. Just as the prosecution could not use in court evidence obtained directly from the unconstitutional search, neither would it be allowed to use evidence obtained indirectly via a subpoena based upon that search. The exclusionary rule was applicable to all evidence "tainted" by the unconstitutional search, and that taint extended to evidence subsequently obtained through the use of information acquired during that search. This *Silverthorne* requirement of exclusion of "secondary" or "derivative" evidence later came to be described as the "fruit of the poisonous tree" doctrine.

Though the "fruits doctrine" was formulated initially in applying the Fourth Amendment's exclusionary rule, it was later applied to other exclusionary rules. Thus, in *U.S. v.Wade* (1967), the Court held that violation of accused's Sixth Amendment right to counsel at a lineup required not only the exclusion of evidence of identification at that lineup but also exclusion of a subsequent in-court identification if it was the fruit of the lineup identification. See § 5.2(c). The Court noted further that the governing standard for determining whether the in-court identification was tainted was the same as that applied in Fourth Amendment cases. So too, in *Nix v. Williams (Williams II)* (1984), considering the admission of secondary evidence (the body of the murder victim) discovered through the Sixth Amendment (*Massiah*) violation presented in *Brewer v. Williams* (§ 4.3(d)), the Court again looked to the "fruits" doctrine (and its "exceptions") as developed in Fourth Amendment cases.

*Kastigar v. U.S.* (§ 8.2(e)), in holding that immunity rendered the self-incrimination privilege inapplicable only if it provided protection against both use and "derivative use" of compelled testimony, established a form of Fifth Amendment "fruits" doctrine. Indeed, *Kastigar's* description of the scope of the prohibition against derivative use ("barring the use of compelled testimony as an 'investigatory lead' and also barring the use of any evidence obtained by focusing on a witness") may prescribe a more stringent exclusion than the Fourth Amendment doctrine. *Kastigar's* derivative evidence ban arguably would not accept either the inevitable discovery or attenuation limitations (discussed in (c) and (d) infra) that are part of the traditional fruits doctrine. *Kastigar* noted that secondary evidence derived from a coerced confession also must be excluded, but whether the scope of that ban is governed by a standard akin to the Fourth Amendment's fruits doctrine or the arguably more rigorous derivative use prohibition of *Kastigar* remains unclear. Cf. *Harrison v. U.S.* (1968) (applying traditional fruits analysis to evidence derived from a *McNabb-Mallory* violation). On the other hand, though the *Miranda* requirements are tied to preservation of the self-incrimination privilege and the administrative need to go beyond the voluntariness standard (see §§ 1.3(f), 4.4(b)), here the Court has made clear that even the Fourth Amendment fruits doctrine does not apply. As discussed in § 6.6(g), when a statement is obtained in violation of *Miranda* alone (i.e., the statement is not also involuntary), evidence derived from that statement ordinarily will not be subject to an exclusionary requirement.

### (b)  The "independent source" limitation

In applying the poisonous tree rule, *Silverthorne* stressed that "facts" obtained through a constitutional violation were not necessarily "inaccessible" for court use. The facts could still be proved, the Court noted, "if knowledge of [the facts] is [also] gained from an independent source." Subsequent Supreme Court opinions have cited the second lower court ruling in *Bynum v. U.S.* (1960) as presenting a classic application of this independent source rule. See *U.S. v. Crews* (1980). The first *Bynum* decision excluded fingerprints obtained from the defendant after he had been illegally arrested. Cf. *Davis v. Miss.* (§ 2.9(e)). At the time of that arrest, the police had reason to suspect the defendant had been involved in the robbery under investigation, although they lacked probable cause. When Bynum was subsequently reprosecuted, the government sought to use an older set of prints obtained from F.B.I. files, which also matched the prints found at the scene of the crime. Since the police had reason to check for Bynum's prints without regard to the illegal arrest, and since the older set of prints had been taken in connection with an unrelated matter, those prints were admitted as independently acquired evidence, "in no way connected with the unlawful arrest." *Bynum v. U.S.* (1960).

The independent source doctrine unlike the purged taint doctrine (see § 6.6(d)), proceeds from the premise that the source producing the evidence stands apart from the influence of the Fourth Amendment violation, with no links between the two. The Supreme Court twice has spoken to assessing the requisite degree of separateness, and in both instances was sharply divided. In *Murray v. U.S.* (1988), the lower court applied the independent source doctrine on the belief that the police in that case (i) initially had probable cause to obtain a search warrant for contraband, (ii) then unlawfully entered the premises without a warrant, where it learned that the contraband sought was indeed there, (iii) then left the premises and obtained a warrant based only on the previously obtained probable cause (i.e., without any reference to information gathered during the unlawful entry), and (iv) then returned with the warrant and seized the contraband in the execution of the warrant. The Supreme Court remanded the case for further findings of fact, but the majority agreed that the independent source doctrine would apply to the situation described by the lower court, provided one additional finding was made. It must also be shown that the police decision to seek the warrant had not been "prompted" by what was learned during the earlier unlawful entry (i.e., the police "would have sought a warrant [even] if they had not earlier entered the [premises]"). The dissenters advocated what the majority described as a "prophylactic rule" that would mandate "per se inadmissibility" absent a police demonstration by some "historically verifiable fact" (e.g., a prior initiation of the warrant process) that the "subsequent search was totally unaffected by the prior illegal search." The majority saw no need for such a requirement, noting that "we see the incentives differently." An officer with probable cause would be "foolish to enter the premises first in an unlawful manner," as that would "add to the normal burden of convincing the magistrate that there is probable cause the much more onerous burden of convincing a trial court that no information gained from the illegal entry affected either the enforcement officers' decision to seek a warrant or the magistrate's decision to grant it."

In *Segura v. U.S.* (1984), the police entered the premises without a warrant, arrested the occupants and then remained on the scene unlawfully for many hours while a search warrant was obtained (see § 2.8(e)). That warrant, however, had been based solely on information acquired prior to the entry, and the only issue before the Court was the suppression of evidence "not observed during the initial entry [but] first discovered" in the execution of the "admittedly valid" search warrant. The dissenters contended that this was not sufficient to establish an independent source, for the agents "access to the evidence" might have rested on the illegal entry (the district court having noted that the evidence "might well" have been destroyed if not for the illegal entry). The majority found this contention unpersuasive and held the independent source doctrine applicable. The possibility that the evidence otherwise would have been removed or destroyed was based on "pure speculation," especially since the police, if they had not entered the premises, presumably would have utilized alternative tactics that would have prevented removal (e.g., a "perimeter stakeout") and avoided alerting the occupants. "Even more important," the majority added, "we decline to extend the exclusionary rule, which already exacts an enormous price from society and our system of justice, to further 'protect' criminal activity, as the dissent would have us do."

### (c) The "inevitable discovery" limitation

In *Nix v. Williams (Williams II)* (1984), the Court concluded that the fruits doctrine did not bar admission of evidence derived from a constitutional violation if such evidence would "inevitably" have been discovered from lawful investigatory activities without regard to that violation. The inevitable discovery rule differs from the independent source rule in that the question presented is not whether the police did in fact acquire the evidence by reliance upon an untainted source but instead whether evidence in fact obtained through a constitutional violation would otherwise inevitably have been discovered from an untainted source. Yet, as the Su-

preme Court explained in *Williams II,* the inevitable discovery rule is analytically similar to the
independent source rule, in that both are intended
to ensure that exclusion does not outrun the deterrence objective: the prosecution is neither "put in a
better position than it would have been if no illegality had transpired" nor "put in a worse position
simply because of some earlier police error or misconduct." Relying on this rationale, *Williams II* also
rejected a lower court ruling that would have allowed the prosecution to justify admissibility on
inevitable discovery grounds only if it first established an absence of "bad faith" on the part of the
police in engaging in the constitutional violation
that actually produced the evidence. Such a limitation, the Court noted, "would place courts in the
position of withholding from juries relevant and
undoubted truth that would have been available to
police absent any unlawful police activity." Contrary to the lower court's assumption, a "bad faith"
exception was not needed to ensure that the inevitable discovery rule did not encourage police to take
unconstitutional short cuts, since "a police officer
who is faced with the opportunity to obtain evidence illegally will rarely, if ever, be in a position to
calculate whether the evidence sought would inevitably be discovered."

*Williams II* does not allow lower courts to apply
the inevitable discovery rule upon the basis of nothing more than a hunch or speculation as to what
otherwise *might* or *could* have occurred. The prosecution must "establish by a preponderance of the

evidence that the information ultimately or inevitably *would* have been discovered by lawful means." The *Williams II* majority concluded that the preponderance standard would suffice here, as it does for most suppression issues (see § 6.9(b)), because "inevitable discovery involves no speculative elements but focuses on demonstrated historical facts capable of ready verification or impeachment." Circumstances justifying application of the inevitable discovery rule are unlikely to be present unless, at the time of the illegal police conduct, there was already in progress an investigation that eventually would have resulted in the discovery of the evidence through routine investigatory procedure. In *Williams II*, a statement illegally obtained from defendant revealed the whereabouts of the murder victim in a roadside ditch, but a group of 200 volunteers was already searching for the body pursuant to a carefully developed plan that eventually would have encompassed the place where the body was found.

### (d) The "purged taint" limitation

Even where the secondary evidence would not have been discovered except for the constitutional violation (i.e., there was no independent source or inevitability of discovery), that evidence need not necessarily be banned as the fruit of the poisonous tree. The Court's decisions clearly indicate that the poisonous tree doctrine does not extend as far as a "but for" causation test might take it. If the means of acquiring the secondary evidence are substantially removed and distinguishable from the initial illegality, neither the "deterrence" rationale nor the "judicial integrity" rationale requires application of the exclusionary rule. *Harrison v. U.S.* (1968). Accordingly, as the Court noted in *Wong Sun v. U.S.* (1963), the controlling question is: "[W]hether, granting establishment of the primary illegality, the evidence to which instant objection is made has been come at by exploitation of that illegality or instead by means sufficiently distinguishable to be purged of the primary taint." This "purged taint" limitation (also described as the "attenuated connection" limitation) most commonly arises in the application of the Fourth Amendment exclusionary rule, but it has also been applied to the Sixth Amendment exclusionary rule. See *U.S. v. Wade* (§ 5.2(c)) (discussing the doctrine as applied to an in-court identification as the fruit of a lineup conducted in violation of the Sixth Amendment).

The application of the "purged taint" limitation in the Fourth Amendment context is well illustrated by the Court's rulings in *Wong Sun*. Narcotics agents there entered a dwelling without probable cause and chased down and arrested A, who almost immediately thereafter made a statement accusing B of having sold narcotics. Narcotics were subsequently seized from B, who in turn, implicated C, who was also arrested illegally. Several days later, after having been arraigned and released on his own recognizance, C voluntarily made an oral confession to a narcotics agent during interrogation. A argued that his statement and the narcotics later seized from B were fruits of the illegal entry into his dwelling and his illegal arrest. The Court agreed and both items were excluded. It rejected, however, C's claim that his statement was the fruit of his illegal arrest. Even though C might never have confessed if he had never been arrested illegally, his voluntary action after having been released and warned of his rights had made the "connection between the arrest and the statement * * * so attenuated as to [have] dissipate[d] the taint."

As *Wong Sun* indicates, the taint of initial illegality may be purged by an "intervening independent act" by the defendant or a third party which breaks the causal chain linking illegality and evidence in such a way that the evidence is not viewed as having been obtained by "exploitation of that illegality." Determining whether there has been such an intervening independent act has proved troublesome in several different settings. The most prominent of these settings are discussed in § 6.6(e), (f).

A quite different kind of attenuation analysis was used in *Hudson v. Mich.* (2006), holding the Fourth Amendment's exclusionary rule inapplicable to knock-and-announce violations. The Court concluded attenuation can also occur when suppression would not serve an interest protected by the constitutional guarantee violated. Such was the case in *Hudson,* the Court concluded, as the interests protected by the knock-and-announce rule were (i) "protection of human life and limb, because an unannounced entry may provoke violence in supposed self-defense by the surprised resident''; (ii) ''protection of property'' by avoidance of forcible entry; and (iii) protection of ''those elements of privacy and dignity that can be destroyed by a sudden entrance,'' but *not* ''one's interest in preventing the government from seeing or taking evidence described in a warrant.'' The four dissenters objected that ''the majority's interest-based approach departs from prior law.''

### (e) The illegal arrest as the poisonous tree

When an unconstitutional arrest leads directly and immediately to a search, the exclusion of evidence seized in that search presents no difficulties. Indeed, a search incident to an unconstitutional arrest is itself unconstitutional, so the Court need not even look to the arrest as the poison tree. The question of exclusion does become complicated, however, where the arrest leads to the production of evidence through the intervening act of the defendant or a third person, as in the case of a confession by the arrestee or an identification of the arrestee by the victim. A similar complication arises when a witness is discovered through an illegal search.

*Post-arrest confessions.* An otherwise legal confession given by a defendant arrested in violation of the Fourth Amendment will be excluded from evidence if it deemed the fruit of the arrest, but will be admitted if it is deemed the product of an ''independent act of free will'' by the defendant. *Brown v. Ill.* (1975) sets forth a multifactored analysis to be applied in determining whether a post-arrest confession falls in one category or the other. The police in *Brown* arrested defendant without probable cause in order to question him concerning a murder. Defendant was then taken to the police station, warned of his *Miranda* rights, and interrogated. He made an initial incriminating statement within two hours after his arrest, was interrogated again several hours later (after the *Miranda* warnings were repeated), and then made a second incriminating statement. The state supreme court upheld the admission of both statements on the ground that the *Miranda* warnings automatically purged the taint of defendant's illegal arrest. The Supreme Court unanimously rejected the state court's view of the impact of the *Miranda* warnings. A majority also found that, on the facts of the case, both statements were the fruit of the illegal arrest.

With respect to the *Miranda* warnings, the *Brown* opinion noted: "[T]he *Miranda* warnings, *alone* and *per se,* cannot always make the act [of confessing] sufficiently a product of free will to break, for Fourth Amendment purposes, the causal connection between the illegality and the confession. * * * The *Miranda* warnings are an important factor, to be sure, in determining whether the confession is obtained by exploitation of an illegal arrest. But they are not the only factor to be considered. The temporal proximity of the arrest and the confession, the presence of intervening circumstances, and, particularly, the purpose and flagrancy of the official misconduct are all relevant."

After examining the *Brown* fact situation in light of the factors noted above, the majority concluded that the prosecution had failed to meet its burden of establishing the dissipation of the initial taint. Defendant's first statement was made within two hours of his arrest and the later, second statement was the fruit of the first. No intervening acts of significance (such as presentment before a magistrate, consultation with counsel, or release from custody) had occurred between the arrest and the first statement. Moreover, the majority emphasized, the illegality had "a quality of purposefulness." The "impropriety of the arrest was obvious"; it had been undertaken as an "expedition for evidence" and had been executed in a manner which "gave the appearance of having been calculated to cause surprise, fright, and confession." Compare *Rawlings v. Ky.* (1980) (where defendant was illegally detained for a short period in the "congenial atmosphere" of a friend's house, *Miranda* warnings were given shortly before he made an incriminating statement, the statement appeared to be a spontaneous reaction to a search of another person, and the police conduct did not rise to the level of "conscious or flagrant misconduct," the state had carried its burden of showing that the statement was not the fruit of the illegal detention).

In *Brown*, the unconstitutionality of the arrest lay in its foundation. In *N.Y. v. Harris* (1990), in contrast, the police had probable cause to make an arrest, but the Fourth Amendment had been violated when the police entered the dwelling to make the arrest without an arrest warrant, contrary to *Payton v. N.Y.* (§ 2.7(a)). The Court here turned from a multifactored analysis of *Brown* and established a per se rule: "where the police have probable cause to arrest a suspect, the exclusionary rule does not bar the State's use of a statement made by the defendant outside of his home, even though the statement is taken after an arrest made in the home in violation of *Payton.*" Once the defendant was removed from his home, the majority reasoned, his continued custody was lawful (as the police did have probable cause) and the statement should not be treated as the fruit of an arrest occurring in the home as opposed to somewhere else.

*Eyewitness identification.* A multifactored analysis similar to that adopted in *Brown* has been applied in determining whether an eyewitness identification following an illegal arrest should be excluded as the fruit of the poisonous tree. Here the temporal proximity is likely to be an insignificant factor as the time which passes between the illegal arrest and the identification has little bearing in itself on the factors that produced the identification, although it may shed light on the purpose of the arrest. The two leading Supreme Court cases on post-illegal-arrest identifications involved arrests that apparently were not motivated by a desire to present the defendant for possible identification, so the Court had no reason to discuss there the element of "purposefulness"; but that element would seem to have a significance in the identification context similar to that which it had in *Brown*. The critical factor in both of the Supreme Court rulings was presence of an "intervening circumstance" that was viewed as having broken the causal connection.

In *Johnson v. La.* (1972), after being subjected to what he alleged to be an unlawful arrest, and before being placed in a lineup, defendant received the assistance of counsel and was brought before a magistrate, who advised him of his rights and set bail. The Supreme Court concluded that "at the time of the lineup, the detention of the [defendant] was under the authority of [the magistrate's] commitment," and "consequently the lineup was conducted not by 'exploitation' of the challenged arrest, but by 'means sufficiently distinguishable to be purged of the primary taint.'" In *U.S. v. Crews* (1980), the Court, on similar grounds, held that an at-trial identification of defendant by a robbery victim was not a fruit of the defendant's earlier illegal arrest. The Court noted that none of the "three distinct elements" of the victim's in-court identification—the victim's presence at trial, her ability to reconstruct the prior criminal occurrence and identify the offender, and the defendant's physical presence in the courtroom—"had been come at by exploitation of the violation of the defendant's Fourth Amendment rights." With respect to the third element, the Court noted that *Frisbie v. Collins* and similar cases had firmly established that a defendant "cannot claim immunity from prosecution simply because his appearance in court was precipitated by an unlawful arrest." See §§ 2.1(b); 6.3(c).

*Witness testimony.* In *U.S. v. Ceccolini* (1978), the potentially tainted witness was a sales clerk in a flower shop who had been present when a visiting patrolman conducted an illegal search by opening an envelope lying on the cash register. The officer found that the envelope contained policy slips, but he did not tell the clerk of his discovery. Several months later, an F.B.I. agent, informed of the patrolman's discovery, questioned the clerk about her employer's activities. She expressed a willingness to help and related the incident involving the patrolman and the envelope. The issue before the Court was whether the sales clerk's subsequent testimony against her employer at trial should be suppressed as the fruit of the officer's search. The Supreme Court held that the fruits doctrine did not bar admission of her testimony.

The *Ceccolini* opinion initially rejected the contention that the case before it should be treated no differently than one in which police discovered physical evidence. The function of the exclusionary rule, the Court noted, requires that special consideration be given to the element of "free will" that might be involved in the witness' decision to testify. The "greater the willingness of the witness to freely testify, the greater the likelihood that he or she will be discovered by legal means and, concomitantly, the smaller the incentive to conduct an illegal search to discover the witness." The exclusion of a tainted witness also involves different considerations because it can "perpetually disable a witness from testifying about relevant and material facts, regardless of how unrelated such testimony might be to the purpose of the originally illegal search."

While *Ceccolini* stressed that the exclusionary rule should be invoked "with much greater reluctance" as applied to "live testimony" than to an "inanimate object," it refused to accept the government's position that the testimony of a witness should always be admissible "no matter how close and proximate the connection between it and a violation of the Fourth Amendment." In determining whether the taint was purged, consideration must be given to the "time, place, and manner," of the initial questioning of the witness and its relationship to the initial illegality. In this case, several factors led to the conclusion that the taint of the illegal search had been dissipated: (i) "the testimony given by the witness was an act of her own free will in no way coerced or even induced by official authority"; (ii) the illegally discovered slips were not used in questioning the witness; (iii) substantial time passed between the search and the F.B.I. officer's contact with the witness and between that contact and her eventual testimony; (iv) the flower shop had been under F.B.I. surveillance even before the patrolman discovered the slips; and (v) there was "not the slightest evidence" that the patrolman made the search "with the intent of finding a willing and knowledgeable witness to testify against [the defendant]."

## (f) Multiple confessions

In *U.S. v. Bayer* (1947) the Supreme Court noted that, "after an accused has once let the cat out of the bag by confessing, no matter what the inducement, he is never thereafter free of the psychological and practical disadvantages of having confessed. * * * In such a sense, a later confession always may be looked upon as a fruit of the first." The Court refused, however, to adopt a "per se rule" that "perpetually disables the confessor from making a usable [confession] after those conditions [which produced the first inadmissible confession] have been removed." Post-*Bayer* rulings dealing with successive confessions have fashioned separate standards for determining the admissibility of the second confession, dependent upon the nature of the illegality that required exclusion of the first confession.

Where the first confession was a fruit of a Fourth Amendment violation, the Court asks whether the second confession is, in turn, the fruit of the first. See *Brown v. Ill.* (discussed in subsection (e) supra). On the other hand, where the original confession is inadmissible under the "voluntariness" standard of due process, the Court asks whether the impact of the coercion that rendered the first confession involuntary has also rendered the second confession involuntary. *Darwin v. Conn.* (1968). This difference in the statement of the governing standard arguably follows from the position that "the exclusionary rule, * * * when utilized to effectuate the Fourth Amendment, serves interests and policies that are distinct from those it serves under the Fifth." *Brown*. In application, the two standards tend to produce the same result, as each looks to whether, "considering the totality of the circumstances," there was a "break in the stream of events * * * sufficient to insulate the final events [producing the second confession] from the effect of all that went before." *Darwin*. However, as discussed in subsection (g) infra, the Court in *Ore. v. Elstad* obviously assumed that application of a voluntariness test in determining the admissibility of the second confession will produce a quite different result than the fruits doctrine where the first confession is inadmissible only because of a *Miranda* violation.

### (g) *Miranda* violations and the fruits doctrine

In *Ore. v. Elstad* (1985), defendant initially made a brief incriminating statement after having been taken into custody at his home and questioned briefly by the arresting officers without *Miranda* warnings. He was questioned again at the police station, after having been given his *Miranda* warnings, and responded with a much more incriminating and extensive second statement. Noting the impact of having let the "cat out of the bag," the lower court held that the second statement was inadmissible as the fruit of the *Miranda* violation which invalidated the first statement. The Supreme Court disagreed, holding that the fruits doctrine was inapplicable to a *Miranda* violation. The admissibility of the second confession depended solely on whether it was voluntary, and the initial failure to provide *Miranda* warnings was insufficient to produce a coerced second confession even though the "cat had been let out of the bag."

In explaining why the fruits doctrine was inapplicable, the *Elstad* majority stressed "fundamental differences between the role of the Fourth Amendment exclusionary rule and the function of *Miranda* in guarding against prosecutorial use of compelled statements as prohibited by the Fifth Amendment." The fruits doctrine had been developed in the context of the Fourth Amendment exclusionary rule, where the objective was to deter unreasonable searches no matter how probative their fruits. *Miranda,* on the other hand, sought to serve the Fifth Amendment prohibition against the use of compelled statements. Moreover, it did so by adopting an exclusionary rule that "sweeps more broadly" than the Fifth itself by establishing an irrebuttable presumption that unwarned statements obtained through custodial interrogation are compelled. This prophylactic element of *Miranda* would not be carried, however, beyond prohibiting the state's use of the unwarned statement in its case in chief. Just as *Miranda* had been held not to bar use of an unwarned but voluntary statement for impeachment use (§ 6.7(b)), so too it should not bar use of a subsequently obtained statement where there was compliance with *Miranda* in obtaining that second statement and the earlier unwarned statement was voluntary. The critical question here simply should be whether the second statement was "knowingly and voluntarily made." (As noted in *Fellers v. U.S.* (2004), the Court has not yet decided whether the *Elstad* rationale applies if the first confession was obtained in violation of defendant's Sixth Amendment right to counsel.)

In *Missouri v. Seibert* (2004), the Court limited the impact of *Elstad*, but did so in a manner not requiring the first confession to be treated as a poisonous tree. *Seibert* involved the increasingly popular police protocol of withholding *Miranda* warnings until interrogation has produced a confession in order "to get a confession the suspect would not make if he understood his rights at the outset," a likely consequence because giving the warnings *after* the defendant has already confessed "could lead to an entirely reasonable inference that what he had just said will be used, with subsequent silence being of no avail." The Court held Seibert's second confession must be suppressed, *not* because it was the fruit of the first confession, but simply because the circumstances in which the *Miranda* warnings were given meant they could not "function 'effectively' as *Miranda* requires." See § 4.8(c).

Although the *Elstad* Court had before it only the question of whether the fruits doctrine should apply to a second confession following an initial *Miranda* violation, the Court's language certainly suggested that the fruits doctrine was not applicable to any type of secondary evidence derived from a *Miranda* violation. The *Elstad* opinion noted, for example, that application of the fruits doctrine assumes a "constitutional violation," but that unwarned questioning in itself violated only prophylactic standards laid down to safeguard against such a violation. The doubts created by *Dickerson v. U.S.* (2000), holding *Miranda* announced a constitutional rule, were tempered by the plurality's conclusion in *Chavez v. Martinez* (2003) that no self-incrimination violation occurs re a confession obtained in violation of *Miranda* unless and until it is admitted against the maker in a criminal trial.

Then came *U.S. v. Patane* (2004), holding the physical evidence obtained as a consequence of such a confession admissible. Three Justices reasoned failure to give the *Miranda* warnings is not itself a violation of a suspect's constitutional rights (or even of the *Miranda* rule), which occurs only if the unwarned confession is admitted into evidence, meaning that exclusion of the confession is itself a sufficient remedy and that there is no need to apply the "fruits" doctrine to the mere failure to warn because there is nothing to deter. Two others deemed it unnecessary to decide such matters; given the important probative value of the physical evidence and the fact that admitting it does not risk admission of the unwarned statement as well, such admission is merely an accommodation of *Miranda* with the other objectives of the criminal justice system. The main dissent stressed that the privilege against self incrimination "extends to the exclusion of derivative evidence" (certainly the case as to compelled testimony; see *U.S. v. Hubbell* (2000)), and that a *Miranda* violation "raises a presumption of coercion" properly applied in the instant context to serve its purpose of freeing courts from "the inherently difficult exercise of assessing the voluntariness of a confession" resulting from custodial interrogation.

## § 6.7  IMPEACHMENT

### (a) Fourth Amendment violations

In *Walder v. U.S.* (1954), the defendant, charged with purchasing and possessing heroin, asserted on direct examination that he had never purchased, sold or handled narcotics at any time "in my life." Responding to that claim, the prosecution sought to impeach defendant by reference to a heroin capsule that had been seized illegally from his home in his presence approximately two years earlier. Defense objected on the ground that the capsule had been suppressed as illegally seized in an earlier prosecution, but the trial court allowed the prosecution's line of questioning (and introduction of direct evidence when defendant denied the previous seizure), advising the jury that it could be considered "solely for the purpose of impeaching the defendant's credibility." The Supreme Court affirmed, noting that "it is one thing to say that the Government cannot make any affirmative use of evidence unlawfully obtained, [but] * * * quite another to say that the defendant can turn the illegal method by which evidence in the Government's possession was obtained to his own advantage, and provide him with a shield against contradiction of his untruths." The

Court reasoned that the defendant "must be free to deny all the elements of the case against him without thereby giving lease to the Government to introduce by way of rebuttal evidence illegally secured to it * * *. Beyond that, however, there is hardly justification for letting the defendant affirmatively resort to perjurious testimony in reliance on the Government's disability to challenge his credibility."

In *Harris v. N.Y.* (1971), a divided Court relied upon *Walder* to uphold the use of defendant's prior statement to a police officer, obtained in violation of *Miranda,* to impeach his trial testimony. Unlike *Walder,* the illegally obtained evidence in *Harris* had been acquired in the investigation of the offense currently charged against defendant. Also, defendant was impeached "as to testimony bearing more directly on the crimes charged" than the "collateral" matter introduced in Walder's testimony. The majority concluded, however, that neither distinction suggested any "difference in principle that warrants a result different from * * * *Walder.*" The *Harris* opinion clearly indicated, as was substantiated in *U.S. v. Havens,* infra, that the same result would have been reached if the impeachment evidence had been obtained by a Fourth Amendment violation.

In *U.S. v. Havens* (1980), the Supreme Court partially accepted and partially rejected another possible limitation upon the impeachment exception to the exclusionary rule. The defendant in *Havens,*

on direct examination, denied that he had been
"engage[d]" in the smuggling activities of his trav-
eling companion. On cross-examination, defendant
was asked whether he had anything to do with his
companion's makeshift underwear pockets in which
the smuggled cocaine was carried. When defendant
gave a negative response, the prosecutor sought to
impeach that denial by reference to an illegal search
of defendant's suitcase in which police found the
material from which the pockets had been cut.
Defendant argued that the illegally seized material
should not be available for impeachment because
that evidence did not "squarely contradict" his direct testimony, as opposed to his cross-examination
testimony. A divided Supreme Court rejected that
argument. It refused to adopt a "flat rule" that
would restrict the impeachment exception to impeachment of direct testimony, but it also noted
that the extension of that exception to impeachment of cross-examination testimony was not without limits. The Court distinguished a pre-*Walder*
ruling, *Agnello v. U.S.* (1925), in which impeachment by reference to illegally seized evidence had
been disallowed. The *Havens* majority noted that
*Agnello* had been a case in which "the government
had 'smuggled in' the impeaching opportunity in
the course of cross-examination." In *Havens,* on the
other hand, the questions asked on cross-examination "would have been suggested to a reasonably
competent cross-examiner by Havens' direct examination." Under that circumstance, prohibiting impeachment by reference to reliable but illegally ob-

tained evidence would be contrary to the emphasis in *Harris* and *Walder* on the "defendant's obligation to speak the truth in response to proper questions."

### (b) Fifth Amendment evidence

As noted above, *Harris v. N.Y.* (1971) held that an impeachment exception also applied to the *Miranda* exclusionary rule. The majority there rejected the contention that the exception had been developed in Fourth Amendment cases and should not apply to *Miranda* violations because of *Miranda*'s Fifth Amendment foundation. Viewing *Miranda*'s exclusionary rule as serving a deterrent function similar to the Fourth Amendment exclusionary rule, the *Harris* majority concluded that function was adequately served by excluding evidence from the prosecution's case-in-chief and did not require providing "a license to use perjury." See also *Ore. v. Hass* (1975) (impeachment use permitted where officer obtained statement, in violation of *Miranda,* by continuing interrogation after defendant asked for a lawyer; "speculative possibility" that this interrogation technique would be employed purposely to gain impeachment evidence was not sufficient to change the "balance * * * struck in *Harris*").

The *Harris* opinion suggested that the ruling there might not apply to involuntary confessions. The Court noted that the case before it did not involve a "coerced confession," and commented that, "of course," the "trustworthiness" of any statement used for impeachment must satisfy "legal standards." In *Mincey v. Ariz.* (1978), the *Harris* suggestion was converted into a direct ruling that involuntary statements could not be used for impeachment purposes. This ruling was later explained as resting on more than the potential untrustworthiness of involuntary confessions. A coerced confession, it was noted, involves the application of the Fifth Amendment privilege "in its most pristine form," while *Miranda* violations involve a rule designed "to deter unlawful police conduct." Because of *Miranda* 's prophylactic function, some balancing was permissible in *Harris,* but not in *Mincey.* See also *N.J. v. Portash* (1979), § 8.1(e) (holding that grand jury testimony given pursuant to a grant of immunity was coerced testimony, similar to an involuntary confession, and therefore could not be used for impeachment even though it was at least as reliable as the statements used for that purpose in *Harris*).

### (c) Sixth Amendment violations

*Mich. v. Harvey* (1990) overturned a state court ruling that had barred impeachment use of defendant's statement because it had been obtained in violation of the ruling in *Mich. v. Jackson* (§ 4.3(f)). *Jackson* held that any statement given by an accused in a discussion initiated by police after the accused had earlier requested counsel was presumptively based on an invalid waiver of his Sixth Amendment right to counsel. That presumption, the majority in *Harvey* noted, operated simply as a "prophylactic rule" designed to ensure "voluntary, knowing, and intelligent waivers of the Sixth Amendment rights," and "did not mark the exact boundary of the Sixth Amendment right itself." The violation of *Jackson* did not invariably mean that the statement was not in fact based on a voluntary, knowing, and intelligent waiver, just as a violation of *Miranda* did not invariably mean a statement was compelled in violation of the Fifth Amendment. Accordingly, the logic of *Harris* applied, and the "shield provided by the prophylactic rule [would not] be perverted into a license to use perjury by way of a defense, free from the risk of confrontation with prior inconsistent utterances."

The *Harvey* ruling was strictly limited to *Jackson* violations. The Court noted that, since the state court had not decided whether the waiver in this case was knowing and voluntary under "traditional standards," it "need not consider the admissibility for impeachment purposes of a voluntary statement obtained in the absence of a knowing and voluntary waiver of the right to counsel." The majority stated that it had previously "mandated the exclusion of reliable and probative evidence for *all* purposes [i.e., including impeachment] only when it is derived from involuntary statements" (citing *Portash* and *Mincey,* discussed supra). Since the majority also assumed that Sixth Amendment waivers invalid under "traditional standards" will not necessarily produce "involuntary" (i.e., "compelled") statements, it viewed a prohibition of impeachment use of all statements obtained without proper waivers as presenting a question quite distinct from that presented in the Fifth Amendment cases. However, the *Harvey* dissenters, who did view the facts there as presenting "a plain violation of respondent's Sixth Amendment rights," suggested that the Sixth Amendment should operate on much the same grounds as the Fifth Amendment in barring all use of statements. Citing some of the cases discussed in § 6.2(b), the dissenters argued that "the exclusion of statements made by a represented and indicted defendant outside the presence of counsel follows not as a remedy for a violation that has preceded trial, but as a necessary incident of the constitutional right itself."

### (d) Defendant's silence

In *Doyle v. Ohio* (1976) and several later cases, the Court moved from impeachment by reference to illegally obtained statements to impeachment by reference to defendant's prior silence. *Doyle* rejected the contention that *Harris* should be extended to allow general impeachment by reference to the fact that defendant, in contrast to his exculpatory testimony at trial, had refused to give any statement to the police after receiving his *Miranda* warnings. The Court stressed that "silence in the wake of warnings may be nothing more than the arrestee's exercise of *Miranda* rights." Moreover, it noted, the implicit message of the warnings is that the defendant's exercise of his right of silence will "carry no penalty"; it therefore would be "fundamentally unfair," after giving the warnings, to then use the silence to "impeach an explanation subsequently offered at trial."

Later cases limited *Doyle* to the special element of unfairness presented where the government had induced defendant's silence through the *Miranda* warnings. Thus, *Anderson v. Charles* (1980) allowed impeachment by prior inconsistent statements given after *Miranda* warnings because "a defendant who voluntarily speaks after receiving *Miranda* warnings has not been induced to remain silent." Also distinguishing *Doyle, Jenkins v. Anderson* (1980) held that due process does not bar impeachment by reference to the defendant's prearrest silence. When the defendant in *Jenkins* testified at trial that he had killed in self-defense, the prosecutor forced him to acknowledge on cross-examination that he had not reported the killing to the police until two weeks later. Here, unlike *Doyle,* the defendant's silence had not been "induced by governmental action" since "the failure to speak occurred before he had been taken into custody and given *Miranda* warnings." *Fletcher v. Weir* (1982) extended *Jenkins* to allow impeachment by post-arrest silence not preceded by *Miranda* warnings. See also *Brecht v. Abrahamson* (1993) (where defendant did not receive warnings until after his arrangement, prosecutor did not violate due process by impeachment reference to silence up to that point).

### (e) Third party impeachment

In *James v. Ill.* (1990), a divided Court refused to extend the impeachment exception to permit the prosecution to introduce unconstitutionally obtained evidence to impeach defense witnesses other than the defendant, even though their testimony was directly contradicted by that evidence. At issue in *James* was the use of an admission obtained from defendant as a fruit of a Fourth Amendment violation, but the Court's rationale was not restricted to the character of the underlying constitutional violation. Expanding the impeachment exception to cover third-party witnesses, the majority reasoned, "would not promote the truth-seeking function to the same extent as did the creation of the original exception, and yet it would significantly undermine the deterrent effect of the general exclusionary rule." The additional contribution to truthfinding would be limited because (1) the threat of subsequent criminal prosecution for false testimony is alone more likely to deter a defense witness than a defendant, and (2) such expansion "likely would chill some defendants from presenting their best defense * * * through the testimony of others," as a variety of factors would make problematic the potential for a defense witness to offer truthful testimony but also "make some statement in sufficient tension with the tainted evidence to allow the prosecution to introduce that evidence for impeachment." On the other side, deterrence through exclusion from the case-in-chief would lose much of its sting, as allowing impeachment use "to *all* witnesses would significantly enhance the expected value to the prosecution of illegally obtained evidence," both by "vastly increas[ing] the number of occasions in which such evidence could be used" and by "deter[ing] defendants from calling witnesses in the first place."

## § 6.8 STANDING

### (a) "Personal rights" analysis

In order to raise a constitutional challenge to governmental action, a litigant must have a sufficient interest in the challenged action to be said to have "standing" to present that claim. The standing requirement demands that the objecting party establish at least that "personal stake in the outcome of the controversy" as will "assure that concrete adversaries which sharpens the presentation of issues upon which the Court so largely depends for illumination of difficult constitutional questions." *Baker v. Carr* (1962). In a criminal case, that minimal requirement presumably is met by the defendant's interest in challenging the admissibility of evidence, for his avoidance of a conviction (obviously a significant personal stake) may rest on the success of his challenge.

In many areas of constitutional law, however, the Court has required for standing more than a minimal adverse interest; it has insisted also that the litigant's adverse interest be based upon a violation of his personal rights, rather than the violation of the rights of a third party which indirectly affects the litigant. *Tileston v. Ullman* (1943). As applied to the exclusionary remedy, this principle would deny standing to defendants who are objecting to the prosecution's use of evidence obtained through the violation of the rights of others. The *Wong Sun* case, described in § 6.6(d), is illustrative. Where the illegal arrest of A led to the illegal seizure of narcotics in B's home and that, in turn, led to the subsequent arrest of C at another location, the narcotics could not be introduced in evidence against A, but could be introduced against C. A had standing because the seizure of the narcotics was the fruit of his illegal arrest, although he could not contest the seizure insofar as it violated the rights of B. C, on the other hand, totally lacked standing because neither the arrest of A nor the subsequent seizure of narcotics in B's home violated his constitutional rights.

The requirement that a litigant assert his "personal rights" and not those of third parties "has not been imposed uniformly as a firm constitutional mandate" of standing. *Flast v. Cohen* (1968). Thus, the argument was advanced that an exception to the "personal rights" requirement should be adopted for claims based upon the Fourth Amendment's exclusionary rule, thereby strengthening the rule's deterrent impact. In *Alderman v. U.S.* (1969), the Supreme Court rejected this argument in the context of claimed "third-party" standing to challenge unconstitutional electronic surveillance.

The *Alderman* majority denied the alternative contentions that (i) all defendants should derive standing to challenge evidence obtained from the illegal wiretapping of others, (ii) at least codefendants and coconspirators should have standing to suppress evidence obtained through illegal wiretapping of other codefendants or coconspirators, or (iii) a special standing rule should be recognized to permit a defendant to exclude evidence obtained unlawfully from the wiretapping of another when that wiretapping was "directed at" obtaining evidence for the prosecution of the defendant. Two dissenters supported the latter position, commonly described as "target standing." However, the Court majority concluded that there was "no necessity" to depart from "the general rule that Fourth Amendment rights are personal rights which * * * may not be vicariously asserted." It did not follow from the adoption of the exclusionary rule "that anything which deters illegal searches [must] thereby [be] commanded by the Fourth Amendment." The majority was "not convinced that the additional benefits of extending the exclusionary rule to other defendants [i.e., non-victims] would justify further encroachment upon the public interest in prosecuting those accused of crime and having them acquitted or convicted on the basis of all the evidence which exposes the truth."

In reaching the above conclusion, the *Alderman* majority relied in part on the deterrent impact of other sanctions against illegal electronic eavesdropping provided in Title III (see § 3.2(b)). However, in *Rakas v. Ill.* (1978), the Court made it clear that the *Alderman* analysis rejected third party standing for all Fourth Amendment cases. See also *U.S. v. Payner* (1980) (federal lower court lacked authority to use its supervisory power to bypass *Alderman* limits by allowing a defendant to gain suppression of evidence obtained through calculated and deliberate violation of the Fourth Amendment rights of another that had been undertaken specifically to obtain evidence against persons such as defendant).

## (b) Identifying the issue

The Court's insistence upon a "personal rights" approach to standing makes the issue of standing a fairly simple one in dealing with challenges based upon the Fifth Amendment, Sixth Amendment, or due process. The nature of the constitutional right involved clearly identifies the person who may be the victim of an alleged violation. In the case of an allegedly coerced confession, for example, the victim is the defendant from whom the confession was obtained, and not those who may have been mentioned in the confession and may now be objecting to use against them of evidence discovered through the confession. In the application of the Fourth Amendment exclusionary rule, however, a determination of whose rights were violated by a particular search or seizure can be much more difficult. A search can invade the justified expectation of privacy of more than one person, and where that is claimed, the Court commonly resolves that issue under the personal rights approach to standing. In *Alderman,* for example, after rejecting third-party standing, the Court had to consider exactly whose rights were violated by an illegal wiretap. The

Court concluded that the violation extended not only to the parties to the unlawfully overheard conversations, but also to the owner of the residence in which the tapped phone was located, even though he had not been a party to those conversations.

Although the question of whether the defendant seeking exclusion was himself the victim of the challenged Fourth Amendment violation had traditionally been discussed under the heading of standing, *Rakas* suggested that separate treatment of standing was no longer necessary after the Court's flat rejection of third-party standing in *Alderman*. *Rakas* saw no "useful analytical purpose" in considering the defendant's victim-status as a matter "apart from the merits of the defendant's Fourth Amendment claim." The appropriate question, the Court noted, is whether the "disputed search infringed an interest of the defendant which the Fourth Amendment was designed to protect." Perhaps because the Court foresaw some confusion between the question asked in determining whether there was a search (did the police intrude upon *anyone*'s justified expectation of privacy) and the question traditionally labeled as one of standing (did the police intrude upon *this defendant's* expectation of privacy), its subsequent opinions have not totally discarded the practice of referring to the latter issue as one of standing. See e.g., *Ark. v. Sanders* (1979).

Whether the issue is described as one of standing or one of defining the scope of Fourth Amendment rights, particular attention must be given to the precise police conduct being called into question. It must be recalled that the fruits doctrine can readily give the defendant the right to challenge evidence obtained during a search of the premises of another, even though the defendant has no expectation of privacy in those premises and clearly was not a victim of that search. In *Wong Sun,* for example, defendant A was allowed to object to the prosecution's use of narcotics found in B's house because the search of B's house was the fruit of the illegal entry into A's home and A's illegal arrest. In the cases discussed below in subsections (c), (d) and (e), the challenges generally were directed at the searches that directly produced the seized evidence, rather than reliance upon the fruits doctrine and some earlier violation. Those cases discuss three types of interests that have been advanced, with varying success, to establish standing in search and seizure cases.

### (c) Legitimate presence at the site of the search

In *Jones v. U.S.* (1960), an occasional occupant of an apartment was held to have standing to object to a search of that apartment conducted while he was present. The *Jones* opinion rejected the view that a party whose privacy was interrupted by an unlawful search only had standing if he had some recognized property right in the premises. The Court noted that property distinctions such as those between "lessee, licensee, invitee, and guest, often only of gossamer strength, ought not to be determinative in fashioning procedures ultimately referable to constitutional safeguards." It concluded that "anyone legitimately on the premises where a search occurs may challenge its legality * * * when its fruits are proposed to be used against him."

In *Rakas v. Ill.* (1978), the majority reexamined and recast the *Jones* ruling. The Court reaffirmed that the "arcane distinctions" of property law were not controlling. It did not follow, however, that any person legitimately on the premises necessarily had an expectation of privacy in the searched portion of the premises. The defendant in *Jones,* the Court noted, occasionally stayed at the apartment searched in that case and had been given a key to the apartment by the owner. At the time of the search, he was the only occupant of the apartment. Under these circumstances, he had a legitimate expectation of privacy in the apartment, but this did not mean that all persons legitimately on the premises would have such an expectation.

Once the *Rakas* majority had rejected legitimate presence as an "automatic measure" of standing, it had little difficulty with the case before it. The defendants in *Rakas* were two passengers in a car that had been stopped in connection with the investigation of a robbery. After the occupants were ordered out of the car, the police searched it and found a sawed-off rifle under the front passenger seat and a box of rifle shells in the glove compartment. The Court found that the defendants had no protected Fourth Amendment interests in the areas searched. The glove compartment and the area under the seat, "like the trunk of the automobile, are areas in which a passenger qua passenger simply would not have a legitimate expectation of privacy." The *Rakas* majority stressed, however, that it was dealing with defendants whose only claim of privacy rested on their status as passengers in the automobile. It noted that the petitioners "asserted neither a property nor a possessory interest in the automobile, nor an interest in the property seized." A concurring opinion further noted that neither had the defendants challenged the "constitutionality of the police action in stopping the automobile" or in ordering the defendants out of the automobile. Cf. *Wong Sun.*

In *Minn. v. Olson* (1990), the Court concluded that defendant's presence came closer to that in *Jones* than in *Rakas*. The Court there held that "an overnight guest has a legitimate expectation of privacy in his guest's home" even though the guest lacks the "complete dominion and control" of an only occupant. Though the host has "ultimate control of the house," and "may admit or exclude from the house as he prefers," the guest is aware that "hosts will more likely than not respect the privacy interests of their guests." In *Minn. v. Carter* (1998), a combination of dissenting and concurring opinions suggested that at least five justices were willing to extend the *Olson* analysis to social guests who were not staying overnight. However, the Court ruled that the defendants there had no reasonable expectation of privacy in light of the character of their presence in the apartment of another, and therefore could not challenge a search through which they were observed bagging cocaine in the apartment. The Court cited "the purely commercial nature of the transaction engaged in here, the relatively short period of time on the premises, \* \* \* the lack of previous connection between the defendants and the householder," and the absence of any other purpose for their visit.

### (d) Possessory interest in the premises

A defendant with a present possessory interest in the premises searched, such as the owner or lessee of a house, thereby commonly has a legitimate expectation of privacy in those premises. That interest gives him standing to challenge the search even though he was not present when the search was made. *Chapman v. U.S.* (1961). The "possessory" interest which provides standing under this analysis ordinarily encompasses any interest which grants the defendant a general right to occupy the premises. That right need not be exclusive. Occupants of hotel rooms have been held to have a sufficient interest, *Stoner v. Cal.* (1964), and *Mancusi v. De-Forte* (1968) deemed sufficient the interest of an employee in an office he shared with several other workers. *Mancusi* reasoned that the defendant clearly would have had standing if the office had been his alone, and the joint use of the office had not so diminished his expectation of privacy as to subject it to a search by government officials acting without the permission of his employer or fellow workers.

### (e) Property interest in the item seized

Various lower court opinions and a few Supreme Court opinions have suggested that, even though a defendant lacks a possessory interest in the premises searched, he still may challenge a search if he has a property interest in the item seized. In support of this conclusion, reliance is placed upon the language of the Fourth Amendment, which refers to protecting an individual's "effects" as well as his home against unreasonable searches and seizures. However, most personal effects, not being containers, are simply seized, without themselves being searched, after a plain view sighting that provided sufficient grounds to justify the seizure (as in the case of apparent contraband). Thus, the seizure of the item is itself lawful (see § 2.7(d)), provided the officer did not violate the rights of the defendant in obtaining the plain view. The defendant's property interest in the item therefore becomes important not to contest the seizure as such, but to establish a reasonable expectation of privacy in the place where his effects are found—i.e., in the premises entered or the container opened.

The Supreme Court decision providing the strongest support for standing tied to an interest in the item seized, *U.S. v. Jeffers* (1951), presented a situation in which the defendant clearly had such an expectation of privacy in the place where the item was located. The defendant in *Jeffers* was allowed to challenge the search of his aunts' hotel room, where police found 19 bottles of cocaine that he had stored in the closet. The Court emphasized that the search and seizure were directed at obtaining defendant's "property" (the fact that he had no lawfully recognized interest in the contraband drugs being irrelevant). The *Jeffers* opinion also noted, however, that the "[aunts] had given [defendant] a key to their room, that he had their permission to use the room as well, and that he often entered the room for various purposes." Subsequently, in *Rakas,* the Court noted that *Jeffers* was a case in which defendant's standing was "based on Jeffers' possessory interest in both the premises searched and the property seized."

The *Rakas* description of *Jeffers* was reiterated and given special emphasis in *U.S. v. Salvucci* (1980). *Salvucci* overturned the previously accepted doctrine of "automatic standing" for cases involving possessory offenses (see § 6.8(f)). In reaching that result, the Court rejected the contention that the prosecution was engaged in self-contradiction when it alleged, on the one hand, that the defendant violated a statute prohibiting possession of contraband and, on the other, that he lacked standing to challenge the search of the home of another in which the contraband was seized. The Court noted that the challenge before it was not to the legality of the seizure in itself, but to the legality of the preceding search of the premises. It could not be assumed that "a person in legal possession of the goods seized during an illegal search has * * * necessarily been subject to a Fourth Amendment deprivation" since such possession "does not invariably represent the protected Fourth Amendment interest" violated by the illegal search. While possession is a factor to be considered, the Court noted, it could not be made into a "substitute" or "proxy" for a factual finding that the defendant had a "legitimate expectation of privacy in the area searched."

*Rawlings v. Ky.* (1980) furnishes an illustration of the point made in *Salvucci* that a possessory interest in the seized goods and an expectation of privacy in the area searched do not invariably coincide. Defendant in *Rawlings* was charged with possession of drugs that he had placed in the purse of an acquaintance [Cox]. Assuming that the search of Cox's purse was illegal, the Court held that the defendant could not challenge the legality of that search. The record below amply supported the lower court's conclusion that Rawlings "had no legitimate expectation of privacy in Cox's purse at the time of the search." When Rawlings "dumped thousands of dollars worth of illegal drugs into Cox's purse," shortly before the police arrived on the scene, he had "known her only a few days" and "had never received access to her purse prior to that sudden bailment." He had no right to exclude others from her purse, and a longtime companion did, in fact, have free access to her purse. While there was some question as to whether Cox had consented to the "bailment," even if she had, "the precipitous nature of the transaction hardly support[ed] a reasonable inference that petitioner took normal precautions to maintain his privacy." Finally, the Court noted, petitioner had "frank[ly] admitt[ed] * * * that he had no subjective expectation that Cox's purse would remain free from government intrusion."

## (f) Establishing standing

In *Simmons v. U.S.* (1968), the defendant, seeking to establish standing to challenge the search of a suitcase, testified that he was the owner of the suitcase. His motion to suppress was subsequently denied, and the government used his testimony at trial in establishing guilt. In finding the use of that testimony unconstitutional, the Supreme Court noted that, at least in marginal cases where the defendant is uncertain as to the probable outcome of his motion, the potential use of such testimony at trial obviously would have a deterrent impact upon his assertion of Fourth Amendment rights. Moreover, the placement of this condition upon the assertion of those rights raised self-incrimination difficulties since "the defendant who wishes to establish standing must do so at the risk that the words which he utters may later be used to incriminate him." Accordingly, the Court held, "when a defendant testifies in support of a motion to suppress evidence on Fourth Amendment grounds, his testimony may not thereafter be admitted against him at trial on the issue of guilt unless he makes no objection."

Prior to *Simmons,* in *Jones v. U.S.* (1960), the Court had held that a defendant charged with a crime requiring proof of his possession of seized property automatically had standing to challenge the search that led to the seizure of that property. Without automatic standing, the *Jones* Court noted, the defendant would face the dilemma of either relinquishing his claim or being forced to "allege facts the proof of which would tend * * * to convict him." In *U.S. v. Salvucci* (1980), the Court discarded the *Jones* automatic standing rule, reasoning that *Simmons* had eliminated the defense dilemma that *Jones* had sought to avoid.

## § 6.9 BURDEN OF PROOF

### (a) Allocation of the burden

At common law, the burden of establishing the factual basis for suppressing otherwise admissible evidence fell upon the party seeking suppression, and the Supreme Court has never questioned the constitutionality of that rule as carried over to the exclusionary rules. Thus, a state may, if it so desires, place upon the defendant the burdens of going forward and of persuasion as to the factual event (i.e., the seizure, the search, the obtaining of a statement, or the identification) which provides the grounding for an exclusionary rule claim. The Supreme Court has held, however, that the prosecution must bear the burden of proof as to certain elements that determine the applicability of an exclusionary rule. Initially, because waiver of a constitutional right is not lightly to be presumed, the prosecution has the burden of establishing that defendant waived his *Miranda* rights or his right to counsel under *Wade.* See §§ 4.4(b), 5.2(b). So too, *Bumper v. N.C.* (1968) held that the burden of establishing a voluntary consent to an otherwise unconstitutional search falls upon the prosecution. For similar reasons, if a constitutional violation is established, and the state contends its evidence is nonetheless admissible under an independent source or inevitable discovery exception to the fruits doctrine, the state has the burden of proving that those exceptions are in fact applicable. *Nix v. Williams* (§ 6.6(b)). See also *Alderman v. U.S.* (1969) (where there has been an illegal wiretap, government has "ultimate burden of persuasion to show that its evidence is untainted"). A similar burden is placed on the state where defendant had been compelled to testify under an immunity order and the government claims its evidence was not directly or indirectly derived from that immunized testimony. See *Kastigar v. U.S.* (§ 8.2(e)) (government's "affirmative duty" is not limited to a "negation of taint," but requires proof that its evidence "is derived from a legitimate source wholly independent of the compelled testimony").

Without speaking directly to the issue, the Court has indicated that the state may also be required to bear the burden as to certain other elements of an exclusionary rule claim. *Lego v. Twomey* (1972), discussed in the next subsection, certainly raises serious doubts as to whether a state could place upon the defendant the burden of persuasion as to the issue of voluntariness. Language in *Beck v. Ohio* (1964), noting that the government there needed to establish probable cause with "more specificity," suggests that the prosecution may be required to establish the existence of probable cause supporting a warrantless search or seizure. At a minimum, since the defendant in such a case does not know what information the police acted upon (unlike the warrant case, there is no probable cause affidavit), the prosecution should have the burden of going forward, if not the ultimate burden of persuasion.

### (b) Quantum of proof

Where the prosecution constitutionally must carry the burden of proof, what is the level of persuasion it must reach? In *U.S. v. Wade,* the Court stated that the prosecution must show by "clear and convincing evidence" that an in-court identification is not the product of an unconstitutional lineup identification. See § 5.2(c). *Wade* stands in contrast, however, to a substantial line of later cases that held satisfactory a preponderance of the evidence standard.

The leading case on the requisite level of proof is *Lego v. Twomey* (1972). The Court there found the preponderance standard constitutionally acceptable as applied to the prosecutor's burden of establishing the voluntariness of a confession. The majority rejected the contention, advanced in the dissent, that proof of admissibility beyond a reasonable doubt was needed "to give adequate protection to those values that the exclusionary rules are designed to serve." The majority found it "very doubtful that escalating the prosecution's burden of proof in

Fourth and Fifth Amendment suppression hearings would be sufficiently productive [in implementing the deterrent impact of the exclusionary rules] to outweigh the public interest in placing probative evidence before juries for the purpose of arriving at truthful decisions about guilt or innocence." Moreover, the defendant had "offer[ed] nothing to suggest that admissibility rulings [based upon a preponderance of the evidence standard] have been unreliable or otherwise wanting in quality because not based on some higher standard."

*Nix v. Williams* (§ 6.6(c)), relying on *Lego,* held that the preponderance standard also was satisfactory in establishing admissibility under the inevitable discovery doctrine. So too, in *U.S. v. Matlock* (1974), the Court commented that the "controlling burden of proof at [Fourth Amendment] suppression hearings should impose no greater burden than proof by a preponderance of evidence." Although *Miranda* spoke of the "heavy burden" that rests on the government to show a knowing and intelligent waiver of *Miranda* rights, *Colo. v. Connelly* (1986) held that here too, the preponderance standard was satisfactory. The Court reasoned: "If, as we held in *Lego v. Twomey,* the voluntariness of a confession need be established only by a preponderance of the evidence, then a waiver of the auxiliary protections established in *Miranda* should require no higher burden of proof."

# CHAPTER 7

# RIGHT TO COUNSEL

## § 7.1 SIXTH AMENDMENT RIGHT

### (a) Right to retained counsel

The Sixth Amendment provides that, "in all criminal prosecutions, the accused shall enjoy the right * * * to have the Assistance of Counsel for his defense." Most of the Supreme Court decisions interpreting the Sixth Amendment right to counsel have dealt with the state's failure to appoint counsel, at its expense, to assist an indigent defendant. The Amendment also guarantees a defendant's right to utilize counsel retained at the defendant's own expense, but that right is so well established by the Sixth Amendment's history and language that it rarely has been directly challenged by statute or judicial practice. The Court has been required to determine its scope only in occasional cases involving practices that impact the right by restricting the defendant's choice of retained counsel. See §§ 7.5(b), 7.6(f).

### (b) Right to appointed counsel

A constitutional right of an indigent defendant to the assistance of court appointed counsel was first recognized by the Supreme Court in *Powell v. Ala.*

(1932), but that ruling was based on due process and was carefully limited to situations similar to that before the Court—a "capital case" in which the defendant was "incapable adequately of making his own defense because of ignorance, feeble-mindedness, illiteracy or the like." *Powell* concluded that, at least under those circumstances, the appointment of counsel to assist the indigent defendant was a "logical corollary" of the defendant's right to a fair hearing.

Despite its limited holding, the *Powell* opinion strongly suggested that in all but exceptional cases, the appointment of counsel would be necessary to ensure the indigent a fair trial. The opinion stressed the inability of even the "intelligent and educated layman" to properly represent himself, and concluded that there was a need for "the guiding hand of counsel at every step of the proceedings." In *Johnson v. Zerbst* (1938), the Court relied heavily upon *Powell*'s discussion of the general need for representation by counsel in holding that the Sixth Amendment required federal courts to provide indigent defendants with appointed counsel in all felony cases. However, in *Betts v. Brady* (1942), the Court refused to apply the *Johnson v. Zerbst* ruling to the states via the Fourteenth Amendment's due process clause. The majority held that due process did not necessarily require appointment of counsel in all felony cases, but only in those cases where the particular circumstances indicated that the absence of counsel would result in a trial lacking "fundamental fairness."

*Gideon v. Wainwright* (1963), adopting a selective incorporation interpretation of the Sixth Amendment (see § 1.2(d)), subsequently overruled *Betts*. *Gideon* held that the Fourteenth Amendment fully incorporated the Sixth Amendment right and accordingly required the state to make appointed counsel available to indigent defendants in all felony cases. The *Gideon* Court deemed it "an obvious truth" that a person denied the assistance of counsel "cannot be assured a fair trial," as evidenced by the fact that "lawyers to prosecute are everywhere deemed essential" and "there are few defendants charged with crime * * * who fail to hire the best lawyers they can get." *Gideon,* like *Johnson v. Zerbst*, viewed the Sixth Amendment right as resting on the defendant's interest in obtaining a fair trial, rather than a defendant's liberty to take advantage of his resources to present his defense through retained counsel if he so preferred. Thus, contrary to earlier due process cases, it recognized a Sixth Amendment right to counsel that had the same grounding and scope as it applied to appointed and retained counsel.

### (c) The misdemeanor, non-incarceration limitation

Prior to *Argersinger v. Hamlin* (1972), some doubt existed as to whether the constitutional right to appointed counsel applied to any misdemeanor prosecutions. *Gideon* involved a felony case, and later opinions had referred to *Gideon* as simply establishing a right to counsel in "felony prosecutions." *Argersinger,* however, held *Gideon* applicable to all indigent misdemeanor defendants who are sentenced to a jail term. The Court rejected the state's contention that the Sixth Amendment right to counsel, like the Sixth Amendment right to a jury trial, should not apply to "petty offenses" (i.e., offenses punishable by no more than six months imprisonment). While there was "historical support" for the jury trial limitation, "nothing in the history of the right to counsel" suggested a "retraction of the right in petty offenses wherein the common law previously did require that counsel be provided." Moreover, there was no functional basis for drawing the line at petty offenses. The legal questions presented in a misdemeanor trial were no less complex because the jail sentence did not exceed six months. Neither was there less need for the advice of counsel prior to entering a plea of guilty. Indeed, the Court noted, petty misdemeanors may create a special need for counsel's assistance because their great volume "may create an obsession for speedy dispositions, regardless of the fairness of the result."

*Argersinger* spoke of the special character of a sentence involving a "loss of liberty," and that led the Court in *Scott v. Ill.* to draw a dividing line between misdemeanor sentences imposing incarceration and those limited to fines. Defendant there was convicted of shoplifting, a misdemeanor punishable by a maximum sentence of imprisonment for one year, but was sentenced to only a fine of $50.00. The Court held that he had not been entitled to appointed counsel since the Sixth Amendment, as to misdemeanor charges, "require[s] only that no indigent criminal defendant be sentenced to a term of imprisonment unless the State has afforded him the right to assistance of appointed counsel." The Court undoubtedly was influenced by the practical problems of providing counsel for all misdemeanor charges, typically a caseload ten times as great as the felony caseload (with only a small percentage resulting in jail sentences). "*Argersinger,*" it noted, "has proved reasonably workable, whereas any extension would create confusion and impose unpredictable, but necessarily substantial cost to 50 quite diverse states."

*Ala. v. Shelton* (2002) concluded that *Argersinger* rather than *Scott* applied where the state imposed a suspended sentence which could "end up in the actual deprivation of a person's liberty" should the defendant subsequently have his probation revoked. The key here was that the defendant would then be imprisoned for the original conviction, on which counsel had not been provided, notwithstanding that the revocation itself was based on some subsequent activity. The Court therefore distinguished *Nichols v. U.S.* (1994), which allowed an uncounseled misdemeanor conviction to be considered under an enhancement provision guiding the sentence imposed for a later conviction. The enhancement provision "did not change the penalty for [the] earlier conviction" (in contrast to *Shelton*), but merely allowed a conviction which had been valid under *Scott* (no incarceration having been imposed) to be considered in determining the appropriate sentence for a subsequent offense, in much the same fashion as other aspects of the defendant's past behavior and criminal record.

### (d) Scope of the "criminal prosecution"

The Sixth Amendment right to counsel is by its terms a right that extends only to "the accused" in a "criminal prosecution." The Court has held that the starting point for the criminal prosecution—i.e., the point at which the individual becomes "an accused"—is the initiation of "adversary judicial proceedings." *Kirby v. Ill.* (1972). Precisely what constitutes the initiation of adversary judicial proceedings is a matter commonly raised in connection with pretrial investigative procedures, and we have discussed it previously in that connection. See §§ 4.3(e), 5.2(e). As noted there, an arrest alone, without the filing of charges in court or the presentation of the arrestee before the magistrate, does not constitute the initiation of adversary judicial proceedings. See also *U.S. v. Gouveia* (1984) (right to counsel did not apply to prison inmates confined in a special unit for several months while prison authorities continued their investigation of the prison murder for which the inmates were eventually indicted; while the lack of counsel at that point could have impaired the inmates' ability to collect favorable evidence, the Sixth Amendment right does not extend to all stages at which counsel's assistance would be helpful, but only to "protecting the unaided laymen at critical confrontations with his adversary"; it therefore does not apply prior to the initiation "adversary judicial proceeding," which marks the point at which the "adverse positions of government and defendant have solidified").

Once started, the criminal prosecution continues through to the end of the trial stage, including sentencing. See *Mempa v. Rhay* (§ 7.3(g)). After that point, however, the criminal prosecution has come to an end for Sixth Amendment purposes. Thus, *Douglas v. Cal.* (§ 7.2(d)) and *Evitts v. Lucey* (§ 7.2(d)), dealing with the right to appointed and retained counsel on a first level appeal, focus only on possible equal protection and due process groundings for those rights. So too, in *Gagnon v. Scarpelli* (§ 7.3(g)), the Court held that a probation revocation proceeding not a part of the initial sentencing (compare *Mempa*) was not a stage in the "criminal prosecution" for Sixth Amendment purposes.

### (e) The "critical stage" requirement

The Court has held that Sixth Amendment right to counsel does not simply start with the initiation of adversary judicial proceedings and then require counsel's assistance at every step in the criminal prosecution thereafter. Rather, the right demands that the assistance of counsel be available only at the "critical stages" in the criminal prosecution—those steps at which substantial rights of the accused may be affected "by counsel's absence." *Mempa v. Rhay* (1967). Applying that test, the Court has held that all of the following present a critical stage:

subjecting the accused to some (but not all) identification procedures (§§ 5.2, 5.3); police or prosecutor attempts to elicit inculpatory statements from the accused (§ 4.3); a first appearance where action taken there (or inaction there) can later be used against the accused (§ 7.3(c)); an arraignment with similar characteristics (§ 7.3(e)); a preliminary hearing (§ 7.3(d)); the trial (§ 7.3(f)); and sentencing, even where imposed in conjunction with a probation revocation (§ 7.3(g)).

## § 7.2  ADDITIONAL CONSTITUTIONAL RIGHTS TO COUNSEL AND OTHER ASSISTANCE

### (a) Due process/fair hearing right to counsel

*Powell v. Ala.* (1932), recognized due process rights to the assistance of appointed and retained counsel at a time when the Sixth Amendment's requirements had not been extended to the states. Today, both rights continue to have significance for those portions of the criminal justice process that are not part of the "criminal prosecution" for Sixth Amendment purposes. Where the defendant is entitled, by constitution or state law, to a hearing at a point in the process not encompassed by the Sixth Amendment, the Court will look to "free-standing due process" (see § 1.2(f)) to determine whether fundamental fairness includes a right to representation by counsel at that hearing.

Traditional due process analysis, as discussed in § 1.2(f), often employs a case-by-case evaluation, looking to all of the facts of the particular case. That was the approach adopted in the pre-*Gideon* cases dealing with the right to counsel at trial, when that issue was governed by a "fundamental fairness" standard rather than the Sixth Amendment. See *Powell v. Ala.* and *Betts v. Brady,* discussed in § 7.1(b). It was also the approach later applied in *Gagnon v. Scarpelli,* dealing with counsel in probation and parole revocation proceedings. See § 7.3(g). On the other hand, *Evitts v. Lucey* adopted a flat due process requirement of counsel on the first appeal as of right. See § 7.2(d) and § 7.3(h). So too, the cases finding no due process right to counsel as to later appeals and collateral attack also were flat rulings that did not look to possible variations in the circumstances of individual cases (apart, perhaps, from the capital case). See § 7.3(h), (i).

## (b) Derivative right to counsel

A constitutional right to the assistance of counsel also can be derived from other constitutional guarantees besides the due process right to a fair hearing. Thus, *Miranda v. Ariz.* (§ 4.4) recognized a right to consult with counsel as a measure protecting the self-incrimination privilege of a person subjected to custodial interrogation. The Court there required that the police inform such a person that "he has a right to consult with a lawyer and to have the lawyer with him during interrogation," and that "if he is indigent, a lawyer will be appointed to present him." This requirement extends beyond the

Sixth Amendment right to counsel since custodial interrogation often occurs before the individual is an "accused" in a "criminal prosecution." The *Miranda* approach of requiring an opportunity to consult with counsel as a means of safeguarding another constitutional guarantee has also been advanced, without success, in other contexts. In *Kirby v. Ill.* (1972) that approach was urged unsuccessfully by the dissenters, who argued that a suspect placed in a lineup, even though not yet an accused, should have a right to the presence of retained or appointed counsel as a means of safeguarding the trial right of confrontation. See § 5.2(a),(e). In *U.S. v. Mandujano* (1976), two justices argued that the self-incrimination privilege of a target-witness before a grand jury carried with it a right to consult with a retained or appointed attorney prior to the questioning. While the Court did not find it necessary to rule on that contention, four justices found it unpersuasive. See § 7.3(b).

### (c) Equal protection and appointed counsel

Although it did not deal with the right to counsel, *Griffin v. Ill.* (1956) provided the doctrinal foundation for the eventual recognition of an equal protection right to appointed counsel. *Griffin* held that where state law conditioned appellate review upon the availability of a stenographic transcript of the trial proceedings, the state had to make such a transcript available without charge to indigent defendants so they would have equal access to appellate review. The plurality opinion stressed that, although the state was not required by due process to afford appellate review, once it did so, it could not condition such review "in a way that discriminates against some convicted defendants on account of their poverty." "There can be no equal justice," the opinion noted, "where the kind of trial a man gets depends on the amount of money he has." In *Douglas v. Cal.* (1963), the Court relied upon the "*Griffin* principle" to hold invalid the California practice of refusing to appoint counsel on an appeal by an indigent when the appellate court, after reviewing the trial record, concluded that "no good whatever could be served" by appointment. The Court noted that the more affluent defendant was not required to run "this gantlet of a preliminary showing of merit" in order to have his appeal presented by counsel. The indigent defendant, it concluded, was entitled to equal treatment, at least on a first appeal granted by the state as a matter of right. The state therefore was required to appoint counsel for all indigent defendants on first appeal, just as it was required by *Gideon* to provide counsel at the trial level.

Construed broadly, the *Griffin-Douglas* concept of equal protection could require the appointment of counsel to assist the indigent at every stage in the administration of criminal justice at which the more affluent defendant is allowed by state law to be represented by privately retained counsel. The question of appointment would rest on the need for providing equal treatment rather than the need for a lawyer's assistance to assure a fair hearing. However, in stressing the importance of the first appeal, and in characterizing a defendant's presentation of that appeal without counsel as a "meaningless ritual," the *Douglas* opinion cited factors that would have been relevant in assessing a due process/fair hearing right to appointed appellate counsel. Subsequently, in *Ross v. Moffitt* (1974), the Court focused on this aspect of the *Douglas* ruling and read the *Griffin* principle as it related to appointed counsel to be closely tied to such a due process right to counsel.

*Ross* involved a state practice of appointing counsel to assist indigent appellants on their appeals to the state intermediate appellate court, but not on their applications for review by the state supreme court or their petitions for certiorari to the United States Supreme Court. A divided Court held that the failure to appoint counsel at these later stages of the appellate process did not deprive the appellants of equal protection. The Court stressed that the indigent defendant did not need counsel to have "meaningful access" to the higher appellate courts. On application for review, the state supreme court would have before it a transcript, the lower court brief, and, in many cases, an opinion of the state intermediate court. These materials, supplemented by any personal statement of appellant, provided an "adequate basis" for the state court to determine whether to grant review—especially since the "critical issue" for that decision was not whether there had been "a correct adjudication of guilt in every individual case," but whether the appeal presented issues of general legal significance. The same factors, the Court noted, also applied to its own consideration of petitions for writ of certiorari.

The *Ross* majority acknowledged that a lawyer skilled in preparing petitions for review "would * * * prove helpful" to an appellant, but went on to add: "The fact that a particular service might be of benefit to an indigent defendant does not mean that service is constitutionally required. * * * [Equal protection] does not require absolute equality or precisely equal advantages. * * * The duty of the state * * * is not to duplicate the legal arsenal that may be privately retained by a criminal defendant in a continuing effort to reverse his conviction, but only to assure the indigent defendant an adequate opportunity to present his claims fairly in the context of the State's appellate process."

*Ross'* characterization of the *Douglas* equal protection analysis as ensuring only that the indigent have an "adequate opportunity" to utilize the state process suggests a standard that comes close to demanding under equal protection only what the indigent defendant would otherwise be entitled to under due process. When *Douglas* was decided, its equal protection analysis might have been viewed as carrying the equal protection right beyond due process by imposing a flat requirement of appointment of counsel for all first appeals granted as a matter of right, without examining the indigent appellant's need for counsel on the case-by-case basis traditionally employed in due process analysis. See § 7.2(a).

However, that view was largely undermined by the subsequent ruling in *Evitts v. Lucey* (1985). As discussed in § 7.3(h), *Evitts* held that due process includes a right to representation by competent counsel on a first appeal as of right, and also did so as a flat requirement.

Today, the Court describes the *Douglas/Ross* line of rulings as resting on "both equal protection and due process concerns," *Halbert v. Mich.* (§ 7.3(h)), and while the Court may separately analyze due process and equal protection claims, see *Pa. v. Finley* (§ 7.3(i)), the analysis of one will bear upon the other. Thus, in *Finley*, the circumstances that led the Court to conclude that due process does not require counsel for a fair hearing also led it to conclude that the indigent denied appointed counsel was not thereby deprived of the "meaningful access" noted in *Douglas*. See § 7.3(i). So too, *Halbert*, in extending *Douglas* to require appointed counsel on a first appeal not of right, relied on the presence of many of the factors cited in *Evitts* as establishing a due process right to the assistance of appellate counsel. See § 7.3(h).

### (d) Assistance other than counsel

Under *Griffin v. Ill.* and its progeny, indigent defendants have been held to have an equal protection right not only to a free trial transcript where needed for appeal, but also to a trial transcript for use in a collateral attack upon a conviction, for a transcript of a habeas proceeding to be used on appeal from a denial of habeas relief, and for a transcript of a preliminary hearing to be used in preparing for trial. See e.g., *Roberts v. LaVallee* (1967). The defendant must, of course, have some need for the transcript, but that is established where the transcript is the common and apparently preferable means of presenting the particular type of claim that defendant desires to advance. See *Draper v. Wash.* (1963). But note *U.S. v. MacCollom* (1976) (free trial transcript for use in collateral attack could be conditioned on judicial certification that indigent petitioner's asserted claim was "not frivolous").

As evidenced by *Mayer v. Chicago* (1971), the right to a free transcript can extend to proceedings which are not part of the "criminal prosecution" for Sixth Amendment purposes nor sufficiently significant to require appointment of counsel under a due process analysis. *Mayer* required that an indigent defendant, fined $500.00 for ordinance violations of disorderly conduct and interference with a police officer, be provided a free transcript needed to challenge on appeal the sufficiency of the evidence supporting his conviction. The Court stressed, inter alia, the potential significance of conviction itself, citing such "collateral consequences * * * as when (as was apparently a possibility in this case) the impecunious medical student finds himself barred from the practice of medicine because of [the] conviction." Under *Scott v. Ill.* (§ 7.1(c)), the defendant would not have been entitled to the appointment of counsel at his trial on the ordinance violations. Providing a transcript may be distinguished from providing a lawyer, however, on the ground that the lack of the transcript would have effectively denied Mayer all access to the appellate process, while Scott still had access to the trial process, albeit through self-representation.

In *Ake v. Okla.* (1985), the Court relied on due process, rather than equal protection, to hold that, "when a defendant has made a preliminary showing that his insanity at the time of the offense is likely to be a significant factor at trial, * * * the state [must] provide access to a psychiatrist's assistance on this issue if the defendant cannot otherwise afford one." This obligation, the Court stressed, was limited to cases in which the defendant's mental condition was "seriously in question" and did not go beyond providing the defense with assistance of a single psychiatrist selected by the trial court. The *Ake* majority noted that the Court had never held that "a State must purchase for the indigent all the assistance that his wealthier counterpart might buy," but due process did require that the indigent defendant be given the "basic tools" needed to present his defense. Taking into consideration the defendant's interest "in the accuracy of the criminal proceeding," the limited financial burden that would be imposed upon the state under the proposed standard for appointment, and the probable value of psychiatric assistance in presenting an insanity defense, a court appointed psychiatrist clearly was such a "basic tool" where insanity is likely to be a serious issue. Although *Ake* dealt only with psychiatric assistance, *Caldwell v. Mississippi*

(1985) held open the possibility of extending the *Ake* analysis to other types of experts (e.g., forensic specialists), given a proper showing of need, and many lower court rulings support that extension.

## § 7.3  RIGHT TO COUNSEL: STAGES OF THE PROCESS

### (a)  Police investigation

Prior to the initiation of adversary judicial proceedings, an individual has no Sixth Amendment right to counsel. See § 7.1(d). However, under *Miranda,* a person subjected to custodial interrogation has a right to consult with counsel prior to and during such interrogation. See § 4.4(b). Once the adversary judicial proceedings have been initiated, the Sixth Amendment applies, and the individual may not be subjected to police action designed to elicit potentially incriminating statements without an appropriate waiver of counsel. See § 4.3. So too, the accused may not be subjected to eyewitness identification in a lineup or show-up without having counsel present or having waived that right. See § 5.2. On the other hand, that right does not extend to other identification procedures involving an accused (e.g., the taking and analyzing of blood samples) as those procedures do not present a "critical stage." See §§ 5.3(b); 7.1(e).

### (b)  Grand jury proceedings

The Supreme Court found it unnecessary in *U.S. v. Mandujano* (1976) to determine whether an indigent "target witness" before the grand jury has a constitutional right to appointed counsel. However, a four-justice plurality opinion argued that there was no such right. Relying on the *Kirby* holding that the starting point for the Sixth Amendment is the initiation of adversary judicial proceedings (see § 7.1(d)), the plurality noted that the Sixth Amendment did not apply here since grand jury witnesses, though targets, have not been charged with any offense.

The *Mandujano* plurality also relied upon the reasoning in *In re Groban's Petition* (1957). In *Groban,* the state refused to permit a witness to have retained counsel present during his examination by a state fire marshall in a proceeding to determine the cause of a fire. In finding that this restriction did not violate due process, the majority cited as an analogy the grand jury proceeding, noting that "a witness before a grand jury cannot insist, as a matter of constitutional right, on being represented by his counsel." Justice Black's dissent in *Groban,* although disagreeing with the majority's conclusion as to the fire marshall's proceeding, agreed with its statement regarding the grand jury. The key there was the presence of the grand jurors as representatives of the community. "It would be very difficult," Justice Black noted, "for officers of the state [i.e., the prosecuting attorney] to seriously abuse or deceive a witness in the presence of the grand jury."

Two dissenters in *Mandujano* contended that the target grand jury witness had a right to counsel (including a right to appointed counsel for the indigent) because the questioning of such a witness "inextricably involves" his privilege against self-incrimination. The *Mandujano* plurality did not speak specifically to a possible Fifth Amendment grounding for a witness' right to counsel, but it did reject an analogy based on *Miranda,* see § 8.2(b). Accordingly, the *Mandujano* plurality opinion, with the support of *Groban,* is generally viewed by lower courts as establishing that no constitutional right to counsel exists at the grand jury stage. Consistent with this position, most jurisdictions do not provide for the appointment of counsel to assist the indigent target witness. However, all jurisdictions will allow a grand jury witness to interrupt his testimony for the purposes of consulting with retained counsel (typically located in an adjoining room, since a substantial majority of jurisdictions, to preserve grand jury secrecy, follow the common law practice of excluding the witness' counsel from the grand jury room). The *Mandujano* plurality had no need to address whether that practice is constitutionally mandated, as the witness there had been informed that he could leave the grand jury room to consult with retained counsel (if he had one, which he did not).

### (c) Initial appearance

With the arrested person's initial appearance (at which the magistrate will set forth the charges, inform the accused of his rights, and set bail), adversary judicial proceedings have been initiated.

See *Mich. v. Jackson* (§ 4.3(e)). Where the state requires the defendant to make an election at the initial appearance that could be prejudicial, *White v. Md.* (1963) establishes that the initial appearance also constitutes a "critical stage," requiring the assistance of counsel. In *White,* the state followed a practice of requesting a felony defendant to enter an initial, non-binding plea before the magistrate. The defendant there, without the assistance of counsel, entered a plea of guilty, and after he shifted his plea to not guilty at his arraignment, that earlier plea was used against him at trial. The Supreme Court reversed the ensuing conviction, holding that the use of the plea rendered defendant's initial appearance a critical stage at which counsel should have been made available to assist the "accused to * * * plead intelligently."

## (d) Preliminary hearing

*Coleman v. Ala.* (1970) ruled that the preliminary hearing is a "critical stage" under the Sixth Amendment. While there was no opinion for the Court, a majority agreed that the failure to appoint counsel at a typical state preliminary hearing resulted in a constitutional violation, though not necessarily requiring reversal of a subsequent conviction. The majority stressed the practical importance of the preliminary hearing and noted five advantages that could result from counsel's assistance at that proceeding: (1) a "lawyer's skilled examination and cross-examination of witness" may lead the magistrate to conclude that the state lacks the probable caused needed for a bindover; (2) "the skilled interrogation * * * by an experienced lawyer can fashion a valuable impeachment tool for use in cross-examination" at trial; (3) the defense counsel may use the preliminary exam to "preserve [favorable] testimony * * * of a witness who does not appear at trial"; (4) "trained counsel can more effectively discover the case the state has against his client and make possible [better] preparation * * * [for] trial"; and (5) "counsel can also be influential at the preliminary hearing in making effective arguments * * * on such matters as the necessity for an early psychiatric examination or bail." The majority added, however, that denial of counsel at preliminary hearing could constitute harmless error where the advantages lost through the lack of counsel had no bearing on the subsequent trial. See § 9.10(a).

### (e) Arraignment

The formal arraignment occurs after the information or indictment is issued, and involves a reading of the charges contained therein and the entry of a plea in response to those charges. Even where the accused enters a plea of not-guilty, the arraignment may be a critical stage due to the consequences of inaction at that point. In *Hamilton v. Ala.* (1961), local law treated certain defenses, such as insanity, as "irretrievably lost" if not raised at arraignment. Finding a constitutional violation in the state's failure to provide defendant with the assistance of counsel, the Court rejected the contention that the critical nature of the proceeding should depend upon a showing of actual prejudice—i.e., a showing that defendant would have raised one of the "lost" defenses if he had been assisted by counsel. It concluded that the degree of prejudice "can never be known" because only counsel present at the time "could have enabled the accused to know all the defenses available to him and to plead intelligently."

## (f) Trial

The earliest right to counsel cases dealt primarily with assistance of counsel at trial, and such assistance is clearly recognized as the "core" of the Sixth Amendment right. Denial of the right to counsel at trial requires the automatic reversal of defendant's conviction, as the defect is "structural."See § 9.10(c). See also *Loper v. Beto* (1972) (where indigent defendant was denied his right to appointed counsel under *Gideon* (§ 7.1), the resulting conviction was void and could not be used to impeach his credibility when he testified at a subsequent trial on a different charge); *Burgett v. Tex.* (1967) (conviction void under *Gideon* could not be used as a prior conviction under recidivist statute).

## (g) Sentencing, probation and parole

*Mempa v. Rhay* (1967) confirmed the implications of prior decisions in holding that sentencing was a "critical stage" of a criminal prosecution, therefore requiring the assistance of appointed counsel. *Mempa* held, moreover, that sentencing remained a "critical stage" even though deferred to a probation revocation proceeding. In *Mempa,* the trial judge placed the defendant on probation without fixing the term of imprisonment that would be imposed if probation were later revoked. The Court concluded that the subsequent determination and imposition of a prison sentence at the probation revocation proceeding was as much a part of the "criminal prosecution" as sentencing imposed immediately after trial. Rejecting the state's contention that counsel was not needed since the length of the prison sentence was set automatically by state law, the Court noted that the trial judge was required to submit a recommendation to the parole board and counsel could assist the defendant in presenting his case on that recommendation. Also, certain legal rights (e.g., withdrawal of a guilty plea) could be lost if not raised at the time the prison sentence was imposed, and counsel also was needed to protect those rights.

In *Gagnon v. Scarpelli* (1973), the Court held that *Mempa* did not extend to a probation revocation proceeding that involved only a determination as to revocation, a prison sentence previously having been imposed and suspended in favor of probation. The probation revocation determination is not based on the commission of the original offense and accordingly is not part of the "criminal prosecution" governed by the Sixth Amendment. The same is true of parole revocation, also covered by the *Gagnon* opinion. However, *Gagnon* concluded that due process requires that the state provide appointed counsel under some circumstances.

The loss of liberty resulting from parole or probation revocation had been held prior to *Gagnon* to be a "serious deprivation" requiring the protection of due process. Under that precedent, due process afforded the parolee or probationer substantial hearing rights, including the rights to present evidence and confront opposing witnesses. *Gagnon* concluded that due process also requires the state to provide appointed counsel where, under the facts of the particular case, counsel is needed to ensure the "effectiveness of the [hearing] rights guaranteed by [due process]." The Court would not attempt to formulate "a precise and detailed set of guidelines" for determining when that need exists, but it did note that counsel ordinarily should be provided where there is a significant factual dispute or the probationer or parolee relies upon a contention that a layman would have difficulty presenting.

Applying traditional due process analysis (see § 7.2(a)), the *Gagnon* opinion refused to impose, a flat requirement of counsel in all revocation cases. While such a requirement "had the appeal of simplicity, it would impose direct costs and serious collateral disadvantages without regard to the need or the likelihood in a particular case for a constructive contribution by counsel." In most revocation cases, the issue presented simply did not require the expertise of a lawyer. Quite often, "the probationer or parolee has been convicted of committing another crime [which automatically establishes grounds for revocation] or has admitted the charges against him." On the other side, "the introduction of counsel" would "alter significantly the nature of the [revocation] proceeding." The state would respond by retaining its own counsel and the role of the hearing body would become "more akin to that of a judge at trial, and less attuned to the rehabilitative needs of the individual probationer."

### (h) Appeals

In *Ross v. Moffitt* (1974), in the course of holding that neither due process nor equal protection requires appointment of counsel to assist a convicted defendant in preparing a petition for second-tier, discretionary appellate review, the Court emphasized the different constitutional status of the trial and the appellate process. While a state could not dispense with the trial stage of criminal proceedings, *McKane v. Durston* (1894) had held it could refuse to provide "any appeal at all." Similarly, while due process requires that the state provide a trial attorney to serve as a "shield to protect [defendant] against being 'haled into court' by the State and stripped of his presumption of innocence," a lesser interest is presented where defendant seeks an attorney to "serve as a sword to upset the prior determination of guilt."

Notwithstanding these differences, the Court has established an automatic constitutional right to counsel in limited appellate settings that is similar to the Sixth Amendment's automatic right to counsel at trial. *Douglas v. Cal.,* as discussed in § 7.2(c), established an equal protection right of the indigent defendant to appointed counsel on a first appeal granted as a matter of right under state law. *Evitts v. Lucey* (1985) held that the *Douglas* ruling also had a due process foundation and therefore established as well a right to representation by retained counsel on first appeal of right. Neither right requires a showing of need under the circumstances of the case (in contrast to the *Gagnon* right at probation revocation). The *Evitts* Court acknowledged the considerations noted in *Ross* as to the distinct character of an appeal, but held that they should not prevail as to the first appeal of right. While the state had no obligation to create an appellate process, a first appeal of right, once established, became "an integral part of [its] system for finally adjudicating the guilt or innocence of a defendant."

*Ross v. Moffit,* as discussed in § 7.2(c), concluded that the character of appellate court consideration of a petition for second-tier, discretionary review rendered inapplicable the considerations that led to the *Douglas* ruling. In *Halbert v. Mich.* (2005), a divided Court concluded that a state law providing for only discretionary appellate review of a first appeal from a guilty-plea (or *nolo*-plea) conviction presented a situation closer to *Douglas* than *Ross*, and therefore required appointment of counsel to assist the plea-defendant in seeking such appellate review. The Court majority stressed: (1) the importance of first-tier appellate review as a protection against errors even in plea cases; (2) the state appellate court's focus on the merits of the petitioner's claim in deciding whether to grant review (in contrast to the emphasis in secondary discretionary review on the general legal significance of the issue presented); (3) the defendant at this stage being without the benefit of the work product of a previous appellate counsel (in contrast to the defendant seeking discretionary second-tier review); and (4) that indigent defendants seeking review of their pleas, as a group, are "particularly handicapped as self-representatives," as a high percentage are "individuals * * * who have little education, learning disabilities, and mental impairment."

Where the *Douglas* doctrine requires appointment of appellate counsel, it also bars the state from adopting a withdrawal procedure that invites counsel to evade her obligation of advocacy on her client's behalf. Thus, *Anders v. Cal.* (1967) found a denial of defendant's rights under *Douglas* when appointed counsel was allowed to withdraw by simply filing a statement noting that the appeal had no merit, and the appellate court, without further briefing, would then examine the record and affirm the conviction. The Court held that, while appointed counsel may request withdrawal when she finds a case to be "wholly frivolous," she cannot do so by simply stating her conclusion that the appeal lacks merit. The Court further stated that, to ensure that counsel was conscientious in arriving at the determination that the appeal was frivolous, the state court should require counsel to file a brief referring to anything in the record that might arguably support the appeal, a copy of the brief should be given to the defendant (who might then respond), and the appellate court should then conduct a "full examination" of the proceedings.

The withdrawal structure announced in *Anders* was later characterized as a "prophylactic framework" which states could modify. The key is that the state withdrawal procedure preserve for the defendant a "fair opportunity to obtain an adjudication on the merits of the appeal." Thus, *McCoy v. Court of Appeals* (1988) held that the state could require counsel's withdrawal brief to cite the authority that led counsel to conclude the appeal was frivolous, as that would provide additional assurance that the attorney's conclusion was based on diligent research. *Smith v. Robbins* (2000) found satisfactory a state procedure under which counsel filed a brief that simply "summarize[d] the procedural and factual history of the case with citations to the record." The Court noted that, before counsel was allowed to withdraw, the state process required the appellate court to independently examine the record and to request briefing on any issues that might be arguable. Thus, counsel was not allowed to withdraw on a statement of "bare conclusion," but had to provide a detailed history of the case (which ensured that "a trained legal eye had searched the record"), and the state appellate court had to agree with counsel's conclusion after conducting its own review. The Court stressed in this regard that the focus of the withdrawal procedure must be on whether the appeal is "frivolous," rather than on whether it simply is not likely to prevail.

### (i) Collateral proceedings

In *Pa. v. Finley* (1987), the Court noted that it has "never held that prisoners have a constitutional right to counsel when mounting collateral attacks to their convictions and we decline to so hold today." Relying on the reasoning of *Ross v. Moffitt,* the Court concluded that "since a defendant has no federal constitutional right to counsel when pursuing a discretionary appeal on direct review of his conviction, *a fortiori* he has no such right when attacking a conviction that has long since become final upon exhaustion of the appellate process."

The *Finley* Court noted that on collateral attack, as in seeking discretionary appellate review, the petitioner retains "meaningful access" to the process even though counsel is not provided. In earlier cases, the Court had imposed several obligations upon state prison authorities to ensure that access to the federal writ of habeas corpus was available to incarcerated defendants. *Johnson v. Avery* (1969) held that a state regulation prohibiting prisoners from assisting each other in preparing habeas corpus petitions violated the prisoner's right of access to federal habeas corpus in the absence of the state providing some alternative form of assistance. *Bounds v. Smith* (1977) later extended *Johnson v. Avery* to hold that "the fundamental right of access to the courts requires prison authorities to assist inmates in the preparation and filing of meaningful legal papers by providing prisoners with adequate libraries or adequate legal assistance from persons trained in the law."

In *Murray v. Giarratano* (1989), the Court was divided as to what due process required for habeas petitioners who were challenging capital convictions. At issue there was the claim of Virginia's death row inmates that they were entitled to appointed counsel to help them prepare habeas challenges to their convictions and sentences. Four justices (per Stevens, J.) argued that the capital case presented a special circumstance which distinguished *Finley*. They stressed the special needs of capital petitioners, as reflected by a success rate on habeas challenges of 60–70% in capital cases, as compared to a rate of 0.25–7% in noncapital cases. Four justices (per Rehnquist, C.J.) thought *Finley* controlling. While the Eighth Amendment and the due process clause required additional procedural safeguards for capital cases at trial, the Court had consistently refused to apply special standards on appellate and collateral review. The deciding vote was cast by Justice Kennedy. He initially accepted Justice Stevens' analysis insofar as it established (1) that "collateral proceedings are a central part of the review process for prisoners condemned to death" and (2) that the "complexity of our jurisprudence in this area * * * makes it unlikely that capital defendants will be able to file successful petitions for collateral relief without the assistance of persons learned in the law." He noted, however, that the necessary assistance can be provided in "various ways" and there was no showing that Virginia's approach (which made available the assistance of "[prison] unit attorneys") had been unsatisfactory. Accordingly, Justice Kennedy concurred in the rejection of the inmates' claim based "on the facts and record of this case."

## § 7.4  WAIVER OF COUNSEL AND THE RIGHT TO PROCEED PRO SE

### (a) The "knowing and intelligent" requirement

The Supreme Court frequently has noted that the defendant may waive his constitutional right to assistance of counsel, but a waiver will be acceptable only if made "knowingly and intelligently." *Johnson v. Zerbst* (1938). It has further noted, that waiver will not be "lightly assumed" on appellate review, and that trial courts, in assessing circumstances suggesting a possible waiver, "must indulge every reasonable presumption against waiver." Id. On the other hand, when a waiver is first challenged on collateral attack (e.g., habeas corpus), "it is the defendant's burden to prove that he did not competently and intelligently waive his right to assistance of counsel." *Iowa v. Tovar* (2004).

What is necessary to establish a valid waiver will vary with the setting in which the waiver occurred. Previous sections have dealt with the waiver of counsel in connection with police investigative practices. See §§ 4.3(f), 4.9, 5.2(b). Our concern here is with waiver in what the Supreme Court has characterized as a "trial-type situation." *Schneckloth v. Bustamonte* (1973). In that setting, *Carnley v. Cochran* (1962) holds that waiver will not be presumed from a "silent record"; the evidence must show that the defendant was informed specifically of his right to the assistance of appointed or retained counsel and that he clearly rejected such assistance. "No amount of circumstantial evidence that the person may have been aware of his right [and intended to silently relinquish it] will suffice" as a replacement for specific notice and rejection on the record.

The Court has described its approach to the assessment of an alleged waiver (beyond requiring the formal prerequisites of *Carnley*) as a " 'pragmatic approach,' * * * one that asks 'what purposes a lawyer can serve at the particular stage of the proceedings in question, and what assistance he could provide to an accused at that stage,' in order to 'determine the * * * type of warnings and procedures that should be required before a waiver * * * will be recognized." *Iowa v. Tovar*. Thus, it has noted, "less rigorous warnings" may be required for a valid waiver at a pre-trial stage, "not because pretrial proceedings are less important than trial, but because at that stage, 'the full dangers and disadvantages of self-representation are * * * less substantial and more obvious to the accused than they are at trial'." In addition to the stage of the proceeding, a series of other factors bear upon "the information that the defendant must possess in order to make an intelligent election," including "the defendant's education or sophistication * * *

[and] the complex or easily grasped nature of the charge." Id.

Waiver of counsel builds upon, and should be distinguished from, the general level of mental competency that a defendant must possess to stand trial. Due process prohibits proceeding against a defendant unless he has "sufficient present ability to consult with his lawyer with a reasonable degree of rational understanding and has a rational as well as factual understanding of the proceedings against him," *Godinez v. Moran* (1993), and under certain circumstances, it will require a psychiatric evaluation in order to assess whether defendant has that level of competency, *Drope v. Mo.* (1975). But once competency is established, no "higher standard" of mental capacity is required for waiving counsel or pleading guilty, although those waivers require separate inquiries to ensure that the defendant has the specific understanding needed for a "knowing and voluntary" relinquishment of the right in question. *Godinez,* supra.

### (b) Waiver prior to the entry of a guilty plea

Very frequently the defendant at arraignment will seek to waive counsel with the obvious intention of entering a plea of guilty. The constitutional limitation upon waiver in this circumstance is supplemented by the due process requirement that the guilty plea be voluntary. See § 9.5(a). As to the waiver of counsel itself, the Court has concluded that the judicial warnings and inquiry here may be less extensive than what is required when the defendant seeks to waive counsel and represent himself at trial. Building upon the waiver requirements of *Faretta v. Cal.* (§ 7.4(d)), which governs the latter situation, the state court in *Iowa v. Tovar* (2004) held that the defendant's waiver in anticipation of entering a guilty plea had been insufficient under the Sixth Amendment because the trial court had: (1) "[failed to] advise the defendant that 'waiving the assistance of counsel in deciding whether to plead guilty entails the risk that a viable defense will be overlooked'; and (2) [failed to] 'admonish' the defendant 'that by waiving his right to an attorney he will lose the opportunity to obtain an independent opinion on whether, under the facts and applicable law, it is wise to plead guilty'." Rejecting this position, a unanimous Supreme Court responded: "[N]either warning is mandated by the Sixth Amendment. The constitutional requirement is satisfied when the trial court informs the accused of the nature of the charges against him, of his right to be counseled regarding his plea, and of the range of allowable punishments attendant upon the entry of a guilty plea." It was sufficient, the Court noted, that the defendant understood how the waived right "would apply *in general* in the circumstances of the waiver."

### (c) The right to proceed pro se

*Faretta v. Cal.* (1975) held that the Sixth Amendment also guarantees to the defendant the right to proceed *pro se* (i.e., to represent himself without counsel). *Faretta* relied upon the "structure of the

Sixth Amendment, as well as * * * the English and colonial jurisprudence from which the Amendment emerged." The Court noted that, while the Sixth Amendment does not specifically refer to the right of self-representation, that right is "necessarily implied" by the Amendment's references to the accused's presentation of his defense. The Sixth Amendment, it noted, refers to the rights of confrontation, compulsory process, and notice as rights of "the accused." Similarly, the counsel provision speaks only of the "assistance" of counsel, and suggests thereby that "counsel, like the other defense tools guaranteed * * * shall be an aid to a willing defendant—not an organ of the State interposed between an unwilling defendant and his right to defend himself personally."

*Faretta* recognized that a constitutional right to proceed *pro se* "seems to cut against the grain" of decisions, like *Gideon,* that are based on the premise that "the help of a lawyer is essential to assure a fair trial." It rejected, however, the dissent's contention that the state's interest in providing a fair trial permitted it to insist upon representation by counsel. An analysis of the historical roots of the Sixth Amendment suggested that the founders had placed on a higher level the right of "free choice." Moreover, where the defendant opposes representation by counsel, "the potential advantage of a lawyer * * * can be realized, if at all, only imperfectly. To force a lawyer on a defendant can only lead him to believe that the law contrives against him."

*Martinez v. Ct. App. Cal.* (2000) distinguished *Faretta* in holding that there is no constitutional right to self-representation on appeal. While *Faretta* had been based on the structure and history of the Sixth Amendment, at the appellate stage of the process, the governing constitutional provision was simply due process. The "autonomy interest" cited in *Faretta* was therefore less compelling, and the Court was "entirely unpersuaded," in light of "the practices that prevail in this nation today," that the "risk of either disloyalty or suspicion of disloyalty [by appointed or retained appellate counsel] is of sufficient concern to conclude that a constitutional right of self-representation is a necessary component of a fair appellate proceeding."

### (d)  Waiver in the pro se situation

*Faretta* stressed that the defendant who proceeds *pro se* must act "knowingly and intelligently" in giving up those "traditional benefits associated with the right to counsel." Thus, "he should be made aware of the dangers and disadvantages of self-representation, so that the record will establish that 'he knows what he is doing and his choice is made with eyes open.'" The also noted that the right to self-representation "is not a license to abuse the dignity of the courtroom." Under *Ill. v. Allen* (§ 9.8(b)), the judge may terminate self-representation by a defendant "who deliberately engages in serious and obstructionist misconduct." Similarly, self-representation is "not a license" for failure to comply with "relevant rules of procedural and substantive law." Thus, "whatever else may or may not be open to him on appeal, a defendant who elects to represent himself cannot thereafter complain that the quality of his own defense amounted to a denial of the 'effective assistance of counsel.' "

Once the trial court is assured that the defendant is knowingly and intelligently giving up the benefits of counsel, it must accept his decision. It matters not that defendant lacks "technical legal knowledge." A person need not "have the skill and experience of a lawyer in order to competently and intelligently choose self-representation." If the defendant is improperly denied a request to proceed pro se (which must be timely made), the state cannot argue that the error was "harmless" because counsel gave defendant better representation than he could have given himself. "Since the right of representation is a right that when exercised usually increases the likelihood of a trial outcome unfavorable to the defendant, its denial is not amenable to 'harmless error' analysis." *McKaskle v. Wiggins* (1984). See § 9.10(c).

### (e) Standby counsel

*Faretta* had noted that "a state may—even over objection by the accused—appoint a 'standby counsel' to aid the accused if and when the accused requests help and to be available to represent the accused in the event that termination of the defendant's self-representation is necessary." *McKaskle v. Wiggins* (1984) added that the standby counsel appointed over defendant's objection was not neces-

sarily limited to a "seen but not heard" role. The
trial court could properly direct counsel to "steer
the defendant through the basic procedures of trial," thereby relieving the judge of that responsibility. In *McKaskle,* however, standby counsel had engaged in unsolicited participation that involved
more than "routine clerical or procedural matters."
Nonetheless, such action was deemed not to violate
defendant's right to proceed pro se because (1) it
did not interfere with defendant's own actions in
such a way as to deprive him of "actual control over
the case he chose to present to the jury," and (2) it
did not "destroy the jury's perception that the
defendant [was] representing himself."

## § 7.5    LAWYER–CLIENT RELATIONSHIP

### (a)  Selection of appointed counsel

*Morris v. Slappy* (1983) concluded that the record
there did not actually present the issue considered
by the appellate court below—whether a defendant
whose originally appointed public defender had
been hospitalized for emergency surgery was entitled to a timely requested delay until that defender
could return to the case, even though a substitute
defender was prepared to go to trial as originally
scheduled. The Court nevertheless went on to criti-
cize the lower appellate court's conclusion that the
refusal to grant such a continuance would deprive
defendant of a "meaningful attorney-client relationship and therefore violate his Sixth Amendment

right to appointed counsel." Flatly rejecting that "novel idea," the Court noted that the Sixth Amendment hardly guaranteed defendant "the kind of rapport with his attorney" that the court below envisaged. It was sufficient that appointed counsel was competent and prepared, and when that was the case, an appellate court must keep in mind "the broad discretion that must be granted trial courts on matters of continuances." The Sixth Amendment, *Slappy* indicates, mandates only that appointed counsel be capable of effective representation, not that she be the counsel in whom the indigent defendant has the most confidence.

### (b) Choice of retained counsel

A defendant's right to retained counsel obviously includes the right to select counsel of his choice, but that right is not absolute. In *Wheat v. U.S.,* discussed in § 7.7(g), the Court stressed that defendant's right to counsel of choice was an aspect of a general right to counsel that was designed to "guarantee an effective advocate" in an adversary system, and defendant's choice therefore could be limited consistent with the fundamental tenets of the adversary system. Thus, a trial court may insist that counsel "be qualified to practice law" under applicable standards, and may, as in *Wheat,* refuse to accept counsel whose joint representation of co-defendants presents a potential conflict of interest.

Other concerns of judicial administration also may prevail over the right to counsel of choice, although here a trial court may have a greater obligation to seek to accommodate defendant's choice. Though *Powell v. Ala.* (1932) held that a "necessary corollary" of the defendant's right is a reasonable delay where needed to employ retained counsel, a trial court may, under appropriate circumstances, restrict defendant's choice through its imposition of scheduling requirements. The right to counsel of one's choice, it frequently is noted, may not be insisted upon at the expense of the trial court's power to ensure that there is an orderly disposition of its docket. See *Ungar v. Sarafite* (1964) (rejecting a constitutional challenge to a continuance denial that resulted in the withdrawal of defense counsel and self-representation by defendant, who was a lawyer, and citing such factors as defendant's delay in seeking the continuance, the allowance of ample time for counsel's preparation in light of the evidence and clearly identified issues, and the need to give deference to the trial judge's judgment).

In *Caplin & Drysdale, Chartered v. U.S.* (1989), the Court sustained a restriction on defendant's ability to retain counsel of choice flowing from a governmental interest totally unrelated to judicial administration. At issue there was the asset forfeiture provisions of a federal statute which subjected to forfeiture all properties "constituting or derived from" the "proceeds" of any drug distribution enterprise. With the forfeiture provisions allowing for both a governmental recapture of all such properties transferred to third parties (including lawyers) and a pretrial freeze on their transfer, the Court assumed that their impact in particular cases would be to render defendants unable to hire any counsel, forcing them to accept court appointed counsel. The dissenters saw these provisions as giving the prosecution an "intolerable degree of power over any private attorney" through the use of a "fictive property law concept." The majority, however, characterized the government's property interest and the petitioner's claim quite differently. The defendant, it noted, certainly "has no Sixth Amendment right to spend another person's money for services rendered by an attorney," and that is what was at stake here. Under the well accepted "taint theory" of forfeiture law, the defendant never had "good title" to the property, as the government obtained a "vested property interest" in the proceeds at the point at which the illegal transactions occurred. The government was fully entitled through the exercise of that interest to "separate a criminal from his ill gotten gains" (which were either returned to defrauded rightful owners or devoted to law enforcement) and thereby to strip the drug enterprise of "undeserved economic power," including "the ability to command high priced legal talent."

*U.S. v. Gonzalez–Lopez* (2006) concluded that, although the Sixth Amendment "right to counsel-of-choice is circumscribed in several important respects," where that right is erroneously denied, a Sixth Amendment violation is "complete" without regard to the adequacy of the representation provided by the substitute counsel. The Court distinguished ineffective assistance of counsel claims, where the defendant must show a prejudicial impact upon the outcome (or special circumstances justifying a presumption prejudice) to establish a Sixth Amendment violation. See § 7.7(c). The "right to select counsel of one's choice * * * [is part of] the root meaning of the [Sixth] Amendment guarantee," and that Amendment "commands not that a trial be fair, but that a particular guarantee of fairness be provided." The requirement that counsel's assistance not be ineffective, in contrast, was initially based on due process (which asks whether "the trial is, in whole, fair"), and subsequently was found to be implicit in the relationship of the counsel guarantee to ensuring a fair trial. Here, the requirement of prejudice to "complete" the violation followed "from the very nature of the specific element of the right to counsel at issue—*effective* (not mistake-free) representation."

### (c)  Counsel's control over defense strategy

Although a defendant has a right to proceed pro se, if the defendant proceeds with counsel, the defendant will have no constitutional complaint if counsel makes strategic decisions contrary to defendant's wishes. Thus, *Jones v. Barnes* (1983) held that a defendant was not denied the effective assistance of counsel where appellate counsel refused to brief a nonfrivolous claim that his client wished to press. Counsel was free to make a strategic choice of contentions, following the time tested advice of advocates that inclusion of "every colorable claim" will "dilute and weaken a good case and will not save a bad one." So too, in *Taylor v. Ill.* (1988), the defendant was stuck with the consequences of counsel's strategy, apparently adopted without consultation with the client, which risked exclusion of evidence rather than give the prosecution advance notice (and time to investigate) as required by the state's discovery rules.

Certain decisions, however, though they may have a strategic element, are so "personal" that counsel must abide by his client's wishes. These include decisions that involve actions by the defendant and basic issues as to the structure of the proceeding. Thus, the Supreme Court has stated, in dictum or holding, that it is for the defendant to decide whether to take each of the following steps: plead guilty or take action tantamount to entering a plea, as in *Brookhart v. Janis* (1966) (where the defense counsel agreed that the state need only produce a prima facie case which the defense would not contest); waive the right to jury trial; waive the right to be present at trial; testify on his own behalf; or forego an appeal. See *Jones,* supra; *Taylor,* supra.

*Fla. v. Nixon* (2004) distinguished from *Brookhart v. Janis* a defense counsel's decision to concede guilt at the guilt phase of a capital trial, and thereby avoid any inconsistency with the case in mitigation to be presented at the penalty phase of the trial. Though counsel had acknowledged in his opening statement that defendant committed the murder, that was not tantamount to a guilty plea (in contrast to *Brookhart*) since defense counsel's actions did not (1) relieve the state of its obligation to prove guilt beyond a reasonable doubt, (2) restrict counsel's ability to object to the admission of prejudicial evidence, or (3) preclude raising on appeal any "errors in the trial or jury instructions." The court in *Nixon* was not required, however, to decide whether counsel could adopt such strategy over the objection of the defendant. Counsel there had discussed the strategy with defendant, and had made a unilateral decision to pursue the strategy only after defendant repeatedly refused to discuss the matter.

Where counsel does fail to follow the instructions of the defendant as to a matter within defendant's control (e.g., fails to file on appeal where defendant directed counsel to do so), that failure will be treated as per se ineffective assistance of counsel. Where, however, counsel never consulted with the defendant and no directions were given, that failure to consult may constitute ineffective assistance, but only if the two-pronged ineffectiveness standard of *Strickland* (see § 7.7(b)) is met. *Roe v. Flores–Ortega* (2000) (failure to consult with defendant on pursuing an appeal).

## § 7.6   STATE INTERFERENCE WITH COUNSEL

### (a)  Restrictions upon counsel's assistance

The "right to the assistance of counsel," the Supreme Court noted in *Herring v. N.Y.* (1975), "has been understood to mean that there can be no restrictions upon the function of counsel in defending a criminal prosecution in accord with the traditions of the adversary factfinding process." Accordingly, state action, whether by statute or trial court ruling, that prohibits counsel from making full use of traditional trial procedures may be viewed as denying defendant the effective assistance of counsel. In considering the constitutionality of such "state interference," courts are directed to look to whether the interference denied counsel "the opportunity to participate fully and fairly in the adversary factfinding process." If the interference had that effect, then the overall performance of counsel apart from the interference, and the lack of any showing of actual prejudice, are both irrelevant.

Three Supreme Court cases illustrate the type of state imposed restriction upon counsel's performance that will be held to violate the Sixth Amendment. *Geders v. U.S.* (1976) found unconstitutional interference when the trial court ordered the defendant not to consult with his attorney during an overnight recess which separated the direct-examination and the cross-examination of the defendant. *Herring v. N.Y.* (1975) held that defendant's Sixth Amendment right to counsel was violated by a statute under which the trial court could refuse to permit a closing argument in a bench trial. The Court reasoned that a final summation by counsel was as basic an element of the adversary process in a bench trial as it was in a jury trial. In *Brooks v. Tenn.* (1972), a statute requiring the defendant to testify as the first defense witness or not at all was held to deprive the defendant of the " 'guiding hand of counsel' in the timing of this critical element of the defense." In each of these cases, it should be noted, the Court might also have found the particular restriction unconstitutional on the ground that it imposed an undue burden on the exercise of a constitutionally protected trial right. See § 8.4(a) (discussing the alternative grounding of *Brooks*).

### (b) Defective appointment

In *U.S. v. Cronic* (1984), the Court noted that there could be situations in which the appointment of counsel was so deficient as to be treated as an automatic violation of the Sixth Amendment, in much the same fashion as a failure to appoint counsel (as in *Gideon*) or a state action that "prevented [counsel] from assisting the accused during a critical stage of the proceeding" (as in the cases discussed in (a) supra). In those two situations, a "breakdown of the adversarial process [is] presumed"; the "circumstances * * * [are] so likely to prejudice the accused that the cost of litigating their effect in a particular case is unjustified." A similar breakdown could be presumed based upon the manner and setting in which counsel is appointed. There may be "occasions when, although counsel is available to assist the accused during trial, the likelihood that any lawyer, even a fully competent one, could provide effective assistance is so small that a presumption of prejudice is appropriate without inquiry into the actual conduct of the trial."

*Cronic* offered one illustration of a case involving an appointment so defective as to be treated as a per se Sixth Amendment violation. That case was *Powell v. Ala.* (1932). The trial court there had utilized such a haphazard process of appointment— ordering admittedly unprepared out-of-state counsel to proceed with whatever help the local bar, appointed en masse, might provide—that there was no need to look at the actual performance of counsel in determining that defendant's constitutional rights had been violated. *Cronic* rejected the contention, however, that the case before it fell in the same category.

The lower appellate court in *Cronic,* without referring to any specific error or inadequacy in counsel's performance, had found that counsel could not have been able to "discharge his duties" in light of five factors: "(1) [T]he [limited] time afforded for investigation and preparation; (2) the [in]experience of counsel; (3) the gravity of the charge; (4) the complexity of possible defenses; and (5) the [in]accessibility of witnesses to counsel." The *Cronic* majority acknowledged that these five factors were "relevant to an evaluation of a lawyer's ineffectiveness in a particular case, but neither separately nor in combination [did] they provide a basis for concluding that competent counsel was not able to provide * * * the guiding hand that the Constitution guarantees." The Court had previously refused to "fashion a per se rule requiring reversal of every conviction following tardy appointment of counsel," *Chambers v. Maroney* (1970), and neither would it find per se ineffectiveness because counsel was young and conducting his first jury trial in a serious, complex case.

## (c) State invasion of the lawyer-client relationship

In *Weatherford v. Bursey* (1977), the Court recognized that a state invasion of a lawyer-client relationship (there an informant's participation in a conference between defendant and his lawyer) could constitute a Sixth Amendment violation, but only if the situation posed a realistic likelihood of the state having gained some advantage (missing here, as the informant did not report anything to his superiors). The *Weatherford* analysis looked to the alleged invasion's actual impact upon the adversarial system. *U.S. v. Morrison* (1981) raised the question of whether a showing of actual adverse impact should also be required where the government had absolutely no justification for the invasion (in comparison to *Weatherford,* where the informant participated in the conference to avoid revealing his true status). In *Morrison,* D.E.A. agents met with the accused in the absence of her retained attorney and disparaged his likely performance. The Court found it unnecessary to rule on the government's contention that a Sixth Amendment violation could not be established without "some [defense] showing of prejudice," because the court below had gone too far in ordering dismissal of the prosecution, a remedy in no way "tailored" to the injury that may have been suffered.

## § 7.7  EFFECTIVE ASSISTANCE OF COUNSEL

### (a)  Constitutional foundation

The Supreme Court has long recognized, with respect to the due process/fair hearing right to counsel, the Sixth Amendment right to counsel, and the equal protection right to counsel, that these rights are not fulfilled if counsel fails to provide effective assistance to the defendant. See e.g., *Powell v. Ala.* (1932); *Jones v. Barnes* (1983). In *U.S. v. Cronic* (1984), the Court explained both the relationship of the effective assistance requirement to the constitutional right to counsel and the general nature of the quality of assistance it demands. *Cronic* noted that the function of the right to counsel, "assur[ing] fairness in the adversary process," necessarily requires that accused have a counsel who acts as his advocate and subjects the prosecution's case to the "crucible of meaningful adversary testing." Accordingly, "when a true adversarial criminal trial has been conducted—even if defense counsel may have made demonstrable errors—the kind of testing envisioned by the Sixth Amendment has occurred." A violation of the right to counsel flows only from a deficiency in counsel that causes "the process [to] lose * * * its character as a confrontation between adversaries."

Consistent with the analysis of *Cronic,* the Court has held that defendant does not have a constitutional basis for complaining about even the most clearly deficient performance of counsel where he lacked an underlying constitutional right to counsel that was tied to ensuring a fair proceeding. Thus, *Wainwright v. Torna* (1982) found that no constitutional right of the defendant had been violated by the negligence of his retained attorney in failing to file a timely application for discretionary review at the state's second level of appeal. At that stage of the proceedings, a defendant has neither a Sixth Amendment, equal protection, nor due process/fair hearing right to the assistance of counsel. See *Ross v. Moffitt* (§ 7.3(h)).

The defendant in a case like *Torna* must bear the consequences of his unwise choice of counsel. The same is not true, however, when defendant has a constitutional right to counsel tied to ensuring a fair proceeding. At one time, it was thought that a deficient trial performance by retained counsel did not present a constitutional violation unless that deficiency was so obvious that the trial judge should have known that the adversarial process was breaking down. This was distinguished from incompetency by appointed counsel, where the state was thought to have greater responsibility since the court had selected counsel. Such a distinction in judging the performance of retained and appointed counsel was rejected in *Cuyler v. Sullivan* (1980), where the Court noted: "Since the State's conduct of a criminal trial itself implicates the State in the defendant's conviction, we see no basis for drawing a distinction between retained and appointed counsel that would deny equal justice to defendants who must choose their own lawyers." While *Cuyler* dealt with the Sixth Amendment right to counsel, the state's responsibility would be similar in those proceedings not a part of the criminal prosecution where the due process/fair hearing rationale, equal protection, or a derivative right analysis guarantees a right to the assistance of counsel. See *Evitts v. Lucey* (§ 7.3(h)).

## (b) The *Strickland* incompetency standard

*Strickland v. Washington* (1984) set forth a two-pronged test for determining whether counsel's performance was so defective as to deny defendant his constitutional right to counsel. Under *Strickland,* to establish constitutionally ineffective representation, the defendant must prove both incompetence (discussed here) and prejudice (discussed in subsection (c) infra). Incompetency is judged by an "objective standard of reasonableness": "Whether in light of all the circumstances, the identified acts or omissions [of counsel] were outside the range of professionally competent assistance."

Prior to *Strickland,* several lower courts had relied heavily upon generally accepted guidelines for counsel's performance, such as the A.B.A. Standards, in judging competency. Indeed, some had suggested that any substantial deviation from those guidelines automatically established incompetency. The *Strickland* majority flatly rejected this approach in explaining its standard of reasonableness. The "performance inquiry" the Court noted, "must be whether counsel's assistance was reasonable under all the circumstances" and "more specific guidelines are not appropriate." Utilizing specific guidelines as a per se test for competent performance was inappropriate because (1) "no particular set of detailed rules for counsel's conduct can satisfactorily take account of the variety of circumstances faced by defense counsel or the range of legitimate decisions regarding how best to represent a criminal defendant," and (2) "reliance on such guidelines * * * could distract counsel from the overriding mission of vigorous advocacy of the defendant's cause." Of course, prevailing norms of practice help to define reasonableness, but the ultimate point of reference is whether counsel's performance met a level consistent with "the proper functioning of the adversarial process"—for that is what sets "the range of competence demanded of attorneys in criminal cases."

Consistent with its emphasis upon a fact-sensitized judgment respecting "the wide latitude counsel must have in making tactical decisions," the *Strickland* majority also warned lower courts against "second-guess[ing]" counsel's performance: "Judicial scrutiny * * * must be highly differential. * * * A fair assessment of attorney performance requires that every effort be made to eliminate the distorting effects of hindsight, to reconstruct the circumstances of counsel's challenged conduct, and to evaluate the conduct from counsel's perspective at the time. Because of the difficulties inherent in making the evaluation, a court must indulge a strong presumption that counsel's conduct falls within the wide range of reasonable professional assistance; that is, the defendant must overcome the presumption that, under the circumstances, the challenged action 'might be considered sound trial strategy.' "

### (c) The *Strickland* prejudice standard

Prior to *Strickland,* lower courts had taken a wide variety of positions on the element of prejudice in an ineffective assistance claim, ranging from presuming prejudice upon a finding of incompetency to placing a heavy burden on defendant to show prejudice. *Strickland* sought to resolve those differences in its explanation of its prejudice prong. The Court initially noted that, since the underlying function of the constitutional right to counsel is to "ensure * * * the assistance necessary to justify reliance on the outcome of the proceeding," any deficiency in counsel's performance "must be prejudicial to the defense in order to constitute ineffective assistance." See also *U.S. v. Gonzalez-Lopez* (§ 7.5(b))(discussing why a showing of prejudice is required here and not for other Sixth Amendment violations).

*Strickland* acknowledged that there were exceptional situations (discussed below) in which prejudice justifiably could be presumed, but that generally was not appropriate for claims based on incompetent performance: "Attorney errors come in an infinite variety and are as likely to be utterly harmless in a particular case as they are to be prejudicial."

Prejudice, under *Strickland*, requires a showing of a "reasonable probability that, but for counsel's unprofessional errors, the result of the proceeding would have been different." The Court described its "reasonable probability" standard as falling between the overly lenient "some conceivable effect" standard (which would invariably lead to a finding of prejudice) and the overly rigorous "more likely than not" test (which would ignore the constitutional grounding of defendant's claim by placing upon it the same burden applied to newly discovered evidence). It also noted that a "reasonable probability" is a "probability sufficient to undermine confidence in the outcome".

In light of the function of the prejudice requirement, the Court has warned against "an analysis focusing solely on mere outcome determination, without attention to whether the result of the proceeding was fundamentally unfair or unreliable." *Lockhart v. Fretwell* (1993). Prejudice does not automatically follow from a reasonable probability of a different result had counsel not taken the action alleged to constitute incompetency. Thus, *Nix v. Whiteside* (1986) held that defendant, "as a matter of law," could not establish prejudice where he claimed that his counsel had improperly prevented him from presenting perjured testimony which could have swayed the jury. So too, in *Lockhart,* the Court held that there was "no 'prejudice' within the meaning of *Strickland*" where counsel's incompetence consisted of failing to present an objection that was supported by precedent at the time of trial, but later was rejected with the overturning of that precedent. Prejudice cannot be based on depriving the defendant of an alleged "substantive or procedural right to which the law does not entitle him."

In *Kimmelman v. Morrison* (1986), counsel's incompetence was in failing to present a Fourth Amendment exclusionary rule claim, and the Court remanded for consideration of the prejudice issue. Arguably implicit in the remand was the assumption that prejudice would be established if there was a reasonable likelihood that the exclusion of the illegally seized evidence would have altered the outcome. However, three concurring justices argued that the failure to gain exclusion of evidence that clearly was reliable, though illegally seized, did not lead to "an unjust or fundamentally unfair result" and therefore could not constitute prejudice.

*Strickland* acknowledged that certain Sixth Amendment violations do not require a showing of prejudice. The most prominent of these are based on violations of obligations or restrictions imposed on the trial court by the Sixth Amendment—e.g., the failure to provide appointed counsel where constitutionally required (§ 7.1), the failure to conduct an inquiry after counsel indicates that a conflict precludes multiple representation (§ 7.7(f)), and the imposition of improper restrictions upon assistance of counsel (7.6(a)). Others, however, are based on a presumption of incompetent performance by counsel. Thus, as discussed in § 7.7(e), a presumption of prejudice attaches in certain conflict of interest situations upon a showing that a conflict of interest adversely affected counsel's representation. So too, as discussed in § 7.7(b), *Cronic* recognized that the appointment of counsel can be so deficient under some circumstances as to establish a Sixth Amendment violation without examining counsel's actual performance.

*Cronic* also noted that prejudice would be presumed where "counsel entirely fails to subject the prosecutor's case to meaningful adversarial testing." In *Bell v. Cone* (2002), the Court stressed that this exception requires a "failure" that is "complete". Thus, it did not apply where counsel failed to introduce mitigating evidence in a capital sentencing proceeding and waived closing argument, but challenged the state's case in other respects (include bringing out mitigating and other favorable evidence in other portions of the proceeding).

### (d) Application of the *Strickland* standards

A series of post-*Strickland* Supreme Court rulings illustrate the application of the *Strickland* standards. *Nix v. Whiteside* (1986) and *Yarborough v. Gentry* (2003) present examples of ineffective assistance claims easily rejected under the *Strickland* standards, *Kimmelman v. Morrison* (1986) a claim easily sustained as to incompetence, and a trio of cases dealing with capital sentencing illustrate the significance of differing judicial perspectives.

The defendant in *Whiteside* alleged ineffectiveness based on counsel's threat to withdraw and reveal defendant's perjury if defendant persisted in his plans to testify falsely, a threat which led defendant to delete false statements from his actual testimony. The Court unanimously concluded that defendant failed to meet the prejudice prong of *Strickland.* Five justices added that defendant had failed as well to meet the incompetency prong of *Strickland.* While the *Strickland* opinion had warned against viewing the breach of an ethical standard or other guideline as incompetency per se, where counsel's action was fully consistent with universally accepted ethical standards (here, those relating to client perjury), that action could hardly be deemed to fall below prevailing professional norms.

In *Yarborough v. Gentry,* a federal habeas court concluded that trial counsel's performance fell below *Strickland*'s competency standard because counsel's closing argument failed to highlight certain exculpatory evidence, mentioned seemingly irrelevant factors, and did not include a direct demand for acquittal. Unanimously reversing that ruling, the Supreme Court noted that as to each supposed weakness in the closing argument, there was a plausible strategic explanation. *Strickland* had emphasized the need for "highly deferential" review of an attorney's strategic choices, and that review had to be "doubly deferential when * * * conducted through the lens of federal habeas corpus" (where the issue is whether the state court, in denying defendant's claim, had applied *Strickland* in an "objectively unreasonable manner," see § 1.4(d)).

In *Kimmelman,* the incompetency claim was based on counsel's failure to file in a timely fashion a defense motion to suppress items obtained through an allegedly unconstitutional search, an error which led to the trial court's refusal to consider the merits of the untimely motion. Counsel's explanation for his failure to make the motion before trial (as required) was that he hadn't previously known that the state had seized those items. Although he could have learned of the seizure through readily available pretrial discovery, counsel hadn't sought such discovery because (1) he had assumed the state had a legal obligation to inform him of its evidence and (2) he had not expected the case to go to trial because the complainant was reluctant to testify (although there had been no court order needed for a dismissal on that ground). These answers, the Court noted, reflected a "startling ignorance" of state law and practice that clearly placed counsel's actions outside "prevailing professional norms." There was no suggestion counsel's decision was tactical, and his error could not be excused by otherwise competent performance during the remainder of the trial.

*Burger v. Kemp* (1987), *Wiggins v. Smith* (2003), and *Rompilla v. Beard* (2005) all involved incompetency claims relating to trial counsel's failure to develop (and present in a capital sentencing hearing) substantial mitigating background evidence that was later uncovered by habeas counsel. The Court was closely divided in each case, with the majority finding *Strickland* violations in *Wiggins* and *Rompella*, but not in *Burger*. In part, the majorities in *Wiggins* and *Rompella* adopted arguments advanced by the dissenters in the earlier *Burger* case, but they also sought to distinguish *Burger* on its facts. *Burger* was characterized as a case in which counsel's preliminary investigation had led to a "reasonable professional judgement" that introducing mitigating background evidence would open the door to harmful counter-evidence, therefore rendering unnecessary further investigation of defendant's background. *Wiggins* was distinguished as a case in which defense counsel's failure to further investigate was based on "inattention rather than a reasoned strategic judgment" (a reading of the record disputed by the dissent) and evidence in the record that the further investigation at issue (obtaining a social history report) was "standard practice" in capital cases in the particular state. In *Rompilla*, only one concurring justice found inattention, but the plurality concluded that counsel should have obtained the full record of a prior conviction that the prosecution intended to rely upon in the sentencing hearing, and if they had done so, they would have discovered new sources of background evidence very favorable to the defendant. Accordingly, counsel were not excused by their having conducted a substantial investigation of background factors that had failed to produce any promising evidence (a factor emphasized by the dissenters, along with their conclusion that counsel had reasonably concluded that further information on the past conviction was not needed in light of their overall strategy). One prominent feature of the various opinions in the three cases is the quite different readings by the justices of the trial and habeas records, particularly as they relate to the factors weighed by counsel.

### (e) Multiple representation and conflicts of interest

One requirement of effective assistance is that counsel's actions stem from his "undivided loyalty" to his client rather than from an attempt to balance his client's interests against the interests of another. While various situations can subject counsel to a conflict of interest, the decisions of the Supreme Court have dealt primarily with the conflict potential in joint representation of codefendants by a single attorney. Although acknowledging that the possibility of prejudice "inheres in almost every instance of multiple representation," the Court has refused to treat joint representation as "per se violative of constitutional guarantees of effective assistance of counsel." *Holloway v. Ark.* (1978). While the obligations of representing codefendants may lead counsel to take action that favors one over the other, there are instances where joint representation may benefit both defendants, as where "a common defense * * * gives strength against a common attack." *Holloway.*

To establish incompetency based upon counsel's performance in a multiple representation situation, defendant must show "an actual conflict of interest [that] adversely affected his lawyer's performance." *Cuyler v. Sullivan* (1980). *Glasser v. U.S.* (1942) is illustrative. The record there showed that counsel had failed to cross-examine a key witness against Glasser and had failed to object to "arguably inadmissible evidence." Both omissions then were found to "have resulted from counsel's desire to diminish the jury's perception of a codefendant's guilt," which established an actual, acted upon conflict. That such a conflict existed is not always evident, as it was in *Glasser*, from the fact that counsel failed to adopt a particular strategy that might have helped defendant while working to the disadvantage of a jointly represented codefendant. Depending upon the available evidence (including counsel's own testimony at any post-trial inquiry), a court may conclude that counsel in fact acted in what he believed to be the defendant's best interests in deciding against that strategy (i.e., he did not act to protect the codefendant). If that is the case, and counsel's decision otherwise was an acceptable professional judgment, then incompetency has not been established. See *Burger v. Kemp* (1987).

The Court has frequently noted that, once a defendant establishes that "a conflict of interest actually affected the adequacy of his representation," he is automatically entitled to relief. *Holloway*. Here, an exception is made to the proof-of-prejudice requirement of *Strickland*. A presumption of prejudice is drawn on the assumption that a counsel who favored a conflicting loyalty in one way may well have done so as well in other, less visible ways. In *Mickens v. Taylor* (2002), the Court left open the possibility that this presumption may apply only to conflicts involving the multiple representation of codefendants, with a *Strickland* showing of prejudice applicable to other types of conflicts, such as the former representation of a prosecution witness.

### (f) Trial court duty to inquire

*Holloway v. Ark.* (1978) established that, under some circumstances, the trial court has a constitutional obligation to inquire into the existence of an actual conflict, and the violation of that duty will constitute in itself an abridgment of the defendant's constitutional right to counsel. In *Holloway,* a public defender made a timely objection to his joint representation of three codefendants. The defender informed the trial court that one or two of the defendants might testify, and he would not be able to cross-examine a testifying defendant on behalf of the other defendants because of "confidential information" he had received from each of the codefendants. The trial court pushed aside counsel's concern, directing him simply to let each defendant testify "to what he wants." This was done and each of the defendants testified (in narrative form) that he was not at the scene of the crime. Reversing the convictions of the three codefendants, the Supreme Court held that, "in the face of the representations made by counsel," the trial court failed to safeguard

the defendants' constitutional right to the assistance of counsel and thereby committed reversible
error. Even if counsel had not provided the trial
court with sufficient information to establish the
constitutional necessity for separate representation,
that court had the obligation to make sufficient
inquiry to ensure that the "risk [of conflict] was too
remote to warrant separate counsel."

The *Holloway* opinion specifically left open the
scope of the trial court's responsibility "where the
trial counsel did nothing to advise the trial court as
to the actuality or possibility of a conflict." In the
subsequent decision of *Cuyler v. Sullivan* (1980),
the Court held that a considerably different standard applied to that situation. *Cuyler* initially rejected the contention that a trial court had a constitutional duty to make some inquiry as to a possible
conflict in all cases of multiple representation. Ordinarily, the Court noted, the trial judge could rely
upon the absence of any objection by counsel, since
counsel has "an ethical obligation to avoid conflicting representations and to advise the court promptly when a conflict arises during the course of the
trial." Thus, "absent special circumstances," where
counsel has raised no objection, the trial court "may
assume either that multiple representation entails
no conflict or that the lawyer and his clients knowingly accept such a risk of conflict as may exist."
The Court noted, however, that there may be cases
where the trial court "reasonably should know"
from the surrounding circumstances that a particular conflict exists and then it would have an obli-

gation to make an inquiry on its own initiative. Such circumstances were not present in *Cuyler,* where the defense attorneys' presentation was consistent on its face with the protection of the interests of all the codefendants they represented.

In *Holloway*, the Court held that the failure of the judge to conduct an inquiry required automatic reversal of the subsequent conviction. *Mickens v. Taylor* (2002) held that the same consequence did not attach to a failure to inquire in violation of the *Cuyler* standard. Presumed prejudice was justified in *Holloway* because the objection there was raised by defense counsel, who "is in the best position to determine when a [disabling] conflict exists", and "the objection came in a case of joint representation,"–a setting which is "inherently suspect," and which places on counsel joint obligations that "effectively seal his lips in crucial matters and make it difficult to measure the precise harm arising from counsel's [conflict]." No similar justification existed for presuming prejudice as to *Cuyler*'s requirement of a *sua sponte* inquiry where the trial court "knows or reasonably should know that a particular conflict exists." Here, on postconviction review, the defendant will be required to make the same showing that would be required where there was no duty to inquire (see § 7.7(e)).

## (g) Disqualification of potentially conflicted counsel

*Wheat v. U.S.* (1988) sets forth the constitutional standards governing a trial court's disqualification of counsel whose multiple representation creates a potential conflict of interest. The Court there found that the trial court had not violated defendant's Sixth Amendment right to counsel of choice when it rejected defendant's motion, "made close to trial," to allow him to be represented by the same lawyer who represented two other codefendants in a complex drug conspiracy, one of whom the government intended to call as a prosecution witness at defendant's trial. The *Wheat* majority initially rejected the defense contention that "the provision of waivers by all affected defendants cures any problems created by multiple representation." A trial court could appropriately prefer not to rely on such a waiver. It could take cognizance of inherent weaknesses in such waivers that could lead to later challenges—recognizing (1) that potential conflicts often reflect "imponderables" that "are difficult enough for a lawyer to assess, and even more difficult to convey by way of explanation to a criminal defendant untutored by the niceties of legal ethics," and (2) that "the willingness of an attorney to obtain such waivers from his clients may bear an inverse relation to the care with which he conveys all the necessary information to them." Moreover, the trial courts also may give weight to the institutional interest of "ensuring that criminal trials are conducted within the ethical standards of the profession and that the legal proceedings appear fair to all who observe them."

The Court stressed, however, that while the trial court must be given "substantial latitude in refusing waivers," that authority was not unlimited. The trial court's findings must establish a sufficient likelihood of conflicted representation to overcome the Sixth Amendment presumption favoring defendant's choice of counsel. Because the likely materialization and dimensions of a conflict are "notoriously hard to predict" in the "murkier pretrial context when relationships between parties are seen through a glass darkly," the authority to disqualify would not be limited to cases in which an actual conflict was apparent. The trial court could properly override the presumption also upon a finding of "a serious potential for conflict", and in making that finding, it could look to its "instinct and judgment based on experience" in evaluating those factors that could produce an actual conflict.

# CHAPTER 8

# THE PRIVILEGE AGAINST SELF–INCRIMINATION

## § 8.1 BASIC ELEMENTS

### (a) Introduction

The Fifth Amendment provides that "[n]o person * * * shall be compelled in any criminal case to be a witness against himself." This prohibition is commonly described as the constitutional "privilege against self-incrimination" because it served to constitutionalize the English common law's evidentiary privilege against compelled self-incrimination. The Fifth Amendment's self-incrimination clause has at times been confined to the elements of that common law privilege, with the Court describing the clause as "a specific provision of which it is particularly true that 'a page of history is worth a volume of logic'." *Ullmann v. U.S.* (1956). At other times, the Court has stressed the need to interpret the clause in light of the general "lessons of [its] history," and to give it a construction "as broad as the mischief against which it seeks to guard." *Counselman v. Hitchcock* (1892). Thus, *Miranda v. Ariz.* (§ 4.4), in extending the privilege beyond it common law boundaries, to encompass the informal compulsion of police station interrogation, stressed the basic policies underlying the privilege and need to recognize that "a noble principle often transcends its origins."

The scope of the constitutional privilege has been set by the Court's interpretation of each of the elements set forth in the language of the self-incrimination clause. Reading that language in light of the history and policies of the common law privilege, the Court has adopted a series of general principles that establish the content of the key terms and phrases of the self-incrimination clause– i.e., "person," "compelled," "to be a witness," "against himself," and "in a criminal case." Those principles are discussed below.

### (b) Protected "persons"

Unlike the Sixth Amendment, which refers to the rights of the "accused," the Fifth Amendment refers to the rights of a "person." The self-incrimination clause, however, carried the potential for a very narrow interpretation of protected persons, as its protection is limited to a person whom the state would "compe[l] * * * in any criminal case to be a witness against himself." It was not until 1892, in *Counselman v. Hitchcock*, that the Court rejected the contention that the clause served only to protect a defendant from being required by the prosecution to appear as witness in his own criminal trial. While the clause clearly includes that protection (described as its "core protection" in *U.S. v. Patane* (2004)), so limiting the clause would have given it no practical significance at the time of its adoption;

for the common law held a defendant to be incompetent to testify as a witness at his own trial under all circumstances. Moreover, the origin of the self-incrimination privilege in English common law is associated with opposition to use of the "oath *ex officio*" in the investigative portion of the proceedings of the English ecclesiastical courts and the Star Chamber (courts which investigated political and religious dissidents in the sixteenth and seventeenth centuries). Thus, *Counselman*, not surprisingly, concluded that the Fifth Amendment privilege protected a person called to testify before the grand jury, reasoning that the grand jury investigation was part of the "criminal case" (a broader term than the "criminal prosecution" used in the Sixth Amendment).

*Counselman* also advanced an analysis suggesting that a person compelled to give testimony in any judicial proceeding was protected by the privilege, even where that proceeding was not itself part of a "criminal case". The compulsion of testimony and the use of that testimony in a criminal case need not occur simultaneously. The privilege, *Counselman* noted, protects against compelling the testimony of a person in any proceeding where that testimony could later be used by the government in a criminal case brought against that person (thereby making him a "witness against himself"). Based on this reasoning, the Court later held that the privilege protects witnesses in a variety of settings not part of the criminal case (e.g., civil cases and administrative hearings), provided that the testimony that would be compelled from the witness might realistically be used against the witness in a subsequent criminal prosecution, see § 8.2(c).

In *Chavez v. Martinez* (2003), the Court majority described a witness' ability to invoke the privilege at the point of compulsion as a court-created procedural safeguard. *Chavez* presented a civil rights damage action based on police compulsion (through coercive interrogation) which led the plaintiff Martinez to make an incriminating statement that was never used in a criminal prosecution (no charges were brought). The *Chavez* majority concluded that the basic prohibition of the self-incrimination clause had not been violated because Martinez was never made a "witness against himself" in a "criminal case." It rejected the contention that the "criminal case * * * encompass[es] the entire investigatory process, including police interrogations."

The *Chavez* majority distinguished the cases that had allowed witnesses in civil and administrative proceedings to refuse to testify when their prospective testimony might be used against them in subsequent criminal prosecutions. The six justices in the majority divided, however, in their characterization of those rulings. Four justices described those rulings as establishing a prophylactic standard (see § 1.3(e)), based on the need to "memorialize the fact" that the witness was not willing to testify voluntarily. Two other justices characterized those rulings as establishing "a law outside the Fifth Amendment core," reflecting the "judgment that the core guarantee, or the judicial capacity to protect it," required the "complementary protection" of allowing the witness to assert the privilege prior to any actual use of the witness' statement. Under either characterization, the majority agreed, there was no need to expand the supplementary protection of the Fifth Amendment right to include a damage remedy where a compelled statement had never been used in a criminal case (although a due process damage remedy might be available if the compulsion in itself violated the free-standing content of due process, see § 1.2(f)).

*Chavez* did not suggest that the plaintiff *Martinez* had lacked the authority to refuse to respond to the coercive police interrogation; indeed, earlier cases had recognized a suspect's "right of silence" (see § 6.7(d)). Supreme Court rulings involving a variety of settings indicate that, as a general rule, any person subject to government compulsion to produce an incriminating statement may assert the privilege in response to that compulsion. See e.g., *Garner v. U.S.* (1976) (assertion on a tax return). Indeed, in many settings, the person must assert the privilege at that point or lose it. See § 8.2(a). If, however, a proper assertion of the privilege is not respected, and an incriminating statement is compelled, *Chavez* indicates that the person then has no Fifth Amendment remedy unless the government subsequently seeks to use that statement against him in a criminal case–at which time, the privilege can be relied upon to preclude that use. See § 8.1(e).

As noted in § 8.3(f), the above discussion of persons protected by the privilege extends only to natural persons, as the privilege is not available to entities.

### (c) Compulsion

Compulsion is a prerequisite to the application of the self-incrimination privilege. A person being questioned can properly rely upon the privilege to refuse to respond only if the person is being compelled by the government to respond. A defendant can assert the privilege to prevent the prosecution from using against him a prior statement only if that statement had been compelled. A statement not compelled is deemed "voluntary" for Fifth Amendment purposes, and the self-incrimination clause does not prohibit the government's subsequent use of a person's voluntary statement to make him, in effect, a witness against himself in a criminal case.

The paradigm for compulsion is the subpoena *ad testificandum* (a court order directing a person to furnish testimony under oath). That subpoena produces what the Court has described as the "core" unfairness which led to the adoption of the privilege—"subject[ing] those suspected of crime to the cruel trilemma of self-accusation, perjury or contempt." *Pa. v. Muniz* (1990). The person under subpoena who is asked a question that would require an incriminating response, if lacking the privilege, would face precisely that trilemma: (1) testifying truthfully and, in effect, acknowledging facts that could give rise to criminal liability (i.e., "self-accusation"); (2) lying under oath and therefore committing the crime of perjury; or (3) refusing to answer and being held in contempt for disobeying a court order.

Compulsion by force of law also can exist without presenting all elements of this "cruel trilemma." It may be present, for example, where the law places regulatory sanctions on a person who fails to provide to the government information that may be incriminating. Illustrative is a law forcing a government employee to chose between disclosing incriminatory information in response to a governmental inquiry and being discharged for failing to respond to that inquiry. See *Garrity v. N.J.* (§ 8.4(a)).

Governmental compulsion may also exist without the formal command of the law. Although a suspect has no legal duty to respond to police questioning, the "informal compulsion" imposed in the course of such questioning may reach the level of the compulsion prohibited by the Fifth Amendment. Thus, the Court today characterizes the constitutional prohibition against admission of involuntary confessions (see § 4.2(a)), which was originally developed as a due process standard, as also resting on the self-incrimination clause. See *Dickerson v. U.S.* (2000). The offensive interrogation techniques that cause a particular confession to be characterized as "coerced" both offend due process and constitute "compulsion" for Fifth Amendment purposes. Indeed, *Miranda v. Ariz.* (§ 4.4) establishes a presumption of compulsion as to all custodial interrogation conducted in violation of the *"Miranda* rules" (§ 4.4(b)), although the Court has also noted that this presumption is "overinclusive" (i.e., covers some instances in which the custodial interrogation did not, in fact, produce compulsion, notwithstanding the violation of the *Miranda* rules). See §§ 1.3(e), 6.6(g), 6.7(b).

As the Court recognized in *Miranda*, even with the *Miranda* warnings, custodial interrogation places a certain degree of psychological pressure on the suspect to explain his actions (even though that explanation may be incriminating), but not all levels of informal governmental pressure rise to the level of the "compulsion" prohibited by the self-incrimination clause. Thus, an offer of charging or sentencing concessions in return for a plea of guilty certainly creates some pressure to admit guilt, but in the context of the "give and take" of plea bargaining, a guilty plea induced by such a concession is not viewed as compelled in violation of the Fifth Amendment. See § 9.5(c).

Neither does compulsion exist where the individual recognizes that unless he testifies in a proceeding (and thereby risks the possibility of incrimination), the case against him is likely to lead to an adverse result. See *Ohio Adult Parole Authority v. Woodward* (1998) (no compulsion where convicted inmate had the option of submitting to an interview in connection with the parole board's consideration of clemency, that interview would create the possibility of incrimination as to the current charge and further charges, but clemency would most likely be denied in the absence of an interview). Relying on this principle, *Williams v. Fla.* (1970) held that a state could require a defendant to give pretrial notice of an alibi defense (including identifying the alibi location and witness who would testify in support of the alibi). The self incrimination clause traditionally was not implicated by the "dilemma demanding a choice between complete silence and presenting a defense" that a defendant faced in deciding how to respond to the prosecution's case-in-chief, and here, the Court reasoned, the state had only accelerated that decision to a pretrial decision. That acceleration did not convert the pressure on the defendant to "compulsion" as "[n]othing in the Fifth Amendment privilege entitles a defendant as a matter of constitutional right to await the end of the state's case before announcing the nature of his defense."

The Fifth Amendment privilege belongs to the person being compelled so a defendant cannot rely on the privilege to oppose the compulsion of a third person to give testimony that would incriminate the defendant. Thus, *U.S. v. Nobles* (1975) held that a defendant could not utilize the privilege to bar a court order requiring a defense investigator, who testified at trial as to statements made to him by various prosecution witnesses, to disclose (for possible impeachment use) the report in which he summarized what these witnesses had said. The defense investigator also could not claim the privilege because, while he was compelled, the potential incrimination did not relate to him personally. See also § 8.3(e).

### (d) Testimonial evidence

The self-incrimination speaks of compelling a person to be a "witness" against himself, and the Court has held that the term "witness," read in light of the common law, restricts the protection of the privilege. The Fifth Amendment does not prohibit the state from compelling production (and subsequently using against a person) all types of evidence, but only evidence of a type that would provided by a "witness"—evidence which is "testimonial" in character. This includes actual testimony and other "evidence of a testimonial or communicative nature." *Schmerber v. Cal.* (§ 5.1(a)).

Compelling non-verbal conduct typically does not involve the compulsion of "testimonial" evidence as opposed to "real or physical evidence." *Schmerber.* Thus, as discussed in § 5.1(b), compelled participation in identification procedures does not fall within the privilege. Under special circumstances, however, the compelled production of physical evidence will be testimonial as the individual's act of production will implicitly speak to his less-than-obvious history with respect to the item produced. See (§ 8.3(b)) (act of producing documents); *Baltimore City Department of Social Services v. Bouknight* (§ 8.3(f)) (act of producing an infant alleged to be in subpoenaed person's custody).

As the Court noted in *Doe v. U.S.* (1988), "[t]here are few instances in which a verbal statement, either oral or written, will not convey information or assert facts," but as to those instances, a verbal statement will not be "testimonial." *Doe* presented such a situation. There, a court order required an individual to sign a form authorizing a foreign bank to release records relating to any account held by the individual. The content of the form was prescribed by the government and it specifically noted that the signing party was acting under court order and did not acknowledge, in signing, the existence of any account in any bank. Thus, the individual was required, in effect, to speak, but the speaking was not testimonial as he was not required engage in "truth telling," thereby revealing "the contents of his mind." Consider also *Pa. v. Muniz* (§ 4.7(d)) (distinguishing between the testimonial character of a response that revealed the individual's mental confusion and the non-testimonial character of slurred-speech, which revealed only a lack of muscular coordination in the tongue and mouth).

### (e) Incriminating use

The Fifth Amendment prohibits compelling a person to be a witness "against himself." This standard is clearly met when a person's compelled statement is used as part of the state's proof of guilt in a subsequent prosecution of the person. The Court has held, however, that the prohibited state use also includes other prosecution uses that operate to the detriment of the individual in his subsequent prosecution. Thus, the privilege bars use of an individual's compelled statement to impeach him when he later testifies as a defendant in his criminal trial. See *N.J. v. Portash* (§ 6.7(b)); *Mincey v. Ariz.* (§ 6.7(b)). So too, it bars use of the compelled statement as a source leading to other evidence, resulting in the privilege prohibiting admission in the criminal case of evidence "derived" from the compelled statement. See *Kastigar v. U.S.* (§§ 6.6(a), 8.2(e)). These further prohibitions do not apply to *Miranda* violations, (see §§ 6.6(g), 6.7(b)), but that is a reflection of the Court's interpretation of *Miranda* as creating an over-inclusive presumption of compulsion. See §§ 1.3(e), 6.2(a), 8.1(c).

Where a witness is required to assert the privilege at the point of compulsion (see § 8.2(a)), a court must consider the entire range of uses prohibited by the privilege in assessing whether the statement being compelled can properly be characterized as potentially incriminatory. Thus as discussed in § 8.2(c), the court must consider not simply whether the witness' statement might itself acknowledge an element of the crime, but whether it could, without such an acknowledgment, nonetheless provide a lead to other evidence that could be used against the witness in a subsequent criminal prosecution (i.e., furnish a "link in the chain of evidence").

### (f) Criminal case

The privilege prohibits the use of the compelled statement only as to a "criminal case." It does not prohibit use in non-criminal proceedings, and a witness cannot claim the privilege when the potential use of the statement does not include use in a criminal case. See § 8.2(e); *Ullmann v. U.S.* (1956) (potential civil disabilities and social stigma, no matter how severe, do not justify reliance on the privilege to refuse to testify). A criminal case necessarily involves the determination of criminal liability and the imposing of criminal sanctions. Thus, *Allen v. Ill.* (§ 4.5(c)) held that the privilege was not available to preclude use of a coerced confession in a civil commitment proceeding for sexually dangerous persons.

## § 8.2    COMPELLING WITNESS TESTIMONY

### (a)  Invoking the privilege

In a criminal trial, the prosecution cannot insist that the defendant take the stand, like any other witness, and invoke the privilege when the response to a particular prosecution question would be incriminating. The defendant at trial may invoke the privilege by simply refusing to testify. The ability to invoke the privilege in this fashion, however, is limited to the defendant. Where a person is subpoenaed to testify as a witness in a judicial or administrative proceeding, the privilege does not allow him to simply refuse to be sworn. The witness intending to exercise the privilege must be sworn and assert the privilege separately as each question calling for an incriminating response. This obligation to appear and respond individually extends even to the witness before the grand jury, who "may himself be the subject of grand jury inquiry" (i.e., a possible "target" of an indictment). *U.S. v. Dionisio* (1973). A person questioned by the police, whether as a possible prosecution witness or a key suspect, may simply refuse to answer any and all questions, but that person is under no legal obligation to provide even non-incriminating answers. The grand jury is given the legal authority, via judicial subpoena, to compel testimony, and having an obligation to "shield against arbitrary accusations," it has a right to be certain that the target's own testimony might not explain away the evidence against him. *U.S. v. Mandujano* (1976). The privilege establishes only a witness' "option of refusal"; it does not create a "prohibition against inquiry."

For the witness, the Fifth Amendment privilege is not self-executing. A suspect subject to police interrogation techniques so coercive as to constitute compulsion can provide an incriminating response and subsequently challenge the government's use of that response in a criminal prosecution as prohibited by the Fifth Amendment. The witness, in contrast, must assert the privilege at the time that question is asked. If the witness answers the question, his answer will be deemed "voluntary." As Justice Frankfurter explained in an often-quoted statement: "[Since the] Amendment * * * does not preclude a witness from testifying voluntarily in matters which may incriminate him, * * * [if the witness] desires the protection of the privilege, he must claim it or, he will not be considered to have been 'compelled' within the meaning of the Amendment." *U.S. v. Monia* (1943) (dis.)

Where the witness responds without asserting the privilege, his statement can subsequently be used against him even if he later claims that he acted under the compulsion of the subpoena, being unaware of the privilege. See *U.S. v. Wong* (1977) (false grand jury testimony could be the grounding for a perjury charge even if, as the witness now claims, she testified only because she misunderstood self-incrimination warnings and believed she was legally required to testify). Moreover, once the witness furnishes incriminating testimony as to a particular subject, she relinquishes the privilege in that proceeding as to further testimony on that subject. As noted in *Rogers v. U.S.* (1951), a witness will not be allowed to disclose a basic incriminating fact and then claim the privilege as to "details." To uphold such use of the privilege would "open the way to distortion of facts by permitting a witness to select any stopping point in her testimony." Although *Rogers* sometimes is described as posing great dangers for the witness who fails to assert the privilege to even seemingly "innocuous questions," the Court there viewed the follow-up questions that the witness failed to answer as only minimally increasing the "danger of prosecution" beyond that created by the witness' earlier response to a question seeking obviously incriminating information.

### (b) Advice as to rights

In general, a witness bears the obligation of recognizing both that the privilege exists and that it applies to a particular response. *U.S. v. Kordel* (1970) (failure to claim privilege in civil proceedings). In *U.S. v. Mandujuano* (1976), the defendant claimed that, where a grand jury witness was a target of the grand jury's investigation, he should be entitled to *Miranda* warnings (see § 4.8), and in the absence of such warnings, the state should be barred from using his grand jury testimony as the basis for a perjury prosecution. The Court unanimously agreed that, even if the warnings were required, that did not excuse the witness' perjury. Six justices also addressed the need for warnings, but divided on that question.

Chief Justice Burger's opinion for four justices distinguished *Miranda* and indicated that no warnings whatsoever were required. The Chief Justice stressed that: (1) grand jury questioning "takes place in a setting wholly different from custodial interrogation" (which occurs in the "hostile" and "isolated" setting of the police station); (2) a grand jury witness has no absolute right to remain silent comparable to that of the suspect interrogated by the police, but rather has an "absolute duty to answer all questions, subject only to a valid Fifth Amendment claim"; and (3) there was no Sixth Amendment basis for advising the witness of a right to consult with appointed counsel (an element of the *Miranda* warnings), as "no criminal proceedings [had] yet been instituted" and "the Sixth

Amendment right to counsel [therefore] had not come into play." Since the witness had been advised that he had a privilege against self-incrimination, the Chief Justice found no need to decide whether a warning limited to that advice might be required as to target witnesses. However, his opinion did stress that the target witness was subject to the same requirements for invoking the privilege as witnesses generally, relying on the explanation of *Monia* (discussed above), which does not call for any warnings.

Two justices (Brennan and Marshall) agreed that *Miranda* was distinguishable, but contended that the *Monia* analysis also did not apply because here the prosecutor "is acutely aware of the potentially incriminating nature of the disclosures sought." They argued that, to ensure that the target witness' response is the product of an "intelligent and intentional" waiver of the privilege, the prosecutor should be required to give complete self-incrimination warnings and also inform the target witness of his target status.

Since it is now commonplace to notify target witness that they may assert the privilege where their answers might be incriminating, the Court has not subsequently been required to rule on the constitutional necessity of such warnings. But note *Minn. v. Murphy* (1984) (noting, in dictum, that the Court has "never held that [warnings] must be given to the grand jury witness"). The Court did subsequently consider the necessity of "target warnings," and in *U.S. v. Washington* (1977) held that no notification of target status was constitutionally required. The Court there reasoned that the failure to provide target notification did not put the witness at a "constitutional disadvantage." His target status "neither enlarge[d] nor diminish[ed] the scope of his constitutional protection," and he "knew better than anyone else" whether his answers would be incriminating.

### (c) Potential incrimination

Since the witness must exercise the privilege at the point of compulsion, before making any statement, there is necessarily uncertainty as to whether the witness' statement, if compelled, would result in a Fifth Amendment violation by its eventual use against the witness in a criminal prosecution. The Court has recognized, in accord with the English common law, that the privilege must be made available to the witness if the danger of such use is "real and appreciable" as opposed to "imaginary and insubstantial." *Brown v. Walker* (1896). If such a danger is posed, the witness' assertion of the privilege must be honored, and the court issuing the subpoena may not hold the witness in contempt for refusing to answer the particular question.

A witness' assertion of the privilege does not, in itself, establish that the testimony the witness would provide, if compelled to answer the particular question, would have the necessary potential for incriminating use in a subsequent prosecution. As *Hoffman v. U.S.* (1951) held, "it is for the court to say whether [the witness'] silence is justified, and to require him to answer 'if it clearly appears to the court that he is mistaken.' " *Hoffman* also indicated, however, that courts are to give the witness every benefit of the doubt in reviewing an assertion of the privilege. "The privilege," the Court noted, applies "not only to answers that would in themselves support a conviction but likewise * * * those which would furnish a link in the chain of evidence needed to prosecute the claimant." The witness must have "reasonable cause" to believe that his testimony would have this potential, but he cannot be expected to "prove * * * [that] hazard in the sense in which a claim is usually required to be established in court," as that would "compel * * * [the witness] to surrender the very protection which the privilege is designed to guarantee." Accordingly, to sustain the witness' claim, "it need only be evident from the implications of the question, in the setting in which it is asked, that a responsive answer to the question or an explanation of why it cannot be answered might be dangerous because injurious disclosure could result."

Under the *Hoffman* standard, unusual circumstances are needed for a court to conclude that a witness' response would not present a "real and appreciable [danger]." As the Court noted in *Ohio v. Reiner* (2001), a witness' assertion that he is innocent is not inconsistent with a claim of potential incrimination, for the witness' statement denying guilt might still acknowledge various potentially incriminating facts (e.g., presence at the scene of the crime, as in *Reiner*). So too, while a question concerning a crime for which the defendant was already convicted might ordinarily suggest a lack of potential for further incrimination, that would not be the case where there was a possibility of ongoing criminality, so that information relating to the offense of conviction might "furnish a link in a chain of evidence sufficient to connect the [witness] with a more recent crime for which he might still be prosecuted." *Malloy v. Hogan* (1964)

In *Hiibel v. Sixth Judicial Dist. Ct.* (2004), the Court did identify one class of questions most unlikely to pose a "real and appreciable fear" of incrimination. *Hiibel* did not involve the assertion of the privilege by a witness, but a case in which a person detained by police on reasonable suspicion refused to identify himself, as required by a "stop and identify statute." The Court questioned whether the detainee actually had relied on the privilege in refusing to provide his name, but went on to note that such a claim typically would fail because "answering a request to disclose a name is likely to be so insignificant in the scheme of things as to be incriminating only in unusual circumstances". It noted that "even witnesses who plan to invoke the Fifth Amendment privilege answer when their names are called to take the stand." Still, the Court also stated that it was not completely foreclosing the possible application of the privilege in the stop and identify situation: "A case may arise where there is a substantial allegation that furnishing identity at the time of the stop would give the police a link in the chain of evidence needed to convict the individual of a separate offense [i.e., other than the failure to identify]" * * * and the court can then consider whether the privilege applies* * *."

## (d) Incrimination under the laws of another sovereign

For many years, American courts took the position that the self-incrimination privilege protected only against incrimination under the laws of the sovereign which was compelling the witness' testimony. Thus, if a witness in a federal proceeding was granted immunity against federal prosecution, he could not refuse to testify on the ground that his answers might be incriminating under the laws of a state or a foreign nation. In *Murphy v. Waterfront Comm'n.* (1964), the Supreme Court rejected this "separate sovereign" doctrine as applied to state and federal incrimination. Noting that the doctrine would allow a witness to be "whipsawed into incriminating himself under both state and federal law," the Court concluded that the "policies and purposes" of the Fifth Amendment require that the privilege protect "a state witness against incrimination under federal as well as state law and a federal witness against incrimination under state as well as federal law."

As *Murphy* noted, where a witness in a federal proceeding claims potential state incrimination, the federal government has the authority to grant the witness immunity that extends to state proceedings, which permits it then to compel the witness' testimony. As for the states, *Murphy* held that where a state granted immunity to a witness, the federal government would be prohibited from making any use of the testimony given under that immunity, so that the state immunity, like the federal, would operate upon both sovereigns. In contrast, neither the federal government nor the states have the authority to grant immunity against foreign prosecution. Elimination of the dual sovereignty doctrine as applied to foreign prosecutions would place the state and federal systems in a position where they could not supplant the privilege and compel the testimony with a grant of immunity. This consideration was noted in *U.S. v. Balysys* (1998), where the Court held that incrimination under the laws of a foreign country was beyond the protection of the self-incrimination clause. The reference to "any criminal case" in the Fifth Amendment, the Court reasoned, extended only to prosecutions in jurisdictions subject to that Amendment (the federal government and the states, via the Fourteenth Amendment), and not to foreign nations.

### (e) Immunity

In *Brown v. Walker* (1896), a sharply divided Court concluded that precluding reliance on the privilege by granting a witness immunity from criminal prosecution was entirely consistent with the purposes of the Fifth Amendment privilege, as illustrated by historical practice. The English had adopted an immunity procedure, known as providing "indemnity" against criminal prosecution, soon after the privilege against compulsory self-incrimination became firmly established, and a similar practice was followed in the colonies. So too, the self-incrimination privilege had been held inapplicable where the witness' compelled testimony would relate only to an offense as to which he had been pardoned or as to which the statute of limitations had run. The thesis of these rulings, like that of the indemnity practice, was that where the witness was assured that his truthful testimony could not lead to his criminal prosecution, the privilege was not available, as the danger against which the privilege protected had been eliminated.

In *Brown v. Walker*, the Court upheld an immunity statute that adopted "transactional immunity," as it guaranteed to the witness that he could not be prosecuted "for or on account of any transaction, matter, or thing concerning which he may testify or produce evidence." Such broad immunity was thought necessary in light of the earlier decision in *Counselman v. Hitchcock* (1892). The Court there had held inadequate an immunity statute that provided the witness with protection only against the immunized testimony being admitted in evidence in a subsequent prosecution for an offense mentioned in that testimony. *Counselman* stressed that the statute failed to provide protection against the derivative use of the witness' testimony, including "the use of his testimony to search out other testimony to be used in evidence against him." However, the Court also spoke of even broader protection which afford "absolute immunity" as to the events noted in the witness testimony (apart from a prosecution for perjury where the witness lied as to those events).

After *Brown*, immunity statutes universally provided for transactional immunity. Then in *Murphy v. Waterfront Comm'n.* (§ 8.2(d)), in holding that a state immunity grant was insufficient if it did not also extend to federal prosecutions, the Court noted that it would be sufficient that the state witness was guaranteed that neither his immunized state testimony nor any fruits derived therefrom would be used against him in a federal prosecution. Following *Murphy*, the federal government and various states adopted immunity provisions that were limited to use-and-derivative-use protection as to prosecutions in the jurisdiction granting the immunity as well as prosecutions in sister jurisdictions (federal or state). These provisions were upheld in the companion cases of *Kastigar v. U.S.* (1972) and *Zicarelli v. N.J.* (1972). The Court there discounted the "broad language in *Counselman*" as inconsistent with *Counselman's* conceptual basis, which was that the immunity grant be "coextensive with the scope of the privilege against self-incrimination." The traditional Fifth Amendment remedy of simply excluding from evidence the compelled statement and its evidentiary fruits (as exemplified by coerced confession cases) indicated that the privilege did not require an absolute bar against prosecution. A prohibition against use and derivative use satisfied the privilege by placing the witness "in substantially the same position as if * * * [the witness] had claimed his privilege."

The *Kastigar* majority rejected the argument, relied upon by the dissenters, that the bar against derivative use could not be enforced so effectively as to ensure that the witness really was placed in the same position as if he had not testified. The statute's "total prohibition on use," it noted, "provides a comprehensive safeguard, barring the use of compelled testimony as an 'investigatory lead,' and also barring the use of any evidence obtained by focusing investigation on a witness as a result of his compelled disclosures." Appropriate procedures for "taint hearings" would ensure that this prohibition was made effective. Once a defendant demonstrates that he previously testified under a grant of immunity, the prosecution must carry "the burden of showing that [its] evidence is not tainted by establishing that [it] had an independent, legitimate source for the disputed evidence." This requirement, the Court noted, would provide the immunized witness with "protection commensurate with that resulting from invoking the privilege itself."

## § 8.3  COMPELLING THE PRODUCTION OF DOCUMENTS

### (a) *Boyd* and "content protection"

*Boyd v. U.S.* (1886) was the first Supreme Court case to consider the applicability of the self-incrimination clause to the compelled production of documents, and for close to a century thereafter, *Boyd* dominated Fifth Amendment analysis of subpoenas directing persons to produce documents (typically before grand juries). At issue in *Boyd* was the constitutionality of a court order requiring an importing firm organized as a partnership to produce the invoice it has received for items alleged to have been illegally imported. The order did not take the form of a subpoena *duces tecum* (a subpoena to produce physical evidence), but it was treated as such. The Court concluded that the subpoena was subject to the Fourth Amendment (see § 2.10), and was unreasonable because it constituted a forcible compulsion that was contrary to the Fifth Amendment's self-incrimination clause. Just as the Fifth Amendment prohibited "compulsory discovery by extorting the party's oath," it also prohibited discovery by "compelling the production of his private books and papers." The documentary production order was simply another form of "forcible and compulsory extortion of a man's own testimony." *Boyd* apparently viewed the compulsory disclosure of a document as equivalent to requiring the subpoenaed party to set forth the content of the document through his testimony. Thus, while *Boyd* also spoke of the protection of personal property, its analysis arguably was limited to documents, which have a testimonial content. On the other hand, though *Boyd* spoke of "private books and papers," it obviously was not limiting its analysis to confidential documents relating to personal matters, as the document at issue there was a business record that had been prepared by a third party.

In the years following *Boyd*, the Court recognized various "exceptions" in which the self-incrimination clause did not apply to the production of documents, such as the "required records" doctrine (§ 8.3(g)), the "entity records" doctrine (§ 8.3(f)), and the seizure-by-search doctrine (see *Andresen v. Md.* § 6.3(b)). In *Fisher v. U.S.* (1976), the Court majority concluded that all that remained of *Boyd* was "a prohibition against forcing the production of private papers [that] has long been a rule searching for a rationale consistent with the prescriptions of the Fifth Amendment against compelling a person to give 'testimony' that incriminating him."

The *Fisher* majority concluded, as discussed in subsection (b), that the act of producing documents "had a communicative aspect of its own, wholly aside from the contents of the paper produced," which could often be subject to the privilege. At the same it noted that the contents of the subpoenaed documents did not fall within the protection of the privilege. The court order of production did not require the subpoenaed party to create the documents, as the documents were pre-existing. Moreover, since the preparation of the pre-existing records had been voluntary, their content "cannot be said to contained compelled testimonial evidence." The records may contain incriminating writing, but whether the writing of the subpoenaed party or another, that writing was not a communication compelled by the subpoena. Accordingly, the prosecution's acquisition of the content of the writing by subpoena no more constituted compelling testimony than the compelled production of other physical evidence with similar incriminating content.

As discussed in subsection (b), the Court in *Fisher* concluded that the act of production, as it occurred in that particular case, did not fall within the protection of the privilege. At the same time, it noted: "Whether the Fifth Amendment would shield the taxpayer from producing his own tax records in his possession is a question not involved here; for the papers demanded here are not 'private papers,' see *Boyd v. United States.*" This statement led some lower courts to view *Fisher's* act-of-production doctrine and *Boyd's* content-based analysis as alternative grounds for applying the privilege. In *U.S. v. Doe* (1984), a case involving a grand jury subpoena for various business records (including some apparently authored by the subpoenaed party), the lower court had relied on both of these grounds in finding the privilege applicable. Although also sustaining the privilege's application, the Supreme Court found erroneous the lower court's reliance on *Boyd's* content analysis. The reasoning of *Fisher*, it noted, had clearly refuted the lower court's argument that the Fifth Amendment created a "zone of privacy" that protects the content of subpoenaed papers.

Justice O'Connor wrote separately in *Doe* "to make explicit what is implicit in the analysis of [the Court's] opinion; that the Fifth Amendment provides absolutely no protection for the contents of private papers of any kind." Justice Marshall, joined by Justice Brennan, expressed disagreement, noting that *Doe* dealt only with business records "which implicate a lesser degree of concern for privacy interests than, for example, personal diaries." The Court has not in subsequent cases dealt with subpoenas for documents as personal as a diary, and it would be a rare situation in which the issue need be faced, as the act-of-production doctrine should almost always work to make the privilege applicable to such a subpoena. Interestingly, in *U.S. v. Hubbell* (2000), Justice Thomas, joined by Justice Scalia, held open the possibility of a complete resurrection of *Boyd*, as a ruling more in tune with the history of the privilege than *Fisher's* act-of-production doctrine.

### (b) Testimony via the act of production

Though rejecting the *Boyd* analysis, *Fisher* concluded that three aspects of the act of producing documents had a "communicative aspect" that could rise to the level of constituting testimonial evidence (see § 8.1(d)) and therefore support the *Boyd* result. The person producing the documents designated in a subpoena was: (1) acknowledging the existence of the documents; (2) acknowledging that the documents were in his "possession or control"; and (3) stating his "belief that the papers are those described in the subpoena" (which, in some instances, could provide evidentiary authentication of the documents). These three elements of production were clearly compelled, but whether they also were "testimonial" and "incriminating" would depend upon "the facts and circumstances of particular cases or classes thereof."

*Fisher* concluded that, in the case before it, the act of production was not testimonial, and even if viewed as testimonial, was not incriminating. On the issue of incrimination, the Court applied the traditional standard of potential incrimination (see § 8.2(c)), and found that a "realistic threat of incrimination" has not been shown, in light of the innocuous character of the documents subpoenaed (an accountant's tax workpapers) and the setting in which they were sought (an IRS investigation). In two subsequent cases involving grand jury subpoenas, the Court has had no difficulty in affirming lower court conclusions that a testimonial act of production did meet the potential incrimination standard, although both subpoenas involved rather standard business records. See *Doe v. U.S.* (1988); *U.S. v. Hubbell* (2000).

In finding that the testimonial component was not met, the *Fisher* Court relied on an analysis of much greater significance, advancing what has come to be known as the "foregone conclusion" doctrine. That doctrine, discussed below, now stands as the primary vehicle advanced by the government to defeat self-incrimination claims as to the compelled document production in criminal investigations.

### (c)  Foregone conclusions

The Court in *Fisher* acknowledged that a taxpayer's act of producing an accountant's tax workpapers, in response to a subpoena, would have communicative aspects, as that act "implicitly admit[ted] the existence and possession of the papers." It concluded, however, that it was "doubtful" that such admissions "rise to the level of testimony within the protection of Fifth Amendment." Explaining that conclusion, it noted:

> The papers belong to the accountant, were prepared by him, and are the kind usually prepared by an accountant working on the tax returns of his client. Surely the Government is in no way relying on the "truthtelling" of the taxpayer to prove the existence of or his access to the documents. The existence and location of the papers are a foregone conclusion and the taxpayer adds little or nothing to the sum total of the Government's information by conceding that he in fact has the papers. Under these circumstances by enforcement of the summons "no constitutional rights are touched. The question is not of testimony but of surrender."

The Court drew an analogy in this connection to the compelled production of a handwriting sample, clearly established by precedent not to be testimonial. Incidental to this act, the suspect necessarily "admits his ability to write and impliedly asserts that the exemplar is his writing." But the government obviously is not seeking this information–the "first would be near a truism and the latter self evident"–and therefore "nothing he has said or done is deemed to be sufficiently testimonial for

purposes of the privilege." Where the communicative aspects of a physical act are a "foregone conclusion," the government is not seeking those assertions in compelling the act, and the act therefore
should not be deemed testimonial. All acts inherently communicate one factual assertion or another,
but unless these assertions are sought by the government in building its case, they should not override the distinction drawn in *Schmerber* and other
cases (see § 8.1(d)) between compelling the production of physical evidence (here a pre-existing document) and compelling "testimony."

*Fisher* offered only limited insight as to what
made the communicative aspects of production a
"foregone conclusion" in a particular case. The
Court's reference to the accountant's workpapers as
a type of document commonly prepared for taxpay-
ers led the government to contend that the existence and location of standard business documents
was always a foregone conclusion. *U.S. v. Doe*
(1984) appeared to reject this contention, as the
documents subpoenaed there were standard business documents and the Court sustained the lower
court findings that the government had failed to
establish "that possession, existence, and authentication were a foregone conclusion." But the Court
in *Doe* did not offer an independent analysis of this
conclusion.

In *U.S. v. Hubbell* (2000), however, the Court
both confirmed the implicit message of *Doe* and
offered a reading of *Fisher* consistent with the

lower court rulings demanding that the government, to meet the foregone conclusion standard, demonstrate with "reasonable particularly that it knows of the existence and location of [the] subpoenaed documents." The subpoena in *Hubbell* called for 11 categories (almost all broadly described) of largely business documents. The Court reasoned that, "given the breadth of the 11 categories, * * * the collection and production of the materials demanded was tantamount to answering a series of interrogatories asking a witness to disclose the existence and location of particular documents fitting broad descriptions." The government responded that this obviously "communicative aspect of production" was nonetheless not sufficiently testimonial "because the existence and possession of such records by any business is a foregone conclusion." Rejecting this contention, the Court reasoned:

> Whatever the scope of this "foregone conclusion" rationale, the facts of this case plainly fall outside of it. While in *Fisher*, the Government already knew that the documents were in the [subpoenaed] attorneys' possession and could independently confirm their existence and authenticity through the accountants who created them, here the Government has not shown that it had any prior knowledge of either the existence or the whereabouts of the 13,120 pages of documents ultimately produced by respondent. The Government cannot cure this deficiency through the overboard argument that a businessman such as respondent will always possess general business

and tax records that fall within the broad categories described in this subpoena. The *Doe* subpoenas also sought several broad categories of general business records, yet we upheld the District Court's finding that the act of producing those records would involve testimonial self-incrimination.

### (d) Act-of-production immunity

Since the testimonial component in the compelled production of documents lies in the act of production, not the contents of the documents, *U.S. v. Doe* (1984) concluded that the government could replace the privilege by providing use-and-derivative use immunity limited to the act of production. *Doe* did not explore the ramifications of such immunity, and the government subsequently took the position that the immunity allowed it to make full use of the documents produced, so long as avoided reference to the source of the documents–i.e., treated the documents as if they "magically appeared before the grand jury from an unknown source." In *U.S. v. Hubbell* (2000), the Supreme Court rejected the government's reliance on that argument.

The prosecution in *Hubbell* argued that its grant of act-of-production immunity (resulting in the production of documents totaling 13,120 pages) did not impact the evidence to be used in its subsequent prosecution of defendant Hubbell. It was not using the documents produced under the immunity order, but other evidence discovered through an examination of the produced documents, and there was no need "to advert to [Hubbell's] act of production in order to prove the existence, authenticity or custody" of the documents that the government would introduce at trial. The Court responded that this explanation failed since the government did not show (and could not show) that it had not made derivative use of the "testimonial aspects" of the act of production. The contention that the produced documents should be useable as if they "magically appeared in the prosecutor's office, like manna from heaven," was not persuasive; in fact those documents "arrived there only after [Hubell] asserted his constitutional privilege, received a grant of immunity, and * * * took the mental and physical steps necessary to provide the prosecutor with an accurate inventory of the many sources of potentially incriminating evidence sought by the subpoena." "It was only through [Hubbell's] truthful reply to the subpoena that the Government received the incriminating documents of which it made 'substantial use . . . in the investigation'."

Certain aspects of *Hubbell*'s discussion of the government's derivative use focused on the special character of the subpoena in *Hubbell*. The subpoena's extreme breadth, the Court noted, required Hubbell to "make extensive use of the 'contents of his own mind' in identifying the hundreds of documents responsive to the subpoena." Such language could be used to distinguish act-of-production immunity where the subpoena sought a single class of easily identified documents. Yet other language in *Hubbell* suggests that even a single document clearly identified in the subpoena would be the fruit of the immunity (and unavailable for use) if its existence and whereabouts were not a forgone conclusion; for without the "truthtelling" involved in the act of production, the government would not have received the document.

### (e)  Third party subpoenas

The Fifth Amendment privilege is personal and therefore applies only to the person compelled to produce the documents. Thus, *Couch v. U.S.* (1973) held that a taxpayer could not assert the privilege as to various financial records that had been delivered to her accountant and subsequently subpoenaed from the accountant. *Fisher v. U.S.* (1976) reached a similar conclusion as to a subpoena directed to the taxpayer's lawyer, (although there the lawyer-client privilege would have allowed the attorney to refuse production if the client would have been able to successfully assert the privilege in response to a subpoena directed to the client). Both *Fisher* and *Couch* did acknowledge, however, that "situations might exist where constructive possession is so clear or the relinquishment of possession is so temporary and insignificant as to leave the personal compulsion upon the accused substantially intact."

### (f)  Entity records

*Hale v. Henkel* (1906), decided two decades after *Boyd*, held that the self-incrimination privilege was not available to a corporation, and therefore the *Boyd* ruling did not operate to bar a grand jury subpoena requiring production of corporate records. The critical element of this ruling, the Court later noted, was not the corporate form as such, but the presence of an organizational structure which created an entity "so impersonal * * * that [it] cannot be said to embody the purely private or personal interests of its constituents, but rather to embody their common or group interests only." *U.S. v. White* (1944) (privilege also not available to a labor union). The end result is an "entity exception," which extends to all organizational forms recognized in the law as establishing "an independent entity [standing] apart from its individual members." *Bellis v. U.S.* (1974). Thus, *Bellis* concluded that a small law firm, organized as a partnership, came within the "entity exception" even though it "embodie[d] little more than the personal legal practice of individual partners."

The Court has cited two factors in explaining the entity exception. First, the self-incrimination clause is grounded on concerns that relate only to the compulsion directed against a human being. The clause has been described, for example, as preventing "inhumane" methods of compulsion (e.g., torture), ensuring "respect for the inviolability of human personality," and establishing a "right of each individual to a private enclave where he may lead a private life." *Murphy v. Waterfront Comm'n.* (1964). An entity is a fictional body, create by the law, and needs no such protection.

Second, as a creation of the law, the entity is subject to a more comprehensive regulatory authority than the individual, and the required production of documents often is essential to the exercise of that authority. Allowing the privilege to preclude the compelled production of entity documents would "largely frustrate legitimate governmental regulation of * * * organizations" as "the greater portion of evidence of wrongdoing by an organization or its representatives is usually found in the official records of that organization." *Braswell v. U.S.* (1988)

Subpoenas to produce entity documents are sometimes directed to an entity employee or other agent in possession of the entity documents, rather than to the entity itself. A series of early 1900s cases held that a corporate employee subpoenaed to produce corporate records could not claim the privilege based on potential incriminating content establishing the employee's personal liability. They reasoned that, by voluntarily accepting possession of the records, the employee (whether or not formally designated a custodian) assumed the responsibility for making the records available upon proper governmental demand. If the rule were otherwise, the Court noted, the entity exception would be meaningless.

*Braswell v. U.S.* (1988) concluded that the reasoning of the entity-agent cases had not been undermined by the Court's recognition in *Fisher* (§ 8.3(b)) that the act of producing documents could have a testimonial content. Any testimonial content in the act of production was properly attributed to the entity, not the individual performing the act, just as the content of the corporate record had been attributed by the early entity-agent cases, applying the *Boyd* analysis, to the entity rather than the employee. Accordingly, the Court noted, "whether one concludes—as did the Court [in *Fisher*]—that a custodian's production of corporate records is deemed not to constitute testimonial self-incrimination or instead that a custodian waives the right to exercise the privilege, the lesson of *Fisher* is clear: A custodian may not resist a subpoena for corporate records on Fifth Amendment grounds."

*Braswell* did add, however, an evidentiary limitation that had not been imposed in the earlier entity-agent cases. Since the agent's act of production is an act of the entity and not the individual, the government "may make no evidentiary use of the 'individual act' against the individual." Illustrating this point, the Court noted that "in a criminal prosecution against the custodian, the Government may not introduce into evidence before the jury the fact that the subpoena was served upon and the corporation's documents were delivered by one particular individual, the custodian." The government would be limited to showing that the entity had produced the document and to using that act of the entity in establishing that the records were authentic entity records that the entity had possessed and had produced.

### (g) Required records

Where individuals engage in a regulated business, they may be required to keep certain records and to make such records open for inspection by public officials. In *Shapiro v. U.S.* (1948), the Court held that the self-incrimination privilege does not provide protection against the compelled disclosure of such records as the records were created for the public benefit, with the government reserving the right to insist upon their production. The *Shapiro* Court acknowledged that "there are limits which the Government cannot constitutionally exceed in requiring the keeping of records which may be inspected," but it had no need to consider those limits in the context of the records before it— records that dealers in various items were required to keep in the implementation of the Wartime Emergency Price Control Act. Subsequently, in *Grosso v. U.S.* (1968), the Court characterized three elements as necessary "premises of the [required records] doctrine."

First, the government's interest in the records must arise out of a regulatory scheme rather than a criminal law enforcement objective. Thus, the doctrine could not be used to impose a reporting requirement on professional gamblers, a "group inherently suspect of criminal activities." Most states make gambling a crime, and looking to the "characteristics of the activity" and "the composition of the group to which inquires are made," the Court could not say that Congress was dealing here with "an essentially non-criminal and regulatory area." *Grosso v. U.S.*

Second, the information that the government seeks by "requiring the preservation of records" must be of a kind which the regulated party has customarily kept. This reduces the burden placed upon the record keeper and often supports the regulatory relevance of the record. "[T]hird, the records themselves must have assumed 'public aspects' which render them at least analogous to public documents." This characteristic was said to exist in *Shapiro* because the "transaction which it [the required record] recorded was one in which petitioner could lawfully engage solely by virtue of the license granted to him under the statute."

The rationale underlying the required records exception may be extended to other types of compelled disclosures as part of a regulatory scheme. Thus, *Cal. v. Byers* (1971) relied largely on that rationale in sustaining a "hit and run" statute which required a driver involved in an accident to stop at the scene and leave his name and address. While the separate opinions contributing to a majority ruling disagreed as whether the required disclosure was "testimonial" and "incriminating," they shared a common grounding based on the state's special interest in requiring disclosure. Thus, the plurality opinion stressed that the required disclosure was part of a "regulatory measure" not intended to facilitate criminal convictions, but to "promote the satisfaction of civil liabilities," as "most automobile accidents occur without creating criminal liability." A concurring opinion similarly stressed the necessity of self-reporting in the "assertedly non-criminal governmental" regulation of automobile driving. Consider also *Baltimore City*

*Dep't. of Social Services v. Bouknight* (1990) (while subpoena directing mother to produce possibly abused infant arguably required an incriminating testimonial communication, as "the act of production would amount to testimony regarding her control over and possession of the child," the privilege was not available, as the mother had received custody under a court order and thereby "assumed custodial duties relating to production").

## § 8.4    ADVERSE CONSEQUENCES

### (a) Rationales prohibiting adverse consequences

The Court has held that certain adverse consequences may not be attached to the exercise of the privilege against self-incrimination, though others are constitutionally permissible. Initially, where the adverse consequences are so significant as to constitute "compulsion," they deny the privilege to the person who would have asserted it. Thus, in *Garrity v. N.J.* (1967), where police officers had been warned that they would be removed from office if they did not waive their privilege and testify in an official inquiry, the Court held that their testimony at that inquiry had been compelled and could not be used against them in subsequent criminal prosecutions.

Secondly, the Court also has held unconstitutional the imposition of adverse consequences, without characterizing those consequences as "compulsion," on the ground that they impose an impermissible burden on the individual's exercise of the privilege. *Brooks v. Tenn.* (1972) relied on this rationale in holding unconstitutional a state law requiring the defendant to choose at the outset of the presentation of his defense whether he would testify or not take the stand. Requiring the defendant to choose before he heard the testimony of his defense witnesses (and the prosecution's cross-examination of these witnesses) placed "a heavy burden on a defendant's otherwise unconditional right not to take the stand," and that burden could not be justified by the state's interest in precluding defendants who testify from "coloring [their] testimony to conform to what has gone before."

As illustrated by *Brooks*, while the Court often speaks of a prohibition against "penalizing" the exercise of the privilege, an adverse consequence may be prohibited constitutionally even though the state's objective is not to penalize the exercise the privilege. On the other hand, where the state can advance a legitimate regulatory interest in attaching an adverse consequence to the individual's failure to disclose certain information, that consequence is less likely to be viewed as constitutionally prohibited. See e.g., *Ohio Adult Parole Authority v. Woodward* (1998) (clemency board has an interest in interviewing the convicted person seeking clemency, and the Fifth Amendment would not be violated if consequence of the individual's decision not to interview, whether on self-incrimination or other grounds, was to be denied clemency).

### (b) Adverse inferences

*Griffin v. Cal.* (1965) held unconstitutional a state practice allowing the prosecutor and trial court to comment adversely on the defendant's failure to take the stand. The state there argued that it was only logical to draw an adverse inference from a defendant's failure to come forward and testify on critical facts "peculiarity within the accused's knowledge," and that the jury would draw that inference whether or not the court or prosecutor suggested it do so. The Court responded that various factors could explain a failure to testify (e.g., concern as to impeachment by reference to prior convictions), and in any event, allowing adverse comment impermissibly operated as a "penalty imposed by courts for exercising a constitutional privilege." The Court subsequently held that, if the defendant requested, the trial court had a constitutional duty to instruct the jury that the defendant's silence must be disregarded, *Carter v. Ky.* (1981), and, indeed, the trial court's interest in ensuring that the jury not draw an adverse inference allowed it to insist on a protective instruction even where the defense objected. *Lakeside v. Or.* (1978).

*Mitchell v. U.S.* (1999) concluded that the concerns underlying the *Griffin* rule extended to the sentencing process, and therefore invalidated a sentence imposed by a sentencing judge who stated that he was "holding against [the defendant] that he didn't come forward and explain [his] side of issue [as to the quantity of drugs involved]." The majority declined, however, to express a view as to whether the defendant's silence at sentencing could nonetheless be considered as it "bears on" two other sentencing considerations—the defendant's "lack of remorse" and "acceptance of responsibility." Arguably silence here plays a different role, as these factors are groundings for leniency, as to which the defendant, in effect, carries the burden of proof.

*Baxter v. Palmigiano* (1976) allowed an adverse inference to be drawn in a prison disciplinary proceeding. A prison inmate charged with a regulatory violation which could also constitute a crime was allowed to "remain silent," but was warned that the disciplinary board might draw an adverse inference from that silence in resolving the disciplinary charge. The Court noted that the Fifth Amendment "does not forbid adverse inferences against parties to civil actions when they refuse to testify in response to probative evidence offered against them," and here too, in a non-criminal proceeding, the disciplinary board was simply being allowed to give to the silence whatever "evidentiary value was * * * warranted by the facts surrounding the case."

### (c) Regulatory sanctions

The Court has held in a variety settings that a state cannot attach a significant adverse regulatory consequence to an individual's exercise of the privilege in an official inquiry. See e.g., *Spevack v. Klein* (1967) (state could not utilize the exercise of the privilege as a basis for disbarring a lawyer who had refused on self-incrimination grounds to provide information relevant to the possible violation of professional disciplinary standards); *Lefkowitz v. Turley* (1973) (similar as to loss of government contract). In *Baxter v. Palmigiano*, (§ 8.3(b)), the Court distinguished these rulings from allowing an adverse evidentiary inference to be based on silence in an administrative inquiry, as the adverse regulatory sanction was automatic, with "a refusal to submit to interrogation and to waive the Fifth Amendment privilege, standing alone and without regard to other evidence, result[ing] in loss of employment or opportunity to contract with the states." *McKune v. Lile* (2002) held, however, that the automatic character of the regulatory sanction is only one factor considered in weighing constitutionality, and in some instances on automatic adverse regulatory consequence will not violate the Fifth Amendment.

In *McKune*, a prison inmate challenged a sexual treatment program which required participants to admit responsibility (and provide details) as to all prior sexual activities, and rendered that information unprivileged (which allowed it to be disclosed to prosecuting officials, although that had not been done in the past). The consequences of the inmate refusing to participate, on self-incrimination or other grounds, was a reduction of his prison privilege status and transfer to a more restrictive facility in the same prison complex. The Court majority concluded that these burdens did not violate the self-incrimination privilege. A plurality reasoned that, in light of the significant restraints inherent in prison life, and the state's legitimate rehabilitation goal, the burdens suffered by the non-participating inmate should not be viewed as a "penalty," but simply as a consequence of the state's need to make room for inmates willing to participate in the treatment program. A concurring justice argued that the consequences did constitute a "penalty," but agreed with the plurality that those consequences were not so significant as to constitute "compulsion" under the Fifth Amendment.

# CHAPTER 9

# THE POST–INVESTIGATORY PROCESS: FROM BAIL TO APPELLATE REVIEW

Once a suspect is arrested, a series of non-investigative steps in the process carry the case to its final disposition. These steps are commonly described as post-investigatory, although very often investigation continues during this post-arrest period. Post-investigatory steps include charging, neutral-body screening of the charge, pre-adjudication procedures, adjudication, sentencing, appeals, and in some instances, a successive prosecution. Each of these steps is subject to constitutional regulation. Several aspects of that regulation have been discussed in chapters 6, 7, and 8. This chapter provides a brief overview of its primary additional components. With so much ground to cover, we will describe in detail only the most prominent Supreme Court rulings.

## § 9.1 PRETRIAL RELEASE

### (a) Eighth Amendment

The Eighth Amendment provides in part: "Excessive bail shall not be required." Although the Court has not had occasion to rule on whether this prohibition is incorporated in the Fourteenth Amendment, *Schilb v. Kuebel* (1971) stated that it "has been assumed to have application to the States through the Fourteenth Amendment." The traditional purpose for setting "bail"—whether it be in the form of a bail bond or some other condition of release—is to assure that the accused will appear at subsequent proceedings. *Stack v. Boyle* (1951). In this context, the prohibition against excessive bail bars imposing conditions for release beyond what is "reasonably calculated" to provide "adequate assurance" of the "presence of the accused" at those proceedings. *Stack.* Setting bail that provides such assurance requires an assessment of the facts of the particular case, and not simply looking to the character of the offense charged. Id.

*U.S. v. Salerno* (1987) rejected the contention that preclusion of flight is the only constitutionally acceptable grounding for setting conditions of bail. The Court there denied a challenge to the constitutionality on its face of a "preventive detention" statute. That statute directed that the setting of bail also take into account the protection of community safety, and authorized denial of release where no set of conditions would "reasonably assure the safety of any other person or the community." The Court found no need to rule on the suggestion, advanced in dictum in *Carlson v. Landon* (1952), that the Eighth Amendment serves only to bar judicial setting of excessive bail for bailable offenses, and does not limit Congress' authority to make non-bailable particular classes of offenses or offenders. For even if it were "to conclude that the Eighth Amendment imposes some substantive limitation on the National Legislature's powers in this area," the "only arguable substantive limitation of the Bail Clause is that the government's proposed conditions of release or detention not be 'excessive' in light of the perceived evil" that informs the release decision. "Nothing in the text of the Bail Clause," the Court noted, "limits permissible government considerations solely to questions of flight." The history of the clause, allowing the refusal of bail in capital cases and as to defendants who present a threat to witnesses, was also cited as supporting Congress' authority to take account of other "compelling interests" beyond flight, as it did in the preventive detention statute.

### (b) Due process

As noted in *Salerno,* denial of pretrial release also may raise substantive due process difficulties. While the presumption of innocence is viewed solely as "a doctrine that allocates the burden of proof" at trial and therefore has "no application * * * before trial has even begun," *Bell v. Wolfish* (1979), substantive due process would bar a pretrial detention provision aimed at punishing individuals thought to be dangerous but not yet found guilty of crimes. *Salerno* concluded that the pretrial detention provision upheld there was not aimed at punishment, but designed to serve the "legitimate regulatory goal" of "preventing danger to the community."

## § 9.2   DECISION TO CHARGE

### (a)  Limitations upon the charging decision

The American prosecutor traditionally has had broad discretion in determining whether to initiate formal charges and in selecting among possible charges. The Supreme Court has frequently recognized the freedom of individual jurisdictions to grant immense charging discretion to the prosecutor. See e.g., *U.S. v. Batchelder* (1979) (holding constitutional a statutory scheme that allowed a prosecutor to choose between two offenses, carrying substantially different punishments, but prohibiting the same conduct). Nonetheless, the Court has also noted that the prosecutor's charging discretion must be exercised consistent with both the equal protection guarantee and the due process prohibition against "vindictiveness."

*Equal protection.* As noted in *Oyler v. Boles* (1962), the prosecutor's "conscious exercise of * * * selectivity in law enforcement" may not be "deliberately based" upon grounds that would violate equal protection, "such as race, religion, or other arbitrary classification." The Court has also noted, however, that because "the decision to prosecute is particularly ill-suited to judicial review," and because "examining the basis of a prosecution delays the criminal proceeding, threatens to chill law enforcement by subjection the prosecutor's motives and decisionmaking to outside inquiry, and may undermine prosecutorial effectiveness by revealing the Government's enforcement policy," the standard for establishing such an equal protection claim is a "demanding one." *U.S. v. Armstrong* (1996); *Wayte v. U.S.* (1985). The defendant must overcome "the presumption that a prosecutor has not violated equal protection" by presenting "clear evidence to the contrary." *Armstrong*. That "clear evidence" must establish that the prosecutor's selective enforcement policy "had a discriminatory effect and that it was motivated by a discriminatory purpose." *Wayte*. To gain discovery from the government, the defendant must first produce "some evidence tending to show the existence" of both of these elements. *Armstrong*. Establishing a discriminatory effect requires a showing both that (1) the persons prosecuted under the particular statute fell disproportionately within the group subjected to the alleged discrimination, and (2) similarly situated offenders not within that group were known to prosecuting officials but nonetheless not prosecuted. Id.

*Vindictive prosecution.* A due process prohibition against prosecutorial vindictiveness in charge selection was first recognized in *Blackledge v. Perry* (1974), a case in which defendant was originally convicted of a misdemeanor assault, exercised his right under local law to a trial de novo, and then was charged before the de novo court with a felony assault based on the same conduct. Striking down the prosecutor's raising of the charge to a felony, the Court noted that defendant was "entitled to pursue his statutory right to a trial de novo without apprehension that the State will retaliate by substituting a more serious charge for the original one." In *Blackledge,* the prosecution initially had gone to trial on the misdemeanor charge, and the Court was willing to assume that the subsequent raising of the charge was vindictive. *U.S. v. Goodwin* (1982) held, however, that a presumption of vindictiveness would not be applied in a pretrial setting because at that stage changes in the charge were so much more likely to be based on non-vindictive grounds. Thus, for the defendant to establish vindictiveness under the facts of *Goodwin* (where defendant, originally charged with a petty offense, sought a jury trial, resulting in the transfer of the case to another court, where a new prosecutor obtained a felony indictment), he would have to show that the raising of the charge against him stemmed from an "actual retaliatory motive" rather than some other factor (e.g., differences in the perspectives of the two prosecutors).

## (b) Grand jury or preliminary hearing review of the charge

Under the Fifth Amendment, a federal prosecutor cannot proceed on a decision to charge for a felony offense ("an infamous crime") unless a grand jury affirms that charging decision by indicting the defendant for that offense or the defendant waives his right to be proceeded against only by indictment. *Hurtado v. Cal.* (1884) held that this Fifth Amendment requirement did not reflect a "fundamental principle of liberty" and therefore was not imposed upon the states by the Fourteenth Amendment. The state in the *Hurtado* case had utilized a preliminary hearing review by a magistrate as a screening alternative to the grand jury, but *Lem Woon v. Ore.* (1913) held that due process was not violated where a state eliminated all independent screening procedures, allowing the prosecution to file felony charges directly in the trial court upon a prosecutorial oath that the charges were fairly grounded. Although *Hurtado* and *Lem Woon* were decided during the early stages of the application of the Fourteenth Amendment to state criminal justice systems, the Court has continued to cite those decisions with approval. See *Gerstein v. Pugh* (1975).

Although states are not constitutionally required to provide for independent screening of the prosecution's decision to charge by grand jury or preliminary hearing, once such a procedure is imposed under local law, it cannot be conducted in a manner that denies equal protection. Thus, the Supreme Court has long held that an indictment is subject to constitutional challenge if the grand jury selection procedure operated to discriminate on racial grounds. See *Ex parte Va.* (1879). Indeed, since racial discrimination "strikes at the fundamental values of our judicial system and our society as a whole," such a challenge is cognizable on appeal or postconviction review even though a fairly selected petit jury subsequently convicted defendant on the charges presented in the grand jury indictment. *Rose v. Mitchell* (1979). See also *Vasquez v. Hillery* (1986) (even though the petit jury's conviction establishes sufficient evidence to indict, a grand jury of a different racial composition may have been willing to exercise its power to "charge a lesser offense than evidence might support").

## § 9.3  TIMING OF THE PROSECUTION

### (a)  Speedy trial requirements

State discretion as to the timing of a trial is limited by the Sixth Amendment requirement that "the accused shall enjoy the right to a speedy trial." Denial of this right automatically requires dismissal of the delayed prosecution with prejudice; the impact of the denial is too diffuse to permit trial courts to seek to tailor the remedy (e.g., by reducing defendant's sentence) to the hardship that may have been caused in the particular case. *Strunk v. U.S.* (1973). Flexibility has been the governing philosophy, however, in determining whether delay constitutes a denial of the right. Thus, the leading speedy trial decision, *Barker v. Wingo* (1972), rejected what it described as "inflexible approaches" (e.g., imposing a specific time limitation) in favor of "a balancing test, in which the conduct of both the prosecution and the defendant are weighed." *Barker* listed four factors to be weighed in determining whether there had been a denial of the speedy trial right: (1) length of the delay; (2) the government's justification for the delay; (3) whether the defendant asserted his right to a speedy trial; and (4) prejudice caused by the delay, such as lengthened pretrial incarceration, lengthened anxiety, and possible impairment of the presentation of a defense.

In discussing those factors, the Court indicated that though a defense demand for a speedy trial is not essential, the absence of a demand will work strongly against the defendant (unless defendant lacked counsel or otherwise was precluded from making a demand). The speedy trial right, it noted, was unlike most other constitutional rights in that the "deprivation of the right may work to the accused's advantage," and it could not be assumed that defendant wanted a speedy trial, delay being a "not uncommon defense tactic."

The absence of a defense demand played a large role in sustaining much of a five year delay in *Barker*, where defendant had been at large on bail through most of that period and pursued the strategy of awaiting the outcome of the ongoing prosecution of his accomplice. On the other hand, a speedy trial violation was found in *Doggett v. U.S.* (1992), where the lack of demand was neutralized because the defendant was not in a position to make a demand (he did not know that charges were pending against him). In *Doggett*, two of *Barker*'s prejudice elements obviously were not present (the accused was not subjected to pretrial incarceration and, being unaware of the charges, he suffered no anxiety), but the extreme length of the delay (six years) was sufficient to presume trial prejudice in the absence of a government showing to the contrary.

Where defendants do demand a speedy trial, the state must respect that demand even if the defendants are incarcerated in another jurisdiction. Though the state lacks authority to compel the other jurisdiction to make the incarcerated defendant available for trial, its failure to request such cooperation over a lengthy period may result in a speedy trial violation. *Dickey v. Florida* (1970).

The Sixth Amendment right to a speedy trial attaches with the "first official act" designating the person as being "accused"—ordinarily, the arrest or the filing of charges, whichever comes first. Delay typically is calculated from that point until trial, but where charges are dismissed (and the defendant released) and then later renewed, the time between dismissal and renewal ordinarily will not be considered because the individual, for that period, was not "an accused." See *U.S. v. MacDonald* (1982). But note *Klopfer v. N.C.* (1967) (holding unconstitutional a state practice that, in effect, suspended prosecution with an automatic leave to reinstate.

### (b)  Due process requirements

Delays which are not covered by the speedy trial guarantee, such as the delay between the investigation of the crime and the institution of prosecution, can violate due process under extreme circumstances. See *U.S. v. Marion* (1971) (although the applicable statute of limitations usually sets the standard as to pre-accusation delay, due process may require dismissal even where the statute of limitations is not violated). To establish such a due process violation, defense must show initially that the prosecution had sufficient evidence to institute prosecution at an earlier point, and that the delay resulted in actual trial prejudice (e.g., the loss of favorable witnesses). *U.S. v. Lovasco* (1977). In addition, the court must find that the reasons for the delay were so unjustified as to "deviate from 'fundamental conceptions of justice.' "*Lovasco* cited as legitimate justifications such administrative needs as "await[ing] the results of additional investigation" to possibly identify other offenders and facilitating joint charging, which will avoid "multiple trials involving a single set of facts." A clearly impermissible grounding for delay would be the prosecution's gain through the hoped for loss of defense evidence over the period of the delay. *Marion.*

## § 9.4  NOTICE, DISCOVERY AND DISCLOSURE

### (a) Notice

The Sixth Amendment requires that the defendant "be informed of the nature and cause of the accusation" against him. This requirement has application primarily to the indictment or information, which must identify the offense charged and "sufficiently apprise the defendant of what he must be prepared to meet." *Russell v. U.S.* (1962). That standard commonly is met by a concise statement in the indictment or information of the essential facts constituting the offense charged. *U.S. v. Debrow* (1953). Having charged the defendant with a particular offense, a state shift to another offense during the course of the proceedings may present a notice violation, depending upon the circumstance surrounding that shift. See *Cole v. Ark.* (1948) (state appellate court violated due process when it affirmed the conviction of the defendants, charged and tried for one offense, on the ground that defendants had actually committed another offense, which was "separate, distinct, and substantially different").

## (b) Defense discovery

The Constitution allows the states considerable flexibility in determining the extent to which they will grant to the defense a right to pretrial discovery of the evidence that the prosecution intends to use at trial. As discussed in subsection (d) infra, the prosecution does have a constitutional duty under the *Brady* doctrine to disclose material exculpatory evidence in its possession, but that disclosure is geared to trial fairness, and typically does not require pretrial disclosure. *U.S. v. Ruiz* (§ 9.5(a)). Also, the evidence that the prosecution intends itself to use at trial ordinarily will be incriminating, rather than *Brady*-encompassed exculpatory evidence. Thus, the Court has stated: "There is no general constitutional right to discovery in a criminal case, and *Brady* did not create one." *Weatherford v. Bursey* (1977). Similarly, the Court has noted that while broad pretrial discovery is the "better practice," the state does not violate due process by refusing to grant pretrial discovery even if the prosecution's evidence will almost certainly take the defendant by surprise. See e.g., *Weatherford* (failure to inform the defendant that an associate was an undercover agent and would testify against him at trial).

### (c) Prosecution discovery

As discussed in § 8.1(c), *Williams v. Fla.* held that the self-incrimination clause does not prohibit a state from requiring a defendant to disclose pretrial his intent to rely on an alibi defense and the character of that defense. Relying on *Williams*, various states require the defense to grant pretrial discovery to the prosecution of the evidence it currently intends to present at trial. Some jurisdictions also require disclosure of statements obtained by the defense from prospective defense witnesses (other than the defendant), which also does not present a self-incrimination issue. See *U.S. v. Nobles* (§ 8.1(c)). Where states impose such requirements, however, due process mandates that the prosecution provide reciprocal pretrial disclosure to the defense. *Wardius v. Ore.* (1973) (due process violated by an alibi-notice provision that required defense disclosure of its alibi witnesses without requiring the prosecution to make reciprocal disclosure of its alibi rebuttal witnesses).

Where the defense fails pretrial to disclose witness names, in contravention of a valid state discovery requirement, the authorized sanctions typically include excluding the testimony of the unlisted witness. *Taylor v. Ill.* (1988) upheld that sanction as applied to a nondisclosure that was "deliberate", "aimed at seeking a tactical advantage" and in "the category of willful misconduct [for] which the severest sanction is appropriate." The Court rejected the contention that exclusion was automatically banned by the Sixth Amendment's compulsory process clause, noting that the pretrial discovery rules are intended to serve "the same high purpose" in "full and truthful disclosure of the facts" as the compulsory process clause and other Sixth Amendment rights. Also rejected was the contention that exclusion should be barred because alternative and less severe sanctions (e.g. allowing the state a continuance to respond to the surprise evidence) were always available. In some instances, those alternatives "would be less effective than the preclusion sanction" and in some instances, they would actually "perpetuate rather than limit the prejudice to the State and [the] harm to the adversary process."

## (d) Disclosure of exculpatory evidence

The prosecution's duty to disclose exculpatory evidence in its possession stems from the ruling in *Brady v. Md.* (1963). The Court there held that due process was violated when the prosecution, in responding to a defense request for recorded statements of a codefendant, failed (perhaps inadvertently) to disclose the statement in which the codefendant admitted that he had done the actual killing. While defendant admitted participation in the crime and was thus guilty of murder in any event, the statement would have lent considerable support to his plea to avoid capital punishment. *Brady* established a constitutional obligation of the prosecution to disclose defense requested evidence that is within the prosecution's possession where that evidence is "favorable to [the] accused" and "material either to guilt or punishment." This obligation was viewed as a logical extension of a line of earlier cases holding that due process was violated where the prosecutor failed to correct perjured testimony which it knew or should have known to be false. See § 9.8(e). Here, by failing to disclose evidence that was material and exculpatory, there was a similar deception of the jury and the trial court. Moreover, the deception existed even though, the failure to disclose "was not the result of guile." The focus of due process was "not punishment of society for misdeeds of a prosecutor, but avoidance of an unfair trial" and therefore the suppression constituted a due process violation "irrespective of the good faith or bad faith of the prosecutor."

A line of cases interpreting *Brady* culminated in *U.S. v. Bagley* (1985) in the announcement of the basic guidelines governing the prosecutor's duty to disclose. The *Brady* obligation of the prosecutor now applies both where the defense makes a specific request for potentially exculpatory evidence, as in *Brady,* and where it fails to make such a request. Moreover, a single standard of materiality applies to both types of cases: "[E]vidence is material * * * if there is a reasonable probability that, had the evidence been disclosed to the defense, the result of the proceeding would have been different. A 'reasonable probability' is a probability sufficient to undermine confidence in the outcome." *Kyles v.*

*Whitley* (1995) added that "four aspects of materiality under *Bagley* bear emphasis": (1) "a showing of materiality does not require demonstration by a preponderance that disclosure of the suppressed evidence would have resulted ultimately in defendant's acquittal"; (2) the materiality test also is not "a sufficiency of evidence test," as the "undermine-confidence-in-the-outcome" standard can be met even though, after discounting the inculpatory evidence in light of the undisclosed exculpatory evidence, there remains sufficient evidence to convict; (3) once a reviewing court has found a due process violation under *Bagley*, there is no need for further harmless error review (see § 9.10(a)); and (4) *"Bagley* materiality" is to be judged by reference to the "suppressed evidence considered collectively, not item by item."

Where the defendant claims that evidence lost or destroyed by the prosecution would have been exculpatory and material, application of the *Brady* doctrine presents obvious difficulties. Not only must the "courts face the treacherous task of divining the import of materials whose contents is unknown and often disputed," but "when evidence has been destroyed in violation of the Constitution", the only available remedies are "barring further prosecution or suppressing * * * the State's most probative evidence." *Cal. v. Trombetta* (1984). Unlike the *Brady* situation, a court cannot simply order a new trial in which the nondisclosed evidence will now be available. Accordingly, the Court has imposed two rigorous standards for such claims. Initially, the defendant cannot gain relief if the lost or destroyed evidence was of such nature that the defendant can replace it with "comparable evidence by other reasonably available means". See *Trombetta* (possible malfunctions in Intoxilyzer test could be raised without resort to the destroyed breath samples). Second, the defense must show "bad faith" by the police or prosecution in their failure to preserve the evidence. "Requiring a defendant to show bad faith," the Court has noted, appropriately restricts the constitutional obligation to preserve evidence to "that class of cases where the interests of justice most clearly require it, i.e. those cases in which the police themselves by their conduct indicate that the evidence would form a basis for exonerating the defendant." *Ariz. v. Youngblood* (1988).

### (e)  Further access to evidence

The Supreme Court has characterized a series of constitutional rulings as combining to create "what might loosely be called the area of constitutionally-guaranteed access to evidence." *Ariz. v. Youngblood* (1988). The primary components of this guarantee of access are the *Brady* duty to disclose and the *Youngblood* restriction on the destruction of potentially exculpatory evidence. Two other components are: (1) the availability of the subpoena power to obtain potentially exculpatory testimonial and physical evidence; and (2) the prohibition against governmental actions that interfere with the defense's utilization of that subpoena power.

Unlike the *Brady* obligation, which extends only to evidence in the possession of the prosecution, the subpoena power extends to evidence in the possession of third persons. The leading case on the state's obligation to make the subpoena power available to obtain evidence is *Pa. v. Ritchie* (1987). The defendant there, charged with sexual assault of his daughter, sought through subpoena to obtain pretrial inspection of the records of a state protective service agency. Although the records had a confidential status, the state intermediate court held that defendant was entitled constitutionally to obtain any verbatim recorded statements the daughter had made to the agency's counselors, and the state high court then took the further step of requiring that the full file be made available to defense so that it could determine whether any other portions were also relevant. The Supreme Court held that the federal constitution required only that the trial court review the agency file in camera to ensure defendant received all evidence that would fit the *Brady* standard of being both exculpatory and material.

The *Ritchie* Court rejected the contention that the right of compulsory process includes a defense right to itself review the evidence for possible relevance even where the evidence enjoyed a confidential status. Noting that it had "never squarely held that the Compulsory Process guarantees the right to discover the *identity* of witnesses or to require the Government to produce exculpating evidence," the Court concluded that if it did exist, any such compulsory process right would provide "no *greater* protections in this area than those afforded by due process," which traditionally allows in camera review. A plurality opinion added that the Sixth Amendment's confrontation clause should have no bearing because it was strictly a trial right, not a "constitutionally-compelled rule of pretrial discovery", and the subpoena here was being used for discovery, as allowed under state law.

A series of cases have dealt with potential constitutional violations in governmental action that undermines the defense's ability to utilize the subpoena authority to gain access to witnesses. The basic approach here has been to weigh the importance of the lost witness to the defense, the strength of the governmental interest underlying the action that precluded access, and the possibility of serving that interest without posing that obstacle to access. The end result has been rulings that vary with the circumstances of the case. See e.g., *Webb v. Tex.* (1972) (due process violated where trial judge used such "unnecessarily strong terms in warning a key defense witness about perjury that he effectively drove the witness from the stand"); *U.S. v. Valenzuela–Bernal* (1982) (while it was proper for the government to promptly deport illegal alien witnesses upon its determination that they possessed no evidence favorable to a defendant charged with transporting them, defendant must be given the opportunity to establish a due process violation by showing "that the evidence lost would be both material and favorable"); *Roviaro v. U.S.* (1957)

(relying on federal supervisory power, but suggesting a basic prosecution obligation to reveal an informer's name where the informer was the "sole participant, other than the accused, in the transaction charged," and thus "was the only witness in a position to amplify or contradict the testimony of government witnesses").

## § 9.5  GUILTY PLEAS

### (a) Voluntariness requirement

A guilty plea is not a constitutionally acceptable basis for a conviction unless that plea is "voluntary." This voluntariness requirement is grounded in due process, being likened by the Court to the requirement that confessions be voluntary (§ 4.2), although its content also is shaped in part by the traditional "knowing and intelligent" standard for waivers of trial rights, *Boykin v. Ala.* (1969). Cf. § 7.4(a). In *Brady v. U.S.* (1970), the Supreme Court noted that "the standard as to voluntariness of guilty pleas must be essentially that defined by * * * [a leading lower court opinion]: '[A] plea of guilty entered by one fully aware of the direct consequences, including the actual value of any commitments made to him by the court, prosecutor, or his own counsel, must stand unless induced by threats (or promises to discontinue improper harassment), misrepresentation (including unfulfilled or unfulfillable promises), or perhaps by promises that are by their nature improper as having no proper relationship to the prosecutor's business (e.g., bribes).' "

*U.S. v. Ruiz* (2002) makes clear that the understanding required for a voluntary plea does not extend to a full appreciation of the strength of the prosecution's case. The Court there held that a prosecutor could condition a plea bargain on the defendant's waiver of the right under *Brady v. Md.* (§ 9.4(d)) to "impeachment information relating to any informants or other witnesses." The Court reasoned that: (1) "impeachment information is special in relation to the *fairness of a trial*, not in respect to whether a plea is *voluntary*," for rights may be waived (as by guilty plea) even by those who "may not know the *specific detailed* consequences" of invoking them; (2) past cases clearly established that a trial judge "may accept a guilty plea * * * despite various forms of misapprehension under which a defendant might labor" (in particular, cases in which the defendant "misapprehended the quality of the State's case" and "misjudged the admissibility" of a confession, see 9.5(e)); and (3) given other "guilty plea safeguards," the risk was slight that, "in the absence of impeachment information, innocent individuals, accused of crimes will plead guilty." The prosecutor in *Ruiz* also had conditioned the plea offer on the defendant's relinquishment of any right to receive information supporting an affirmative defense, and the Court concluded that much the same reasoning sustained that condition. It further noted, however, that the prosecutor there had recognized a continuing duty, pursuant to

Brady, *to disclose information regarding the defendant's "factual innocence."*

## (b) Acceptance of a guilty plea

The voluntariness requirement imposes a duty upon the trial judge to ensure that the guilty plea is made knowingly and without coercion. The Court has emphasized that the scope of that duty, like the definition of voluntariness itself, is set by constitutional standards. However, the leading cases examining the trial court's responsibilities are quite limited in their holdings. Thus, *Boykin v. Ala.* (1969) held that a guilty plea could not be assumed to be voluntary based on a "silent record" (one which indicated the trial judge "asked no questions of [defendant] and the [defendant] did not address the court"), but *N.C. v. Alford* (1970) later suggested that the state could also establish a knowing waiver by counsel's testimony in a later proceeding that counsel, prior to the plea, had informed defendant of the rights relinquished by pleading guilty. That issue is unlikely to arise today because all jurisdictions require the trial judge to inform the defendant as to at least the three relinquished rights noted in *Boykin* (the right to jury trial, the right to confront one's accusers, and the right to refuse to testify at trial).

As for the determination that the defendant is aware of the "nature of the charge," *Henderson v. Morgan* (1976) found a fatal flaw in a trial court's failure to explain the elements of the offense to which the defendant pled, but there the elements of that offense were not charged in the indictment, they had not been explained by defense counsel, and defendant's explanation of his actions implicitly negotiated the presence of a key element. So too, *Bousley v. U.S.* (1998), discussing a judicial explanation of the offense that misinformed by failing to note a key element, indicated that such an omission would render the plea invalid only if the defendant had not otherwise been made aware of the element (e.g., by counsel). Such a complete lack of understanding is most likely to arise where, as in *Bousley*, the offense in question was first interpreted as including the particular element in a case decided subsequent to the defendant's plea.

Most jurisdictions also require that the trial court determine that there is a "factual basis" for the plea before accepting it. *N.C. v. Alford* (1970) suggests that a finding of a factual basis may be necessary constitutionally, but the Court there was dealing only with the situation in which the defendant desires to plead guilty, but claims that he is innocent. *Alford* found no constitutional violation in the acceptance of a plea from a defendant who claimed to be innocent where (1) the defendant desired to enter the plea to a lesser offense to avoid the possibility of a substantially harsher penalty (the death sentence) on a higher offense and (2) the trial court had received a summary of the state's case which contained "strong evidence of actual guilt." The defendant's position as to his innocence was not substantially different from that of a defendant who pleads *nolo contendere*, and the "strong factual basis" indicated that the "plea was being intelligently entered."

### (c) Negotiated pleas

Prior to the decision in *Brady v. U.S.* (1970), some uncertainty existed as to the voluntariness of a guilty plea that was the product of "plea bargaining"—i.e., a negotiated arrangement under which the defendant pleads guilty in return for certain concessions, such as the reduction of charges or the promise of a more lenient sentence. *Brady* did not itself involve a negotiated plea, but the Court, in discussing the voluntariness of Brady's plea, drew an analogy between that plea (which allowed Brady to avoid the possibility of a death sentence) and a negotiated plea. The *Brady* opinion stressed in particular what it described as the "mutuality of advantage" in plea bargaining. From the state's view, the granting of concessions to those pleading guilty was consistent with the administrative as well as the rehabilitative goals of the criminal justice system. The state was "extend[ing] a benefit to a defendant who in turn extends a substantial benefit to the state and who demonstrates by his plea that he is ready and willing to admit his crime and to enter the correctional system in a frame of mind which affords hope for success in rehabilitation over a shorter period of time than might otherwise be necessary." Guilty pleas would not be treated as involuntary simply because they were "motivated by the defendant's desire to accept the certainty * * * of a lesser penalty rather than * * * [a trial that might result in] conviction and a higher penalty." Indeed, to reject all pleas induced by promises of more lenient treatment would be, in large part, to "forbid guilty pleas altogether."

*Bordenkircher v. Hayes* (1978) explored the relationship between *Brady*'s approval of plea bargaining and the prohibition against prosecutorial vindictiveness in charge selection (see § 9.2(a)). The prosecutor there charged defendant with a crime that carried a sentence of ten years imprisonment, but noted at the outset that a recidivist charge, carrying a mandatory sentence of life imprisonment, would be added if the defendant did not plead guilty to the initial charge. The Court held that this was not a situation suggesting a vindictive attempt by the prosecutor to punish the defendant for exercising his right to demand a trial. Rather, it reflected the "give and take" of plea bargaining, with the prosecutor agreeing to forego a legitimate recidivist charge to produce the "mutuality of advantage" of a negotiated plea. The recidivist charge fell within the legitimate scope of prosecutorial discretion, being supported by probable cause. "To hold that the prosecutor's desire to induce a guilty plea is an 'unjustifiable standard,' which like race or religion, may play no part in his charging decision, would contradict the very premises that underlie the concept of plea bargaining." The *Bordenkircher* opinion also stressed that the prosecutor's intention was known to the defendant before he decided to go to trial, and that defendant, represented by counsel, was "presumptively capable of intelligent choice in response to prosecutor persuasion."

## (d) Broken bargains

As was noted in *Brady*'s definition of voluntariness (9.5(a)), an "unfulfilled or unfulfillable promise" renders a guilty plea involuntary. Thus, if as part of the plea agreement the prosecutor has promised to recommend a particular disposition, the plea becomes subject to challenge if the prosecutor fails to make that recommendation or makes a contrary recommendation. *Santobello v. N.Y.* (1971). The Court left open in *Santobello,* however, the possibility that the prosecutor could resurrect the bargain by now performing as promised (i.e., going before a new sentencing judge and making the promised recommendation) even though the defendant insists upon the withdrawal of the plea. The Court also has not had occasion to discuss the opposite side of that question, whether the defendant can insist upon specific performance of an unfulfilled bargain where the prosecution takes the position that only withdrawal should be permitted. Where the defendant had broken the bargain after entry of the plea (by failing to give testimony against codefendants as promised), and the plea agreement included a provision allowing the prosecutor to invalidate the plea and reinstate the original charge on such a breach, the Court concluded that neither the double jeopardy prohibition nor due process precluded enforcement of that provision. *Ricketts v. Adamson* (1987).

Whether there has in fact been a breach of the plea bargain is an issue for the courts to decide, but the Court has warned against "imply[ing] as a matter of law a term which the parties themselves did not agree upon." *U.S. v. Benchimol* (1985) (lower court erred in finding a breach where the prosecutor simply made the promised recommendation of probation, but did so without comment, as the government had not made an express commitment either to make the recommendation enthusiastically or to state reasons for it). *Mabry v. Johnson* (1984) held that there was no breached agreement where the prosecution made an initial offer of a 21 year concurrent sentence, withdrew that offer when defense counsel sought to accept it three days later, and then submitted a second offer of a 21 year consecutive sentence that the defense eventually accepted. In the absence of detrimental reliance by the defense, due process did not preclude the prosecution from withdrawing its original offer, which had not been finalized through judicial acceptance of the guilty plea.

## (e) Collateral challenges

In general, "a voluntary and intelligent plea of guilty made by an accused person, who has been advised by competent counsel, may not be collaterally attacked" by reference to procedural errors that occurred prior to the entry of the plea. *Mabry v. Johnson* (1984). This is true even though such errors were constitutionally grounded. See e.g., *McMann v. Richardson* (§ 6.6(h)) (coerced confession); *Tollett v. Henderson* (1973) (racial discrimination in grand jury selection). Where a defendant chooses to take "the benefit, if any, of a guilty plea," he "accepts the inherent risk that good-faith evaluations of a reasonably competent attorney will turn out to be mistaken either as to the facts or as to what a court's judgment might be on given facts." *McMann.* In determining whether the defendant actually received the competent assistance of counsel in entering his guilty plea, *Strickland*'s two-pronged ineffective assistance of counsel standard is applied (see § 7.7(b)). *Hill v. Lockhart* (1985).

Notwithstanding the general rule prohibiting collateral attacks where the defendant had the competent assistance of counsel, a voluntary guilty plea may be challenged collaterally where defendant's constitutional claim rests on a "right not to be hailed into court at all" as to the offense to which he pleaded. *Blackledge v. Perry* (1974) (plea did not bar collateral challenge where the prosecution acted vindictively in bringing the charge). While a voluntary guilty plea admits "factual guilt" and thereby "renders irrelevant those constitutional violations not logically inconsistent with the valid establishment of factual guilt," that is not the case for a claim that argues "that the State may not convict petitioner no matter how validly his factual guilt is established." *Menna v. N.Y.* (1975) (guilty plea did not preclude collateral challenge based on double jeopardy bar to the prosecution). Where the claim goes to "the very power of the State to bring the defendant into court to answer the charge," the error is not one which the state might have "cured" except for its reliance upon the guilty plea. *Blackledge*. This stands in contrast to the *Tollett* and *McMann* errors, which could have been "cured" through new pretrial proceedings (*Tollett*) or a prosecution without use of the tainted evidence (*McMann*). This exception applies, however, only where the state's lack of authority to bring the charge is apparent on the face of the record. *U.S. v. Broce* (1989) (guilty plea to two counts facially indicating separate offenses cannot be challenged as violating double jeopardy because both counts were, in fact, for the same offense).

## § 9.6    IMPARTIAL JURY AND JUDGE

### (a)  Right to a jury trial

While the Sixth Amendment declares that an accused shall have the right to a jury trial "in all criminal prosecutions," that provision has always been read in light of the common law tradition which did not provide juries for "petty offenses." *D.C. v. Clawans* (1937). The Court has held that the most "relevant criteria" in characterizing a crime as "petty" is the "severity of the maximum authorized penalty", as it reflects a legislative judgement about the relative seriousness of the offense. *Blanton v. North Las Vegas* (1989). An authorized punishment of imprisonment for more than six months establishes per se that the offense is outside the petty offense category, *Baldwin v. N.Y.* (1970), and while an authorized punishment of six months imprisonment or less does not automatically place the offense in the petty offense category, it is "presum[ed] for purposes of the Sixth Amendment that society views such an offense as 'petty'." *Blanton*. See also *Frank v. U.S.* (1969) (as to criminal contempts, which ordinarily do not have a statutorily prescribed penalty, the contempt falls within the petty offense category when the penalty actually imposed does not exceed six months imprisonment). Where the defendant has a Sixth Amendment right to a jury trial, that does not include a correlative right to insist upon a trial before a judge alone. *Singer v. U.S.* (1965) (jurisdiction may grant prosecutor or trial court a right to insist upon a jury trial even though defendant prefers to waive in favor of a bench trial).

Although most jurisdictions provide for a 12 person jury in felony cases, that is not a constitutional requirement. *Williams v. Fla.* (1970) upheld the use of a six person jury for non-capital felony cases. The key to constitutional acceptance, the Court noted, was that the jury be large enough to fulfill its traditional functions, i.e., "to promote group deliberation, free from outside attempts at intimidation, and to provide a fair possibility for obtaining a representative cross section of the community." In *Ballew v. Ga.* (1978), the Court held that a 5–member jury was too small to serve these functions and therefore was not allowable for a non-petty offense. Placing a similar emphasis on the jury's function, the Court has sustained state acceptance of less-than-unanimous verdicts for both acquittal and conviction where the state required sufficient supporting votes to assure adequate deliberations. See *Apodaca v. Ore.* (§ 1.2(e)); *Johnson v. La.* (1972) (upholding a 9–3 felony conviction); *Burch v. La.* (1979) (rejecting a 5–1 vote for non-petty offenses).

The right to a jury trial, like other trial rights, cannot be subjected to a "needless" burden that has a "chilling effect" on the exercise of that right. See *U.S. v. Jackson* (1968) (sentencing provision that allowed capital punishment only where defendant chose a jury trial "needlessly penalized" the exercise of that right, as the state's objective of having only juries issue capital sentences could be achieved in bench trials by use of advisory juries on sentencing). In *Ludwig v. Mass.* (1976), the Court held that the right to a jury trial was not unconstitutionally burdened by a state's "two-tier" trial system under which a defendant was not entitled to a jury in his initial trial before a magistrate's court, but then, if convicted, received a trial de novo with a jury before a higher trial court.

The right to jury trial also cannot be narrowed by having elements of the offense determined by the trial judge. *U.S. v. Gaudin* (1995) (on prosecution of defendant for making false statement, as to which materiality is an element of the offense, the trial judge could not instruct the jury that the statements in question were material). This safeguard does not include the determination of the sentence, which may be assigned to the judge even as to capital punishment. *Spaziano v. Fla.* (1984) (state law could allow judge to override jury recommendation favoring life sentence over capital punishment). However, *Apprendi v. N.J.* (2000) warns that the state cannot convert what historically has been an element of the offense into a "sentencing factor" and thereby take the issue from the jury. The Court there concluded that, "other than the fact of a prior conviction, any fact that increases the penalty for a crime beyond the prescribed statutory maximum must be submitted to a jury and proven beyond a reasonable doubt." This principle was carried forward to capital sentencing in *Ring v. Arizona* (2002) (where death penalty may be imposed only on a finding of enumerated aggravating factors, those factors must be found by a jury), and to guideline sentencing in *Blakely v. Wash.* (2004) (where guideline system permits enhanced sentence, though within statutory maximum, to be imposed only on a finding of facts that take the case outside the standard-range sentencing, existence of those facts must be found by jury). See also *U.S. v. Booker* (2005) (*Blakely* rendered invalid federal sentencing guidelines insofar as they conditioned guideline sentencing levels on judicial findings; to preserve the constitutionality of the guidelines scheme, though judicial findings would still be required, the guideline levels would thereafter be treated as simply "advisory," with judicial discretion controlling).

## (b) Equal protection

Long before the Sixth Amendment guarantee was applied to the states, the Court relied on the equal protection guarantee to reject racial discrimination in jury selection. *Strauder v. W.Va.* (1879). A long line of cases since then have dealt with the troublesome problem of establishing proof of discrimination where the jury selection system does not, on its face, authorize exclusion on racial grounds. The Court has refused to bar state selection criteria that are susceptible to manipulation, at least where there is "no suggestion" those criteria were "originally adopted or subsequently carried forward for the purpose of fostering racial discrimination" *Carter v. Jury Comm'n.* (1970). But where states utilize such criteria, a prima facie case of discrimination is established by showing that only a small percentage of blacks have been called to jury duty despite a much larger percentage in the community. The burden then shifts to the state to prove that this pattern did not result from purposeful discrimination. *Turner v. Fouche* (1970). The same standards for establishing presumed discrimination apply to alleged discrimination based on ethnicity. *Castaneda v. Partida* (1977).

*Batson v. Ky.* (1986) and *Ga. v. McCollum* (1992) hold that the prohibition against racial and ethnic discrimination applies not only to the selection of the jury venire, but also to the selection of individual jurors through the exercise of peremptory challenges. *Batson* held that the prosecutor could not use peremptory challenges to exclude prospective jurors because of their race. That applied not only where the prosecutor did so generally, in the belief persons of a particular race should not sit as jurors, but also where the prosecutor acted in the particular case "on the assumption—as his intuitive judgment—that [the group discriminated against] would be partial to the defendant because of their shared race." *McCollum* held that the defense's exercise of peremptory challenges to strike black jurors on the basis of their race was equally forbidden. Though *Batson* spoke only to racial discrimination, *J.E.B. v. Ala. ex rel T.B.* (1994) extended *Batson* to the government's exercise of peremptory challenges on the basis of gender (in that case the exclusion of men).

The equal protection claim under *Batson*, as with other equal protection claims, applies only to a purposeful discrimination on racial grounds. However, *Batson,* following the lead of the cases dealing with discrimination in the selection of the venire, recognized a process of establishing a "prima facie case of purposeful discrimination" based on the manner in which the peremptories were exercised. Initially, the defense must show that the "pattern of strikes" and other "relevant circumstances" raise "an inference that the prosecutor * * * excluded veniremen on account of their race". If a prima facie case is established, then "the burden shifts to the State to come forward with a neutral explanation for challenging * * * [the excluded group of] jurors." The ultimate burden of persuasion that the strike was based on race rather than on the neutral explanation then rests on "the oppo-nent of the strike." *Purkett v. Elem* (1995). In *Hernandez v. N.Y.* (1991), the plurality emphasized that a "neutral explanation" means simply an "ex-planation based on something other than the race of the juror," and that the issue is whether "a dis-criminatory intent" was present, not whether there was a "racially disproportionate impact." Such a neutral reason existed where the prosecutor's per-emptory challenges "rested neither in the intention to exclude Latino or bilingual jurors, nor in stereo-typical assumptions about Latinos or bilinguals," but rather in an intent to exclude only those bilin-guals who "might have difficulty in accepting the translator's rendition of Spanish-language testimo-ny." However, the neutral reason should be com-pared against the prosecutor's actual practice in striking and accepting jurors of different races, and consideration also must be given to other factors suggesting the neutral reason was actually a pretext (e.g., the prosecutor's mischaracterization of the voir dire testimony of the struck jurors). *Miller-El v. Dretke* (2005).

For over a century, equal protection objections were thought to be available only to defendants who were of the same race as the excluded prospective jurors. *Powers v. Ohio*, in 1991, rejected any such limitation. The Court reasoned that the guarantee of equal protection was designed to preclude not merely the potential unfairness to a defendant tried by a jury from which members of his race are excluded, but also the harm to the community at large and to the excluded prospective jurors kept "solely by reason of their race" from a "significant opportunity to participate in civil life." Accordingly, defendants in criminal cases, whether or not members of the group discriminated against, have standing to raise the equal protection rights of excluded jurors, who would themselves confront "considerable practical barriers" to challenging their exclusion. See also *Campbell v. La.* (1998) (same principle applies to equal protection challenges to grand jury composition).

### (c) The "fair cross-section" requirement

Relying on the Sixth Amendment, the Court had gone beyond racial discrimination to hold that a jury's representative function requires that it be selected from a "fair cross-section of the community." *Taylor v. La.* (1975). Since all defendants are entitled to this representative potential of the jury, the cross-section objection can be raised whether or not the defendant is a member of the distinctive class allegedly excluded. *Taylor* (male may object to exclusion of women). The objection is limited, however, to the selection of the venire; it does not encompass the use of peremptory challenges or challenges for cause. *Holland v. Ill.* (1990). Its purpose, noted the Court in *Holland*, is to "deprive the State of ability to 'stack the deck in its favor' "in that part of the jury selection process that the government alone controls, and that function does not run counter to allowing each side, "once a fair hand is dealt, [to] use peremptory challenges to eliminate prospective jurors belonging to groups it believes would unduly favor the other side." Limits on the latter practice stem solely from *Batson* and its progeny.

The fair cross-section requirement does not give the defendant a right to a jury venire of any particular composition, but only to one drawn from the community in a manner that does not systematically exclude or substantially reduce the representatives of a particular class of possible jurors. Moreover, that restriction does not go so far as to protect every possible group in the community, and while it can be violated by a discriminatory impact that is not the product of purposeful discrimination, the government is given a certain degree of administrative latitude in justifying that impact.

The leading case, *Taylor,* held that the cross-section requirement was violated by a state practice of excluding females unless they volunteered for jury service. See also *Duren v. Mo.* (1979) (*Taylor* applied to a state granting an automatic exemption to women when all but a small portion of the women claimed the exemption). The Court in *Taylor* referred to the exclusion of "large, distinctive groups" and "identifiable segments playing major roles in the community." In *Hamling v. U.S.* (1974), the Court ruled that, even if "the young" should be "an identifiable group entitled to a group-based protection under * * * prior decisions," the defendant had not been denied a representative jury simply because the jury selection list was compiled every four years and therefore excluded young persons who had become eligible during the interim period. The cross-section requirement, the Court noted, does not deny the government sufficient "play in the joints of the jury selection process" to accommodate "the practical problems of judicial administration." In *Lockhart v. McCree* (1986), the Court held that the cross-section requirement did not apply to challenges for cause, but also noted that the group at issue there—jurors firmly opposed to the death penalty—would not fall within the protection of the requirement in any event.

### (d) Jury impartiality

The Sixth Amendment guarantees a right to trial by an "impartial" jury. The primary procedures used to ensure jury impartiality are the voir dire of the prospective jurors and the exercise of challenges for cause and peremptory challenges. The constitutional regulation of the voir dire is quite limited, being directed primarily at racial bias. In *Ham v. S.C.* (1973), the Court held that a bearded civil rights worker, convicted of marijuana possession, had no constitutional right to insist that the trial judge allow voir dire questions concerning defendant's wearing of a beard. The Court acknowledged that it was possible that one or more potential jurors may have been prejudiced against bearded persons, but it stressed that the state must be allowed to give trial courts "broad discretion" in conducting the voir dire. *Ham* also ruled, however, that possible racial prejudice presented a special problem because, inter alia, a principal purpose of the Fourteenth Amendment was to bar racial discrimination. Here, voir dire questioning directed to possible prejudice would be mandated constitutionally on a proper defense showing.

Even as to racial prejudice, the Court has noted, there is no constitutional right to voir dire questioning unless "special circumstances" create a "significant likelihood that racial prejudice might affect [the] trial." *Ristaino v. Ross* (1976). Those circumstances were present in *Ham,* where the defendant, who was black, claimed that he had been "framed because of his civil rights activities." *Ristaino* (involving a black defendant and white victim in a robbery case) held that the fact that the crime is interracial does not in itself establish such special circumstances. But *Turner v. Murray* (1986) held that, because of the jury's special role in capital sentencing, "a capital defendant accused of an interracial crime * * * [is] entitled to have prospective jurors * * * questioned on the issue of racial bias" (although the plurality also concluded that denial of such voir dire required reversal only of the death sentence, not the conviction). See also *Rosales-Lopez v. U.S.* (1981) (a defendant of Mexican descent, charged with aiding members of his own ethnic group in gaining illegal entry into the United States, was not entitled constitutionally to requested voir dire questions aimed at racial or ethnic prejudice).

Apart from the pretrial publicity cases discussed in subsection (e) infra, the leading Supreme Court cases on challenges for cause have dealt with the exclusion of prospective jurors in capital cases. *Witherspoon v. Ill.* (1968) concluded that the defendant had been denied his Sixth Amendment right to an impartial jury where the trial court excluded on the prosecution's challenges for cause "all who expressed conscientious or religious scruples against capital punishment or all who opposed it in principle." The result was not a jury simply "neutral" as to penalty, but one "uncommonly willing to condemn a man to die." As subsequently interpreted in *Wainwright v. Witt* (1985), the *Witherspoon* principle does allow exclusion of jurors even though they might not "automatically" vote against the death penalty. The critical question is "whether the juror's views would 'prevent or substantially impair the performance of his duties in accordance with his instructions and his oath.' " A lengthy line of subsequent cases have dealt with the application of the *Witherspoon–Witt* standard to challenges for cause. See e.g., *Gray v. Miss.* (1987) (death penalty nullified by a single juror excluded improperly by the prosecution); *Lockhart v. McCree* (1986) (state could apply *Witherspoon–Witt* to remove completely firmly anti-capital-punishment jurors, thereby excluding them as to both the guilty and sentencing determinations, even though it utilized a bifurcated capital trial); *Ross v. Okla.* (1988) (trial judge erred in denying a reverse-*Witherspoon* motion of the defense to exclude for cause a juror unwilling to consider any penalty short of death, but defense's striking of that juror with one of nine peremptories cured that error).

### (e) Prejudicial publicity and jury selection

Where a pending prosecution has received considerable newspaper or television publicity, the selection of an impartial jury requires extra care. The Court has never insisted that prospective jurors be totally unaware of all adverse publicity. Such a standard, it has noted, would be impossible "in these days of swift, widespread, and diverse methods of communications." On the other hand, the jurors must not have been so influenced by the publicity that they cannot put aside any "preconceived notions" and "render a verdict based on the evidence presented in court." *Irvin v. Dowd* (1961). Where prospective jurors state that they can put aside preconceived notions, trial courts must determine whether the character of the pretrial publicity and the circumstances surrounding its dissemination create "such a presumption of prejudice * * * that the jurors' claims that they can be impartial should not be believed."

*Irvin* found that circumstances there created such a presumption and the trial judge therefore committed constitutional error in seating such jurors. In two later cases in which such jurors were seated, *Murphy v. Fla.* (1975) and *Patton v. Yount* (1984), the Court held that such a presumption was not justified. Although the Court stressed that each case rested on the totality of the circumstances, the primary factors that appeared to distinguish *Mur-*

*phy* and Patton from *Irvin* were: (1) the strength of the voir dire responses with respect to preconceived notions (looking to the responses of both the seated jurors and the complete panel of prospective jurors); (2) the nature of the pretrial publicity (whether "largely factual" as in *Murphy*, or highly inflammatory and likely to have created a "pattern of deep and bitter prejudice" in the community, as in *Irvin*); and (3) the time elapsed between the height of the publicity and the jury selection (critical in *Patton*, where four years had elapsed and "community sentiment had softened").

In *Mu'Min v. Va.* (1991), the Court considered the bearing of the *Irvin* line of cases on the scope of voir dire in pretrial publicity cases. It concluded that the Sixth Amendment did not require the trial judge to allow the questioning of each prospective juror out of the presence of others so the juror safely could be asked specific questions about what she had learned from the media coverage. The majority opinion stressed that a trial judge must be given "great latitude" in structuring voir dire questioning, but it also noted that the depth and extent of the publicity in this case was not of the extreme type found in *Irvin*. A concurring opinion by the justice providing the majority's critical fifth vote added that the trial judge had been in a position to conclude that, even if the seated jurors had read all the publicity, there would be no reason to doubt their credibility in claiming impartiality.

*Rideau v. La.* (1963) adopted an approach quite different from the above rulings, an approach which has been described as resting on "presumptive prejudice" rather than "actual prejudice." The Court there found a constitutional violation without looking to the voir dire and the responses of the jurors. The entire community had been "exposed repeatedly and in depth to the spectacle of Rideau personally confessing in detail to the crimes with which he was later charged" as a result of a police "interview" being thrice broadcasted on local television, and the Court held that, under such exceptional circumstances, due process had been violated by failing to grant defendant's request for a change of venue.

### (f) The right to an impartial judge

Just as the Sixth Amendment requires an impartial jury, due process requires an impartial judge, particularly in cases involving a bench trial. *Ward v. Village of Monroeville* (1972). However, a judge ordinarily is subject to a due process challenge only if he has a financial interest or some other "personal involvement" in the case. It is not objectionable, for example, that the trial judge presided at a pretrial proceeding and therefore has already considered some of the evidence in the case. *Withrow v. Larkin* (1975). It is objectionable, however, that the judge's salary will depend upon the fines he assesses. *Tumey v. Ohio* (1927). Similarly, where a contempt charge is based upon defendant's highly personal attack against the trial judge, that judge is constitutionally precluded from presiding at a subsequent non-summary contempt proceeding. *Mayberry v. Pa.* (1971). In neither case is it necessary to establish that the judge is in fact prejudiced. The guiding standard on personal involvement, the Court has emphasized, must be the "likelihood or appearance of bias" rather than "proof of actual bias." *Taylor v. Hayes* (1974).

## § 9.7　FAIR TRIAL AND FREE PRESS

### (a) "Gag orders"

*Sheppard v. Maxwell* (1966), commenting upon a trial court's failure to control publicity prejudicial to defendant's right to a fair trial, noted that "the trial court might well have proscribed extra-judicial statements by any lawyer, party, witness, or court official." There was no mention of restricting the media, and in *Nebraska Press Ass'n v. Stuart* (1976), the Court flatly rejected a "gag order" directed at the press. Barring the reporting of what occurred at an open preliminary hearing violated the "settled principle" that "once a public hearing has been held, what transpired there could not be subject to prior restraint." As for prohibiting media publication of information received from other sources (e.g., police or counsel), the heavy First Amendment presumption against prior restraints made such an order virtually impossible to sustain in light of numerous other measures (e.g., change of venue) that might be taken to ensure that defendant receives a fair trial notwithstanding adverse pretrial publicity.

*Gentile v. State Bar of Nevada* (1991) held that the potential for eliminating prejudice through these other alternatives did not require a state to impose a "clear and present danger" standard upon its prohibition of certain public statements by counsel in pending cases. Because counsel have "a fiduciary responsibility not to engage in public debate that will redound to the detriment of the accused or that will obstruct the fair administration of justice," and because their statements pose a special threat in this regard, since "they are likely to be received as especially authoritative" in light of the lawyer's "special access to information through discovery and client communication", the First Amendment was not violated by a standard prohibiting those statements that posed a "substantial likelihood of material prejudice." However, in the case before the Court, the state's prohibition was held to be void for vagueness because it also included a vague "safe harbor" provision (allowing defense counsel to set forth in a media statement, "without elaboration", the "general nature" of the client's "defense"), upon which the defense counsel had relied.

## (b) Public right of access

*Gannett Co. v. DePasquale* (1979) held that the Sixth Amendment right to a public trial was the personal right of the accused, but *Richmond Newspapers, Inc. v. Va.* (1980) recognized a press/public constitutional right of access to the criminal trial based upon the First Amendment interest in "ensur[ing] that the individual citizen can effectively participate in and contribute to our republican system of government." Although also dealing with the trial, *Globe Newspaper Co. v. Superior Court* (1982) established the foundation for extending the reach of this public access right. The Court there noted that the keys to defining the reach of the right were a historic tradition of openness for the particular proceeding and the contribution of public access to the functioning of the proceeding. Relying on these two factors, *Press-Enterprise Co. v. Superior Court (Press Enterprise I)* (1984) held that the right of access extended to the voir dire examination of jurors, and *Press-Enterprise Co. v. Superior Court (Press Enterprise II)* (1986) held the right applicable to the preliminary hearing. The same conclusion would seem to follow for a wide range of pretrial hearings (e.g., bail and suppression hearings), with the one exception being the historically closed grand jury proceeding (recognized as such in *Press Enterprise II*).

As noted in *Globe Newspaper,* the First Amendment right of access "is not absolute." Closure of a proceeding subject to the right can be justified upon a showing that closure is "necessitated by a compelling government interest, and is narrowly tailored to serve that interest." *Globe* held that protecting minor victims of sex crimes "from further trauma" was such an interest, but it would not justify a general statutory prohibition requiring exclusion whenever a victim under 18 testified. To ensure that closure is narrowly tailored to that interest, a state procedure must require the trial court to "determine on a case-by-case basis" whether closure is "necessary" to protect the particular minor. So too, *Press Enterprise I* acknowledged that a prospective juror's privacy interest as to personal matters might justify closing a very limited segment of the voir dire, but the proper procedure was to inform the prospective jurors of their opportunity to make such a request, and to have the judge respond to such a request by first deciding if there is a "valid basis" for the juror's concern, and if so, to then decide whether to excuse the juror or order limited disclosure.

As for closure in order to avoid prejudicial publicity, *Press Enterprise II* set forth the governing standard: "If the [compelling] interest asserted is the right of the accused to a fair trial, the * * * [proceeding] shall be closed only if specific findings are made that first, there is substantial probability that the defendant's right to a fair trial will be prejudiced by publicity that the closure would prevent and second, reasonable alternatives to closure cannot adequately protect the defendant's free trial rights." For pretrial proceedings that would produce prejudicial publicity (e.g., a suppression hearing), the relevant alternatives to closure would include extensive voir dire to identify biased petit jurors, continuances, and change of venue; as to publicity during the trial, the key alternatives would be admonitions to the jurors and sequestration.

### (c)  Media interference

*Sheppard v. Maxwell* (1966) found a denial of due process in the trial judge's failure both to respond adequately to massive publicity and to prevent certain media interference with the trial. As to the element of interference, the Court cited the judge's failure to provide privacy for the jury, to insulate witnesses from newsmen, and to control various media activities that contributed substantially to the carnival atmosphere of the trial.

In *Estes v. Tex.* (1965), a divided Court held that defendant had been denied due process by the televising of his trial over his objection. Relying on *Rideau* (§ 9.6(e)), the majority found that the likely prejudicial impact upon the jury of a cumbersome and conspicuous televising procedure eliminated the need for a showing of specific instances of "isolatable prejudice." Indeed, four members of the majority expressed the view that public television of a trial was inherently prejudicial, but the fifth justice limited his concurrence to "criminal trial[s] of great notoriety" such as that involved in *Estes.* Subsequently, in *Chandler v. Fla.* (1981), the Court relied upon that concurrence to hold that a state may permit televising and still photographing, over the objection of the accused, under the restricted conditions prescribed there by state rule. Those restrictions included placing on the trial judge "positive obligations to be on guard to protect the fundamental right of the accused to a fair trial." Moreover, it would remain open to the particular defendant "to show that the media's coverage of his case * * * compromised the ability of the jury to judge him fairly," or to "show that broadcast coverage of his particular case had an adverse impact on the trial participants sufficient to constitute a denial of due process."

## § 9.8 THE TRIAL

### (a) Right to a public trial

The defendant's Sixth Amendment right to a public trial exists apart from the press/public right of access discussed in § 9.7(b). Whether it has a broader reach than the First Amendment right of access has not been considered by the Court. It has been held to apply to criminal contempt proceedings, *In re Oliver* (1948), and to certain pretrial proceedings, such as a suppression hearing, which bear a resemblance to a trial, *Waller v. Ga.* (1984). In *Waller,* the Court held that the standards adopted in *Globe Newspaper* and *Press-Enterprise I* for overriding the right of access also governed the closure of a suppression hearing over defendant's objection. See § 9.7(b). The defendant's constitutional right to a public trial has been characterized as serving the defendant's interest by: (1) providing "a safeguard against an attempt to employ our courts as instruments of persecution" (the knowledge that the trial "is subject to contemporaneous review in the form of public opinion" serving as "an effective restraint on possible abuse of judicial power"); (2) assuring testimonial trustworthiness by inducing a fear in witnesses that false testimony will be detected; and (3) making the proceedings known to possible material witnesses who might otherwise be unknown to the defense. *Oliver,* supra.

## (b) Right of presence

While "rooted to a large extent in the confrontation clause of the Sixth Amendment," the defendant's constitutional right to be present also has a due process component. *U.S. v. Gagnon* (1985). Accordingly, it is not restricted to those parts of the trial in which the defendant is "actually confronting witnesses or evidence against him," but encompasses all trial-related proceedings at which defendant's presence "has a relation, reasonably substantial, to the fullness of his opportunity to defend against the charge." *Gagnon.* In determining whether the right extends to a particular proceeding apart from the trial itself, the Court has looked to the function of the right as it relates to the context of the particular case. Thus, while an in-chambers inquiry into a juror's possible prejudice would generally require defendant's presence, *Gagnon* held that was not the case where the trial judge (with defense counsel present) did no more than first explain to the juror that defendant's continuous sketching during trial was innocuous and then receive from the juror an assurance of continued impartiality. See also *Ky. v. Stincer* (1987) (in-chamber examination of two young victims of alleged sex offense, to determine solely whether they were competent to testify, did not constitutionally require defendant's presence, where defense counsel participated and further questions concerning competency could be raised at trial with defendant present).

The state cannot unnecessarily condition defendant's presence at trial in such a way as to create possible juror bias against him. Thus, it cannot insist that he stand trial in prison garb, *Estelle v. Williams* (1976), but it can insist upon reasonable security precautions, *Holbrook v. Flynn* (1986). Also, defendant can forfeit his right to be present by his disruptive misconduct. See *Ill. v. Allen* (1970) (where defendant had continued in his disruptive behavior despite due warning, the trial court acted appropriately in banishing him from the courtroom rather than resorting to less desirable remedies (e.g., binding and gagging him) simply to ensure his physical presence during the remainder of the trial). So too, once the trial has started, defendant cannot preclude its continuation by his voluntary absence. *Taylor v. U.S.* (1973).

## (c) Presentation of evidence

The constitutional regulation of the presentation of evidence presents a complex series of standards that are commonly studied in courses on evidence. For our purposes, it is sufficient to note that these standards flow from three sources—the confrontation clause of the Sixth Amendment, the compulsory process clause of the Sixth Amendment, and freestanding due process. The constitutional regulation bears upon various aspects of state evidentiary law including the range of cross-examination, the admission of testimonial hearsay (and in some instances, non-testimonial hearsay), and the limitation of competency to testify.

## (d)  Joint trials

Where several persons have participated in a single offense or a series of related offenses, state law ordinarily allows for a joint trial. Where, however, the prosecutor desires to use a confession of one of the participants, *Bruton v. U.S.* (1968) may pose a significant obstacle to a joint trial. *Bruton* held that where the confession of one codefendant contains references to a second codefendant, and the confessor refuses to take the stand, the use of that confession in a joint trial violates the second codefendant's Sixth Amendment right of confrontation; it is not sufficient simply to inform the jury that the confession constitutes admissible evidence only against the confessor. The *Bruton* prohibition applies even though the prosecution uses interlocking confessions of each of the non-testifying codefendants. *Cruz v. N.Y.* (1987).

*Richardson v. Marsh* (1987) limits *Bruton* to cases in which the non-testifying codefendant's confession refers directly to the other codefendant. Where the confession has only an evidentiary linkage to the other codefendant (i.e., it contains information that could be viewed, in light of other evidence in the case, as linking the other codefendant to the crime, but it does not refer to the codefendant or his actions), sufficient protection is provided by the judicial charge to the jury that the confession is evidence only against the confessing codefendant. In *Gray v. Maryland* (1998), however, the Court refused to extend the distinction drawn in *Richardson* as to "inferential incrimination" to a confession that referred to the defendant but then had been redacted to substitute "a blank space, the word deleted, or a similar symbol" for that name. The redaction could not eliminate the confession's potential for direct incrimination since the jury "will often realize that the [redacted] confession refers specifically to the defendant" and the "obvious deletion may well call the juror's attention specifically to the removed name," thus "encouraging the jury to speculate about the reference." *Richardson* reflected an accommodation of administrative concerns (e.g., the difficulty of determining pretrial whether an evidentiary linkage would exist, and the value of joinder in avoiding inconsistent verdicts), and that accommodation would not be carried over to a setting posing far greater potential for improper use of the confession to incriminate other codefendants.

### (e) Defendant's right to testify and not testify

As discussed in Chapter 8, the Fifth Amendment's self-incrimination clause gives the defendant the option of not testifying in his criminal trial, and also not having the prosecutor or court make adverse comments on defendant's exercise of that right. See §§ 8.2(a), 8(4)(b). In contrast to the common law, which barred the defendant from testifying as a witness, the defendant today also has a constitutionally protected right to testify. That right stems from three sources: (1) the guarantee of due process (which ensures a "fair adversary process," including a "right to be heard and to offer testimony"); (2) the Sixth Amendment's compulsory process clause (which "logically include[s]" defendant's "right to testify himself"); and (3) the Fifth Amendment's guarantee against compulsory self-incrimination (a "necessary corollary" of which is the defendant's right to testify "in the unfettered exercise of his own will"). *Rock v. Ark.* (1987).

The defendant's right to testify may be restricted to accommodate other "legitimate interests in the criminal trial process," but those restrictions, as *Rock* noted, "may not be arbitrary or disproportionate to the purposes they are designed to serve." Thus, *Rock* held that, though the state has a legitimate interest in imposing evidentiary restrictions designed to exclude unreliable evidence, that interest could not justify a per se exclusion of a defendant's hypnotically refreshed testimony. Such a rule was excessive because it operated without regard either to procedural safeguards employed in the hypnosis process to reduce inaccuracies or to the availability of corroborating evidence and other traditional means of assessing the accuracy of the particular testimony. *Perry v. Leeke* (1989), on the other hand, held that it was permissible to treat a testifying defendant like any other witness and bar consultation with counsel during a short recess prior to the start of cross-examination. Distinguishable was the constitutional violation in *Geders v.*

*U.S.,* (see § 7.6(a)), for the defendant/witness there was barred from consultation during an overnight recess, where general matters of defense strategy (rather than simply defendant's testimony) would have been discussed. *Portuondo v. Agard* (2000) held that defendant's right also was not burdened impermissibility by the prosecutor's argument that defendant's presence during the testimony of other witnesses allowed him to tailor his testimony to theirs.

**(f) Prosecutorial misconduct**

Apart from the responsibilities imposed by the more specific constitutional guarantees, the prosecution is subject at trial to due process requirements relating to its role as the representative of the state "whose interest in a criminal prosecution is not that it shall win a case, but that justice shall be done." *Berger v. U.S.* (1935). Building upon this obligation, a series of cases hold the prosecution must correct any material perjured testimony of its witnesses when it knows, or should know from information that it has received, that the testimony is false. See e.g., *Giglio v. U.S.* (1972) (due process violated when the prosecutor, not realizing that promises had been made by his predecessor, failed to correct a witness' statement that no promises had been made in return for his testimony). The test of "materiality" for this purpose reaches more than that applied to the prosecution's duty to disclose exculpatory testimony. See § 9.4(d). False testimony is material if there is "any reasonable likelihood * * * [it] could have affected the judgment of the jury"—a standard the Court has characterized as synonymous with the "reasonable doubt" as to an adverse impact that precludes a finding of "harmless error" under the harmless error standard of *Chapman v. Cal.* (§ 9.10(b)). See *U.S. v. Bagley* (1985).

In presenting argument to the jury, particularly closing argument, the prosecutor is also subject to due process limitations. Here due process prohibits statements so prejudicial and inflammatory as to produce a "fundamentally unfair" trial. *Darden v. Wainwright* (1986). In making this assessment, the Court will consider a variety of factors, including the presence or absence of trial court instructions advising the jury to disregard the prosecutor's improper remarks, the frequency of those remarks, the general tenor of the trial, and the likely impact of the remarks in light of the strength of the evidence against the accused.

### (g) Proof

Due process requires the prosecution to prove beyond a reasonable doubt each element of the crime charged. *In re Winship* (1970). This requirement, in turn, leads to a series of implementing constitutional standards that typically are considered in courses on evidence and substantive criminal law (and therefore will not be explored in detail here). They deal with such subjects as the sufficiency of jury instructions on the meaning of proof beyond a reasonable doubt and the presumption of innocence, the use of evidentiary presumptions, the distinction between elements of the crime and affirmative defenses, and limitations on submitting to the jury alternative elements for a single offense.

## § 9.9   POST–TRIAL PROCEDURES

### (a) Sentencing

Apart from the area of capital sentencing, where the Eighth Amendment introduces special considerations, the Supreme Court consistently has held that the sentencing process, while not "immune" from the restrictions of due process, is subject to considerably less extensive procedural requirements than the trial process. That conclusion is based, in part, on the historical separation of the trial and sentencing stages, as reflected in the many constitutional guarantees that clearly refer only to the trial. It also has been justified on the ground that fulfillment of the basic objectives of sentencing, particularly the emphasis on relating punishment to the individual as well as the crime, often requires more flexible procedures than those applied to the determination of guilt. Thus, *Williams v. Okla.* (1959) held that a sentencing judge could "consider responsible unsworn or 'out-of-court' information relative to the circumstances of the crime and to the convicted person's life and characteristics." And, in *Williams v. N.Y.* (1949), the Court held that the defendant had no constitutional right to an adversary sentencing proceeding in which he could cross-examine persons who had supplied information to the sentencing court. Consider also *U.S. v. Grayson* (1978) (in considering "the defendant's whole person and personality," the sentencing judge may give consideration to defendant's untruthfulness in his trial testimony, notwithstanding defendant's complaint that he has never been indicted, tried, or convicted for the alleged perjury).

The Court also has identified, however, several factors that cannot be considered in sentencing. *McClesky v. Kemp* (1987) indicates that the race of neither the defendant nor the victim may be a consideration in setting a sentence, although the defendant bears the difficult burden of showing such purposeful discrimination. *Dawson v. Delaware* (1992) concluded that, while "the Constitution does not erect a per se barrier" to considering "evidence concerning one's beliefs and associations," the First Amendment did prohibit the introduction in a capital proceeding of such information (there the defendant's membership in the Aryan Brotherhood) when it was "totally without relevance" to the sentencing proceedings. Compare *Barclay v. Fla.* (1983) (defendant's membership in Black Liberation Army and desire to provoke a "race war" was relevant to several aggravating factors in state's capital sentencing structure). Consider also *Mitchell v. U.S.* (§ 8.4(b)); *N.C. v. Pearce* (§ 9.9(b)).

The Supreme Court has stated that, outside of special sentencing structures (e.g., for dangerous sex offenders), the Fourteenth Amendment has never been held to "require a judge to have sentencing hearings and to give the convicted person an opportunity to participate in these hearings." *Specht v. Patterson* (1967). However, it has held that the defendant has a "due process right not to be sentenced on the basis of materially untrue information," *Townsend v. Burke* (1948), and the Sixth Amendment right to counsel has been extended to sentencing, as a critical stage, in part because of counsel's function in presenting information to the sentencing judge and challenging information presented by the prosecution. See § 7.3(g).

While sentencing hearings traditionally have not been trial-type hearings, where the sentencing structure calls upon the judge to make a specific finding of fact (as in the case of guideline sentencing, sentencing enhancements, and mandatory minimum provisions), adversary hearings are commonly utilized if the critical fact is contested. It also is common to impose upon the prosecution a preponderance-of-the-evidence standard of proof as to the critical fact. *McMillan v. Pa.* (1986) upheld that standard under a statute that mandated a minimum sentence upon proof that defendant visibly possessed a weapon during the commission of the crime. The Court distinguished the proof requirement for elements of the offense, noting that the preponderance standard was sufficient for sentencing. The *McMillan* reasoning was held to apply in *Almendarez-Torres v. U.S.* (1998) to a recidivist enhancement that increased the defendant's maximum sentence from two to twenty years. But the

Court drew the line in *Apprendi v. N.J.* (2000). Noting that the longstanding common law tradition was to treat factors that increased a maximum sentence as an element of the offense (in effect creating a higher level offense), the *Apprendi* Court concluded that such a factor was subject to the general constitutional standards applicable to elements of the offense. That included not only a right to a jury trial, as discussed in § 9.6(a), but also proof beyond a reasonable doubt. *Apprendi* distinguished *Almendarez-Torres* as possibly reflecting a different history and special considerations relevant to recidivist statutes.

The double jeopardy clause also has been held to bear upon sentencing. The Court has frequently noted that double jeopardy "protects against multiple punishment for the same offense". *N.C. v. Pearce* (1969). At the same time, however, it has held that the *Blockburger* definition of "same offense" (see § 9.11(b)) does not limit sentencing. Thus, while it ordinarily is presumed that the legislature did not intend to prescribe separate punishments for statutory violations that constitute the same offense under *Blockburger*, the state retains the authority to specifically direct that separate punishments be imposed for separate statutory violations even though all the elements of one are included in the other. *Mo. v. Hunter* (1983) (separate sentences authorized for armed robbery and enhancement offense of armed criminal action).

The prohibition against multiple punishment does serve to limit the capacity of a sentencing judge to alter a sentence previously imposed for the same offense when that alteration operates to the prejudice of the defendant. The leading case applying this protection is *Ex parte Lange* (1873), which invalidated a trial judge's attempt to correct an original sentence of both prison and a fine to simply prison (the statute not allowing both) after the defendant had already paid his fine. *Lange* was later limited in *Jones v. Thomas* (1989). *Jones* found no double jeopardy bar where a trial court originally sentenced defendant to consecutive terms on two offenses, the defendant fully served the shorter term on the lesser offense, an appellate court then ruled that separate sentences for both offenses was not permissible and the trial judge then vacated the sentence on the lesser offense and gave the defendant credit for the time served against the longer term remaining on the greater offense. By giving credit for the time served, the trial court here, unlike the trial court in *Lange,* had made certain that the total punishment imposed was not beyond that legislatively authorized.

*U.S. v. DiFrancesco* (1980) held that *Lange* has no bearing on prosecution appeals of sentences claimed to be illegal, even though the result of the appeal may be to impose a new, higher sentence. *N.C. v. Pearce,* supra, similarly held that where a defendant's conviction is overturned, he starts anew and double jeopardy does not prohibit a higher sentence on reconviction—although the defendant must be given credit for time previously served (and the higher sentence, under due process, cannot be vindictive, see (b) infra).

## (b) Appeals

The Supreme Court continues to recognize the ruling in *McKane v. Durston* (1894) that a state is not constitutionally required to provide appellate review of criminal convictions. See *Ross v. Moffitt* (§ 7.2(d)). All states now provide for appellate review, however, and the Court has held that, once established, appellate review cannot be restricted or burdened on arbitrary grounds. *N.C. v. Pearce* (1969) found such a violation where defendants who had gained appellate reversal of their initial convictions, were then given higher sentences on the same charges following a retrial and reconviction. *Pearce* held that due process prohibited the imposition of a more severe sentence for the purpose of punishing the defendants for having exercised their statutory right to appeal. Moreover, to facilitate attack on such improper motivation, the Court imposed a "prophylactic" safeguard of requiring the trial judge to set forth reasons for a higher sentence, with these reasons based on factors that refute vindictiveness.

Subsequent decisions have limited the applicability of the prophylactic portion of the *Pearce* ruling. The Court has held that a statement of reasons for the higher second sentence is not required as to: (1) a higher second sentence by a jury, *Chaffin v. Stynchcombe* (1973); (2) a higher second sentence imposed following a trial de novo, *Colten v. Ky.*

(1972); and (3) a higher second sentence imposed by a judge who herself granted the new trial order that resulted in the retrial, *Tex. v. McCullough* (1986). Moreover, *McCullough* strongly suggests that a higher second sentence following an appellate reversal would fall in the same category where (in contrast to *Pearce*) the judge who presided at the second trial (and imposed the higher sentence) was not the same judge who presided at the overturned first trial. In all of these situations the likelihood of vindictiveness is viewed as not sufficient to justify a presumption of vindictiveness that the sentencer must rebut by setting forth grounds for the higher sentence. As for the grounds that will justify a higher sentence when *Pearce* requires that reasons be set forth, *McCullough* referred to new testimony which has "a direct effect on the strength of the state's case" and new sentencing information revealing that defendant's background was worse than previously assumed.

### (c) Newly discovered evidence

*Herrera v. Collins* (1993) held that due process was not violated by a state's application of a 60 day time limit to preclude a motion for new trial based on newly discovered evidence presented eight years after trial. The Court also rejected the defendant's claim that the Eight Amendment would be violated by imposing the death penalty where the precluded evidence merely suggested his "actual innocence." The majority concluded that, assuming a "truly persuasive demonstration of actual innocence would render the execution of the defendant unconstitutional" (and therefore require federal habeas relief if the state process was unavailable), the "threshold showing for such an assumed right would be necessarily high" and defendant's showing fell far short of that threshold.

## § 9.10    HARMLESS ERROR

### (a) Application to constitutional errors

All jurisdictions have "harmless error" provisions that prohibit appellate reversal based upon errors that did not "affect the substantial rights" of the convicted defendants. Prior to *Chapman v. Cal.* (1967), it frequently was assumed that the harmless error principle did not apply to the review of constitutional errors because such errors were "per se injurious." *Chapman,* however, rejected that position. The *Chapman* opinion acknowledged that a rule of automatic reversal had been applied to certain constitutional errors (see (c) infra), but concluded that there was no grounding in theory or past precedent for granting all constitutional errors a blanket exemption from the traditional requirements for appellate reversal of a conviction. The Court noted in this respect that harmless error statutes serve "a very useful purpose insofar as they block setting aside convictions for small errors or defects that have little, if any, likelihood of having changed the result of the trial." That purpose was equally served where, "in the setting of a particular case," constitutional errors are "so unimportant or insignificant" as to fall within a narrowly confined harmless error standard.

The harmless error standard serves to determine whether the possible influence of a constitutional violation is so unlikely that a new trial need not be ordered. Thus, the harmless error standard has no bearing on constitutional violations that are not remedied by a new trial, but call for a remedy of precluding prosecution (e.g. double jeopardy or speedy trial violations).

Even where a new trial is the appropriate remedy, there is no need to consider the possible application of the *Chapman* standard if the finding of a constitutional violation rests on a showing of specific prejudice to defense in the outcome of the case. Accordingly, harmless error analysis also is not applied to a constitutional violation that requires a finding that the challenged behavior presented a "reasonable probability" of having affected the outcome of the proceeding—as in ineffective assistance of counsel claims under *Strickland* (§ 7.7), and due process claims for the nondisclosure of exculpatory evidence, *Kyles v. Whitley* (§ 9.4(d)). The presence of the violation in itself establishes that the likely impact was more than enough to meet *Chapman's* reasonable doubt standard ((b) infra). The same analysis extends to ineffective assistance claims that are based on the special circumstances that justify a presumption of prejudicial impact. See *Holloway v. Ark.* (§ 7.7(f)); *Cuyler v. Sullivan* (§ 7.7(e)). See also *Geders v. U.S.* (§ 7.6(a)).

As to those constitutional violations that are remedied by a new trial and that do not require a showing of prejudicial impact (or circumstances producing a presumption of prejudice) in establishing the violation, application of the *Chapman* standard has become the general rule. As discussed in subsection (c), there remain a group of such violations that require automatic reversal without applying *Chapman,* but "they are the exception and not the rule". *Rose v. Clark* (1986). Thus *Chapman* has been held applicable to all violations involved in the use of unconstitutionally obtained evidence, including: the improper admission of evidence obtained in violation of the Fourth Amendment, including unconstitutional electronic surveillance (chs. 2 and 3); the admission of confessions obtained in violation of the Sixth Amendment right to counsel and in violation of *Miranda,* and the admission of confessions that are involuntary (ch. 4); and the admission of identification evidence that was obtained in violation of the Sixth Amendment right to counsel or that is excludable under due process (ch. 5). So too, *Chapman* applies to many of the constitutional errors discussed in this chapter, such as an adverse comment on defendant's failure to testify (the constitutional violation in *Chapman* itself).

As to the right-to-counsel violations discussed in ch. 7, *Chapman* generally does not apply to those violations that do not relate to the acquisition of evidence, as they tend to fall either in the automatic reversal category discussed in subsection (c) or to require a finding of prejudicial impact (or circumstances producing a presumption of prejudice) in establishing the violation. Consider, however, *Coleman v. Ala.* (§ 7.3(d)), where the harmless error standard of *Chapman* was held applicable to the denial of a Sixth Amendment right to counsel at a preliminary hearing.

## (b) The reasonable doubt standard

The state court in *Chapman* had applied a harmless error standard that placed primary emphasis upon the presence of evidence that rendered the proof of guilt "overwhelming," but the Supreme Court concluded that the constitutional harmless error standard should emphasize the impact of the error upon the "substantial rights" of the defendant. Accordingly, the Court ruled that a constitutional error could be viewed as harmless only if the "beneficiary" of the error (i.e., the prosecution) could "prove beyond a reasonable doubt that the error * * * did not contribute to the verdict obtained."

The *Chapman* opinion clearly indicated that its harmless error standard looked not to whether a jury could have convicted without regard to constitutional error, or whether the appellate court judges believe the conviction is justified by the admissible evidence, but to whether the error had influenced the jury in reaching its verdict. The Court did not clearly indicate, however, precisely what weight could be given to properly admitted, "overwhelming evidence of guilt" in making that determination. Early cases dealt with constitutional error in the admission of evidence, and where that inadmissible evidence was roughly matched by similar admissible evidence that clearly pointed to guilt, the constitutional error was viewed at harmless, even where the inadmissible evidence had been a confession. *Harrington v. Cal.* (1969); *Milton v. Wainwright* (1972).

Determining the influence of the constitutional error on the conviction proved more difficult in evaluating errors that did not relate to the admission of evidence, such as unconstitutional charging errors that took issues from the jury by using unconstitutional presumptions. The Court here noted that "to say an error did not 'contribute' to the ensuing verdict is not * * * to say the jury was totally unaware of that feature of the trial [that constituted constitutional error]," but only "to find that error unimportant in relation to everything else the jury considered." *Yates v. Evatt* (1991). In some instances, the jury may have found the same ultimate fact under another count as to which the unconstitutional presumption did not apply, but absent such an obvious indication of harmlessness, the Court would look to the weight of the evidence and ask "whether the force of the evidence presumably considered by the jury in accordance with the instructions is so overwhelming as to leave it beyond a reasonable doubt that the verdict resting on the evidence would have been the same in the absence of the presumption." Id. See also *Neder v. U.S.* (1999) (to conclude that constitutional error in failing to submit an element of the crime to the jury was harmless, court must find "beyond a reasonable doubt that the omitted element was uncontested and supported by overwhelming evidence, such that the jury verdict would have been the same absent the error").

#### (c) Automatic reversal

*Chapman* noted that "there are some constitutional rights so basic to a fair trial that their infraction can never be treated as harmless error." Included in this category are: violation of the right to trial before an impartial judge, *Tumey v. Ohio* (§ 9.6(f)); denial of the constitutional rights to appointed counsel at trial and on first appeal of right, *Gideon v. Wainwright* (§ 7.1(b)), *Penson v. Ohio* (1988); denial of the Sixth Amendment right to representation by a retained counsel of choice, *U.S. v. Gonzalez–Lopez* (2006); denial of a defendant's right to public trial, *Waller v. Ga.* (§ 8.8(a)); denial of defendant's right to proceed to pro se, *McKaskle v. Wiggins* (§ 7.4(d)); constitutional violations in the selection of the petit jury, *Gray v. Miss.* (§ 9.6(d)); constitutionally deficient jury instructions on the need for proof beyond a reasonable doubt, *Sullivan v. La.* (1993); and racial discrimination in the selection of a grand jury, *Rose v. Mitchell* (§ 9.2(b)).

The Court has cited several different features in explaining why particular constitutional errors require automatic reversal, rather than the application of the *Chapman* standard. *McKaskle,* supra, explained the refusal to apply a harmless error analysis there as flowing logically from the nature of the right to proceed pro se, which allows the defendant to control his own destiny even if it works to his disadvantage. See § 7.4(d). *Rose v. Mitchell* "reasoned that racial discrimination in the selection of the grand jury is so pernicious, and other remedies so impracticable, that the remedy of automatic reversal was necessary as a prophylactic means of deterring grand jury discrimination in the future." *U.S. v. Mechanik* (1986). Explaining automatic reversal for the *Tumey* and *Gideon* violations, *Rose v. Clark* (1986) noted that such violations deprive defendants of "basic protections" without which "a criminal trial cannot reliably serve its function as a vehicle for determination of guilt or innocence." *Gray* characterized a constitutional violation in jury selection, even where it involves only one juror, as falling in the same general category as *Tumey* and *Gideon* violations; since jury selection standards are "rooted in the constitutional right to an impartial jury, and because the impartiality of the adjudicator goes to the very integrity of the legal system, the *Chapman* harmless error standard cannot apply." *Sullivan,* supra, reasoned that a deficient reasonable doubt instruction deprived the defendant of his Sixth Amendment right to a jury finding of guilt beyond a reasonable doubt, and an appellate court holding such error harmless would be substituting its own judgment for the constitutionally required judgment of a jury.

A common characteristic of many of these errors is that their impact upon the outcome of the proceeding cannot readily be isolated, rendering that impact "necessarily unquantifiable and indeterminate." *U.S. v. Gonzalez–Lopez* (2006). This quality led the Court in *Ariz. v. Fulminante* (1991) to categorize the automatic-reversal errors as "structural defects affecting the framework within which the trial proceeds." On the other hand, *Fulminante* noted, violations subject to *Chapman's* harmless error analysis were tied together by the "common thread" of "involv[ing] 'trial error'—error which occurred during the presentation of the case to the jury and which therefore may be quantitatively assessed in the context of other evidence presented in order to determine whether its admission was harmless beyond a reasonable doubt." Applying its "structural defect" standard, the *Fulminante* majority rejected earlier precedent suggesting that the admissibility of a coerced confession should be in the automatic-reversal category. Subsequent cases have continued to apply the "structural error/trial error" dichotomy, while giving the structural category a broad enough cast to encompass the rationales advanced in the pre-*Fulminante* cases, such as *McKaskle* and *Rose*. See *U.S. v. Gonzales–Lopez* (2006) (denial of representation by counsel of choice is a structural defect, as "it is impossible to know what different choices the rejected counsel would have made, and then to quantify the impact of these different choices on the outcome of the proceedings"); *Neder v. U.S.* (1999) (not submitting one element of the crime to the jury is not a structural error and therefore can be harmless; contrasted to *Sullivan* error, which was structural, since jury instruction flaw there "vitiated all of the jury's findings"); *Wash. v. Recuenco* (2006) (*Neder* analysis applies as well where a fact triggering a higher sentencing maximum was erroneously decided by the sentencing judge rather than submitted to the jury).

## § 9.11  SUCCESSIVE PROSECUTIONS

### (a)  The double jeopardy prohibition

The Fifth Amendment provides: "[N]or shall any person be subject for the same offence to be twice put in jeopardy of life or limb". As discussed in § 9.9(a), this "double jeopardy" prohibition bears upon the imposition of multiple sentences, but its primary significance lies in its restriction of successive prosecutions. To be subject to the double jeopardy prohibition, a criminal prosecution must meet four prerequisites. First, it must be a second instance in which the individual was placed in jeopardy of "life or limb." That jeopardy is not limited to possible conviction for an offense carrying a capital or corporal punishment, but it does require a possible conviction for a "crime" (including crimes subject to lesser penalties). *Hudson v. U.S.* (1997) holds that proceedings designated as "civil," though bearing significant "penalties" (e.g., heavy fines), will be subject to the double jeopardy clause only upon "the 'clearest proof' that the penalty [actually] * * * is punitive." Accordingly the double jeopardy clause does not bar the combination of a criminal prosecution and a separate civil penalty proceeding, though based on identical criminal and civil prohibitions.

Second, a second criminal prosecution will not present double jeopardy difficulties unless the first prosecution reached the point in the proceedings where "jeopardy attached." *Serfass v. U.S.* (1975). In jury trials, jeopardy attaches once the jury is "empaneled and sworn," and in bench trials, it attaches when "the first witness is sworn." *Crist v. Bretz* (1978). Third, apart from the collateral estoppel doctrine discussed in subsection (c), double jeopardy applies only when the multiple prosecutions are for "same offense"—a concept which goes beyond the same criminal statute, as explained in subsection (b).

Fourth, the multiple prosecutions for the same offense must be by the "same sovereign." In keep with the English common law, violations of the laws of different governments are viewed as separate offenses, even when those laws use identical definitions of a particular offense. Under this "dual sovereignty" doctrine, a local unit of government is not viewed as distinct from the state government, so prosecutions under local ordinances and state laws will be barred if for the same offense. *Waller v. Fla.* (1970). Each state and the federal government are separate sovereigns, however, so each may prosecute the same crime under its own statute. See *Bartkus v. Ill.* (1959) (federal and state prosecutions for same bank robbery); *Heath v. Ala.* (1985) (successive prosecutions by two states for the same murder).

Even if the four prerequisites noted above are met, double jeopardy will not necessarily prohibit the second prosecution. The double jeopardy clause is based upon the common law pleas of *autrefois acquit* and *autrefois convict*, and neither those pleas nor the concepts underlying their establishment at common law necessarily apply to all instances of successive prosecutions for the same offense. The precise impact of the double jeopardy clause varies in large part with the character of the ruling that ends the first prosecution. The standards applicable to the different types of endings are discussed in subsections (d)-(g) infra.

### (b) The "same offense" limitation

While separate prosecutions based on the same events and charging violations of precisely the same statute clearly constitute multiple prosecutions for the "same offense," that can also be true of prosecutions for the same events under two distinct criminal provisions. "[To] determine whether there are two offenses or only one," the Court applies the "same-elements" test of *Blockburger v. U.S.* (1932): "whether each [criminal] provision requires proof of an additional fact which the other does not." An obvious illustration of separate provisions that are part of the same offense under this test are the higher and lower degrees of the same crime (e.g., first degree and second degree homicide). However, the two provisions need not be part of a formal degree classification scheme in order to constitute the "same offense" under the *Blockburger* test. Thus *Brown v. Ohio* (1977) found that the crimes of theft of a vehicle and joyriding in that vehicle were part of the same offense since, as defined by state law, theft was simply joyriding with an additional element (an intent to permanently deprive the owner of the property). On the other hand, two crimes can be part of the same statutory grouping, building upon the same core offense, and not be the "same offense" under the *Blockburger* standard. Thus, in *U.S. v. Dixon* (1993), Justice Souter (in a dissent arguing for a conception of "same offense" broader than *Blockburger*) offered the illustration of the crimes of robbery in a dwelling and robbery with a firearm. While both have the common element of robbery, each has a different additional element, and therefore, under *Blockburger*, separate prosecutions could be brought for a single robbery involving both additional elements (although if a prosecution initially was brought for the core crime of robbery, subsequent prosecutions for the firearm and dwelling offenses would be barred because the simple robbery would be the "same offense" as to each).

Where a statutory offense includes alternative elements, determining whether two crimes constitute the same offense requires an inquiry beyond the language of the statutory provisions. Thus in *Harris v. Okla.* (1977), defendant was initially prosecuted under a felony murder statute that made all felonies predicate offenses for felony murder. Since that prosecution was premised on the murder having occurred in the perpetration of a robbery with a firearm, the Court held that a second prosecution for the underlying offense of robbery with a firearm was barred. Although commission of that particular felony was not essential to a felony murder, the Court looked to the theory of the earlier prosecution as establishing the relevant statutory elements for that case, and applied *Blockburger* to those elements. In *Grady v. Corbin* (1990), the Court went beyond *Harris* (and *Blockburger*) to hold that a defendant who had been prosecuted for driving while intoxicated and crossing the median could not subsequently be prosecuted for negligent homicide if the element of negligence was to be proven by the "same conduct" as charged in the earlier prosecution. However, *U.S. v. Dixon* (1993) overruled the "same conduct" standard of *Grady,* and held that double jeopardy protection did not go beyond the *Harris* application of *Blockburger*.

If the two crimes are the "same offense" under the *Blockburger* test, the double jeopardy prohibition applies—without regard to whether the more serious or less serious came first (or second). There are, however, special circumstances under which the prohibition will not be available to a defendant. The defendant, in effect, forfeits the protection of the prohibition where the defendant was responsible for splitting the two charges into separate trials. *Jeffers v. U.S.* (1977) (defense successfully opposed government motion to consolidate). Similarly, the government will not be held responsible for failing to bring the two charges together when the elements of the second offense charged did not exist or could not have been known at the time the first charge was resolved (a situation that would be presented in a felony-murder situation if the charge on the predicate offense was resolved before the victim died). *Diaz v. U.S.* (1912). See also *Garrett v. U.S.* (1985) (separate continuing enterprise charge not barred because that offense was still ongoing when defendant pled guilty to included narcotics transaction).

### (c) Collateral estoppel

Multiple prosecutions, even where not for the same offense, will be barred under certain circumstances by the doctrine of collateral estoppel, which was recognized as an aspect of double jeopardy in *Ashe v. Swenson* (1970). The collateral estoppel doctrine bars prosecution for a second offense where the defendant was previously acquitted on a factually related offense and that acquittal was based on a factual element that is also an essential element of the second offense. Thus, in *Ashe,* a defendant charged with robbing the initial victim in a single, multi-victim robbery, and acquitted by the jury on the ground that he had not been present at the robbery, could not subsequently be prosecuted on a charge of robbing the other victims. Under the collateral estoppel doctrine, the earlier acquittal only bars use of the same critical facts as an element of another offense; it does not preclude use of the same evidence for another purpose requiring a lesser standard of proof, such as a civil forfeiture, or showing similar past behavior in a prosecution for an unconnected offense. *Dowling v. U.S.* (1990). Also, it applies only to the ultimate fact on which the jury acquitted and not as to some subsidiary issue. Id. Of course, as an aspect of double jeopardy, collateral estoppel serves only to protect the defendant; the prosecution cannot use a guilty verdict to relieve it of the burden of establishing beyond a reasonable doubt the same ultimate fact in a prosecution for another offense involving that fact. *Simpson v. Fla.* (1971).

### (d) Mistrials

Where the initial prosecution ends in a mistrial (the judicial discharge of the jury prior to verdict), a subsequent prosecution for the same offense may be barred by double jeopardy, notwithstanding that mistrials typically are ordered under the assumption that there will be a retrial. That assumption most often holds true, but there are certain situations in which the double jeopardy concerns applicable even before a verdict has been reached—the "minimization of harassing exposure to the harrowing experiences of a criminal trial, and the valued right [of the defendant] to continue with the chosen jury"—will lead to prohibiting a new trial. *Crist v. Bretz* (1978).

If the mistrial was ordered at the request of the defense, a new trial will not be barred unless the defense acted in response to prosecutorial or judicial overreaching that was "intended to 'goad' the defendant into moving for a mistrial." *Ore. v. Kennedy*

*Burks v. U.S.* (1978). The double jeopardy principle allowing retrials following appellate reversals is often described as the "*Ball* principle," after *Ball v. U.S.* (1896). It is justified as serving "defendant's rights as well as society interests," since a contrary position would obviously discourage appellate courts from granting reversals. *U.S. v. Tateo* (1964). The *Ball* principle does not allow retrial following a reversal based on the insufficiency of the prosecution's evidence since that appellate ruling is equivalent to a directed verdict of acquittal at trial. *Burks.* However, this only applies when all of the evidence before the trial court is insufficient to sustain a conviction, not where the trial court erred in admitting certain evidence and the insufficiency only exists without that evidence. *Lockhart v. Nelson* (1988).

†

appeal is permitted. Generally, jurisdictions do not allow appeals following an acquittal because appellate review would be meaningless; even if the appellate court concluded that the acquittal was erroneous, double jeopardy would prohibit a retrial on the charge. Where the acquittal is granted postconviction, however, there is no need for a retrial; in overturning the acquittal, the appellate court can merely reinstitute the jury's verdict. That does not violate the double jeopardy prohibition because it does not subject the defendant to a second trial. *U.S. v. Wilson* (1975).

### (g) Convictions

Where the trial ends in a verdict of guilty, reprosecution also is barred unless the defendant successfully challenges that verdict. If he chooses, the defendant may accept the guilty verdict and thereby prevent the government from subjecting him to the "embarrassment, expense, and ordeal" of another trial. *Wilson.* The same ordinarily is true of a conviction on a guilty plea. *Ohio v. Johnson* (1984) (exception recognized where trial judge, over the prosecution's objection, accepted a plea to a lesser-included offense, and sought to thereby terminate the prosecution; dismissal of the higher offense was, basically a pre-jeopardy ruling).

If the defendant appeals a conviction based on a guilty verdict or guilty plea, and gains a reversal, he then may be retried—with the one exception being a reversal of a guilty verdict grounded on the insufficiency of the evidence to support the verdict.

*v. U.S.* (1978). As the Court noted in *Scott*, "to permit a second trial after an acquittal, however mistaken the acquittal may have been, would present an unacceptably high risk that the Government, with its vastly superior resources, might wear down the defendant so that 'even though innocent he may be found guilty.' "

Not all jury verdicts amounting to an acquittal take the form of an acquittal. An acquittal is implied as to a higher offense where a jury is charged on both higher and lesser included offenses and returns a verdict of guilty only on the lesser included offense, without announcing a verdict on the higher offense. *Green v. U.S.* (1957). An implied acquittal precludes a reprosecution on the higher offense, even if the defendant appeals and successfully overturns the conviction on the lesser offense (which permits a reprosecution only on that offense). *Morris v. Mathews* (1986).

Ordinarily, as a consequence of the double jeopardy prohibition, an acquittal precludes further prosecutorial action on the offense charged. That is not the case, however, as to two special types of judicial acquittals. If a trial judge dismisses a charge pretrial based on the insufficiency of the evidence, that fits the definition of an acquittal, but it is a prejeopardy ruling and therefore does not bar reprosecution if an appellate court reverses that pretrial ruling. *Serfass v. U.S.* (1975). Where a jury convicts and the judge subsequently enters a judgment of acquittal notwithstanding the verdict, here again an not, in fact, an "acquittal." Where the dismissal is based on some preliminary error that does not permanently terminate the prosecution, but allows the prosecution to reprosecute after curing the error (as where dismissal is based on a defective joinder), the dismissal clearly will not be an acquittal and will be governed by the mistrial standards (typically permitting a reprosecution since the dismissal will be on the motion of the defense). *Lee v. U.S.* (1977). A dismissal based on grounds permanently terminating the prosecution (e.g., denial of a speedy trial) also is treated in the same fashion as a mistrial. *U.S. v. Scott* (1978). Here, however, the reviewing court must be certain that ruling labeled a dismissal is truly that and not an acquittal, for "the trial judge's characterization of his own action cannot control the classification of [his] action." *Smalis v. Pa.* (1986) (demurrer to the evidence, though labeled a dismissal, actually was an acquittal). An acquittal for this purpose occurs "when the ruling of judge, whatever its label, represents a resolution in defendant's favor, correct or not, of some of the factual elements of the charge." *Scott.* If the "dismissal" is in fact an "acquittal," the subsequent prosecution for the same offense is barred.

### (f) Acquittals

A jury or judge-directed acquittal bars reprosecution. The state cannot gain reversal of the acquittal even if it probably was based on some error in the instructions or the admission of evidence. *Sanabria*

(1982). Where the mistrial was ordered over defense objection (or without giving the defense an opportunity to object), a retrial will be barred unless the "declaration of the mistrial was dictated by 'manifest necessity' or the 'ends of public justice.' " *Ill. v. Somerville* (1973). If the mistrial was due to an uncontrolled event (e.g., the illness of a juror, or a jury that could not agree on a verdict), that ordinarily will meet this "manifest necessity" standard and a retrial will be permitted. Where the mistrial was due to some error by counsel or the trial judge, the Court will look to several factors in applying the "manifest necessity" standard. These include: (1) if the error was by the prosecutor, whether it was the type of error that might be intentionally manipulated to gain a new trial at which the prosecution could strengthen its case, *Downum v. U.S.* (1963); (2) whether the trial court could have utilized alternative remedies for the error that would have permitted the trial to continue to an impartial verdict that could be sustained on appeal, *U.S. v. Jorn* (1971); and (3) whether the trial judge's rejection of alternatives to a mistrial involved the assessment of factors (e.g., jury reaction to a prejudicial remark) that are not particularly "amenable to appellate scrutiny." *Ariz. v. Washington* (1978).

### (e) Dismissal

Where the trial court dismisses a prosecution after jeopardy has attached and before a verdict is reached, the principles applicable to mistrials will apply, but only if the dismissal is truly that, and